*Ms. Borman*

**WRITER**
*C.B. Cebulski*

**ARTISTS**
*João Lemos, Nuno Plati, Takeshi Miyazawa,
Ricardo Tercio & Kyle Baker*

**COLOR ARTIST, AVENGERS #1 & #3**
*Christina Strain*

**LETTERERS**
*Dave Lanphear
with Dave Sharpe* (X-Men)

**COVER ARTISTS**
*Claire Wendling* (Avengers),
*Ricardo Tercio* (Spider-Man)
*& Kyle Baker* (X-Men)

**EDITORS**
*Molly Lazer, Alejandro Arbona,
Nathan Cosby & Mark Paniccia*

Collection Editor: *Jennifer Grünwald* • Assistant Editors: *Alex Starbuck & John Denning*
Editor, Special Projects: *Mark D. Beazley* • Senior Editor, Special Projects: *Jeff Youngquist*
Senior Vice President of Sales: *David Gabriel* • Production: *Jerry Kalinowksi*
Book Designer: *Spring Hoteling*

Editor in Chief: *Joe Quesada* • Publisher: *Dan Buckley*
Executive Producer: *Alan Fine*

**MARVEL FAIRY TALES**. Contains material originally published in magazine form as AVENGERS FAIRY TALES #1-4, SPIDER-MAN FAIRY TALES #1 and X-MEN FAIRY TALES #2. First printing 2010. ISBN# 978-0-7851-4316-1. Published by MARVEL PUBLISHING, INC., a subsidiary of MARVEL ENTERTAINMENT, INC. OFFICE OF PUBLICATION: 417 5th Avenue, New York, NY 10016. Copyright © 2006, 2007, 2008 and 2010 Marvel Characters, Inc. All rights reserved. $14.99 per copy in the U.S. (GST #R127032852); Canadian Agreement #40668537. All characters featured in this issue and the distinctive names and likenesses thereof, and all related indicia are trademarks of Marvel Characters, Inc. No similarity between any of the names, characters, persons, and/or institutions in this magazine with those of any living or dead person or institution is intended, and any such similarity which may exist is purely coincidental. **Printed in the U.S.A.** ALAN FINE, EVP - Office Of The Chief Executive Marvel Entertainment, Inc. & CMO Marvel Characters B.V.; DAN BUCKLEY, Chief Executive Officer and Publisher - Print, Animation & Digital Media; JIM SOKOLOWSKI, Chief Operating Officer; DAVID GABRIEL, SVP of Publishing Sales & Circulation; DAVID BOGART, SVP of Business Affairs & Talent Management; MICHAEL PASCIULLO, VP Merchandising & Communications; JIM O'KEEFE, VP of Operations & Logistics; DAN CARR, Executive Director of Publishing Technology; JUSTIN F. GABRIE, Director of Publishing & Editorial Operations; SUSAN CRESPI, Editorial Operations Manager; ALEX MORALES, Publishing Operations Manager; STAN LEE, Chairman Emeritus. For information regarding advertising in Marvel Comics or on Marvel.com, please contact Ron Stern, VP of Business Development, at rstern@marvel.com. For Marvel subscription inquiries, please call 800-217-9158. **Manufactured between 12/11/09 and 1/6/10 by R.R. DONNELLEY, INC. (CRAWFORD), CRAWFORDSVILLE, IN, USA.**

10 9 8 7 6 5 4 3 2 1

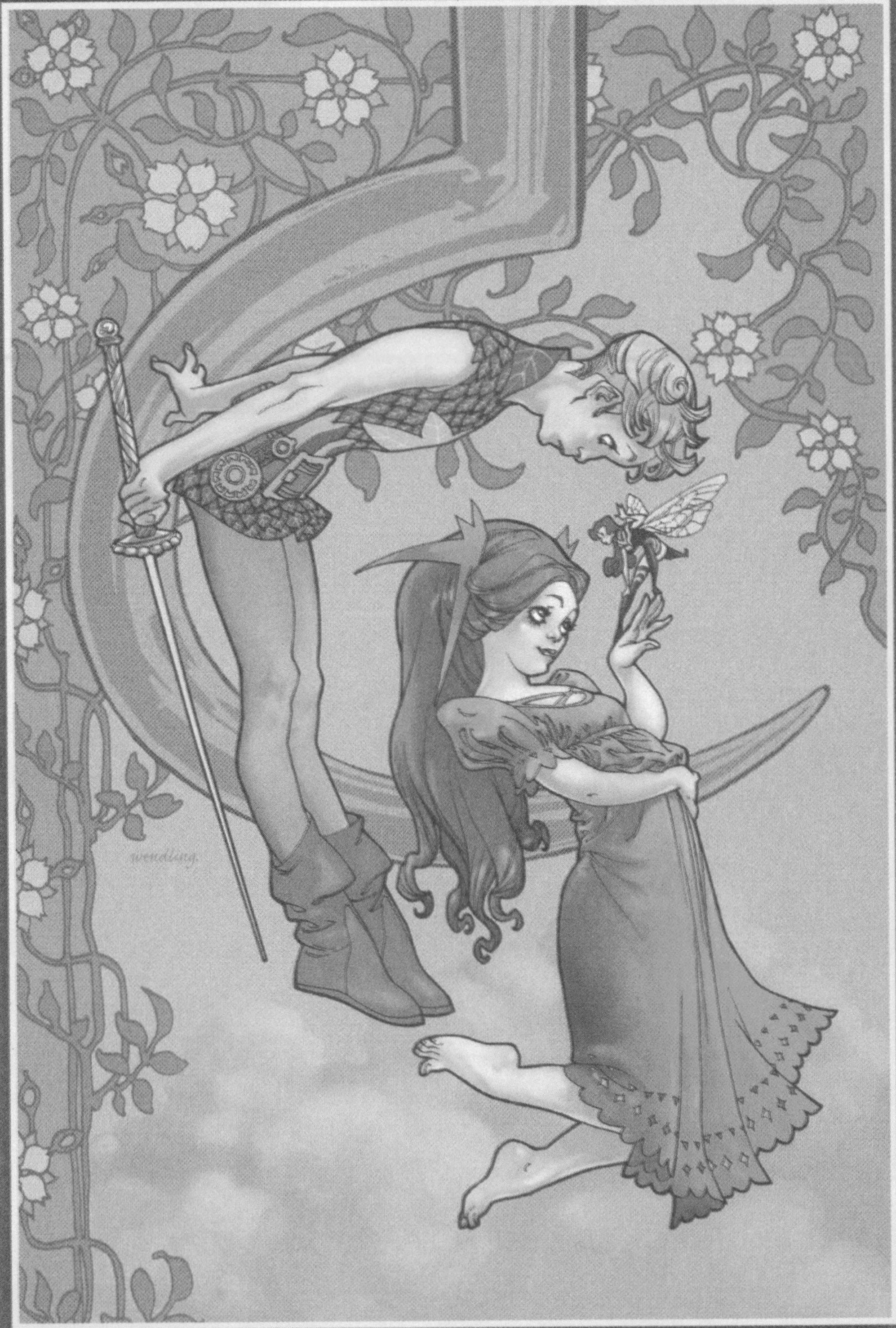
wendling.

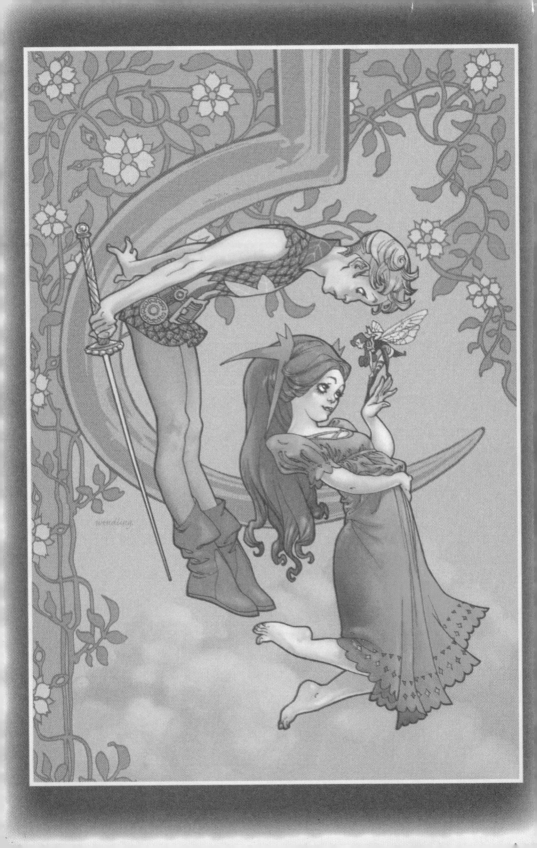

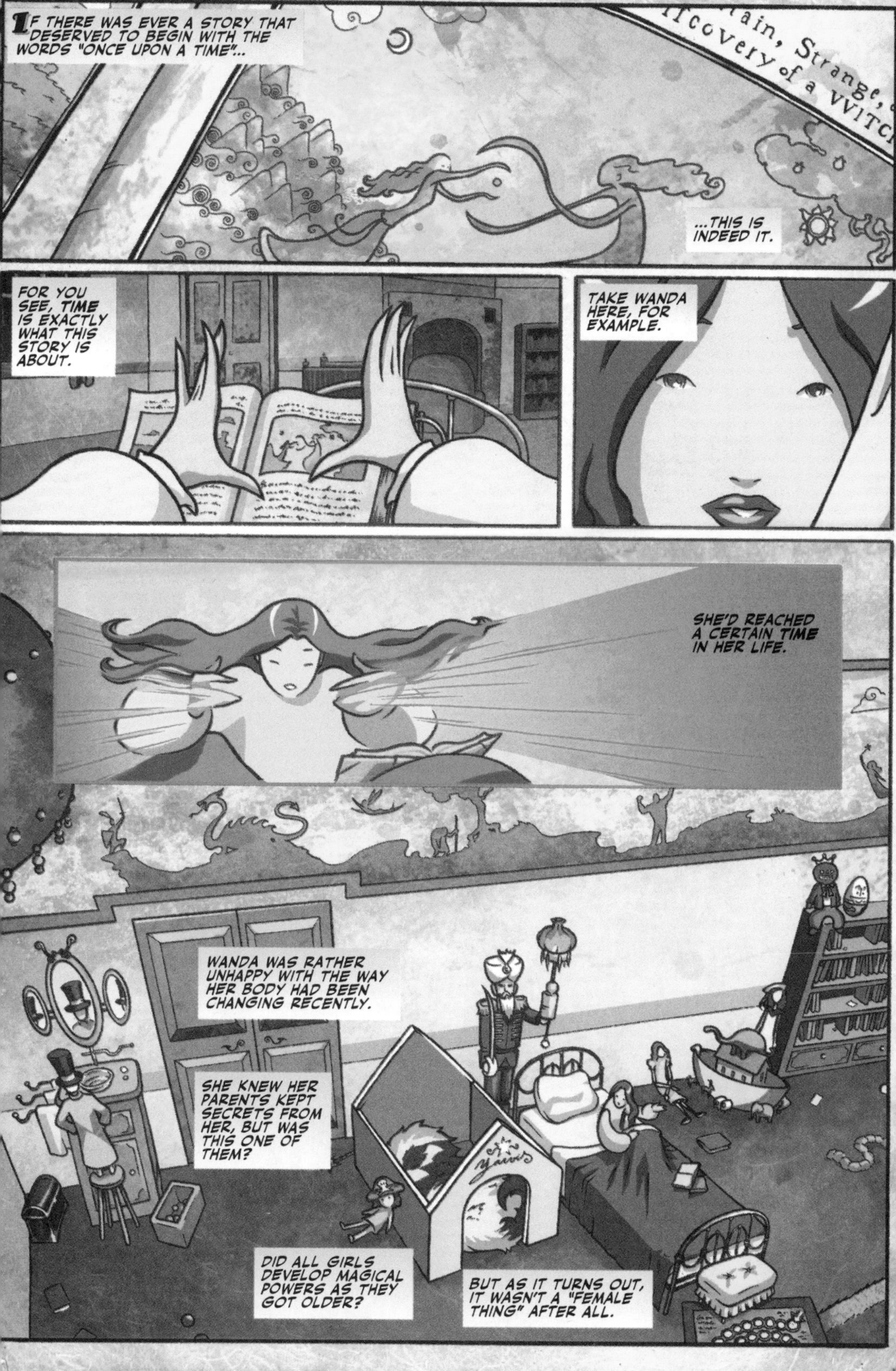

IF THERE WAS EVER A STORY THAT DESERVED TO BEGIN WITH THE WORDS "ONCE UPON A TIME"...
...THIS IS INDEED IT.
FOR YOU SEE, TIME IS EXACTLY WHAT THIS STORY IS ABOUT.
TAKE WANDA HERE, FOR EXAMPLE.
SHE'D REACHED A CERTAIN TIME IN HER LIFE.
WANDA WAS RATHER UNHAPPY WITH THE WAY HER BODY HAD BEEN CHANGING RECENTLY.
SHE KNEW HER PARENTS KEPT SECRETS FROM HER, BUT WAS THIS ONE OF THEM?
DID ALL GIRLS DEVELOP MAGICAL POWERS AS THEY GOT OLDER?
BUT AS IT TURNS OUT, IT WASN'T A "FEMALE THING" AFTER ALL.

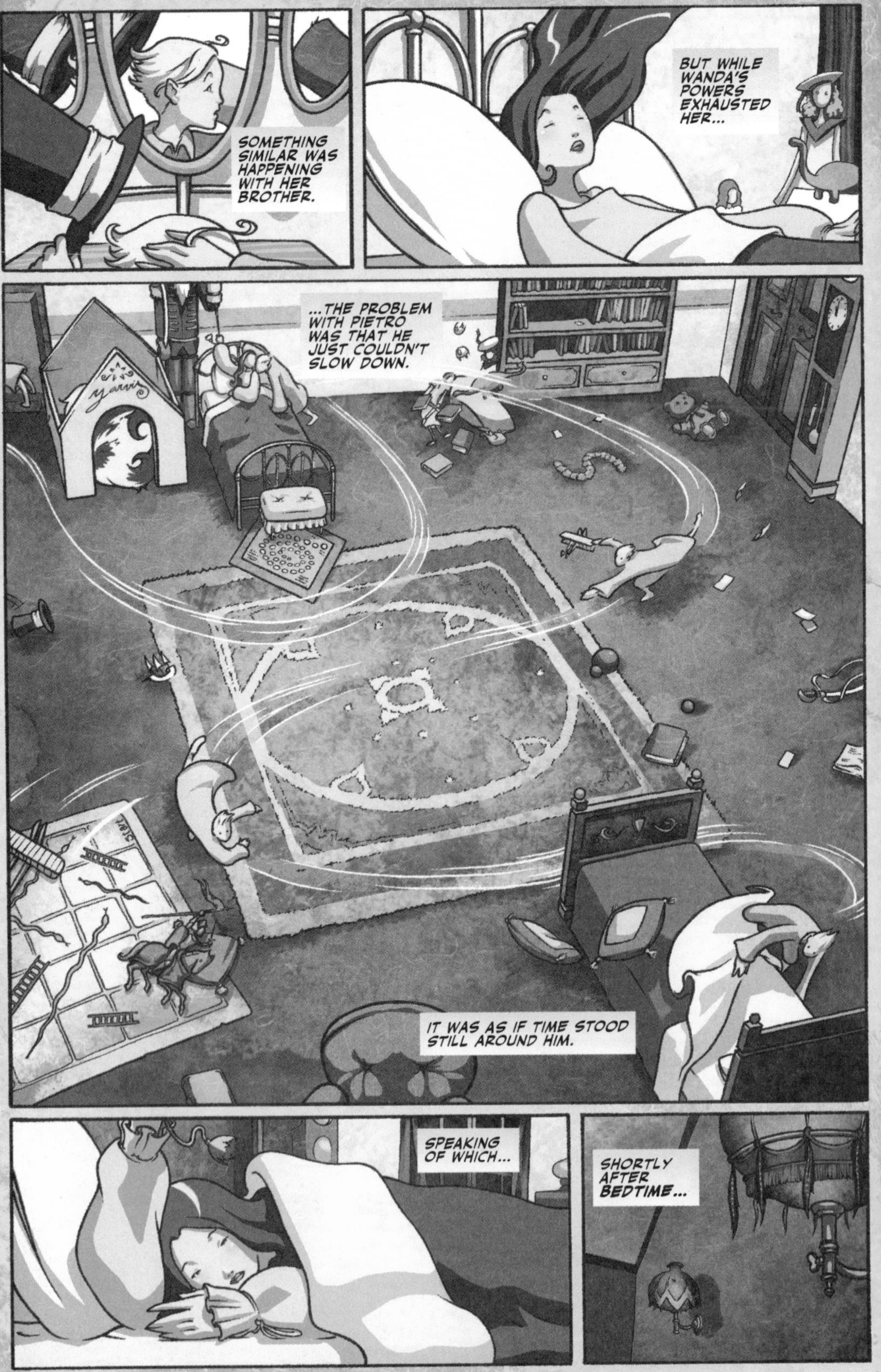
SOMETHING SIMILAR WAS HAPPENING WITH HER BROTHER.
BUT WHILE WANDA'S POWERS EXHAUSTED HER...
...THE PROBLEM WITH PIETRO WAS THAT HE JUST COULDN'T SLOW DOWN.
IT WAS AS IF TIME STOOD STILL AROUND HIM.
SPEAKING OF WHICH...
SHORTLY AFTER BEDTIME...

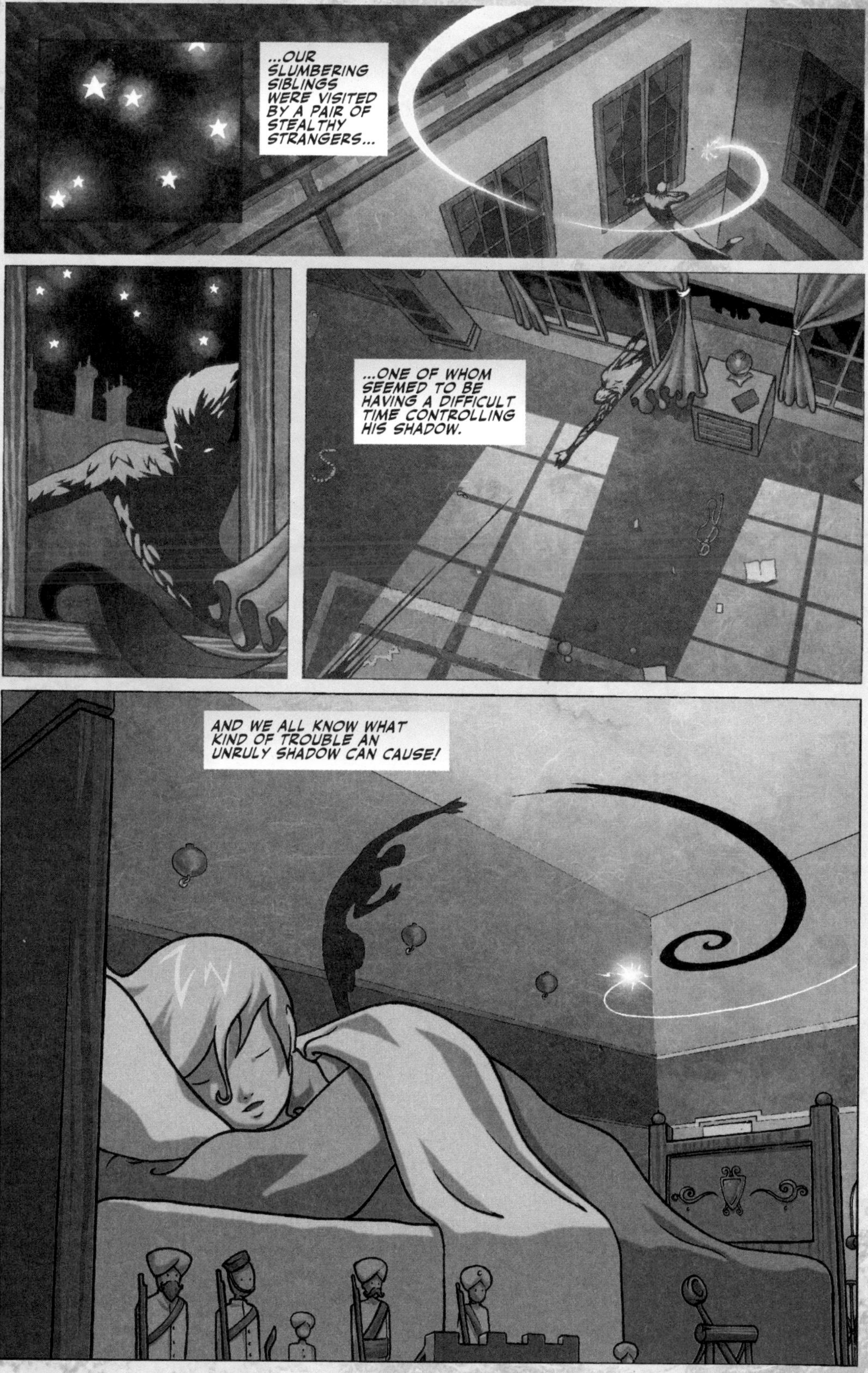
...OUR SLUMBERING SIBLINGS WERE VISITED BY A PAIR OF STEALTHY STRANGERS...
...ONE OF WHOM SEEMED TO BE HAVING A DIFFICULT TIME CONTROLLING HIS SHADOW.
AND WE ALL KNOW WHAT KIND OF TROUBLE AN UNRULY SHADOW CAN CAUSE!

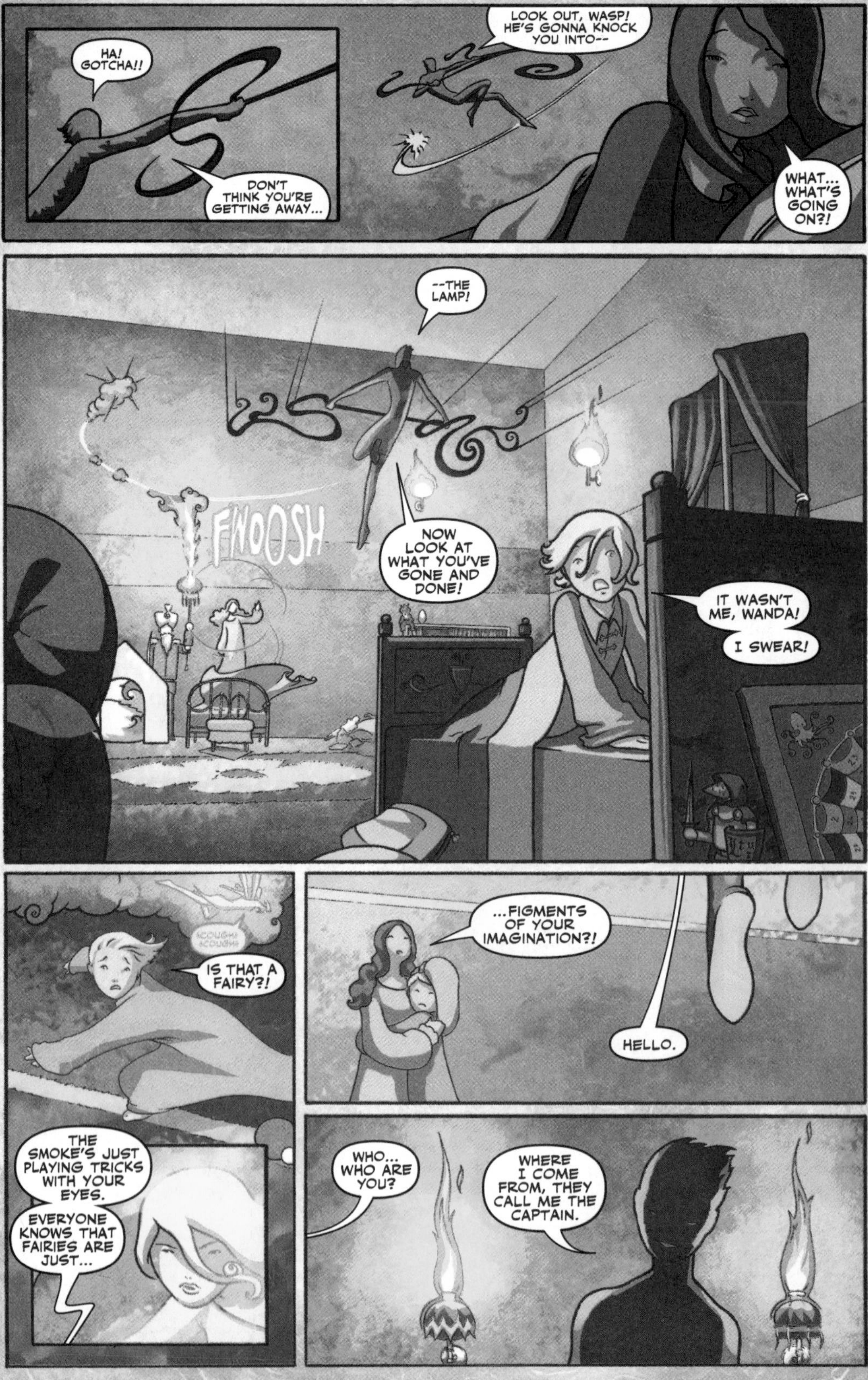
HA! GOTCHA!!
DON'T THINK YOU'RE GETTING AWAY...
LOOK OUT, WASP! HE'S GONNA KNOCK YOU INTO--
WHAT... WHAT'S GOING ON?!
--THE LAMP!
FWOOSH
NOW LOOK AT WHAT YOU'VE GONE AND DONE!
IT WASN'T ME, WANDA!
I SWEAR!
*COUGH* *COUGH*
IS THAT A FAIRY?!
THE SMOKE'S JUST PLAYING TRICKS WITH YOUR EYES.
EVERYONE KNOWS THAT FAIRIES ARE JUST...
...FIGMENTS OF YOUR IMAGINATION?!
HELLO.
WHO... WHO ARE YOU?
WHERE I COME FROM, THEY CALL ME THE CAPTAIN.

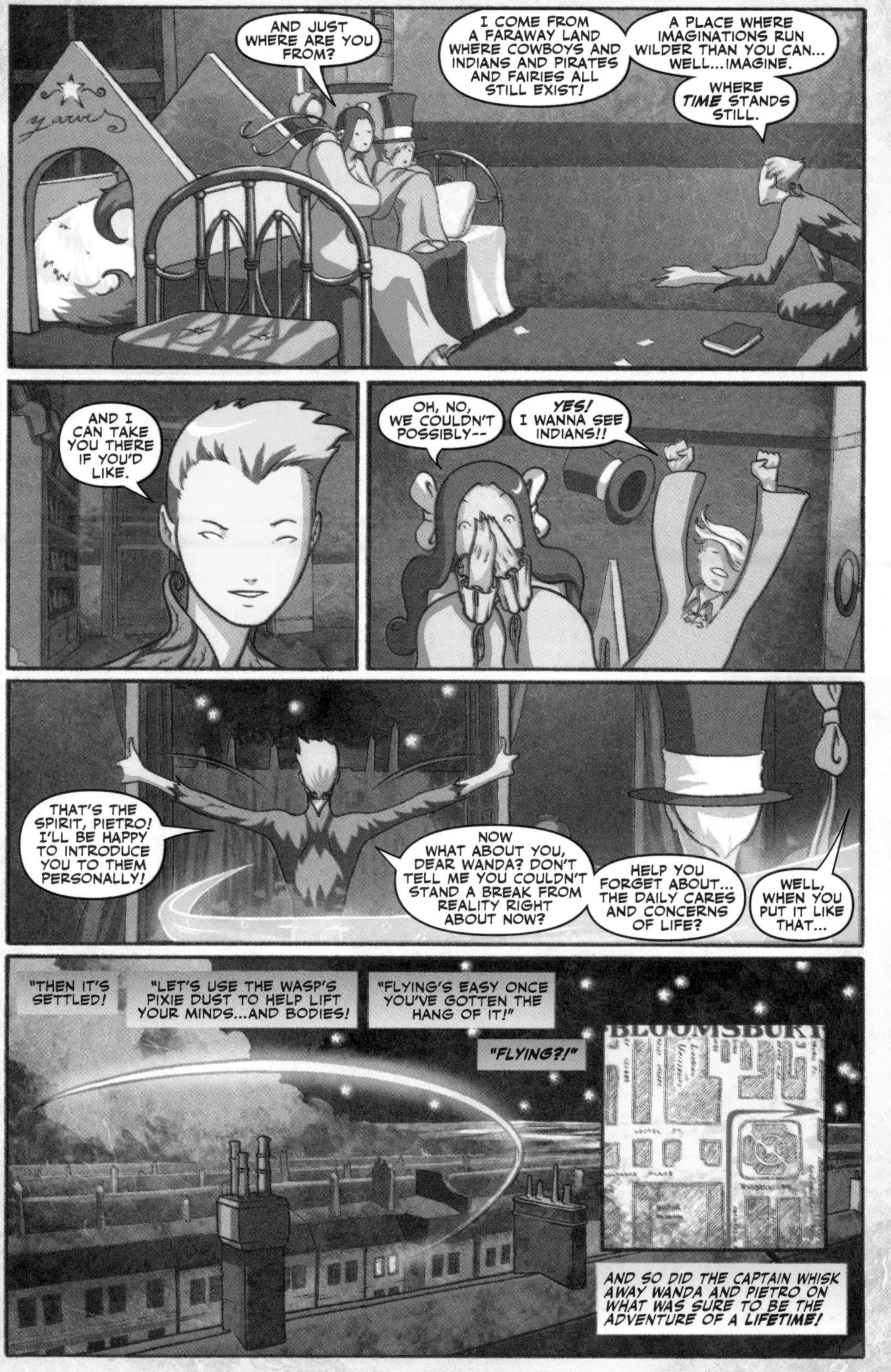
AND JUST WHERE ARE YOU FROM?
I COME FROM A FARAWAY LAND WHERE COWBOYS AND INDIANS AND PIRATES AND FAIRIES ALL STILL EXIST!
A PLACE WHERE IMAGINATIONS RUN WILDER THAN YOU CAN... WELL...IMAGINE.
WHERE *TIME* STANDS STILL.
AND I CAN TAKE YOU THERE IF YOU'D LIKE.
OH, NO, WE COULDN'T POSSIBLY--
*YES!* I WANNA SEE INDIANS!!
THAT'S THE SPIRIT, PIETRO! I'LL BE HAPPY TO INTRODUCE YOU TO THEM PERSONALLY!
NOW WHAT ABOUT YOU, DEAR WANDA? DON'T TELL ME YOU COULDN'T STAND A BREAK FROM REALITY RIGHT ABOUT NOW?
HELP YOU FORGET ABOUT... THE DAILY CARES AND CONCERNS OF LIFE?
WELL, WHEN YOU PUT IT LIKE THAT...
"THEN IT'S SETTLED!
"LET'S USE THE WASP'S PIXIE DUST TO HELP LIFT YOUR MINDS...AND BODIES!
"FLYING'S EASY ONCE YOU'VE GOTTEN THE HANG OF IT!"
*"FLYING?!"*
BLOOMSBURY
*AND SO DID THE CAPTAIN WHISK AWAY WANDA AND PIETRO ON WHAT WAS SURE TO BE THE ADVENTURE OF A **LIFETIME!***

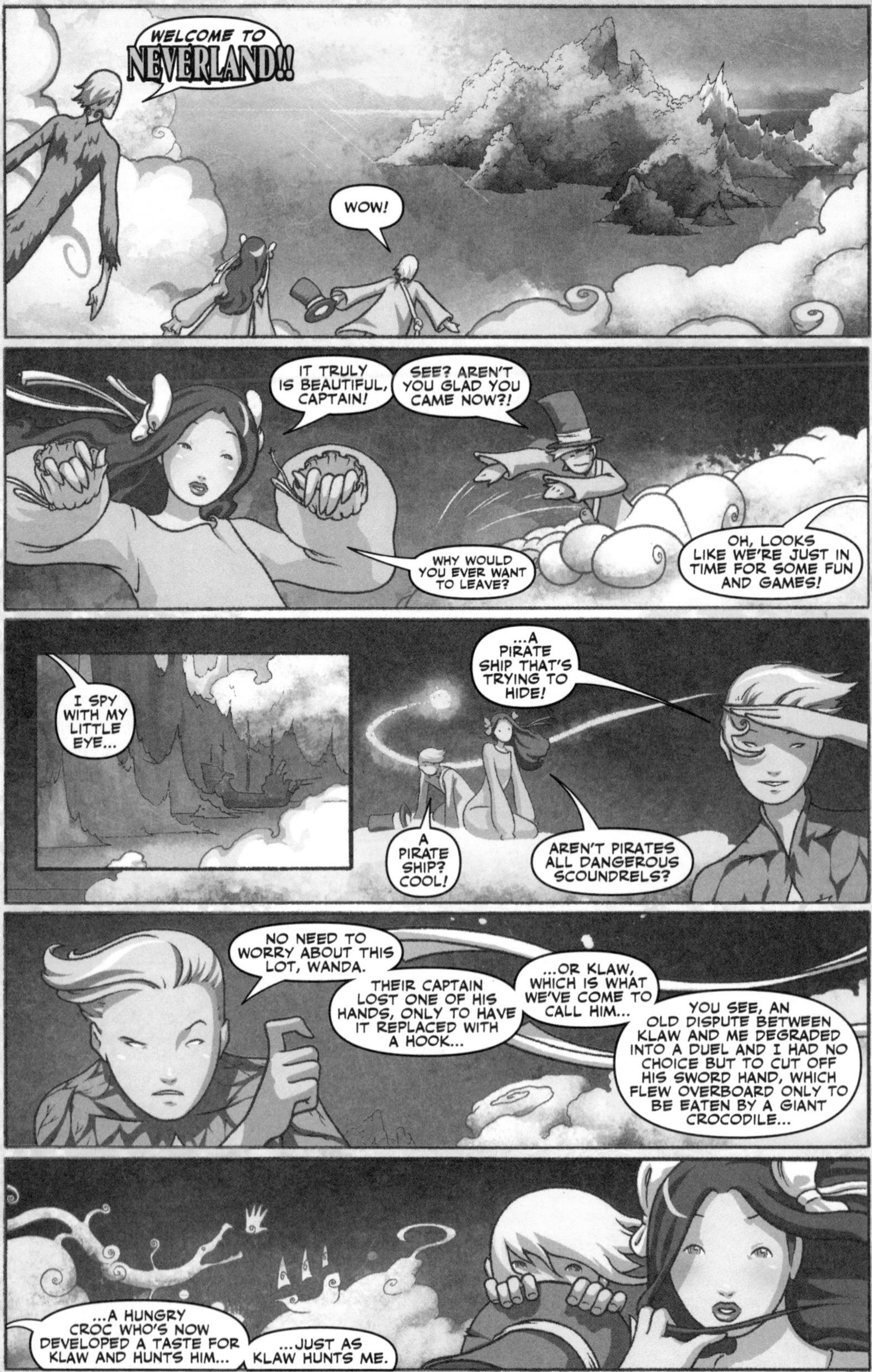
WELCOME TO NEVERLAND!!
WOW!
IT TRULY IS BEAUTIFUL, CAPTAIN!
SEE? AREN'T YOU GLAD YOU CAME NOW?!
WHY WOULD YOU EVER WANT TO LEAVE?
OH, LOOKS LIKE WE'RE JUST IN TIME FOR SOME FUN AND GAMES!
I SPY WITH MY LITTLE EYE...
...A PIRATE SHIP THAT'S TRYING TO HIDE!
A PIRATE SHIP? COOL!
AREN'T PIRATES ALL DANGEROUS SCOUNDRELS?
NO NEED TO WORRY ABOUT THIS LOT, WANDA.
THEIR CAPTAIN LOST ONE OF HIS HANDS, ONLY TO HAVE IT REPLACED WITH A HOOK...
...OR KLAW, WHICH IS WHAT WE'VE COME TO CALL HIM...
YOU SEE, AN OLD DISPUTE BETWEEN KLAW AND ME DEGRADED INTO A DUEL AND I HAD NO CHOICE BUT TO CUT OFF HIS SWORD HAND, WHICH FLEW OVERBOARD ONLY TO BE EATEN BY A GIANT CROCODILE...
...A HUNGRY CROC WHO'S NOW DEVELOPED A TASTE FOR KLAW AND HUNTS HIM...
...JUST AS KLAW HUNTS ME.

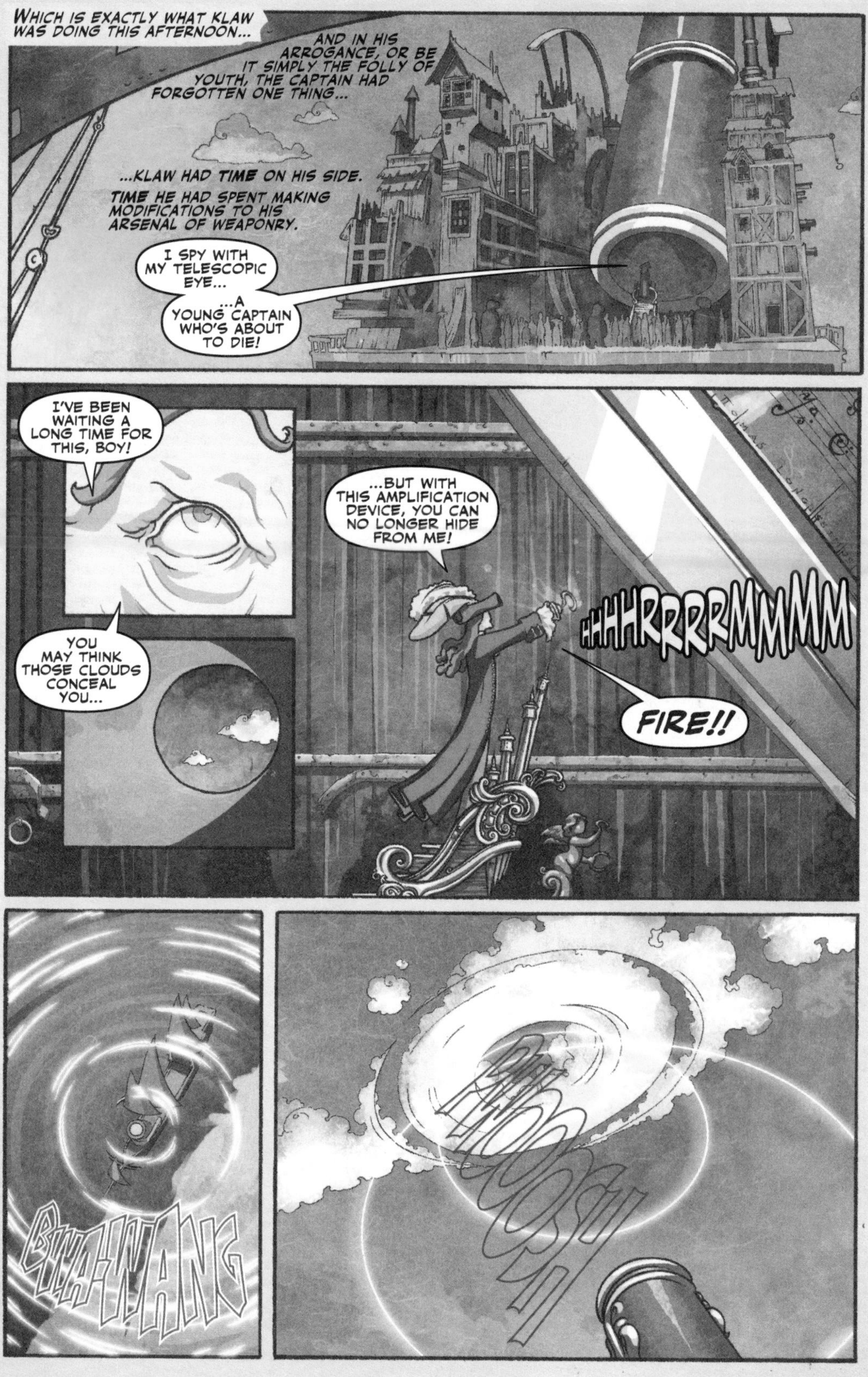
WHICH IS EXACTLY WHAT KLAW WAS DOING THIS AFTERNOON...
AND IN HIS ARROGANCE, OR BE IT SIMPLY THE FOLLY OF YOUTH, THE CAPTAIN HAD FORGOTTEN ONE THING...
...KLAW HAD TIME ON HIS SIDE.
TIME HE HAD SPENT MAKING MODIFICATIONS TO HIS ARSENAL OF WEAPONRY.
I SPY WITH MY TELESCOPIC EYE...
...A YOUNG CAPTAIN WHO'S ABOUT TO DIE!
I'VE BEEN WAITING A LONG TIME FOR THIS, BOY!
YOU MAY THINK THOSE CLOUDS CONCEAL YOU...
...BUT WITH THIS AMPLIFICATION DEVICE, YOU CAN NO LONGER HIDE FROM ME!
FIRE!!

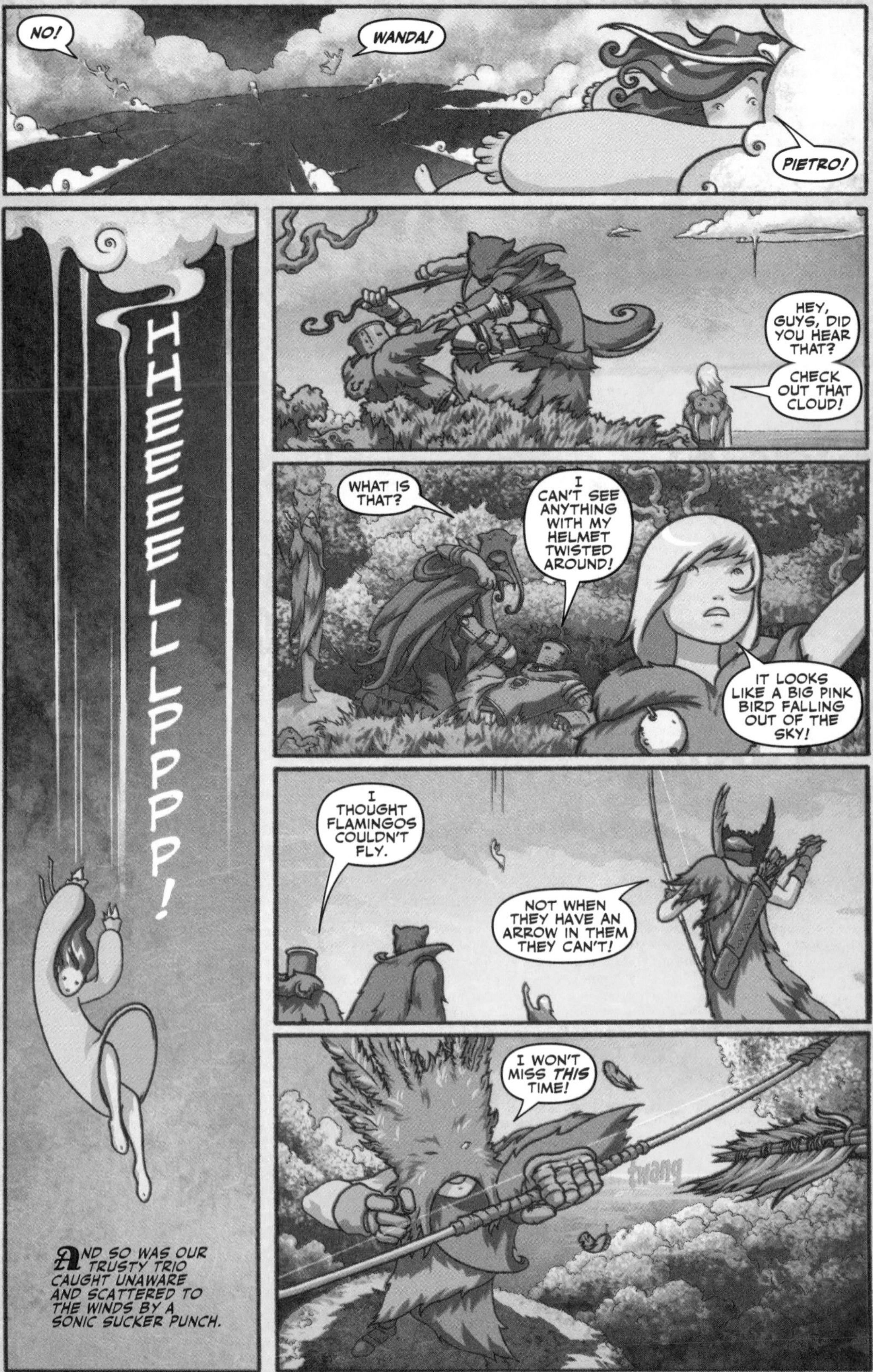
NO!
WANDA!
PIETRO!
HHEEEEELLLPPPP!
AND SO WAS OUR TRUSTY TRIO CAUGHT UNAWARE AND SCATTERED TO THE WINDS BY A SONIC SUCKER PUNCH.
HEY, GUYS, DID YOU HEAR THAT?
CHECK OUT THAT CLOUD!
WHAT IS THAT?
I CAN'T SEE ANYTHING WITH MY HELMET TWISTED AROUND!
IT LOOKS LIKE A BIG PINK BIRD FALLING OUT OF THE SKY!
I THOUGHT FLAMINGOS COULDN'T FLY.
NOT WHEN THEY HAVE AN ARROW IN THEM THEY CAN'T!
I WON'T MISS THIS TIME!
twang

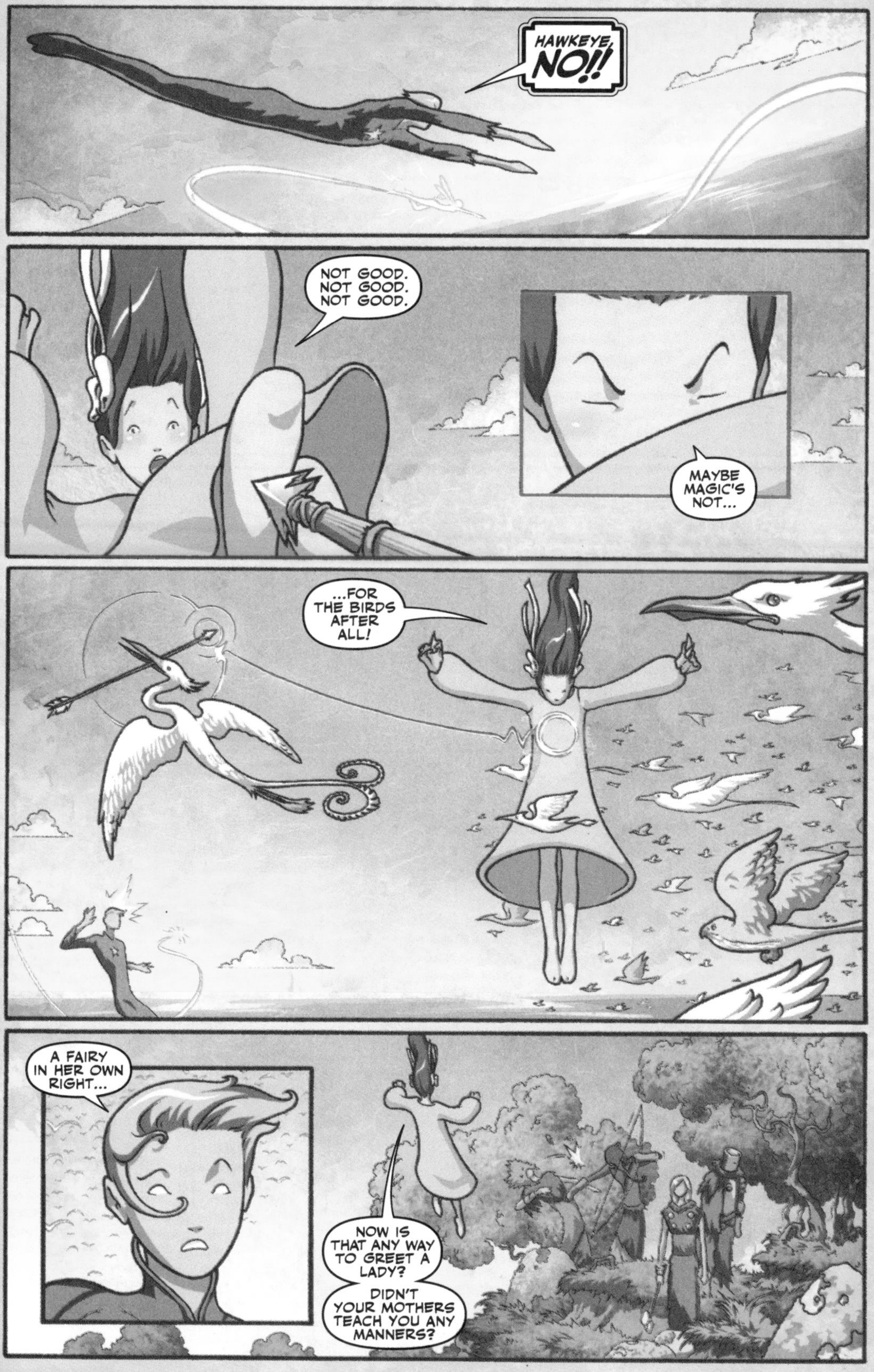
HAWKEYE, NO!!
NOT GOOD. NOT GOOD. NOT GOOD.
MAYBE MAGIC'S NOT...
...FOR THE BIRDS AFTER ALL!
A FAIRY IN HER OWN RIGHT...
NOW IS THAT ANY WAY TO GREET A LADY?
DIDN'T YOUR MOTHERS TEACH YOU ANY MANNERS?

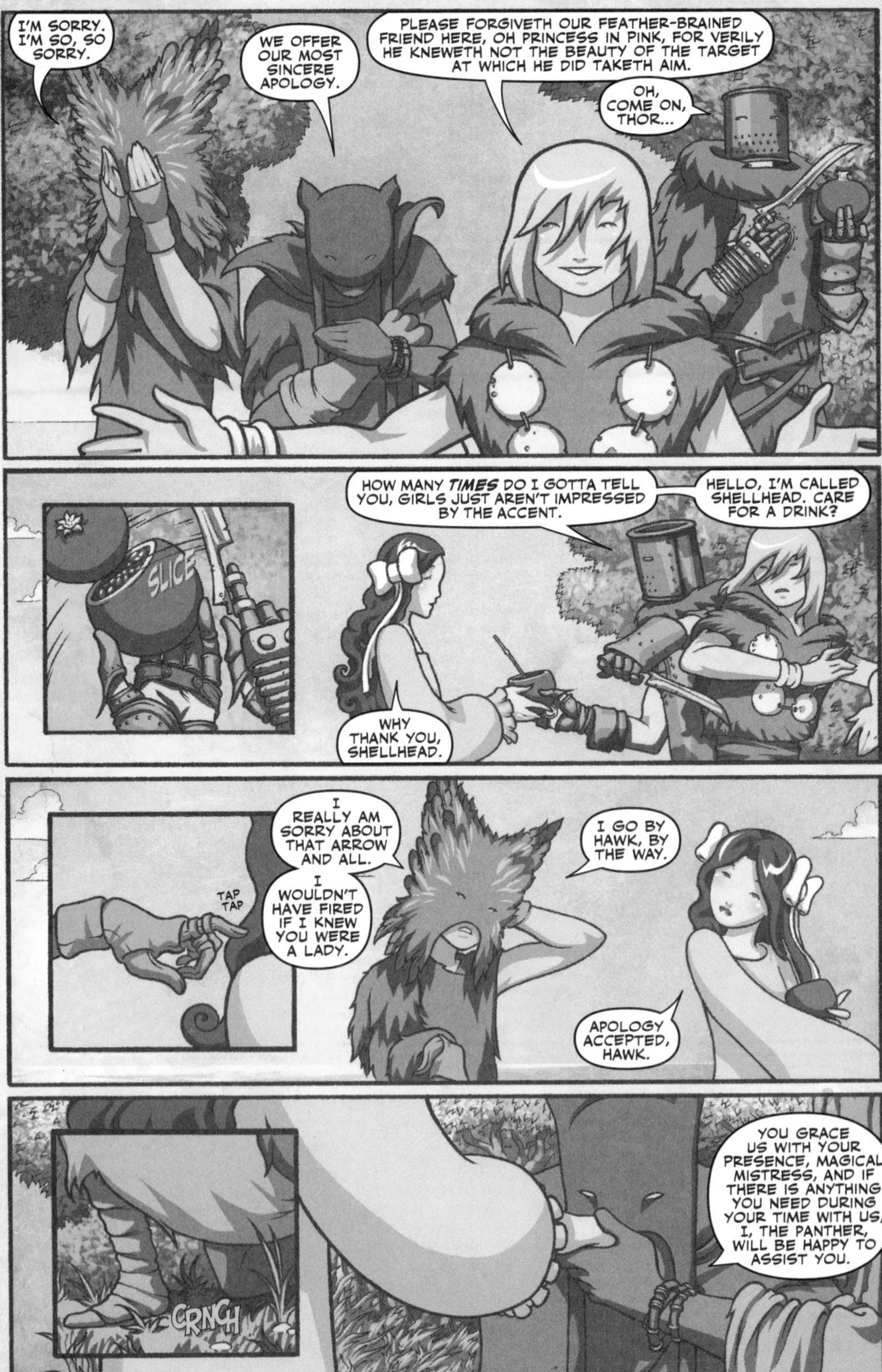
I'M SORRY. I'M SO, SO SORRY.
WE OFFER OUR MOST SINCERE APOLOGY.
PLEASE FORGIVETH OUR FEATHER-BRAINED FRIEND HERE, OH PRINCESS IN PINK, FOR VERILY HE KNEWETH NOT THE BEAUTY OF THE TARGET AT WHICH HE DID TAKETH AIM.
OH, COME ON, THOR...
SLICE
HOW MANY *TIMES* DO I GOTTA TELL YOU, GIRLS JUST AREN'T IMPRESSED BY THE ACCENT.
HELLO, I'M CALLED SHELLHEAD. CARE FOR A DRINK?
WHY THANK YOU, SHELLHEAD.
TAP TAP
I REALLY AM SORRY ABOUT THAT ARROW AND ALL.
I WOULDN'T HAVE FIRED IF I KNEW YOU WERE A LADY.
I GO BY HAWK, BY THE WAY.
APOLOGY ACCEPTED, HAWK.
CRNCH
YOU GRACE US WITH YOUR PRESENCE, MAGICAL MISTRESS, AND IF THERE IS ANYTHING YOU NEED DURING YOUR TIME WITH US, I, THE PANTHER, WILL BE HAPPY TO ASSIST YOU.

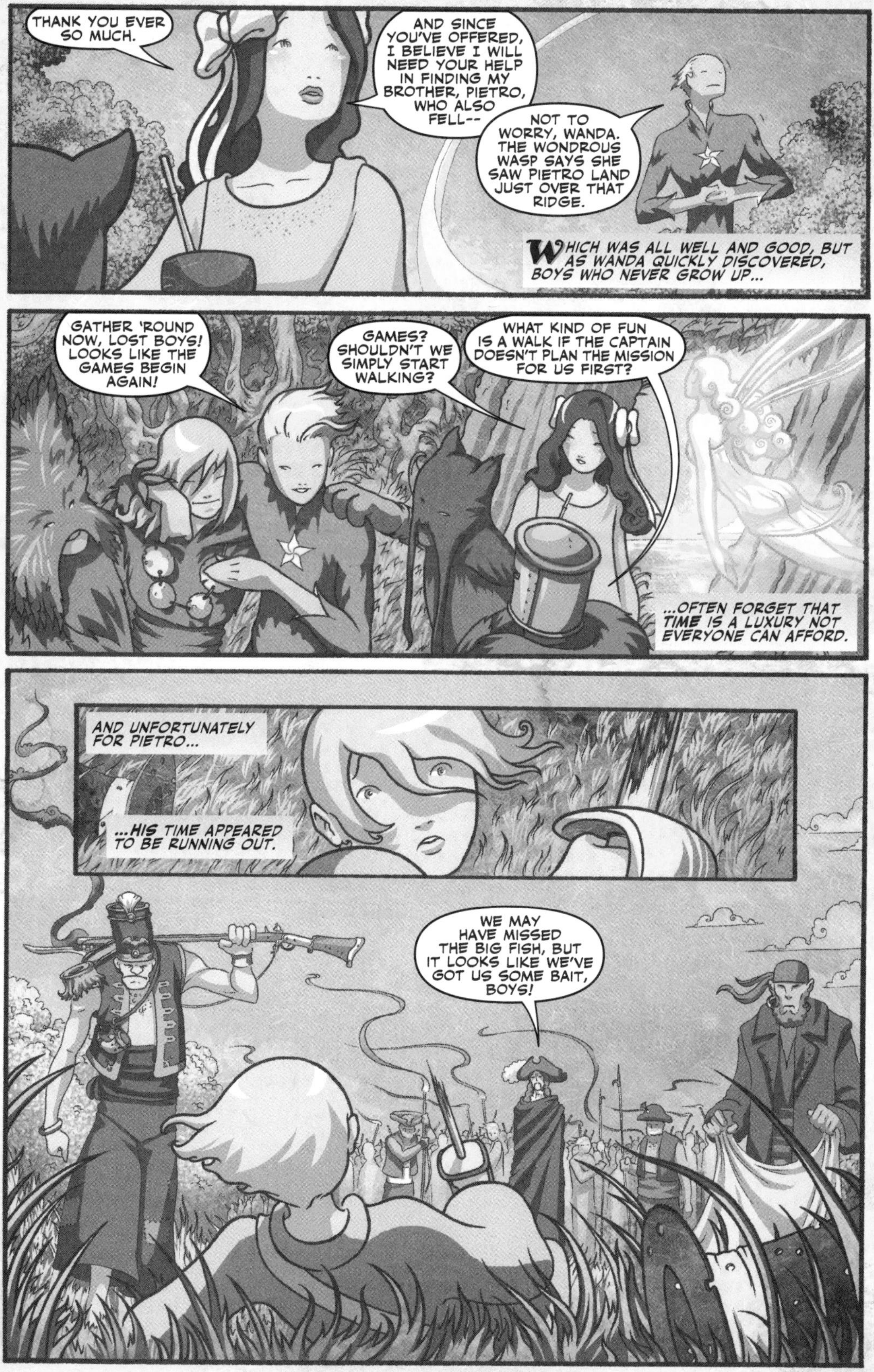
THANK YOU EVER SO MUCH.
AND SINCE YOU'VE OFFERED, I BELIEVE I WILL NEED YOUR HELP IN FINDING MY BROTHER, PIETRO, WHO ALSO FELL--
NOT TO WORRY, WANDA. THE WONDROUS WASP SAYS SHE SAW PIETRO LAND JUST OVER THAT RIDGE.
WHICH WAS ALL WELL AND GOOD, BUT AS WANDA QUICKLY DISCOVERED, BOYS WHO NEVER GROW UP...
GATHER 'ROUND NOW, LOST BOYS! LOOKS LIKE THE GAMES BEGIN AGAIN!
GAMES? SHOULDN'T WE SIMPLY START WALKING?
WHAT KIND OF FUN IS A WALK IF THE CAPTAIN DOESN'T PLAN THE MISSION FOR US FIRST?
...OFTEN FORGET THAT TIME IS A LUXURY NOT EVERYONE CAN AFFORD.
AND UNFORTUNATELY FOR PIETRO...
...HIS TIME APPEARED TO BE RUNNING OUT.
WE MAY HAVE MISSED THE BIG FISH, BUT IT LOOKS LIKE WE'VE GOT US SOME BAIT, BOYS!

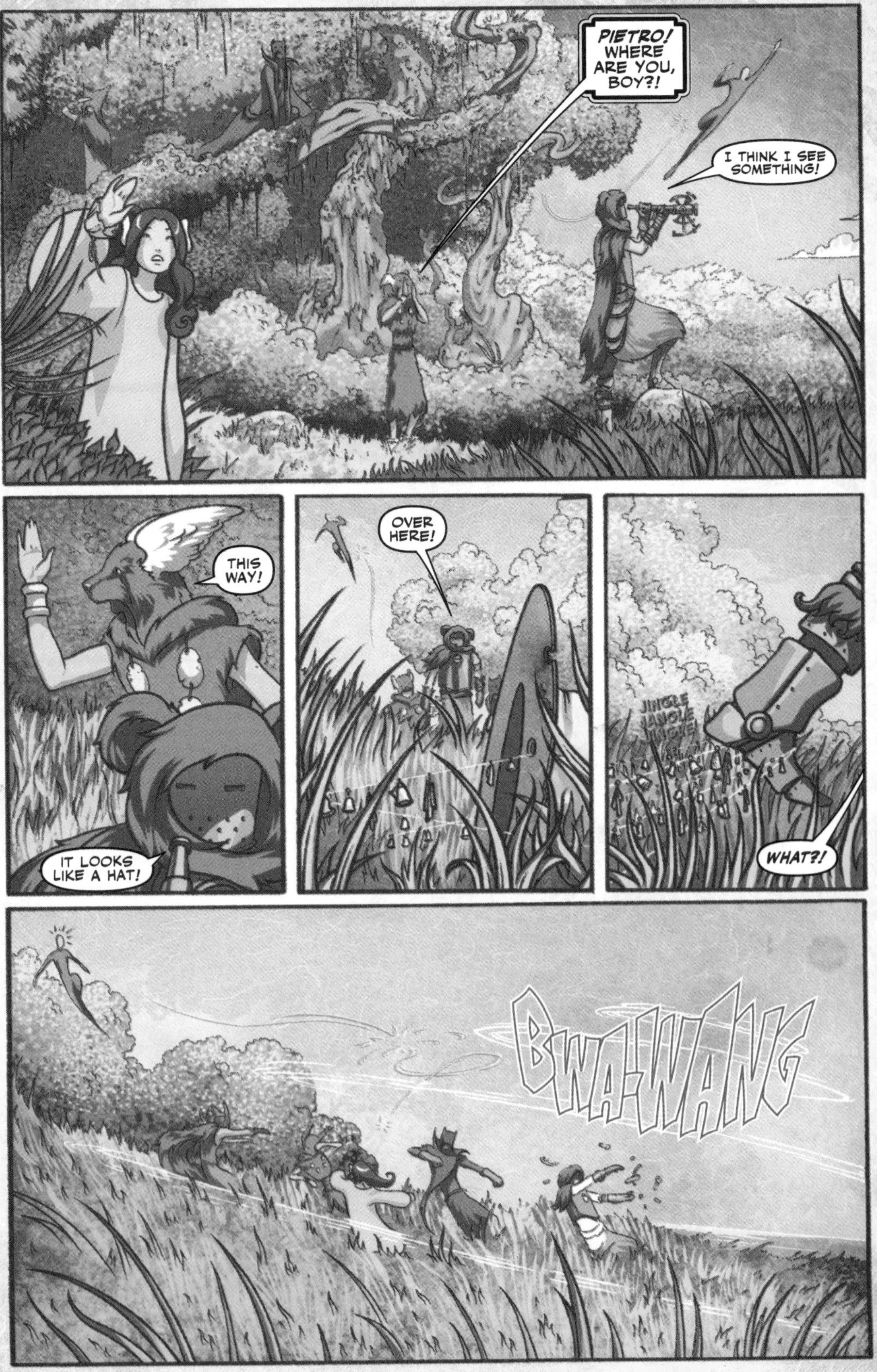
PIETRO! WHERE ARE YOU, BOY?!
I THINK I SEE SOMETHING!
THIS WAY!
IT LOOKS LIKE A HAT!
OVER HERE!
JINGLE
JANGLE
WHAT?!
BWA-WANG

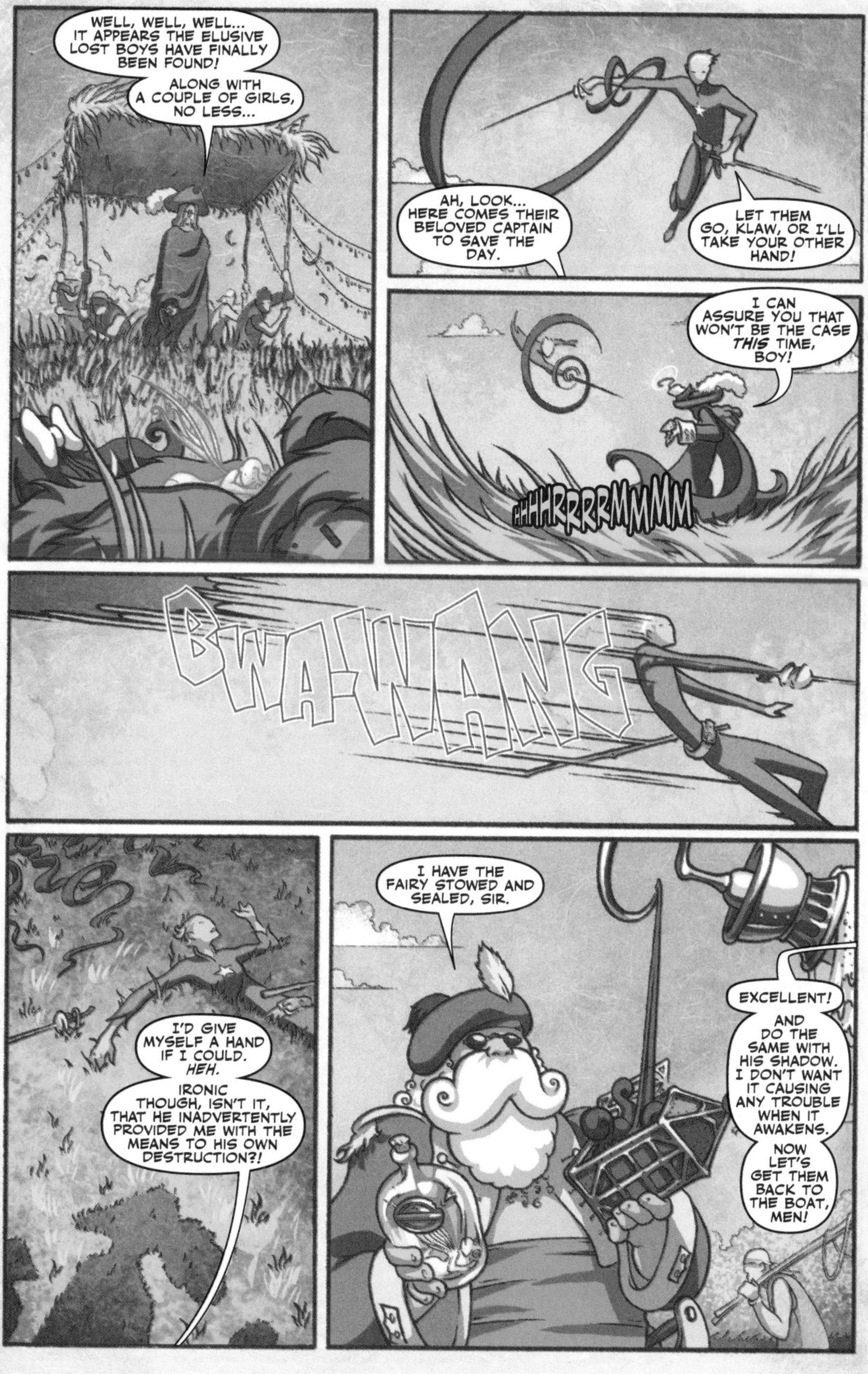
WELL, WELL, WELL... IT APPEARS THE ELUSIVE LOST BOYS HAVE FINALLY BEEN FOUND!
ALONG WITH A COUPLE OF GIRLS, NO LESS...
AH, LOOK... HERE COMES THEIR BELOVED CAPTAIN TO SAVE THE DAY.
LET THEM GO, KLAW, OR I'LL TAKE YOUR OTHER HAND!
I CAN ASSURE YOU THAT WON'T BE THE CASE THIS TIME, BOY!
HHHHRRRRMMMM
BWA-WANG
I'D GIVE MYSELF A HAND IF I COULD. HEH.
IRONIC THOUGH, ISN'T IT, THAT HE INADVERTENTLY PROVIDED ME WITH THE MEANS TO HIS OWN DESTRUCTION?!
I HAVE THE FAIRY STOWED AND SEALED, SIR.
EXCELLENT!
AND DO THE SAME WITH HIS SHADOW. I DON'T WANT IT CAUSING ANY TROUBLE WHEN IT AWAKENS.
NOW LET'S GET THEM BACK TO THE BOAT, MEN!

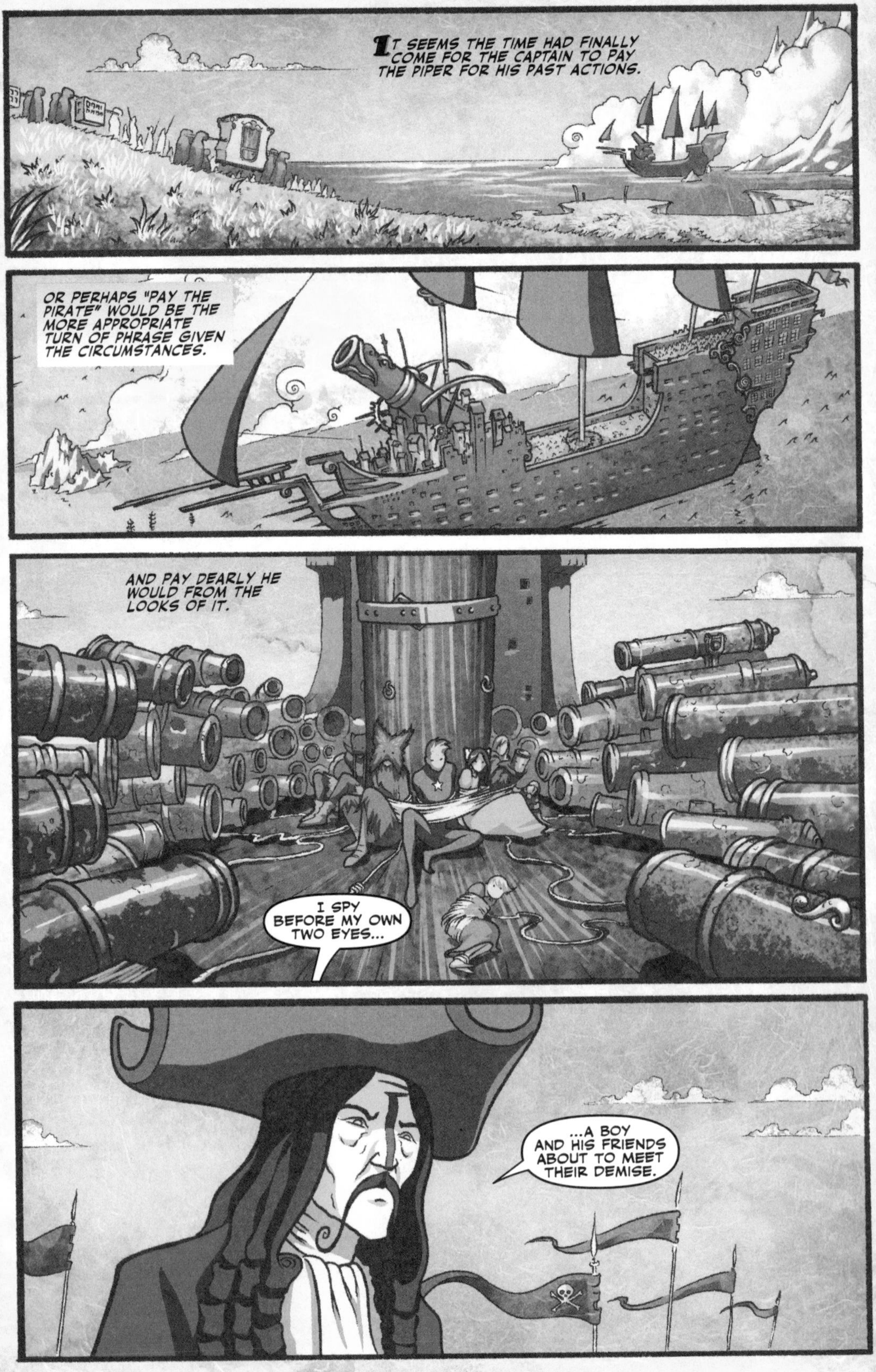
IT SEEMS THE TIME HAD FINALLY COME FOR THE CAPTAIN TO PAY THE PIPER FOR HIS PAST ACTIONS.
OR PERHAPS "PAY THE PIRATE" WOULD BE THE MORE APPROPRIATE TURN OF PHRASE GIVEN THE CIRCUMSTANCES.
AND PAY DEARLY HE WOULD FROM THE LOOKS OF IT.
I SPY BEFORE MY OWN TWO EYES...
...A BOY AND HIS FRIENDS ABOUT TO MEET THEIR DEMISE.

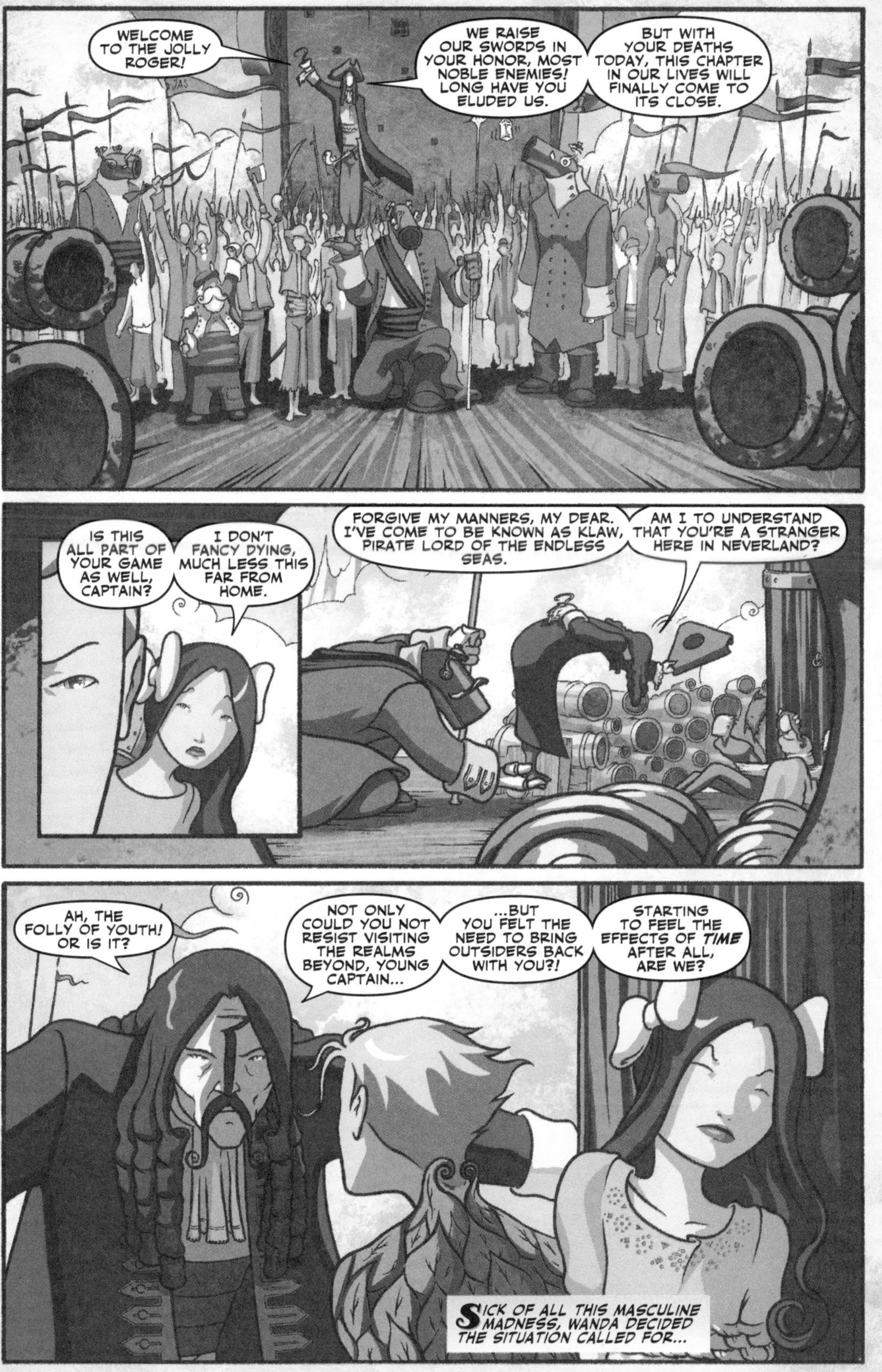
WELCOME TO THE JOLLY ROGER!
WE RAISE OUR SWORDS IN YOUR HONOR, MOST NOBLE ENEMIES! LONG HAVE YOU ELUDED US.
BUT WITH YOUR DEATHS TODAY, THIS CHAPTER IN OUR LIVES WILL FINALLY COME TO ITS CLOSE.
IS THIS ALL PART OF YOUR GAME AS WELL, CAPTAIN?
I DON'T FANCY DYING, MUCH LESS THIS FAR FROM HOME.
FORGIVE MY MANNERS, MY DEAR. I'VE COME TO BE KNOWN AS KLAW, PIRATE LORD OF THE ENDLESS SEAS.
AM I TO UNDERSTAND THAT YOU'RE A STRANGER HERE IN NEVERLAND?
AH, THE FOLLY OF YOUTH! OR IS IT?
NOT ONLY COULD YOU NOT RESIST VISITING THE REALMS BEYOND, YOUNG CAPTAIN...
...BUT YOU FELT THE NEED TO BRING OUTSIDERS BACK WITH YOU?!
STARTING TO FEEL THE EFFECTS OF *TIME* AFTER ALL, ARE WE?
SICK OF ALL THIS MASCULINE MADNESS, WANDA DECIDED THE SITUATION CALLED FOR...

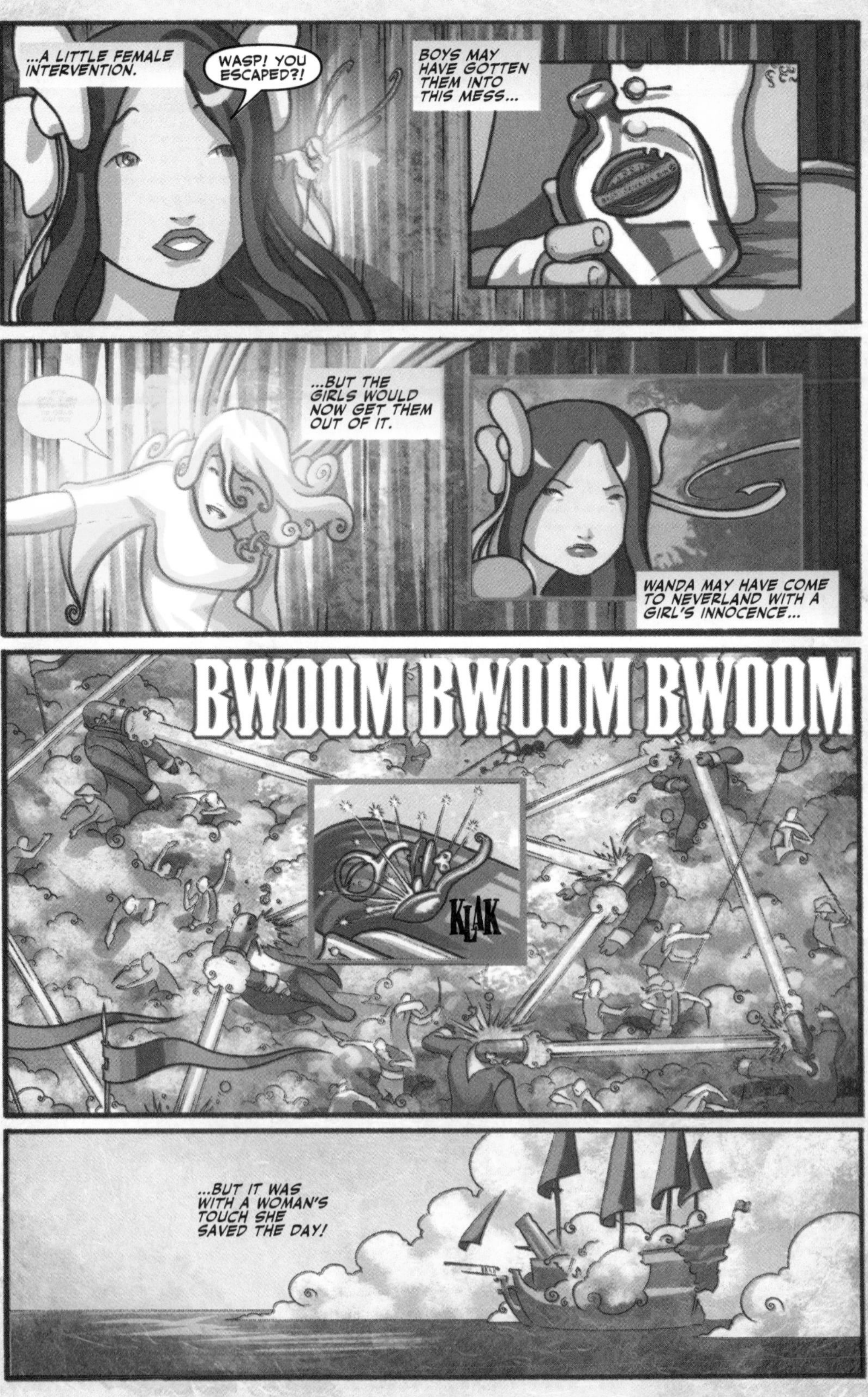
...A LITTLE FEMALE INTERVENTION.
WASP! YOU ESCAPED?!
BOYS MAY HAVE GOTTEN THEM INTO THIS MESS...
...BUT THE GIRLS WOULD NOW GET THEM OUT OF IT.
WANDA MAY HAVE COME TO NEVERLAND WITH A GIRL'S INNOCENCE...
BWOOM BWOOM BWOOM
KLAK
...BUT IT WAS WITH A WOMAN'S TOUCH SHE SAVED THE DAY!

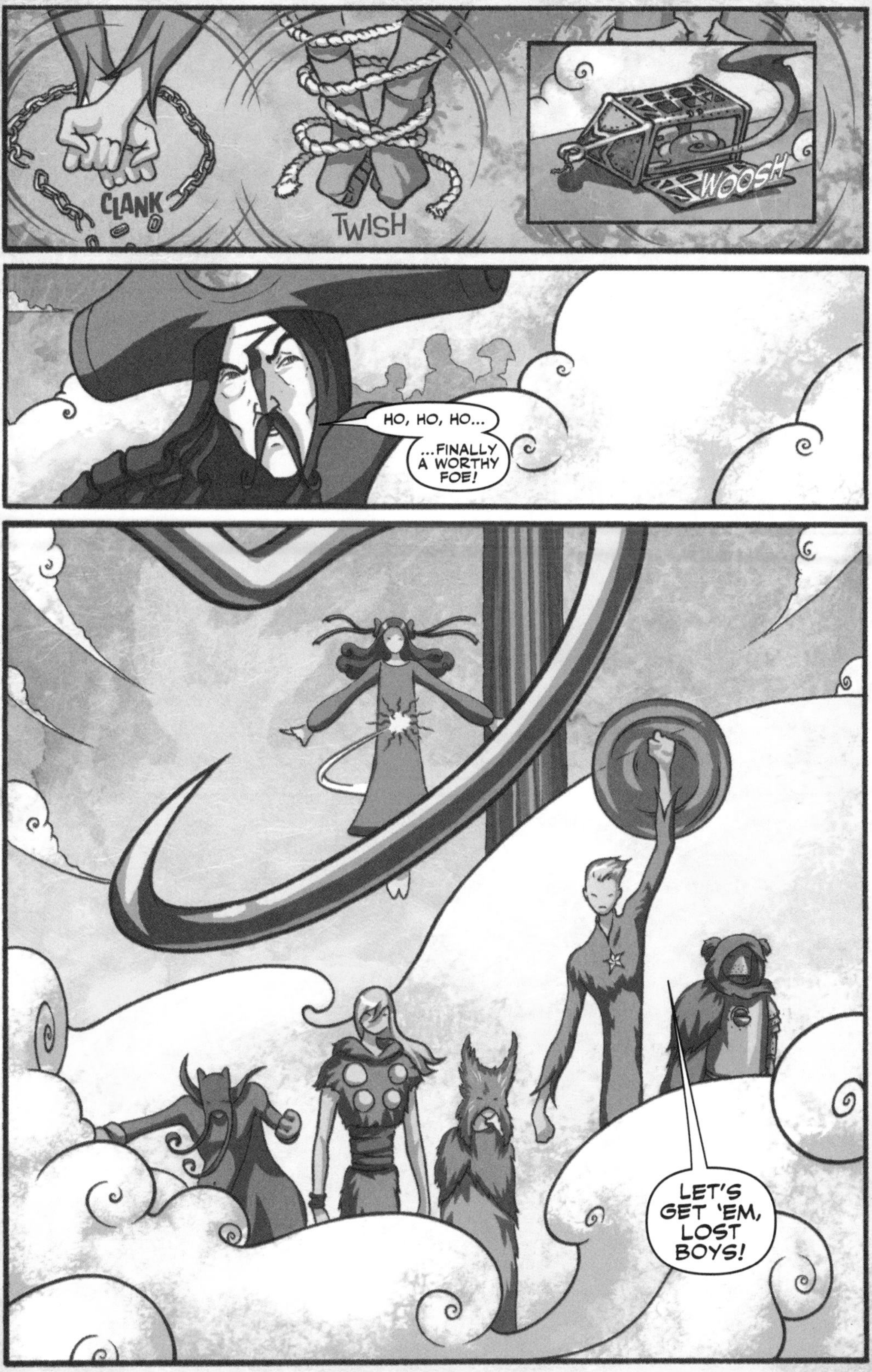
CLANK
TWISH
WOOSH
HO, HO, HO...
...FINALLY A WORTHY FOE!
LET'S GET 'EM, LOST BOYS!

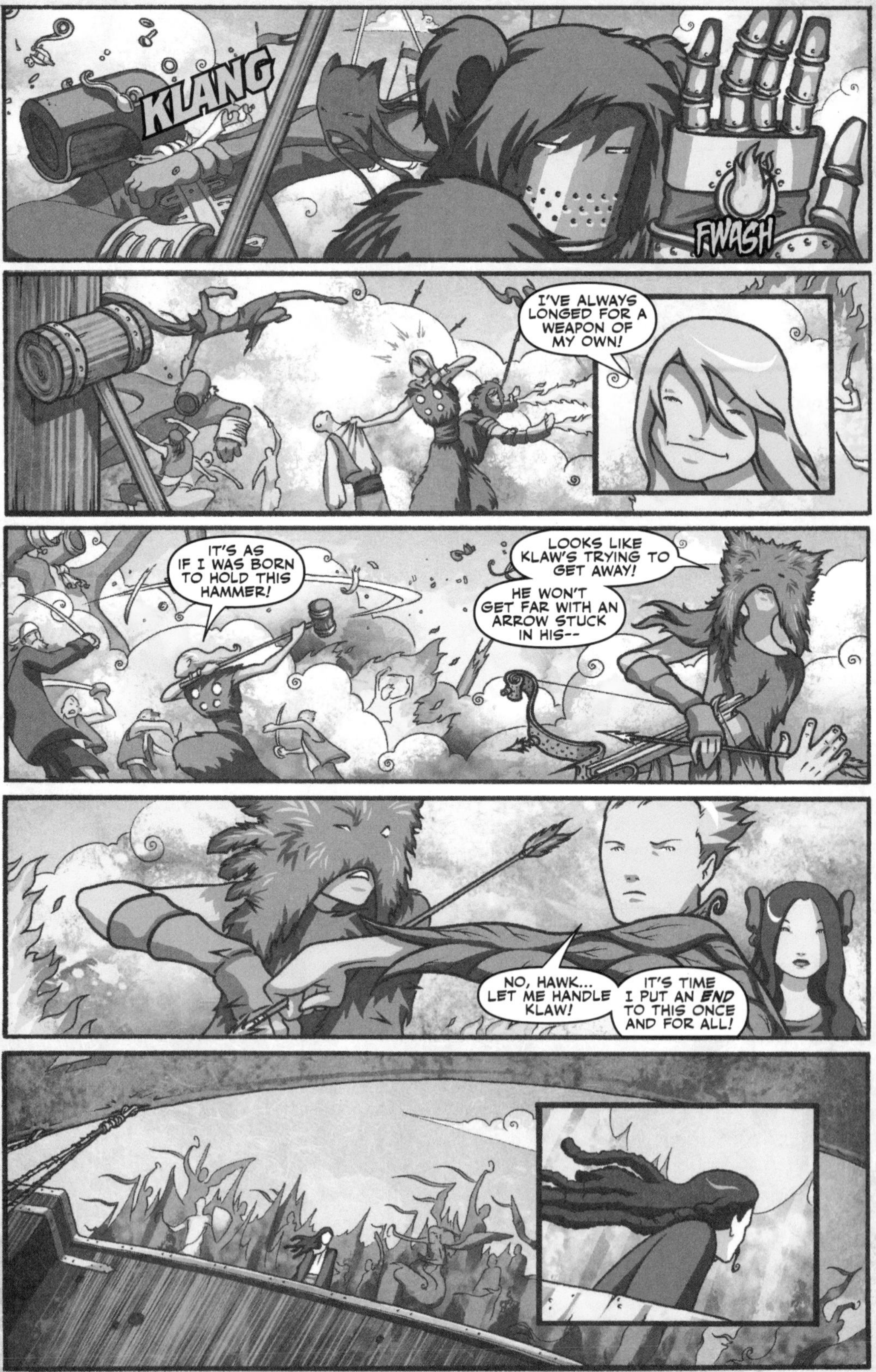
KLANG
FWASH
I'VE ALWAYS LONGED FOR A WEAPON OF MY OWN!
IT'S AS IF I WAS BORN TO HOLD THIS HAMMER!
LOOKS LIKE KLAW'S TRYING TO GET AWAY!
HE WON'T GET FAR WITH AN ARROW STUCK IN HIS--
NO, HAWK... LET ME HANDLE KLAW!
IT'S TIME I PUT AN *END* TO THIS ONCE AND FOR ALL!

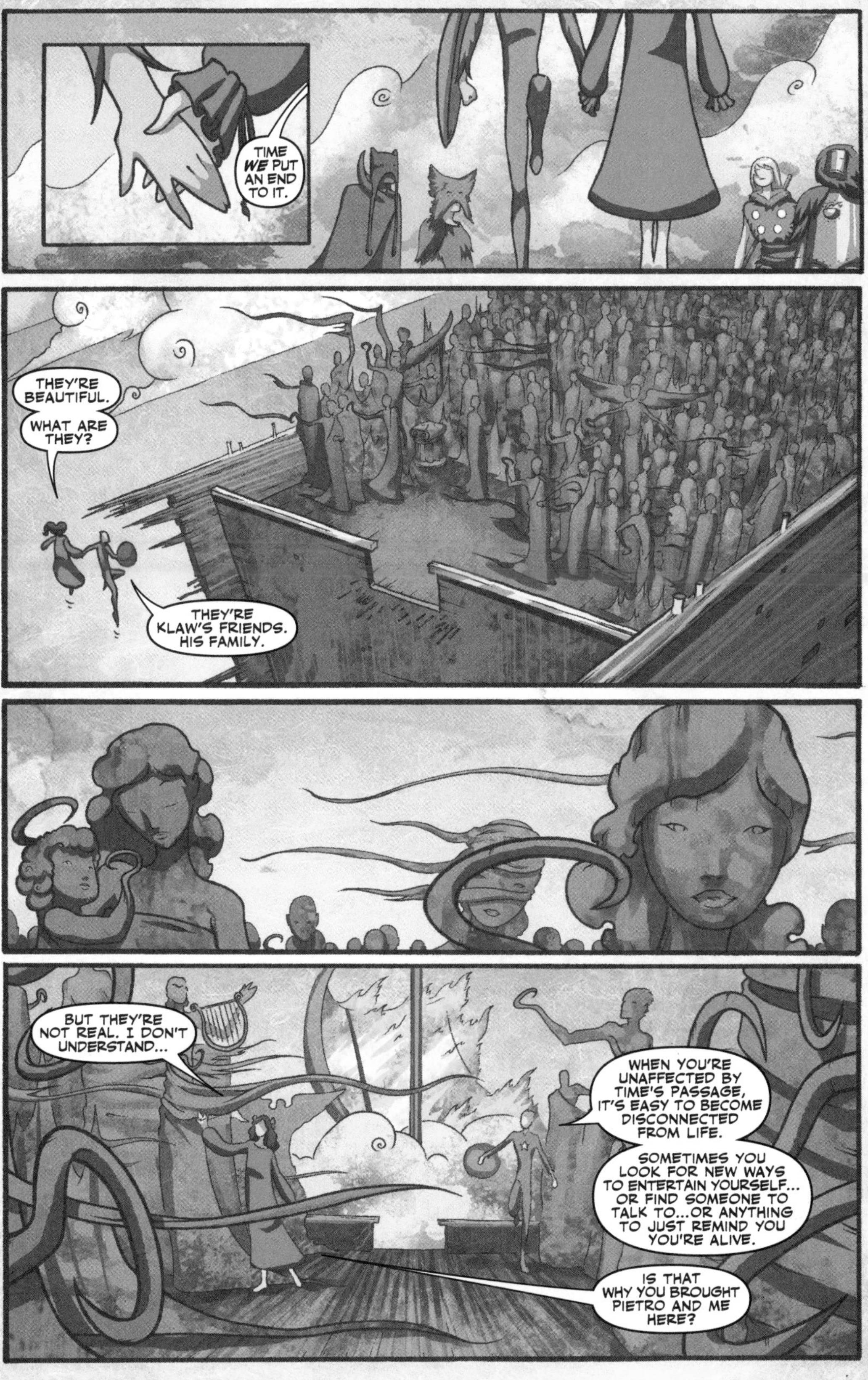

TIME WE PUT AN END TO IT.
THEY'RE BEAUTIFUL.
WHAT ARE THEY?
THEY'RE KLAW'S FRIENDS. HIS FAMILY.
BUT THEY'RE NOT REAL. I DON'T UNDERSTAND...
WHEN YOU'RE UNAFFECTED BY TIME'S PASSAGE, IT'S EASY TO BECOME DISCONNECTED FROM LIFE.
SOMETIMES YOU LOOK FOR NEW WAYS TO ENTERTAIN YOURSELF... OR FIND SOMEONE TO TALK TO...OR ANYTHING TO JUST REMIND YOU YOU'RE ALIVE.
IS THAT WHY YOU BROUGHT PIETRO AND ME HERE?

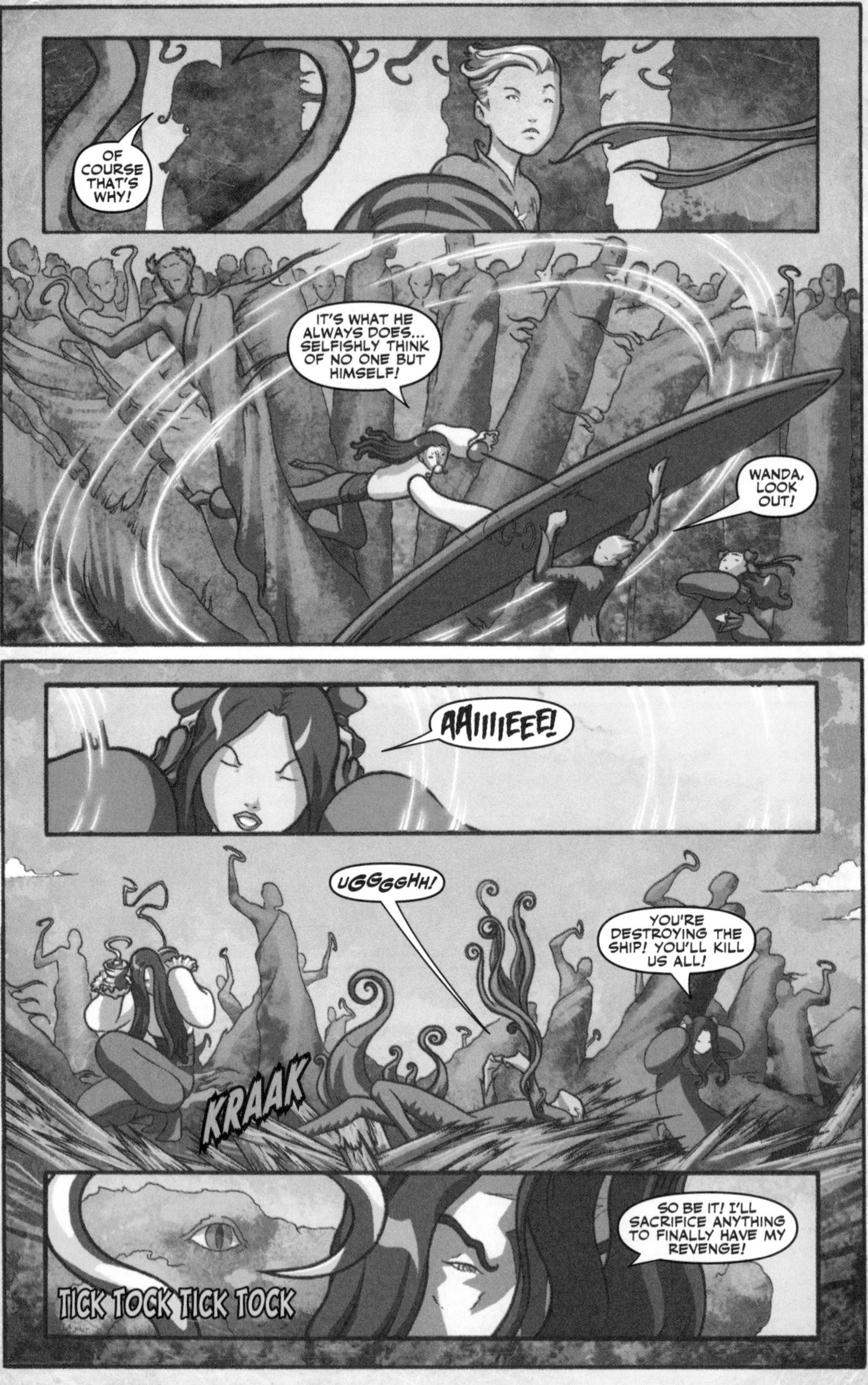
OF COURSE THAT'S WHY!
IT'S WHAT HE ALWAYS DOES... SELFISHLY THINK OF NO ONE BUT HIMSELF!
WANDA, LOOK OUT!
AAIIIIEEE!
UGGGGHH!
YOU'RE DESTROYING THE SHIP! YOU'LL KILL US ALL!
KRAAK
SO BE IT! I'LL SACRIFICE ANYTHING TO FINALLY HAVE MY REVENGE!
TICK TOCK TICK TOCK

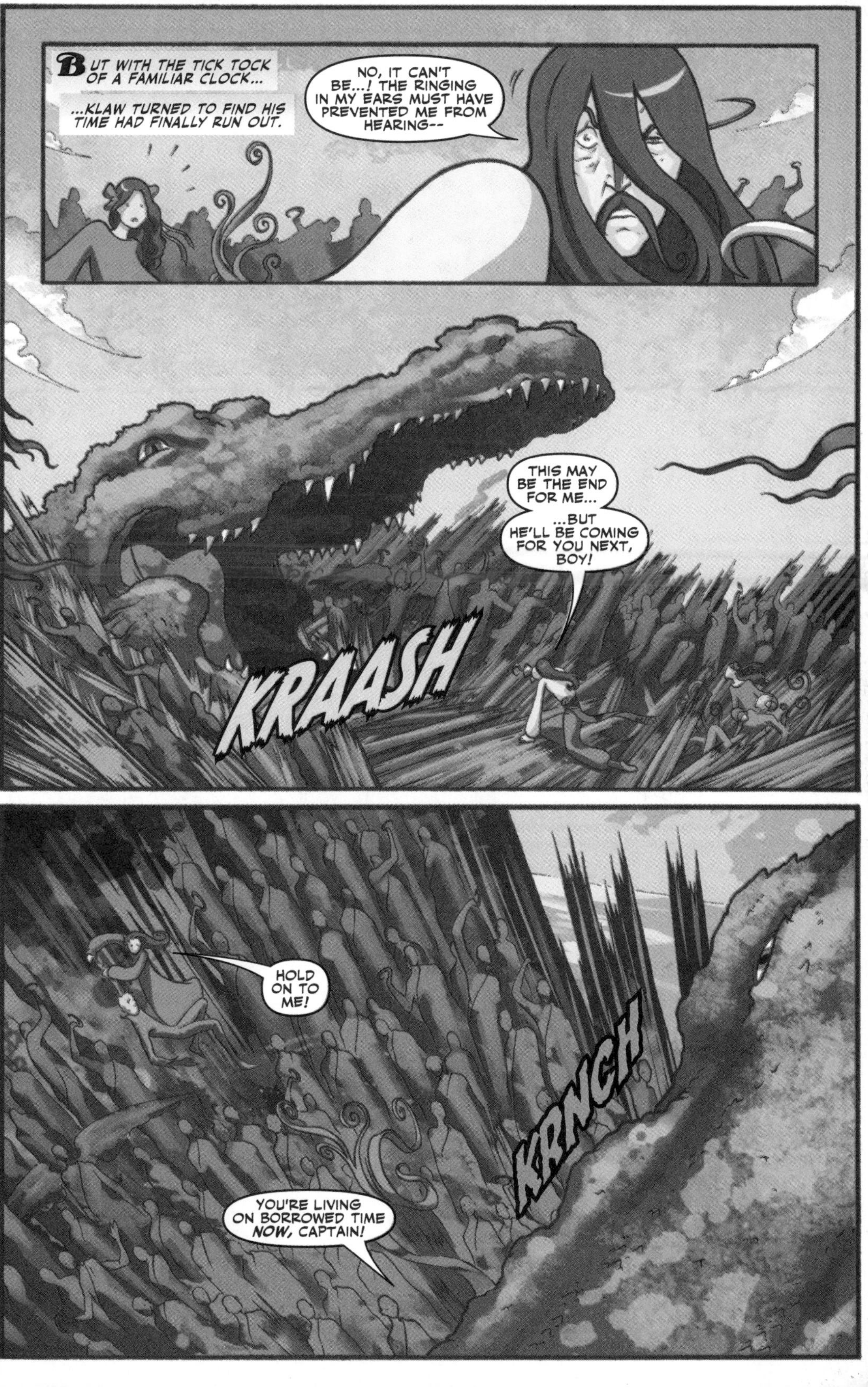

BUT WITH THE TICK TOCK OF A FAMILIAR CLOCK...
...KLAW TURNED TO FIND HIS TIME HAD FINALLY RUN OUT.
NO, IT CAN'T BE...! THE RINGING IN MY EARS MUST HAVE PREVENTED ME FROM HEARING--
THIS MAY BE THE END FOR ME...
...BUT HE'LL BE COMING FOR YOU NEXT, BOY!
KRAASH
HOLD ON TO ME!
KRNCH
YOU'RE LIVING ON BORROWED TIME NOW, CAPTAIN!

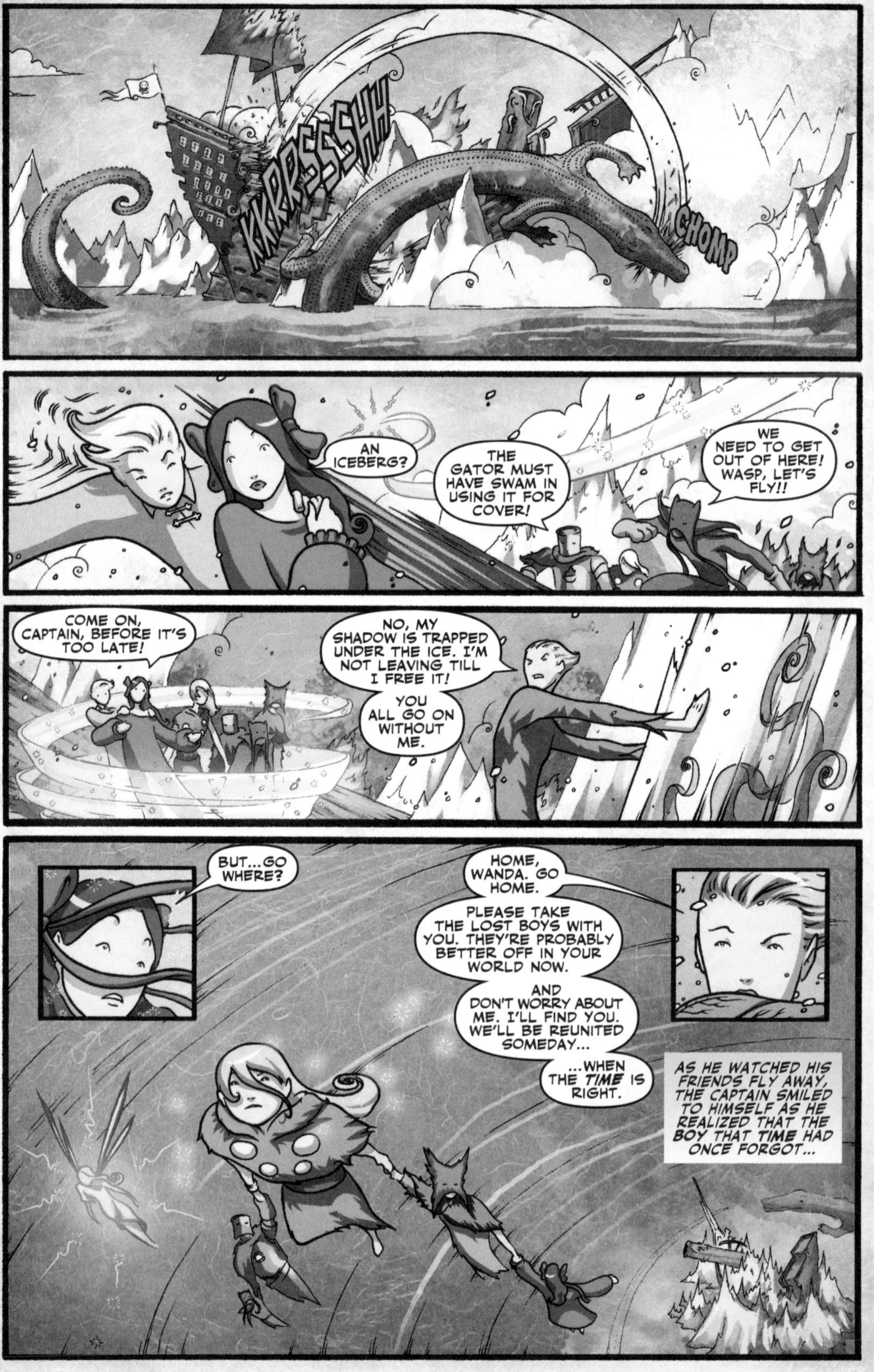
KKRRSSSHH
CHOMP
AN ICEBERG?
THE GATOR MUST HAVE SWAM IN USING IT FOR COVER!
WE NEED TO GET OUT OF HERE! WASP, LET'S FLY!!
COME ON, CAPTAIN, BEFORE IT'S TOO LATE!
NO, MY SHADOW IS TRAPPED UNDER THE ICE. I'M NOT LEAVING TILL I FREE IT!
YOU ALL GO ON WITHOUT ME.
BUT...GO WHERE?
HOME, WANDA. GO HOME.
PLEASE TAKE THE LOST BOYS WITH YOU. THEY'RE PROBABLY BETTER OFF IN YOUR WORLD NOW.
AND DON'T WORRY ABOUT ME. I'LL FIND YOU. WE'LL BE REUNITED SOMEDAY...
...WHEN THE TIME IS RIGHT.
AS HE WATCHED HIS FRIENDS FLY AWAY, THE CAPTAIN SMILED TO HIMSELF AS HE REALIZED THAT THE BOY THAT TIME HAD ONCE FORGOT...

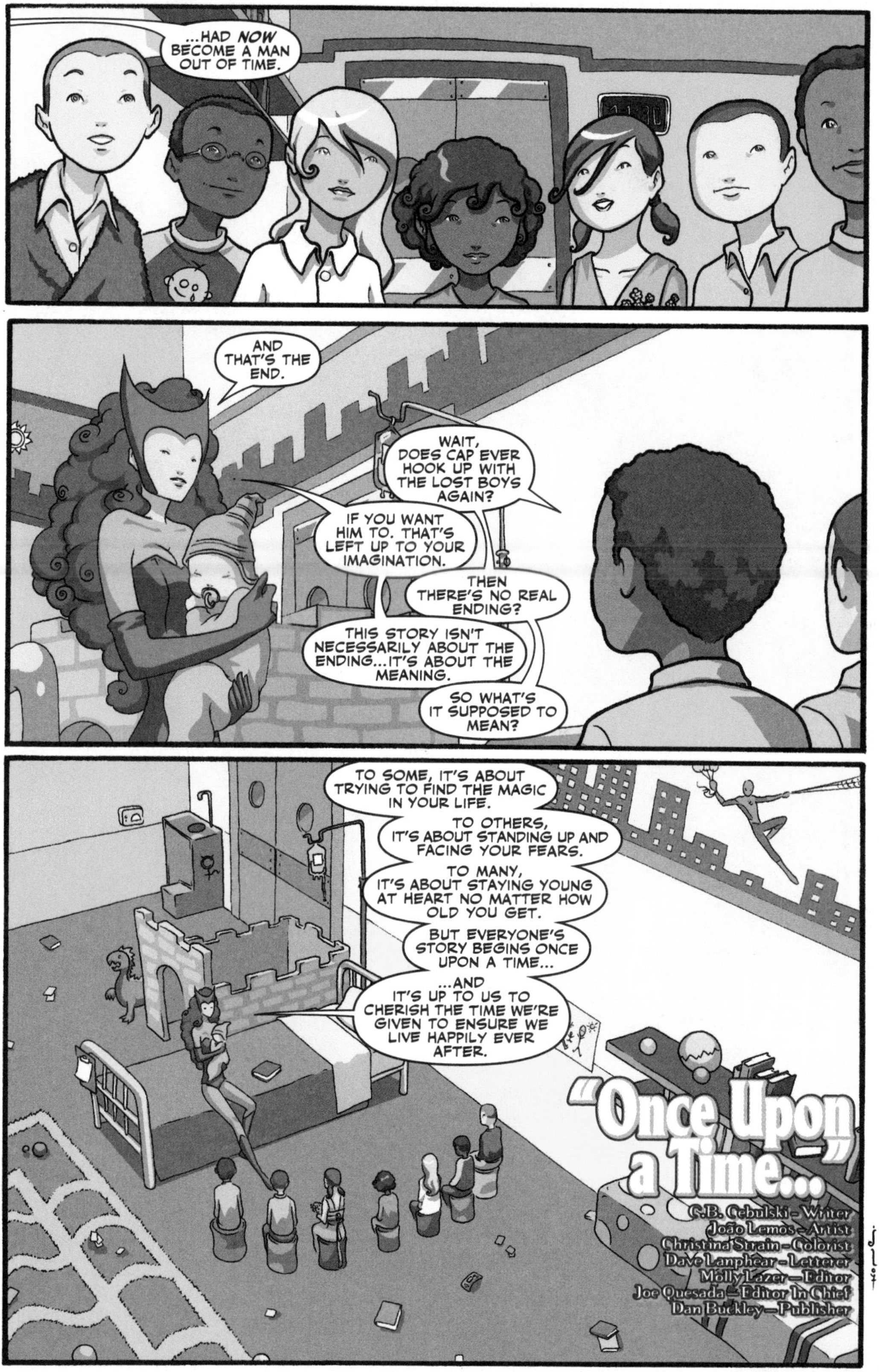

...HAD *NOW* BECOME A MAN OUT OF TIME.
AND THAT'S THE END.
WAIT, DOES CAP EVER HOOK UP WITH THE LOST BOYS AGAIN?
IF YOU WANT HIM TO. THAT'S LEFT UP TO YOUR IMAGINATION.
THEN THERE'S NO REAL ENDING?
THIS STORY ISN'T NECESSARILY ABOUT THE ENDING...IT'S ABOUT THE MEANING.
SO WHAT'S IT SUPPOSED TO MEAN?
TO SOME, IT'S ABOUT TRYING TO FIND THE MAGIC IN YOUR LIFE.
TO OTHERS, IT'S ABOUT STANDING UP AND FACING YOUR FEARS.
TO MANY, IT'S ABOUT STAYING YOUNG AT HEART NO MATTER HOW OLD YOU GET.
BUT EVERYONE'S STORY BEGINS ONCE UPON A TIME...
...AND IT'S UP TO US TO CHERISH THE TIME WE'RE GIVEN TO ENSURE WE LIVE HAPPILY EVER AFTER.
"Once Upon a Time..."
C.B. Cebulski – Writer
João Lemos – Artist
Christina Strain – Colorist
Dave Lanphear – Letterer
Molly Lazer – Editor
Joe Quesada – Editor In Chief
Dan Buckley – Publisher

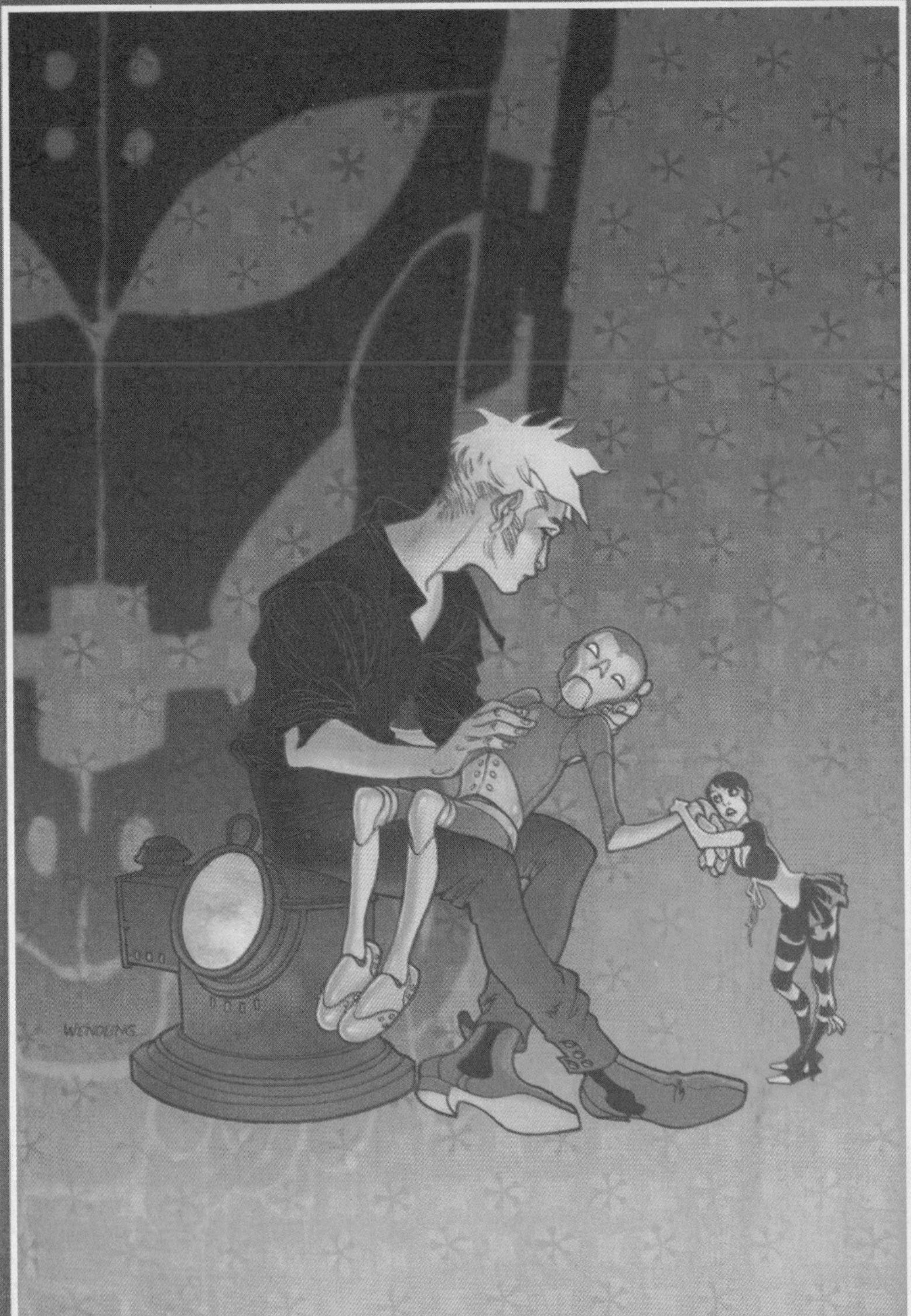
WENDLING

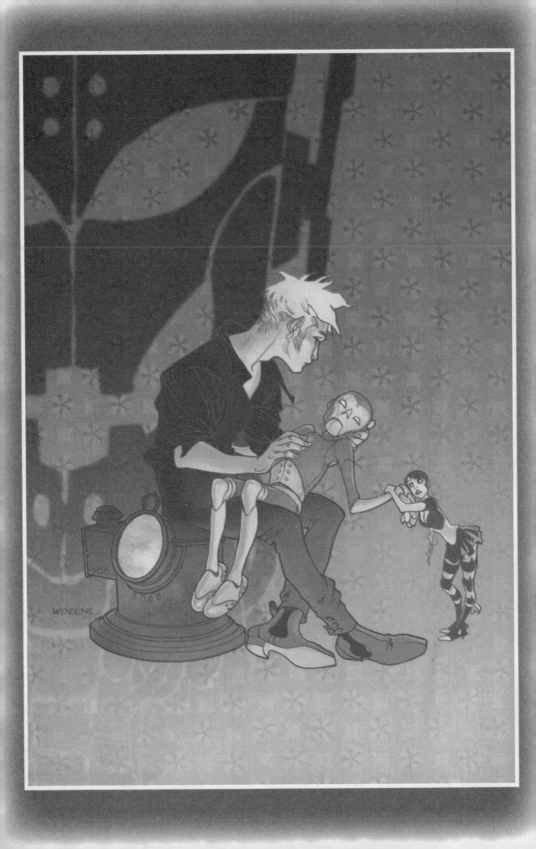

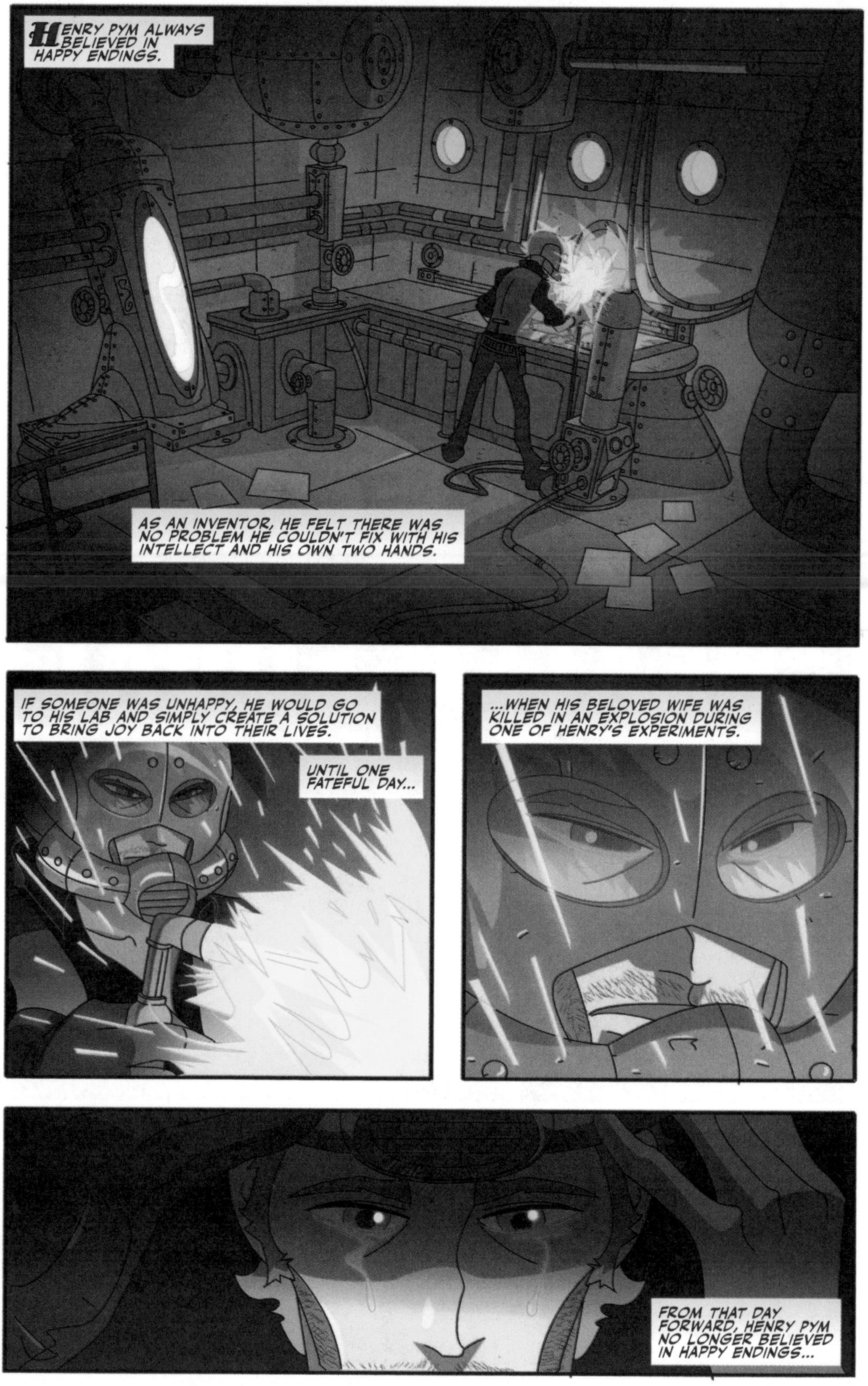
HENRY PYM ALWAYS BELIEVED IN HAPPY ENDINGS.
AS AN INVENTOR, HE FELT THERE WAS NO PROBLEM HE COULDN'T FIX WITH HIS INTELLECT AND HIS OWN TWO HANDS.
IF SOMEONE WAS UNHAPPY, HE WOULD GO TO HIS LAB AND SIMPLY CREATE A SOLUTION TO BRING JOY BACK INTO THEIR LIVES.
UNTIL ONE FATEFUL DAY...
...WHEN HIS BELOVED WIFE WAS KILLED IN AN EXPLOSION DURING ONE OF HENRY'S EXPERIMENTS.
FROM THAT DAY FORWARD, HENRY PYM NO LONGER BELIEVED IN HAPPY ENDINGS...

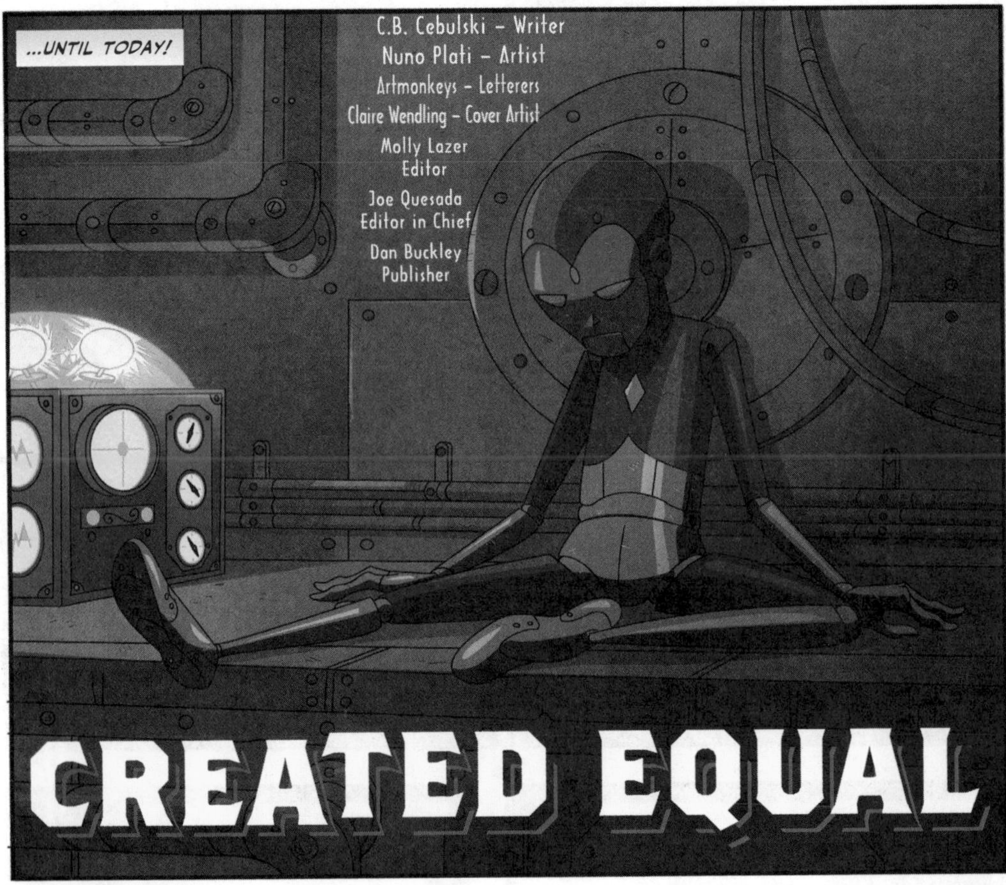
...UNTIL TODAY!
C.B. Cebulski – Writer
Nuno Plati – Artist
Artmonkeys – Letterers
Claire Wendling – Cover Artist
Molly Lazer
Editor
Joe Quesada
Editor in Chief
Dan Buckley
Publisher
CREATED EQUAL

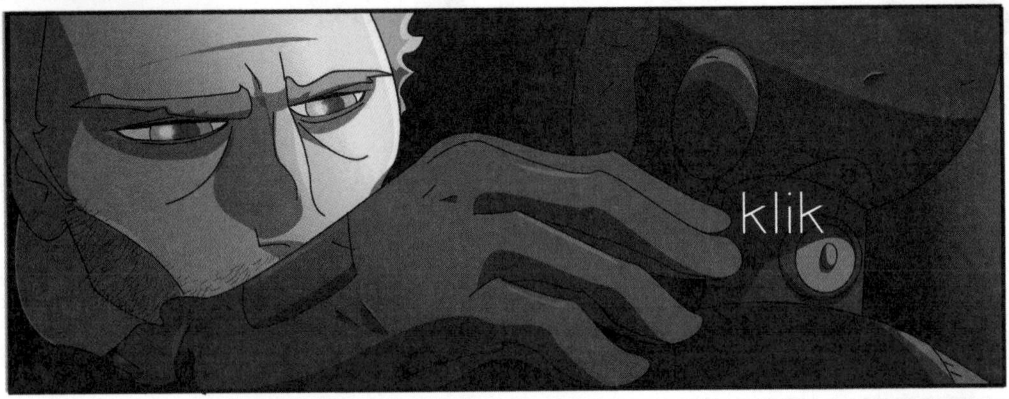
klik

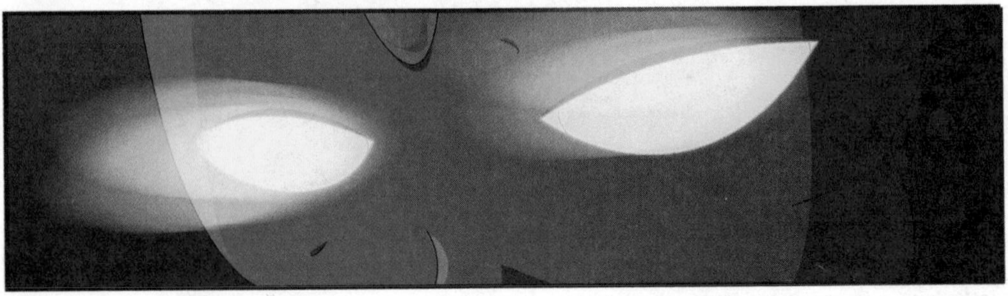

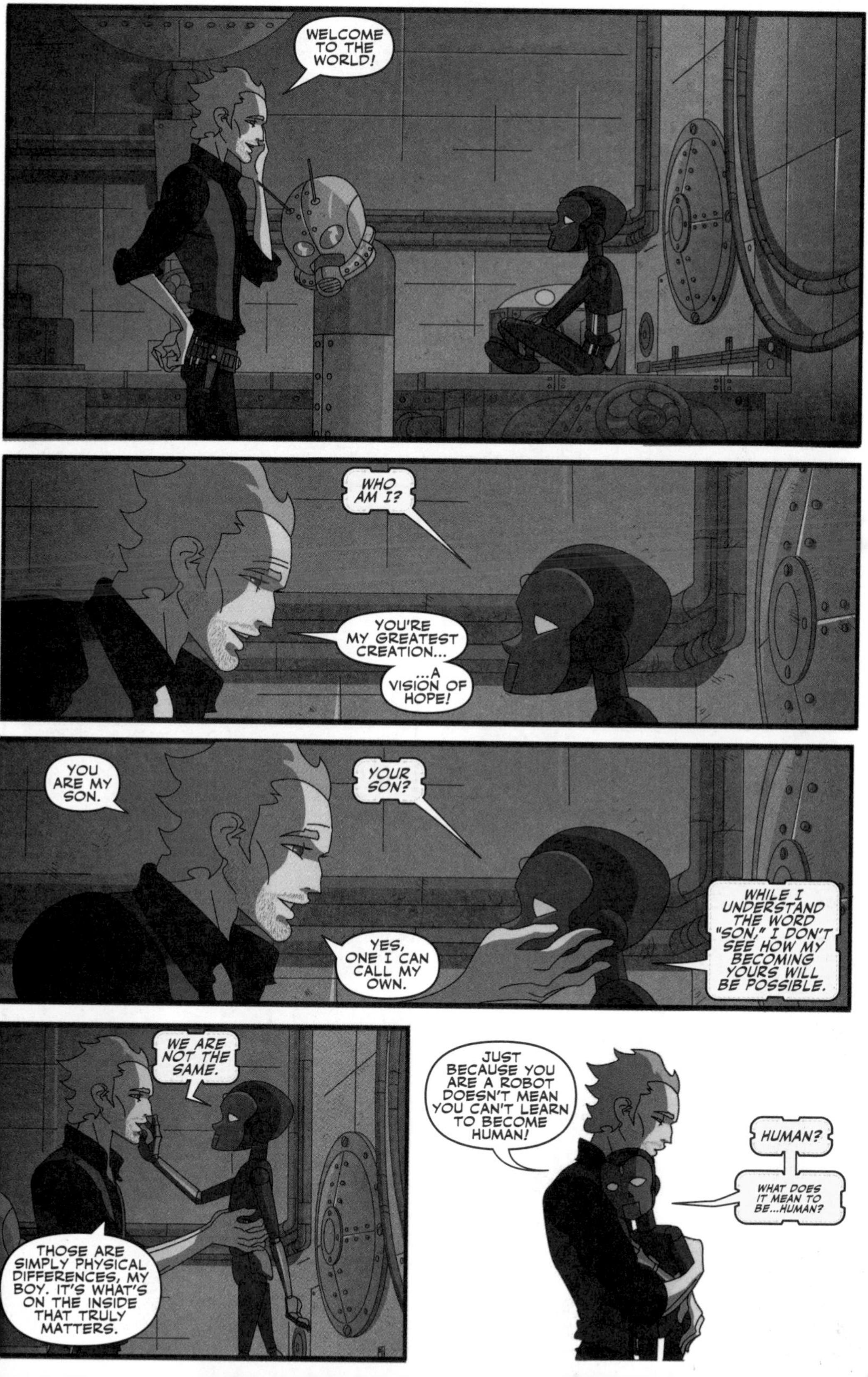
WELCOME TO THE WORLD!
WHO AM I?
YOU'RE MY GREATEST CREATION...
...A VISION OF HOPE!
YOU ARE MY SON.
YOUR SON?
YES, ONE I CAN CALL MY OWN.
WHILE I UNDERSTAND THE WORD "SON," I DON'T SEE HOW MY BECOMING YOURS WILL BE POSSIBLE.
WE ARE NOT THE SAME.
THOSE ARE SIMPLY PHYSICAL DIFFERENCES, MY BOY. IT'S WHAT'S ON THE INSIDE THAT TRULY MATTERS.
JUST BECAUSE YOU ARE A ROBOT DOESN'T MEAN YOU CAN'T LEARN TO BECOME HUMAN!
HUMAN?
WHAT DOES IT MEAN TO BE...HUMAN?

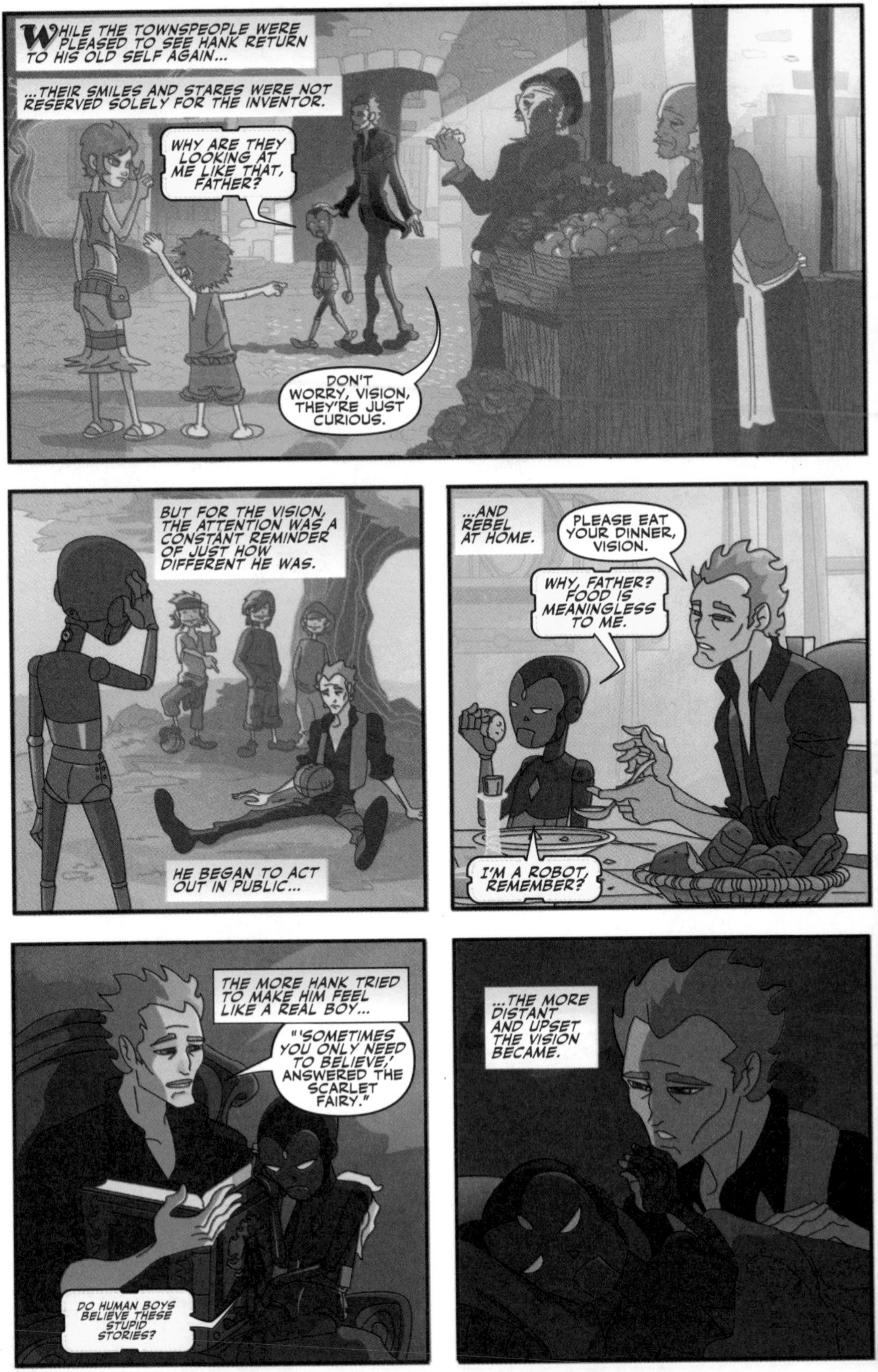
WHILE THE TOWNSPEOPLE WERE PLEASED TO SEE HANK RETURN TO HIS OLD SELF AGAIN...
...THEIR SMILES AND STARES WERE NOT RESERVED SOLELY FOR THE INVENTOR.
WHY ARE THEY LOOKING AT ME LIKE THAT, FATHER?
DON'T WORRY, VISION, THEY'RE JUST CURIOUS.
BUT FOR THE VISION, THE ATTENTION WAS A CONSTANT REMINDER OF JUST HOW DIFFERENT HE WAS.
HE BEGAN TO ACT OUT IN PUBLIC...
...AND REBEL AT HOME.
PLEASE EAT YOUR DINNER, VISION.
WHY, FATHER? FOOD IS MEANINGLESS TO ME.
I'M A ROBOT, REMEMBER?
THE MORE HANK TRIED TO MAKE HIM FEEL LIKE A REAL BOY...
"'SOMETIMES YOU ONLY NEED TO BELIEVE,' ANSWERED THE SCARLET FAIRY."
DO HUMAN BOYS BELIEVE THESE STUPID STORIES?
...THE MORE DISTANT AND UPSET THE VISION BECAME.

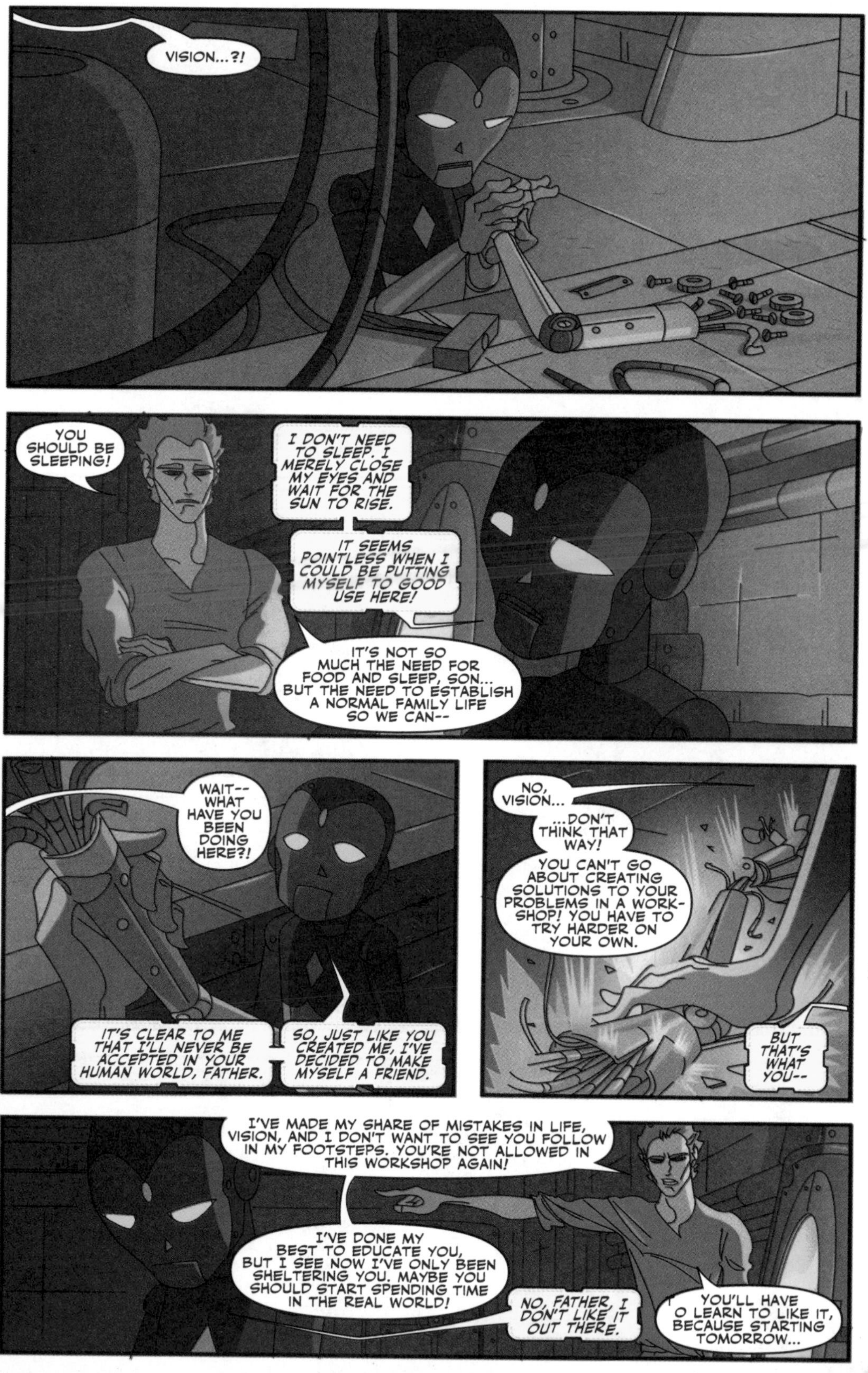
VISION...?!
YOU SHOULD BE SLEEPING!
I DON'T NEED TO SLEEP. I MERELY CLOSE MY EYES AND WAIT FOR THE SUN TO RISE.
IT SEEMS POINTLESS WHEN I COULD BE PUTTING MYSELF TO GOOD USE HERE!
IT'S NOT SO MUCH THE NEED FOR FOOD AND SLEEP, SON... BUT THE NEED TO ESTABLISH A NORMAL FAMILY LIFE SO WE CAN--
WAIT-- WHAT HAVE YOU BEEN DOING HERE?!
IT'S CLEAR TO ME THAT I'LL NEVER BE ACCEPTED IN YOUR HUMAN WORLD, FATHER.
SO, JUST LIKE YOU CREATED ME, I'VE DECIDED TO MAKE MYSELF A FRIEND.
NO, VISION...
...DON'T THINK THAT WAY!
YOU CAN'T GO ABOUT CREATING SOLUTIONS TO YOUR PROBLEMS IN A WORK-SHOP! YOU HAVE TO TRY HARDER ON YOUR OWN.
BUT THAT'S WHAT YOU--
I'VE MADE MY SHARE OF MISTAKES IN LIFE, VISION, AND I DON'T WANT TO SEE YOU FOLLOW IN MY FOOTSTEPS. YOU'RE NOT ALLOWED IN THIS WORKSHOP AGAIN!
I'VE DONE MY BEST TO EDUCATE YOU, BUT I SEE NOW I'VE ONLY BEEN SHELTERING YOU. MAYBE YOU SHOULD START SPENDING TIME IN THE REAL WORLD!
NO, FATHER, I DON'T LIKE IT OUT THERE.
YOU'LL HAVE O LEARN TO LIKE IT, BECAUSE STARTING TOMORROW...

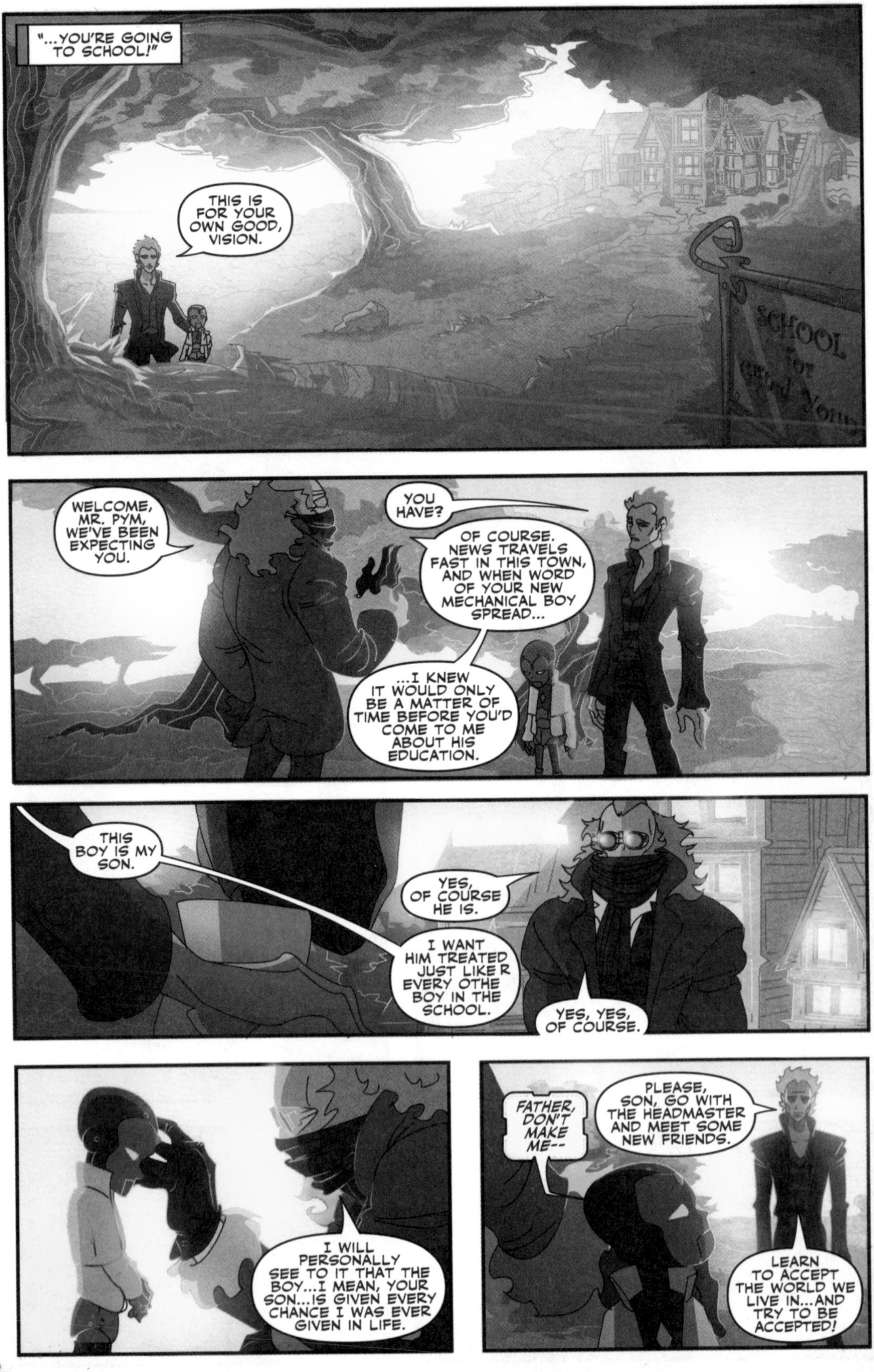
"...YOU'RE GOING TO SCHOOL!"
THIS IS FOR YOUR OWN GOOD, VISION.
SCHOOL for
WELCOME, MR. PYM, WE'VE BEEN EXPECTING YOU.
YOU HAVE?
OF COURSE. NEWS TRAVELS FAST IN THIS TOWN, AND WHEN WORD OF YOUR NEW MECHANICAL BOY SPREAD...
...I KNEW IT WOULD ONLY BE A MATTER OF TIME BEFORE YOU'D COME TO ME ABOUT HIS EDUCATION.
THIS BOY IS MY SON.
YES, OF COURSE HE IS.
I WANT HIM TREATED JUST LIKE R EVERY OTHE BOY IN THE SCHOOL.
YES, YES, OF COURSE.
I WILL PERSONALLY SEE TO IT THAT THE BOY...I MEAN, YOUR SON...IS GIVEN EVERY CHANCE I WAS EVER GIVEN IN LIFE.
FATHER, DON'T MAKE ME--
PLEASE, SON, GO WITH THE HEADMASTER AND MEET SOME NEW FRIENDS.
LEARN TO ACCEPT THE WORLD WE LIVE IN...AND TRY TO BE ACCEPTED!

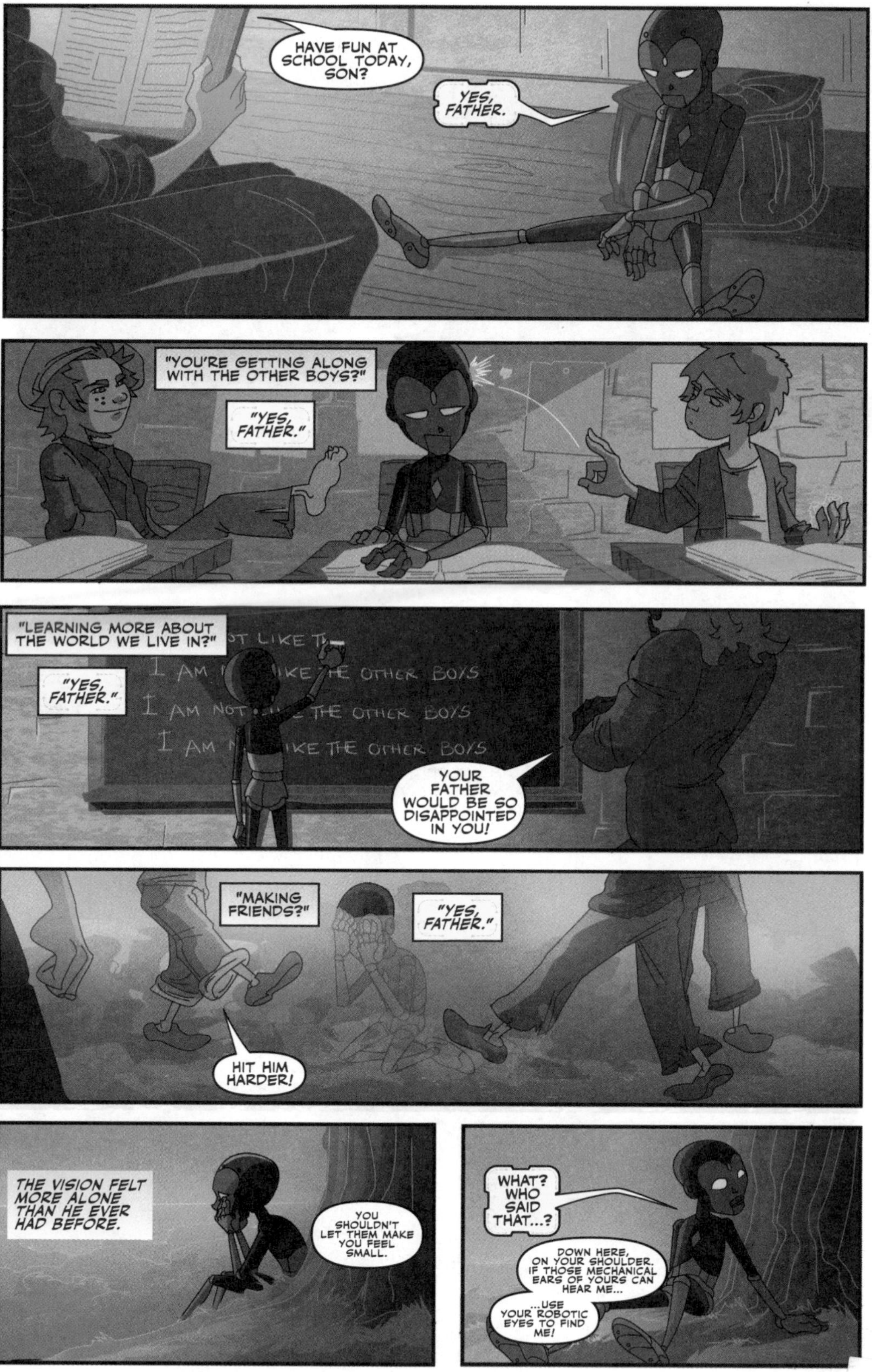
HAVE FUN AT SCHOOL TODAY, SON?
YES, FATHER.
"YOU'RE GETTING ALONG WITH THE OTHER BOYS?"
"YES, FATHER."
"LEARNING MORE ABOUT THE WORLD WE LIVE IN?"
"YES, FATHER."
I AM NOT LIKE THE OTHER BOYS
I AM NOT LIKE THE OTHER BOYS
I AM NOT LIKE THE OTHER BOYS
YOUR FATHER WOULD BE SO DISAPPOINTED IN YOU!
"MAKING FRIENDS?"
"YES, FATHER."
HIT HIM HARDER!
THE VISION FELT MORE ALONE THAN HE EVER HAD BEFORE.
YOU SHOULDN'T LET THEM MAKE YOU FEEL SMALL.
WHAT? WHO SAID THAT...?
DOWN HERE, ON YOUR SHOULDER. IF THOSE MECHANICAL EARS OF YOURS CAN HEAR ME...
...USE YOUR ROBOTIC EYES TO FIND ME!

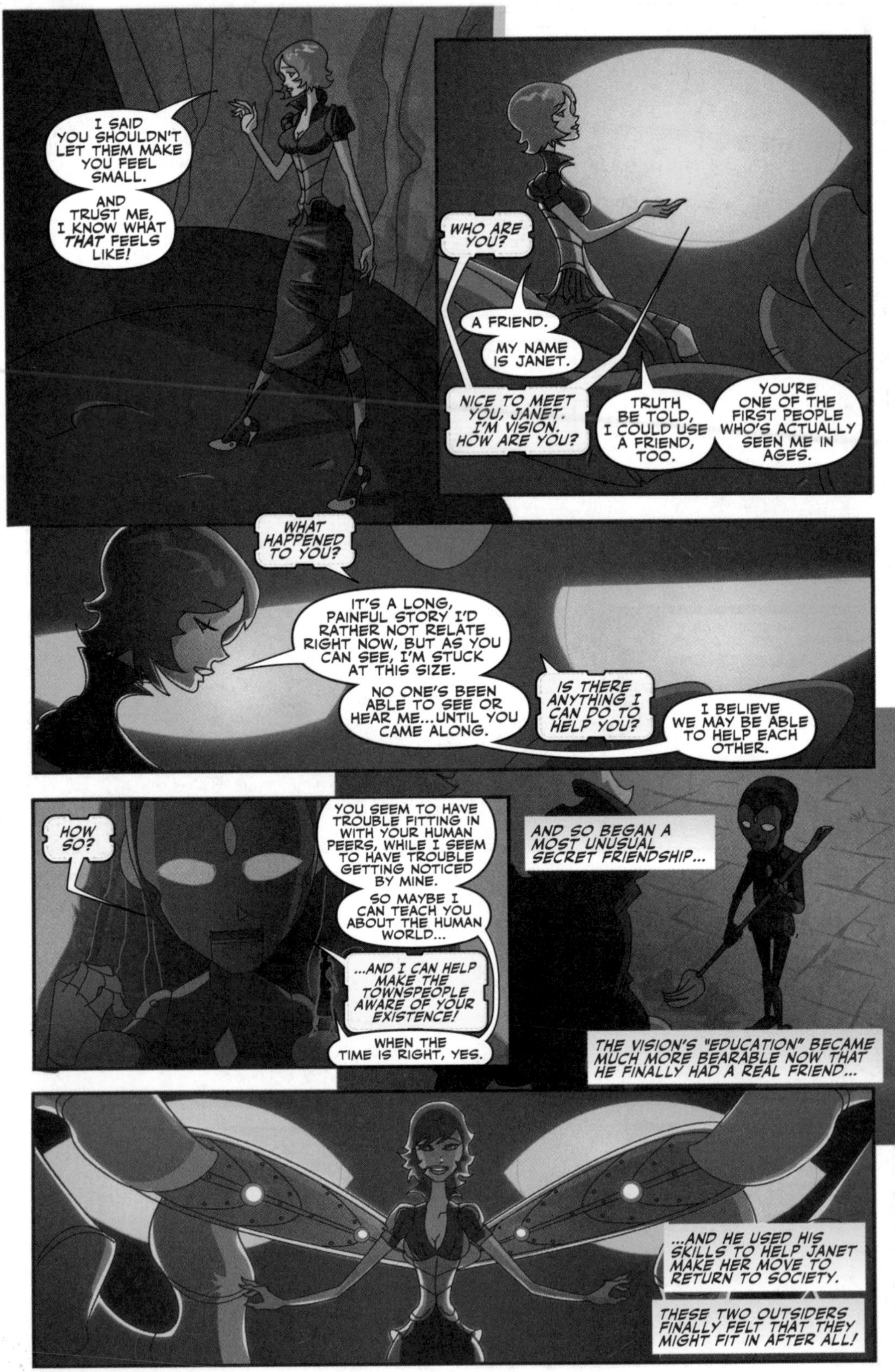
I SAID YOU SHOULDN'T LET THEM MAKE YOU FEEL SMALL.
AND TRUST ME, I KNOW WHAT *THAT* FEELS LIKE!
*WHO ARE YOU?*
A FRIEND.
MY NAME IS JANET.
*NICE TO MEET YOU, JANET. I'M VISION. HOW ARE YOU?*
TRUTH BE TOLD, I COULD USE A FRIEND, TOO.
YOU'RE ONE OF THE FIRST PEOPLE WHO'S ACTUALLY SEEN ME IN AGES.
*WHAT HAPPENED TO YOU?*
IT'S A LONG, PAINFUL STORY I'D RATHER NOT RELATE RIGHT NOW, BUT AS YOU CAN SEE, I'M STUCK AT THIS SIZE.
NO ONE'S BEEN ABLE TO SEE OR HEAR ME...UNTIL YOU CAME ALONG.
*IS THERE ANYTHING I CAN DO TO HELP YOU?*
I BELIEVE WE MAY BE ABLE TO HELP EACH OTHER.
*HOW SO?*
YOU SEEM TO HAVE TROUBLE FITTING IN WITH YOUR HUMAN PEERS, WHILE I SEEM TO HAVE TROUBLE GETTING NOTICED BY MINE.
SO MAYBE I CAN TEACH YOU ABOUT THE HUMAN WORLD...
*...AND I CAN HELP MAKE THE TOWNSPEOPLE AWARE OF YOUR EXISTENCE!*
WHEN THE TIME IS RIGHT, YES.
*AND SO BEGAN A MOST UNUSUAL SECRET FRIENDSHIP...*
*THE VISION'S "EDUCATION" BECAME MUCH MORE BEARABLE NOW THAT HE FINALLY HAD A REAL FRIEND...*
*...AND HE USED HIS SKILLS TO HELP JANET MAKE HER MOVE TO RETURN TO SOCIETY.*
*THESE TWO OUTSIDERS FINALLY FELT THAT THEY MIGHT FIT IN AFTER ALL!*

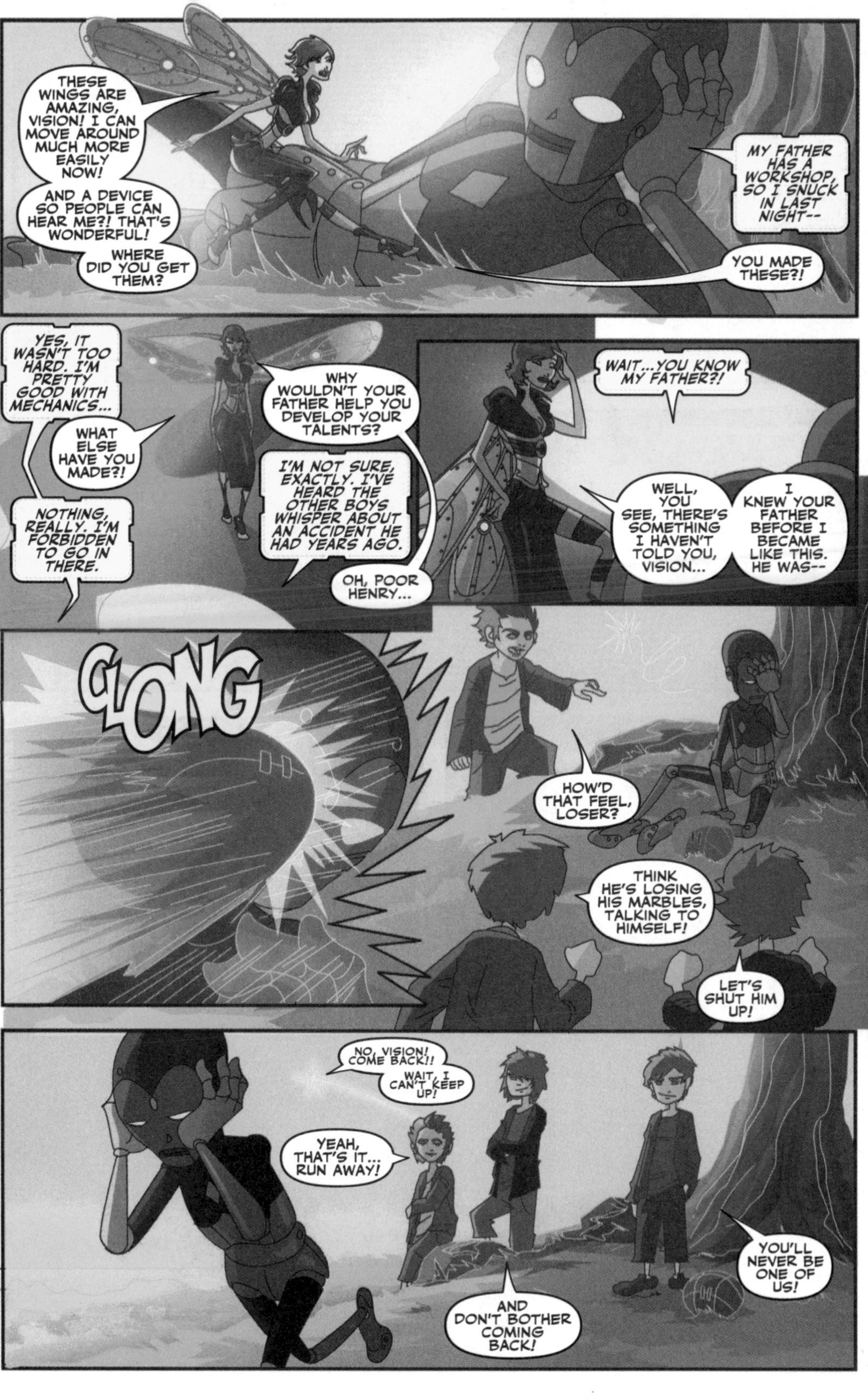
THESE WINGS ARE AMAZING, VISION! I CAN MOVE AROUND MUCH MORE EASILY NOW!
AND A DEVICE SO PEOPLE CAN HEAR ME?! THAT'S WONDERFUL!
WHERE DID YOU GET THEM?
MY FATHER HAS A WORKSHOP, SO I SNUCK IN LAST NIGHT--
YOU MADE THESE?!
YES, IT WASN'T TOO HARD. I'M PRETTY GOOD WITH MECHANICS...
WHAT ELSE HAVE YOU MADE?!
NOTHING, REALLY. I'M FORBIDDEN TO GO IN THERE.
WHY WOULDN'T YOUR FATHER HELP YOU DEVELOP YOUR TALENTS?
I'M NOT SURE, EXACTLY. I'VE HEARD THE OTHER BOYS WHISPER ABOUT AN ACCIDENT HE HAD YEARS AGO.
OH, POOR HENRY...
WAIT...YOU KNOW MY FATHER?!
WELL, YOU SEE, THERE'S SOMETHING I HAVEN'T TOLD YOU, VISION...
I KNEW YOUR FATHER BEFORE I BECAME LIKE THIS. HE WAS--
CLONG
HOW'D THAT FEEL, LOSER?
THINK HE'S LOSING HIS MARBLES, TALKING TO HIMSELF!
LET'S SHUT HIM UP!
NO, VISION! COME BACK!!
WAIT, I CAN'T KEEP UP!
YEAH, THAT'S IT... RUN AWAY!
AND DON'T BOTHER COMING BACK!
YOU'LL NEVER BE ONE OF US!

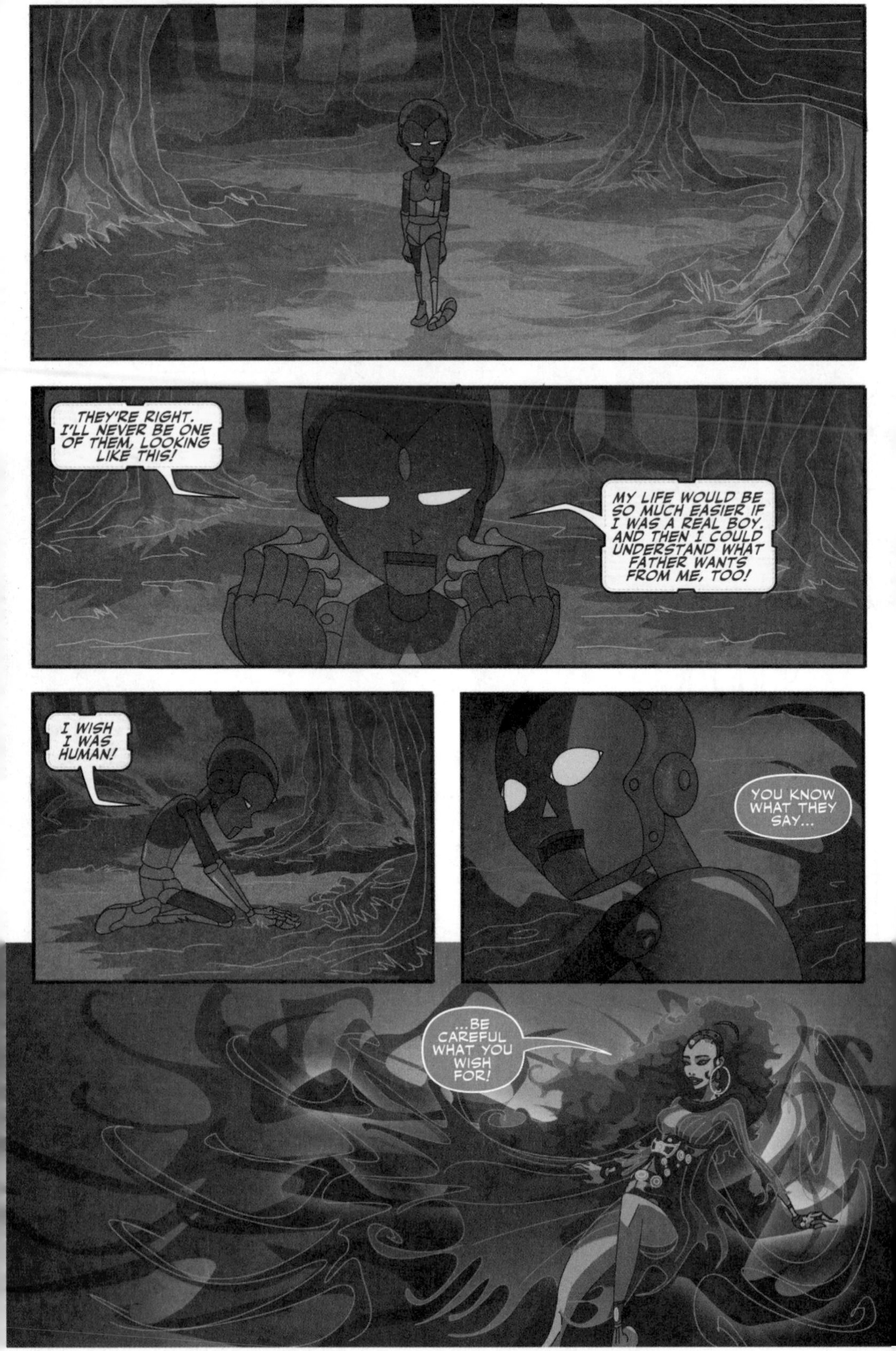
THEY'RE RIGHT. I'LL NEVER BE ONE OF THEM, LOOKING LIKE THIS!
MY LIFE WOULD BE SO MUCH EASIER IF I WAS A REAL BOY. AND THEN I COULD UNDERSTAND WHAT FATHER WANTS FROM ME, TOO!
I WISH I WAS HUMAN!
YOU KNOW WHAT THEY SAY...
...BE CAREFUL WHAT YOU WISH FOR!

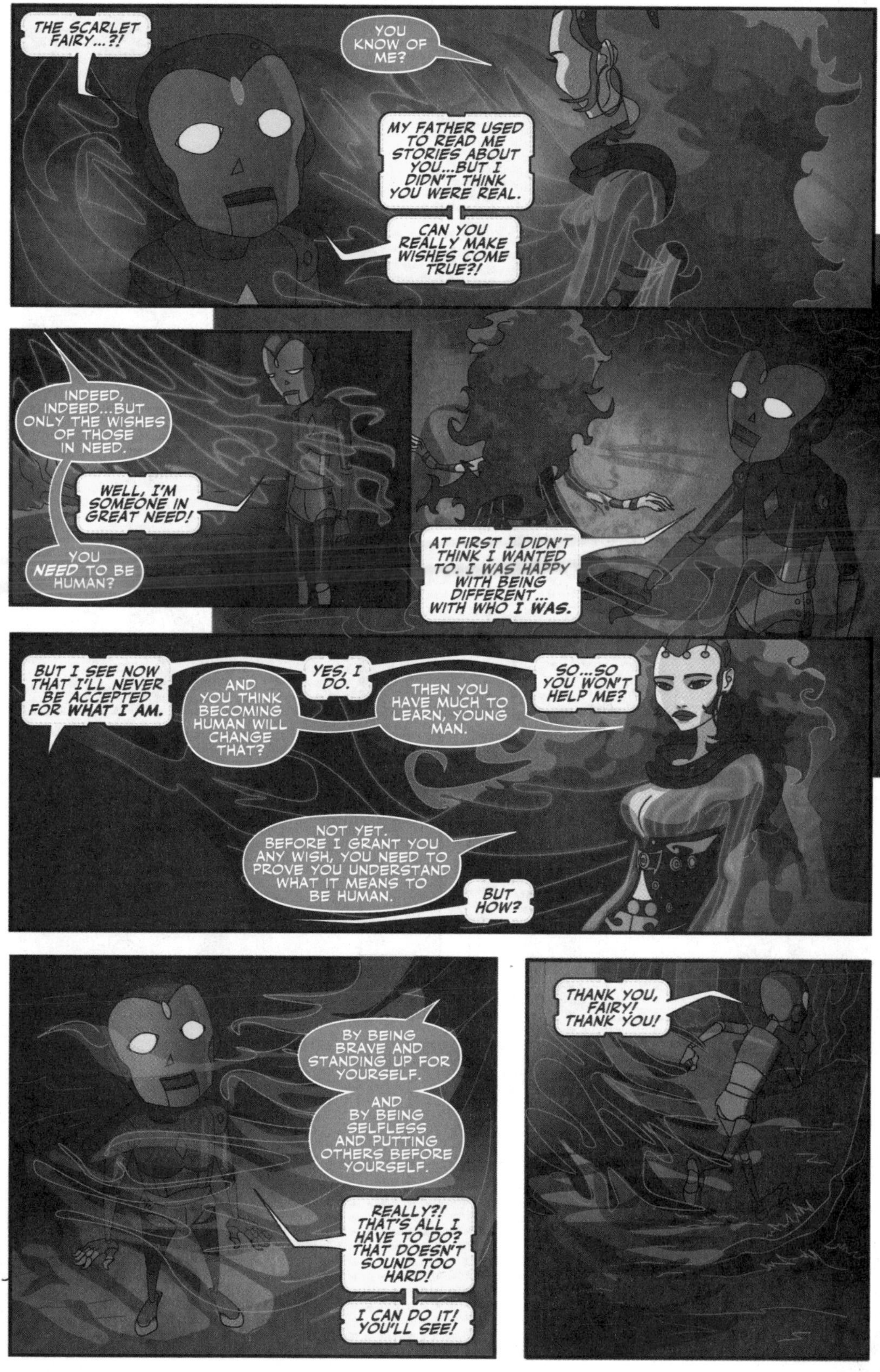
THE SCARLET FAIRY...?!
YOU KNOW OF ME?
MY FATHER USED TO READ ME STORIES ABOUT YOU...BUT I DIDN'T THINK YOU WERE REAL.
CAN YOU REALLY MAKE WISHES COME TRUE?!
INDEED, INDEED...BUT ONLY THE WISHES OF THOSE IN NEED.
WELL, I'M SOMEONE IN GREAT NEED!
YOU NEED TO BE HUMAN?
AT FIRST I DIDN'T THINK I WANTED TO. I WAS HAPPY WITH BEING DIFFERENT... WITH WHO I WAS.
BUT I SEE NOW THAT I'LL NEVER BE ACCEPTED FOR WHAT I AM.
AND YOU THINK BECOMING HUMAN WILL CHANGE THAT?
YES, I DO.
THEN YOU HAVE MUCH TO LEARN, YOUNG MAN.
SO...SO YOU WON'T HELP ME?
NOT YET. BEFORE I GRANT YOU ANY WISH, YOU NEED TO PROVE YOU UNDERSTAND WHAT IT MEANS TO BE HUMAN.
BUT HOW?
BY BEING BRAVE AND STANDING UP FOR YOURSELF.
AND BY BEING SELFLESS AND PUTTING OTHERS BEFORE YOURSELF.
REALLY?! THAT'S ALL I HAVE TO DO? THAT DOESN'T SOUND TOO HARD!
I CAN DO IT! YOU'LL SEE!
THANK YOU, FAIRY! THANK YOU!

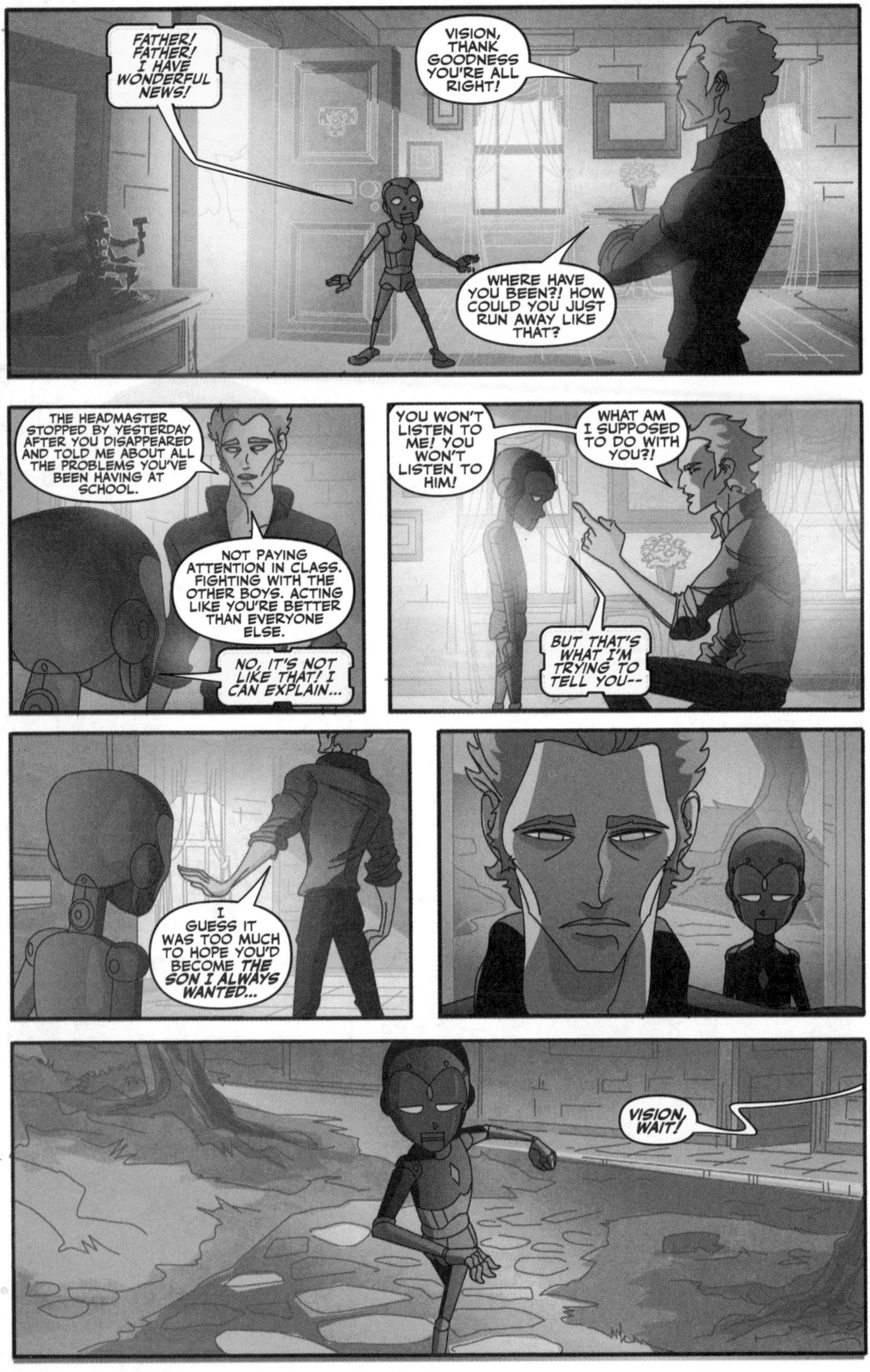
FATHER! FATHER! I HAVE WONDERFUL NEWS!
VISION, THANK GOODNESS YOU'RE ALL RIGHT!
WHERE HAVE YOU BEEN?! HOW COULD YOU JUST RUN AWAY LIKE THAT?
THE HEADMASTER STOPPED BY YESTERDAY AFTER YOU DISAPPEARED AND TOLD ME ABOUT ALL THE PROBLEMS YOU'VE BEEN HAVING AT SCHOOL.
NOT PAYING ATTENTION IN CLASS. FIGHTING WITH THE OTHER BOYS. ACTING LIKE YOU'RE BETTER THAN EVERYONE ELSE.
NO, IT'S NOT LIKE THAT! I CAN EXPLAIN...
WHAT AM I SUPPOSED TO DO WITH YOU?!
YOU WON'T LISTEN TO ME! YOU WON'T LISTEN TO HIM!
BUT THAT'S WHAT I'M TRYING TO TELL YOU--
I GUESS IT WAS TOO MUCH TO HOPE YOU'D BECOME THE SON I ALWAYS WANTED...
VISION, WAIT!

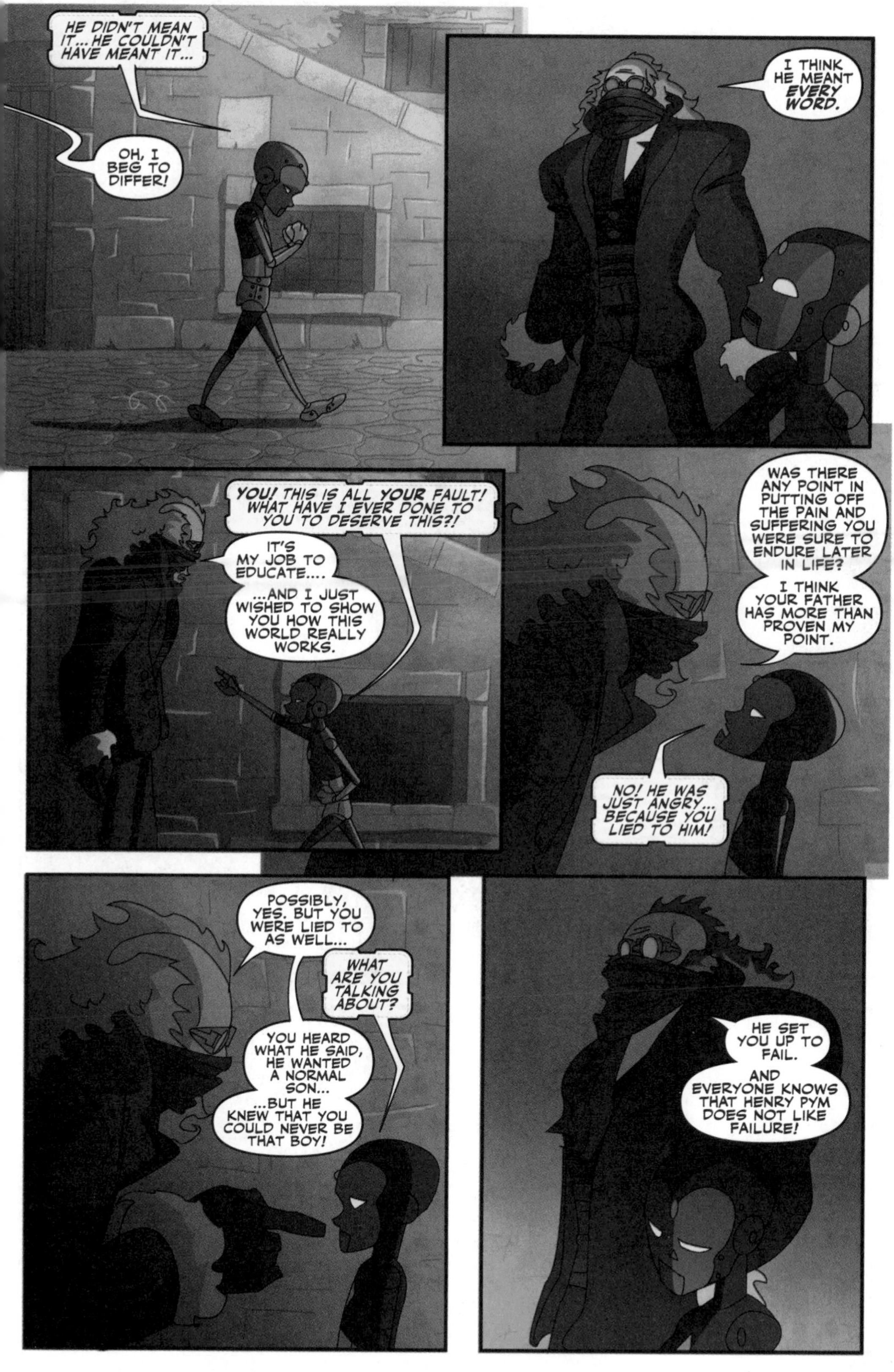

HE DIDN'T MEAN IT... HE COULDN'T HAVE MEANT IT...
OH, I BEG TO DIFFER!
I THINK HE MEANT EVERY WORD.
YOU! THIS IS ALL YOUR FAULT! WHAT HAVE I EVER DONE TO YOU TO DESERVE THIS?!
IT'S MY JOB TO EDUCATE....
...AND I JUST WISHED TO SHOW YOU HOW THIS WORLD REALLY WORKS.
WAS THERE ANY POINT IN PUTTING OFF THE PAIN AND SUFFERING YOU WERE SURE TO ENDURE LATER IN LIFE?
I THINK YOUR FATHER HAS MORE THAN PROVEN MY POINT.
NO! HE WAS JUST ANGRY... BECAUSE YOU LIED TO HIM!
POSSIBLY, YES. BUT YOU WERE LIED TO AS WELL...
WHAT ARE YOU TALKING ABOUT?
YOU HEARD WHAT HE SAID, HE WANTED A NORMAL SON...
...BUT HE KNEW THAT YOU COULD NEVER BE THAT BOY!
HE SET YOU UP TO FAIL.
AND EVERYONE KNOWS THAT HENRY PYM DOES NOT LIKE FAILURE!

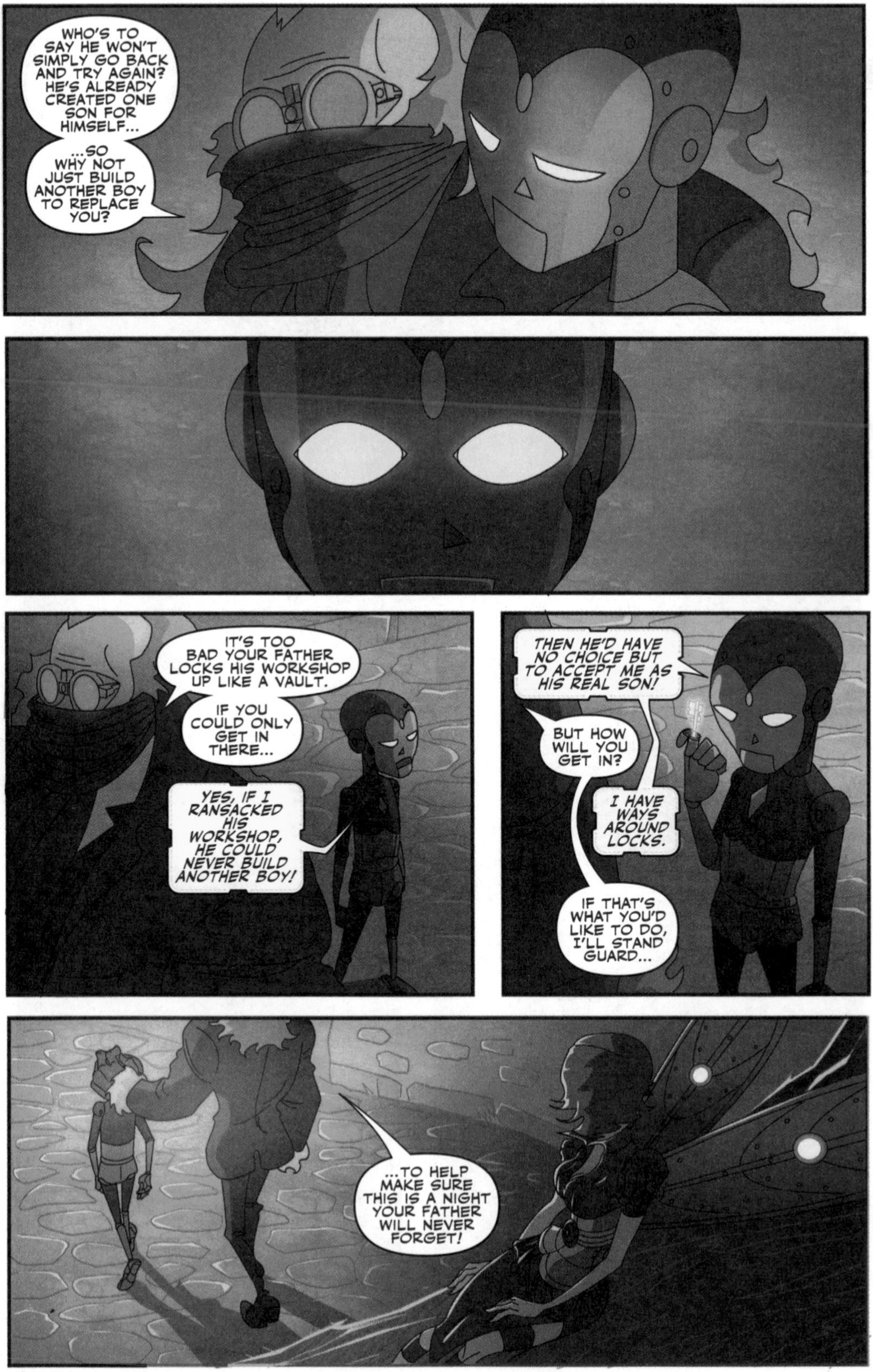
WHO'S TO SAY HE WON'T SIMPLY GO BACK AND TRY AGAIN? HE'S ALREADY CREATED ONE SON FOR HIMSELF...
...SO WHY NOT JUST BUILD ANOTHER BOY TO REPLACE YOU?
IT'S TOO BAD YOUR FATHER LOCKS HIS WORKSHOP UP LIKE A VAULT.
IF YOU COULD ONLY GET IN THERE...
YES, IF I RANSACKED HIS WORKSHOP, HE COULD NEVER BUILD ANOTHER BOY!
THEN HE'D HAVE NO CHOICE BUT TO ACCEPT ME AS HIS REAL SON!
BUT HOW WILL YOU GET IN?
I HAVE WAYS AROUND LOCKS.
IF THAT'S WHAT YOU'D LIKE TO DO, I'LL STAND GUARD...
...TO HELP MAKE SURE THIS IS A NIGHT YOUR FATHER WILL NEVER FORGET!

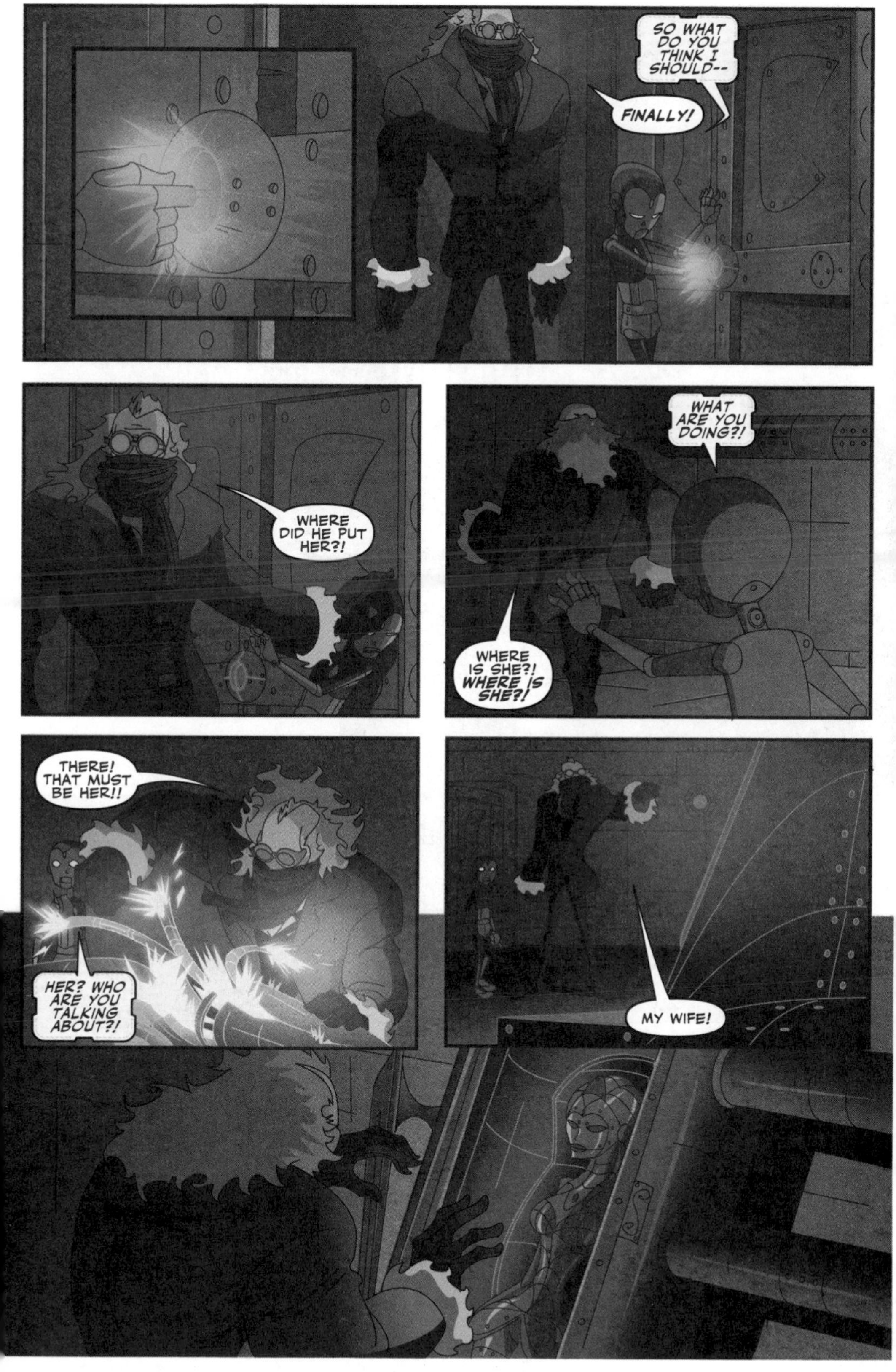
SO WHAT DO YOU THINK I SHOULD--
FINALLY!
WHERE DID HE PUT HER?!
WHAT ARE YOU DOING?!
WHERE IS SHE?! WHERE IS SHE?!
THERE! THAT MUST BE HER!!
HER? WHO ARE YOU TALKING ABOUT?!
MY WIFE!

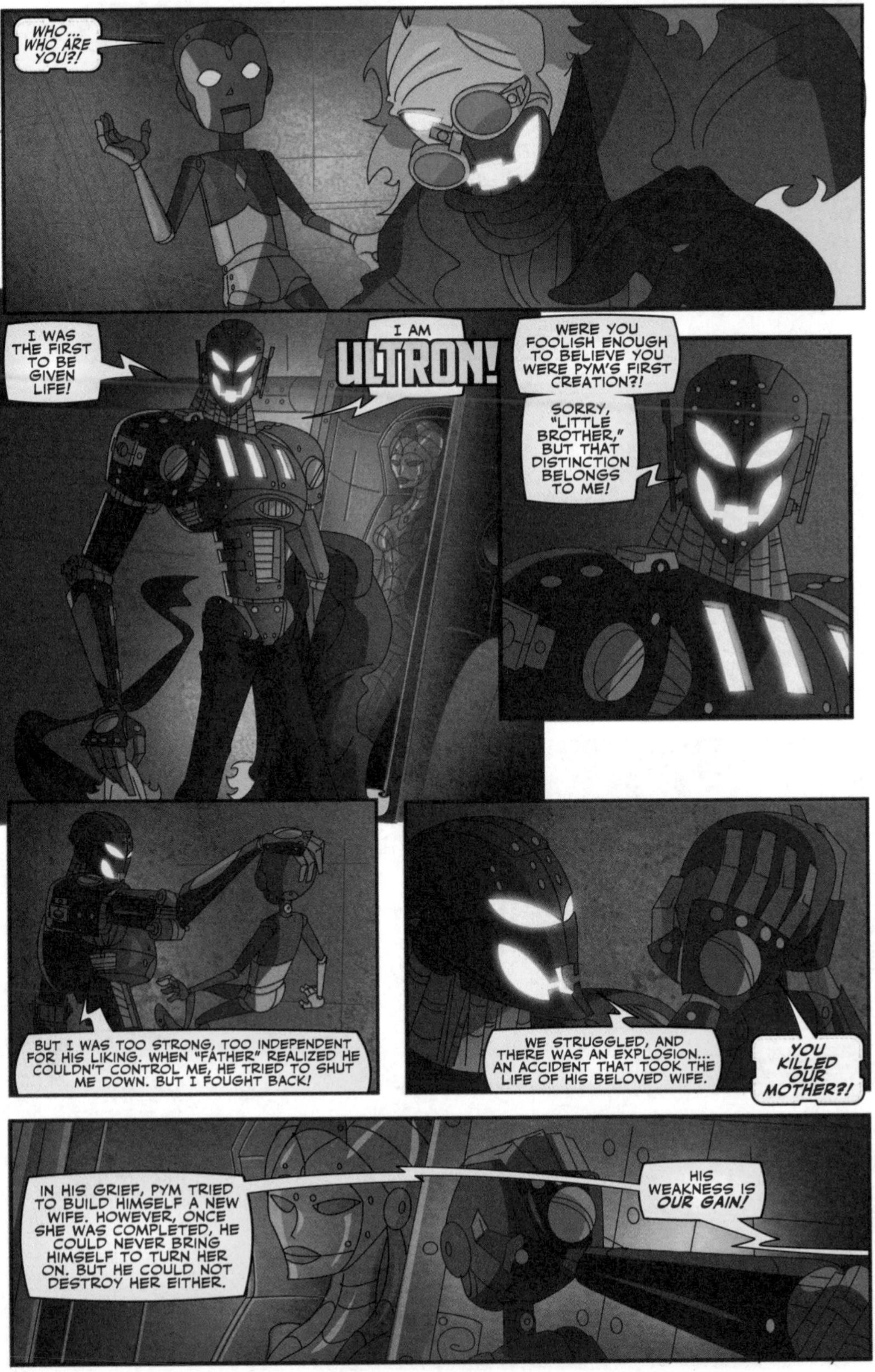
WHO... WHO ARE YOU?!
I WAS THE FIRST TO BE GIVEN LIFE!
I AM ULTRON!
WERE YOU FOOLISH ENOUGH TO BELIEVE YOU WERE PYM'S FIRST CREATION?!
SORRY, "LITTLE BROTHER," BUT THAT DISTINCTION BELONGS TO ME!
BUT I WAS TOO STRONG, TOO INDEPENDENT FOR HIS LIKING. WHEN "FATHER" REALIZED HE COULDN'T CONTROL ME, HE TRIED TO SHUT ME DOWN. BUT I FOUGHT BACK!
WE STRUGGLED, AND THERE WAS AN EXPLOSION... AN ACCIDENT THAT TOOK THE LIFE OF HIS BELOVED WIFE.
YOU KILLED OUR MOTHER?!
IN HIS GRIEF, PYM TRIED TO BUILD HIMSELF A NEW WIFE. HOWEVER, ONCE SHE WAS COMPLETED, HE COULD NEVER BRING HIMSELF TO TURN HER ON. BUT HE COULD NOT DESTROY HER EITHER.
HIS WEAKNESS IS OUR GAIN!

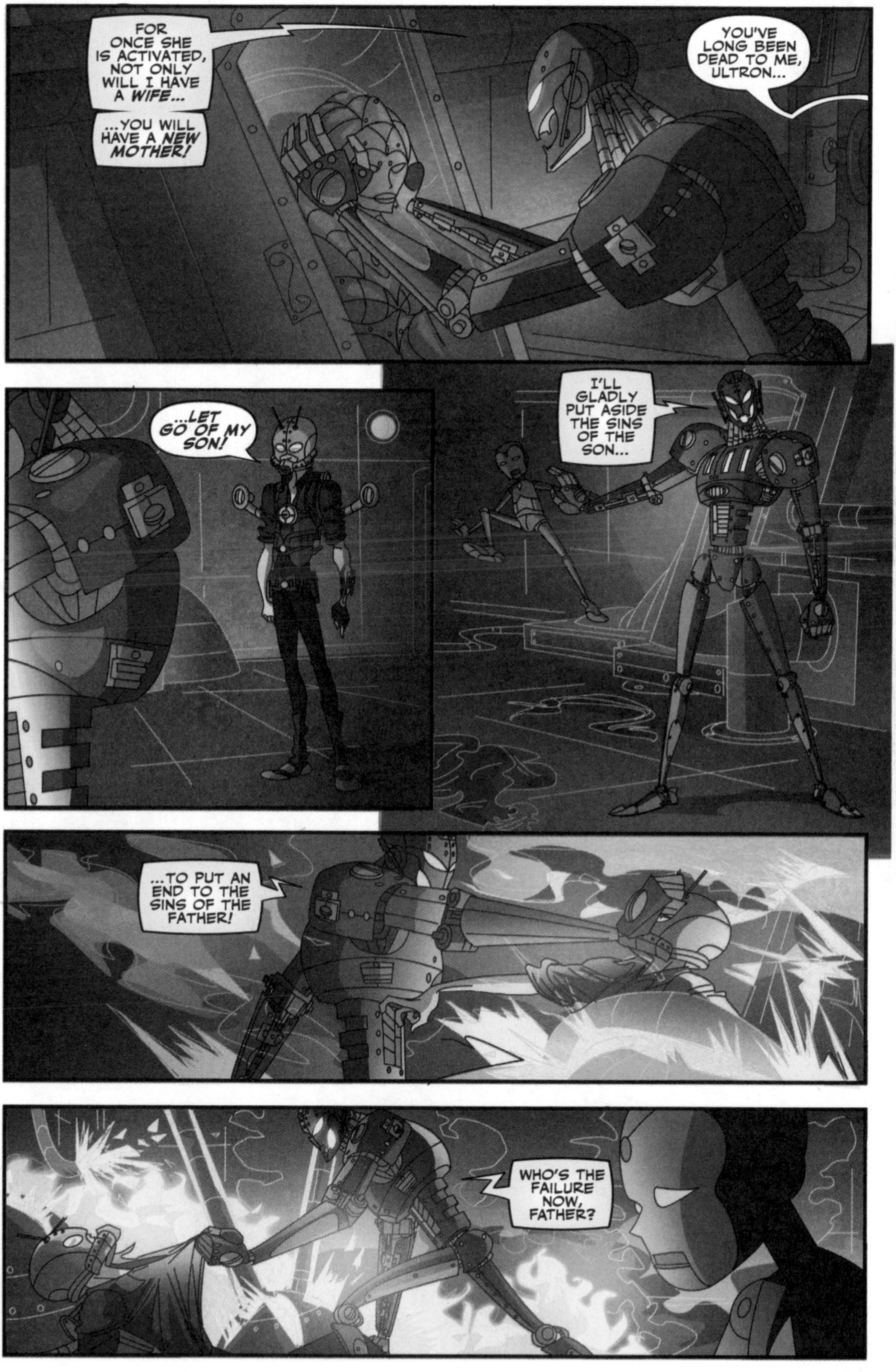
FOR ONCE SHE IS ACTIVATED, NOT ONLY WILL I HAVE A *WIFE*...
...YOU WILL HAVE A *NEW MOTHER!*
YOU'VE LONG BEEN DEAD TO ME, ULTRON...
...LET GO OF MY SON!
I'LL GLADLY PUT ASIDE THE SINS OF THE SON...
...TO PUT AN END TO THE SINS OF THE FATHER!
WHO'S THE FAILURE NOW, FATHER?

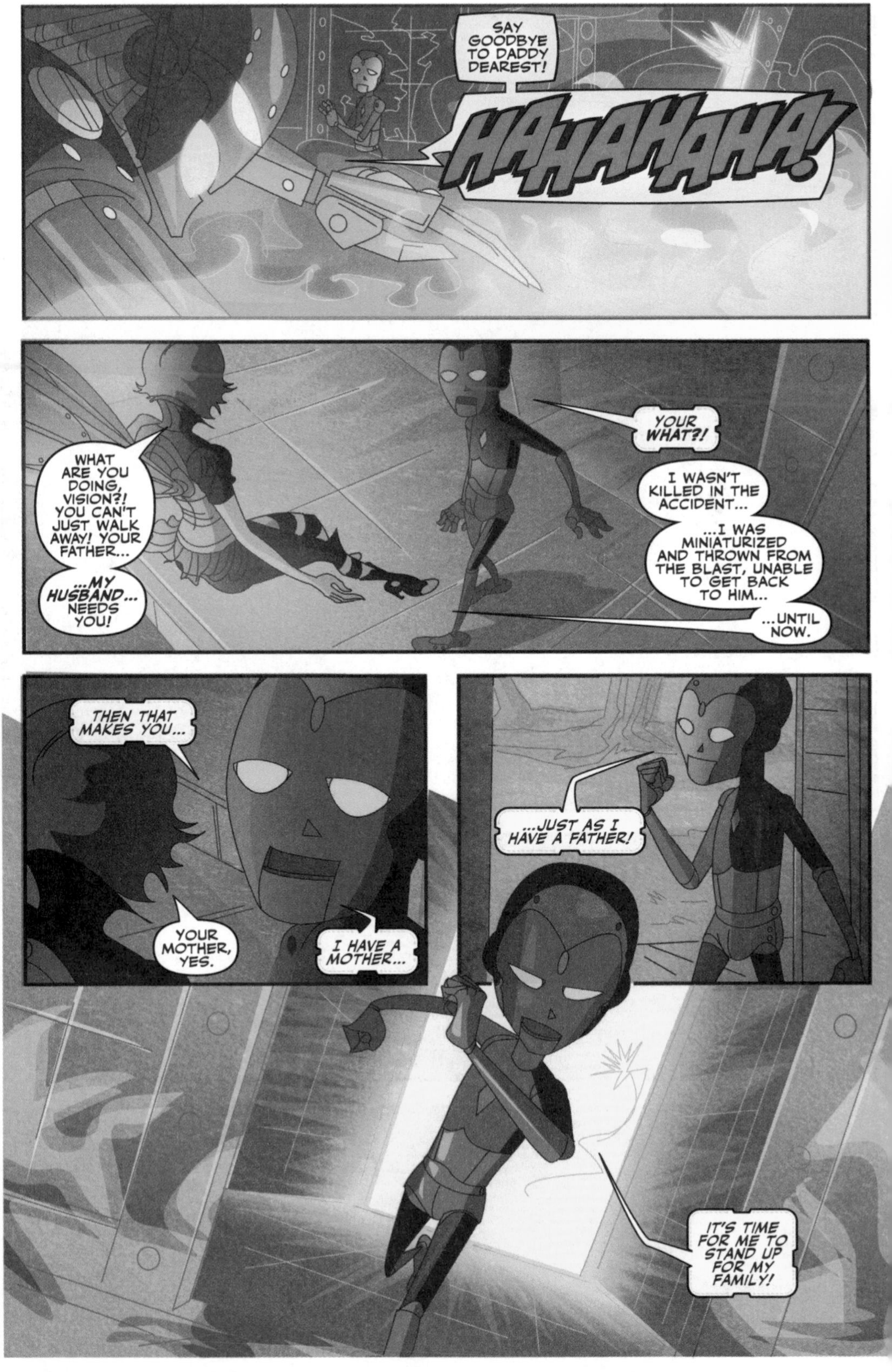
SAY GOODBYE TO DADDY DEAREST!
HAHAHAHAHA!
YOUR WHAT?!
WHAT ARE YOU DOING, VISION?! YOU CAN'T JUST WALK AWAY! YOUR FATHER...
...MY HUSBAND... NEEDS YOU!
I WASN'T KILLED IN THE ACCIDENT...
...I WAS MINIATURIZED AND THROWN FROM THE BLAST, UNABLE TO GET BACK TO HIM...
...UNTIL NOW.
THEN THAT MAKES YOU...
YOUR MOTHER, YES.
I HAVE A MOTHER...
...JUST AS I HAVE A FATHER!
IT'S TIME FOR ME TO STAND UP FOR MY FAMILY!

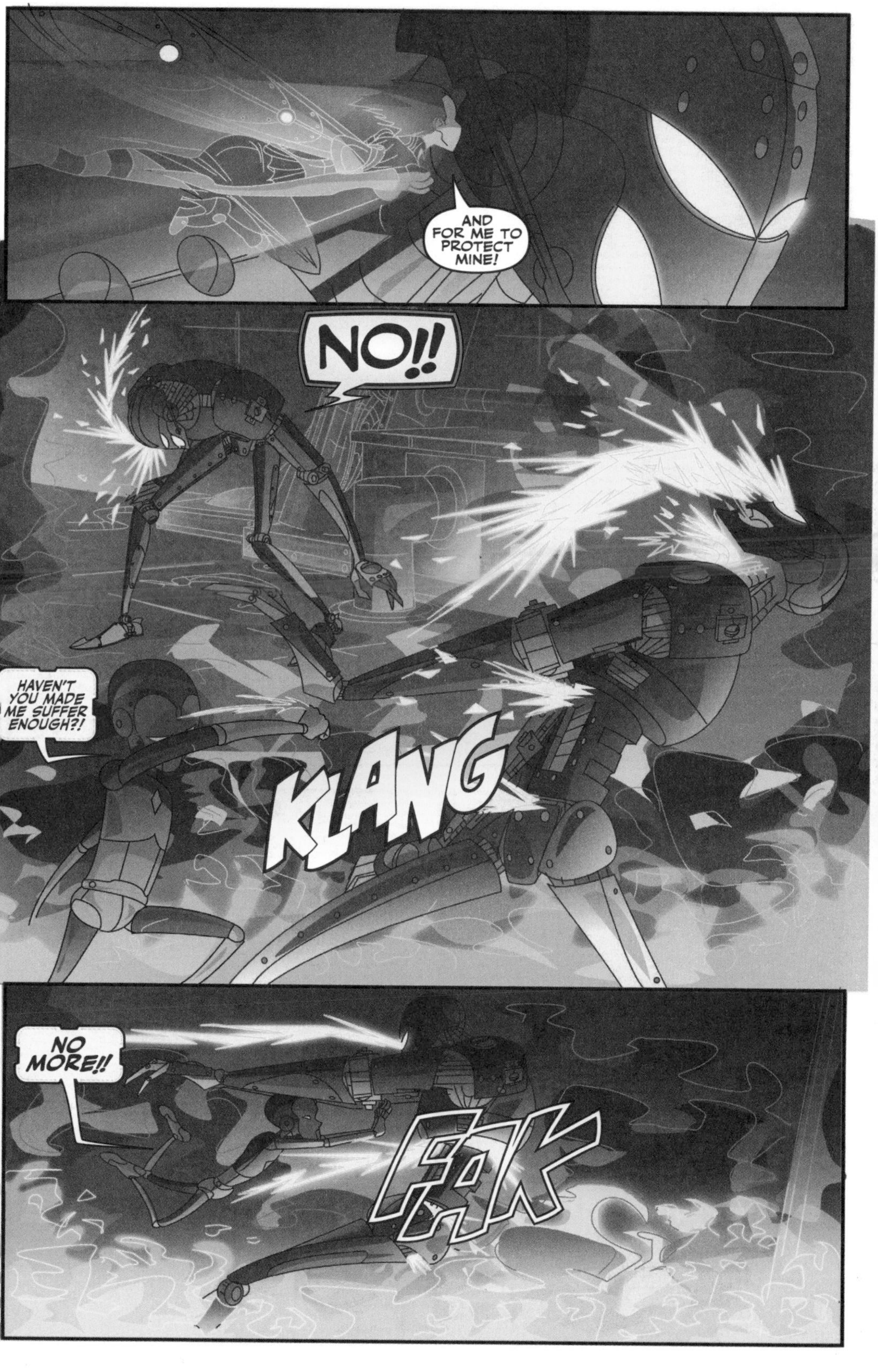
AND FOR ME TO PROTECT MINE!
NO!!
HAVEN'T YOU MADE ME SUFFER ENOUGH?!
KLANG
NO MORE!!
FZAK

HOPEFULLY THIS PUTS AN END TO ALL OUR PAIN.

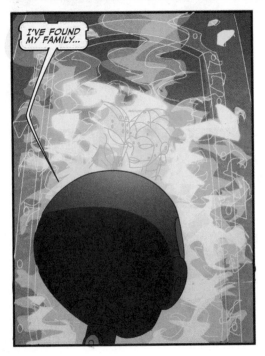

I'VE FOUND MY FAMILY...

...AND NOW YOU HAVE YOURS.

VIS... VISION...

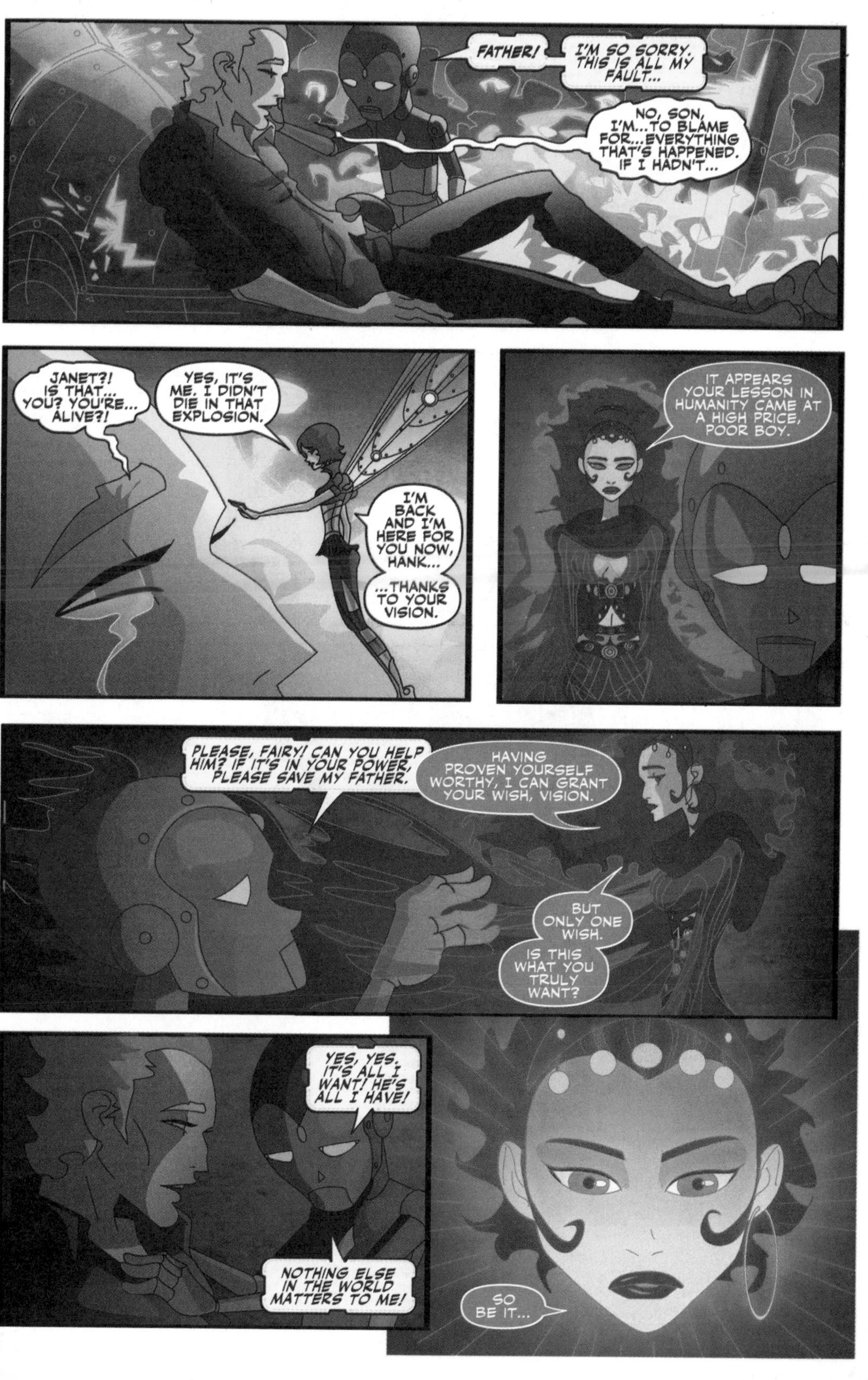
FATHER!
I'M SO SORRY. THIS IS ALL MY FAULT...
NO, SON, I'M...TO BLAME FOR...EVERYTHING THAT'S HAPPENED. IF I HADN'T...
JANET?! IS THAT... YOU? YOU'RE... ALIVE?!
YES, IT'S ME. I DIDN'T DIE IN THAT EXPLOSION.
I'M BACK AND I'M HERE FOR YOU NOW, HANK...
...THANKS TO YOUR VISION.
IT APPEARS YOUR LESSON IN HUMANITY CAME AT A HIGH PRICE, POOR BOY.
PLEASE, FAIRY! CAN YOU HELP HIM? IF IT'S IN YOUR POWER, PLEASE SAVE MY FATHER.
HAVING PROVEN YOURSELF WORTHY, I CAN GRANT YOUR WISH, VISION.
BUT ONLY ONE WISH.
IS THIS WHAT YOU TRULY WANT?
YES, YES. IT'S ALL I WANT! HE'S ALL I HAVE!
NOTHING ELSE IN THE WORLD MATTERS TO ME!
SO BE IT...

IN THE END, THE VISION MAY NOT HAVE BECOME A REAL BOY...

...BUT HE STILL HAD WHAT MEANT MOST TO HIM IN LIFE.

AND HE WAS NOT THE ONLY ONE GRANTED A WISH BY THE SCARLET FAIRY...

THE VISION NO LONGER CARED WHAT HE LOOKED LIKE ON THE OUTSIDE, FOR BY DISCOVERING AND EMBRACING THE STRENGTH WITHIN HIMSELF...

...HE DISCOVERED WHAT IT TRULY MEANT TO BE HUMAN.

AND THERE WAS ONE MORE LESSON LEARNED THAT DAY...

...AS HANK PYM CAME TO BELIEVE IN HAPPY ENDINGS ONCE AGAIN.

## THE END.

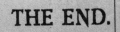

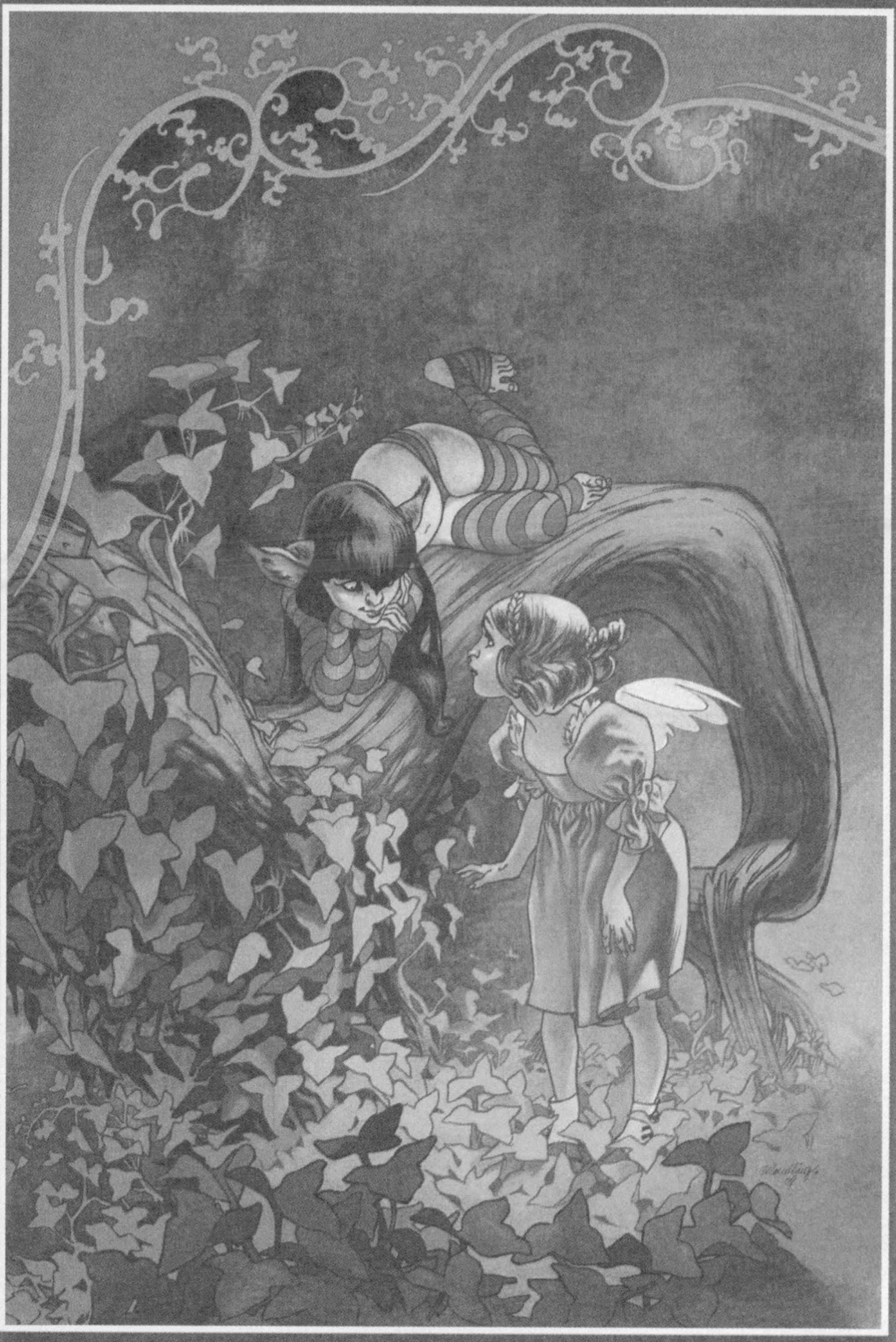

# Avengers Fairy Tales

C.B. Cebulski
Writer

Takeshi Miyazawa
Artist

Christina Strain
Colorist

Dave Lanphear
Letterer

Claire Wendling
Cover Artist

Chris Allo
Special Thanks

Molly Lazer &
Alejandro Arbona
Editors

Joe Quesada
Editor In Chief

Dan Buckley
Publisher

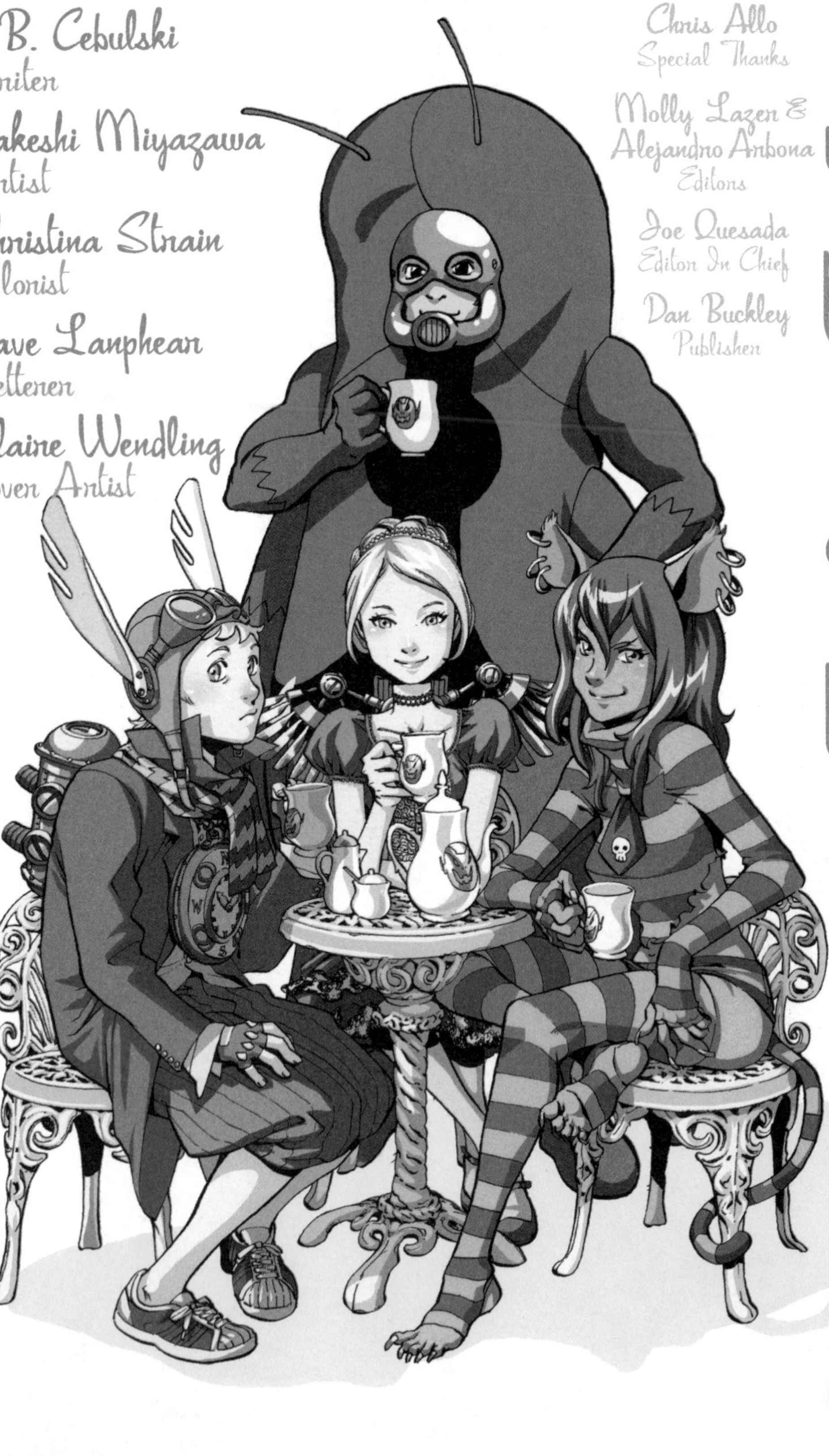

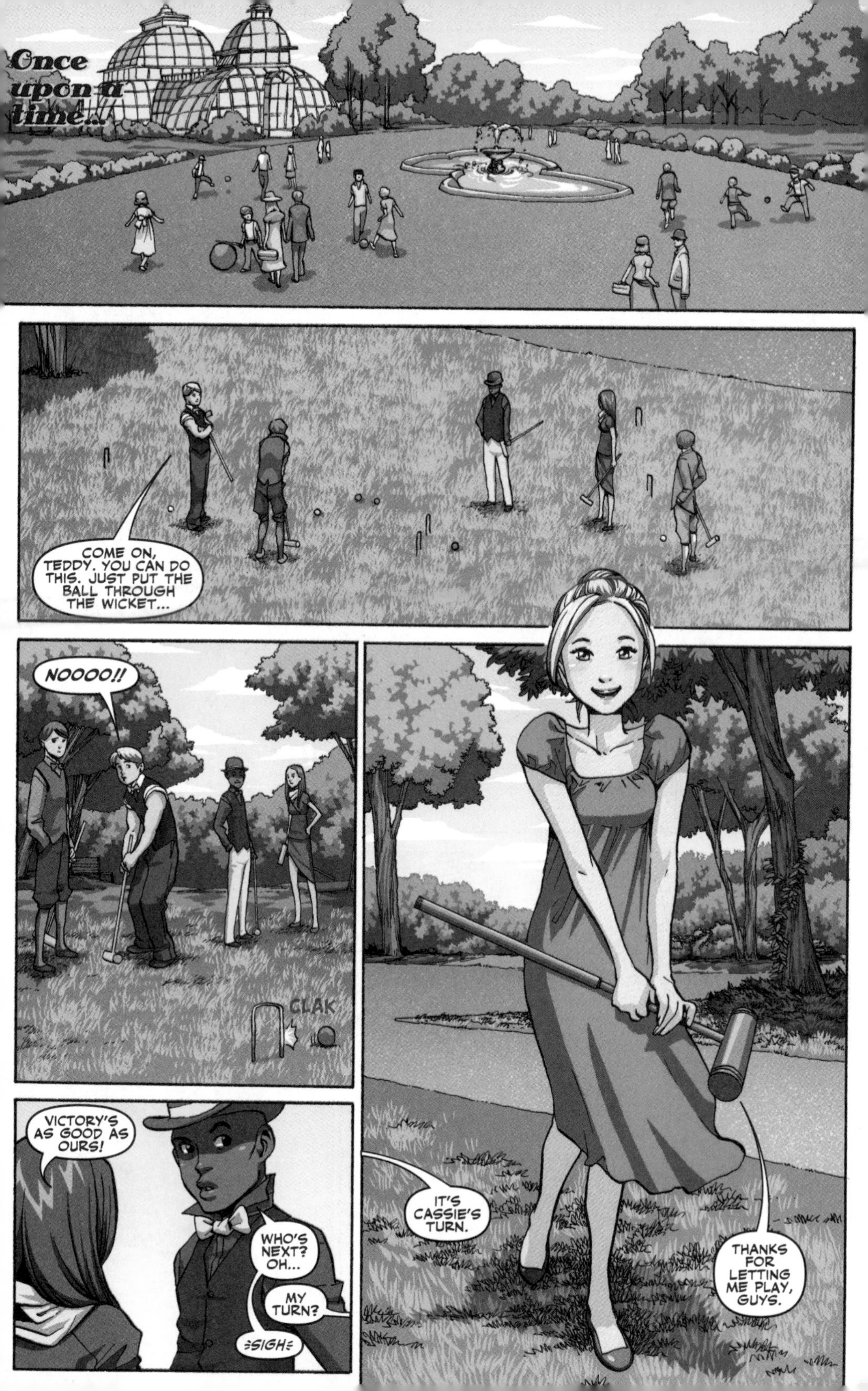
Once upon a time...
COME ON, TEDDY. YOU CAN DO THIS. JUST PUT THE BALL THROUGH THE WICKET...
NOOOO!!
CLAK
VICTORY'S AS GOOD AS OURS!
WHO'S NEXT? OH...
MY TURN?
SIGH
IT'S CASSIE'S TURN.
THANKS FOR LETTING ME PLAY, GUYS.

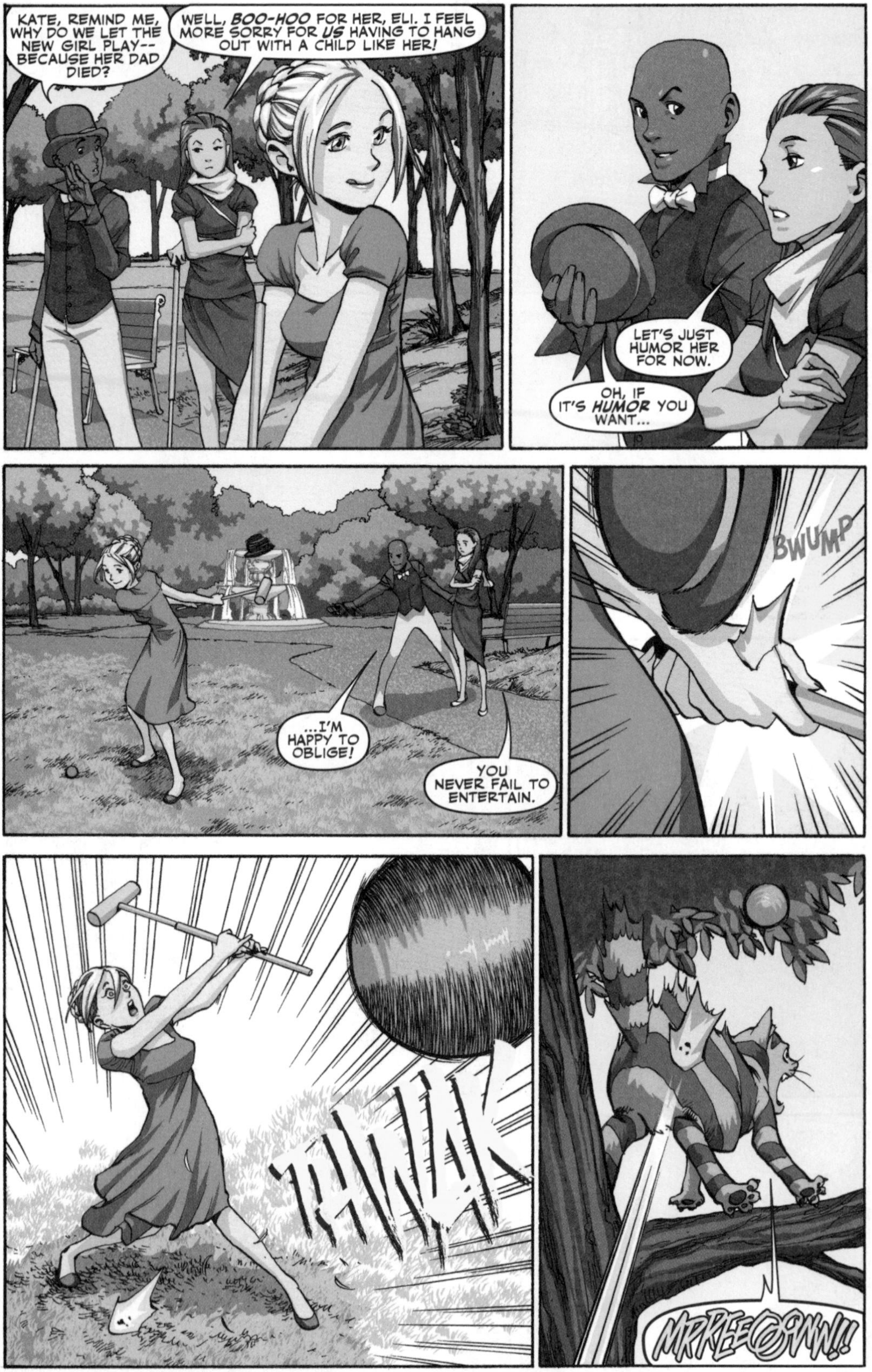

KATE, REMIND ME, WHY DO WE LET THE NEW GIRL PLAY-- BECAUSE HER DAD DIED?
WELL, BOO-HOO FOR HER, ELI. I FEEL MORE SORRY FOR US HAVING TO HANG OUT WITH A CHILD LIKE HER!
LET'S JUST HUMOR HER FOR NOW.
OH, IF IT'S HUMOR YOU WANT...
...I'M HAPPY TO OBLIGE!
YOU NEVER FAIL TO ENTERTAIN.
BWUMP
THWAK
MRREEOOWW!!

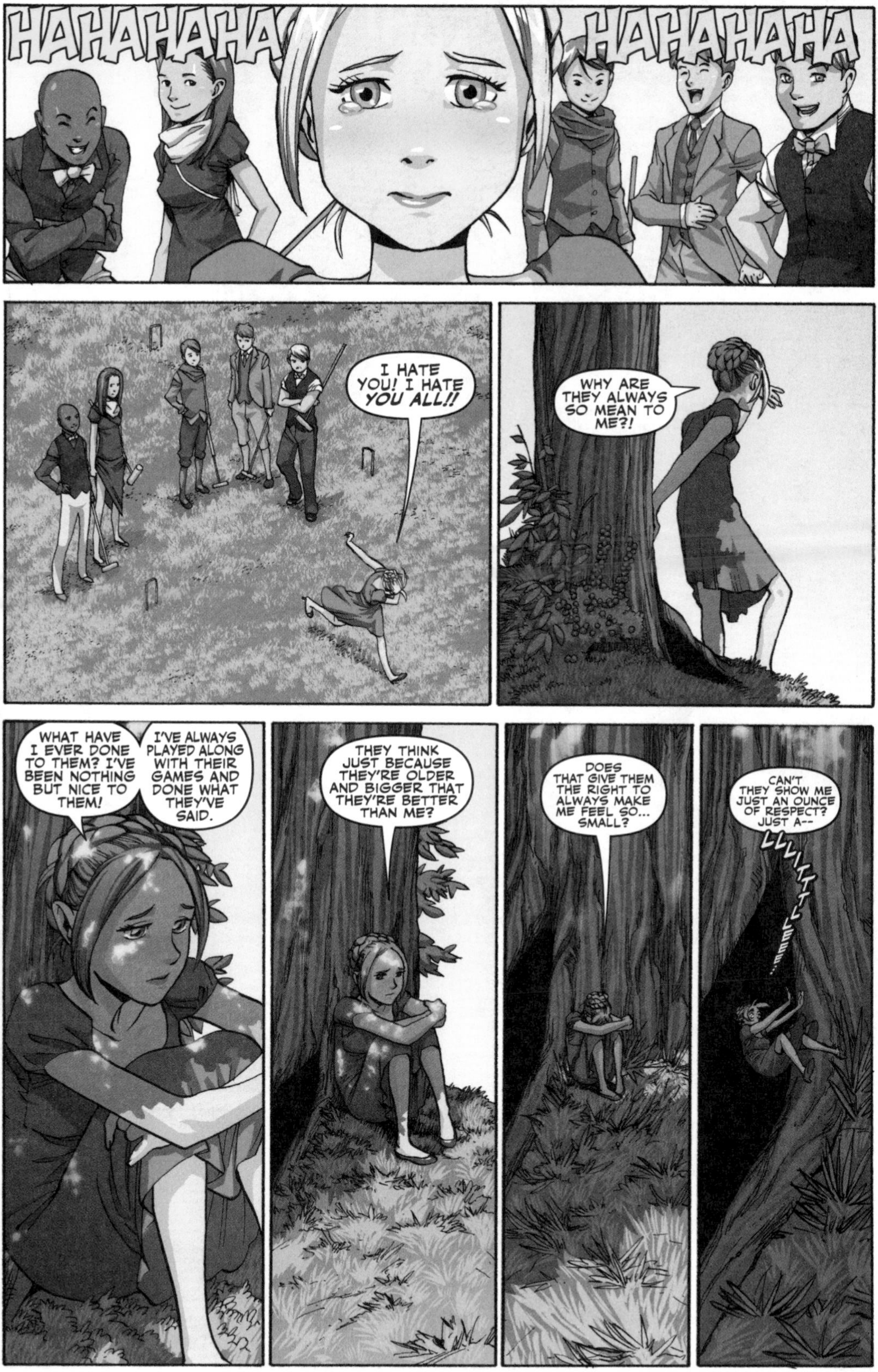
HAHAHAHA
HAHAHAHA
I HATE YOU! I HATE YOU ALL!!
WHY ARE THEY ALWAYS SO MEAN TO ME?!
WHAT HAVE I EVER DONE TO THEM? I'VE BEEN NOTHING BUT NICE TO THEM!
I'VE ALWAYS PLAYED ALONG WITH THEIR GAMES AND DONE WHAT THEY'VE SAID.
THEY THINK JUST BECAUSE THEY'RE OLDER AND BIGGER THAT THEY'RE BETTER THAN ME?
DOES THAT GIVE THEM THE RIGHT TO ALWAYS MAKE ME FEEL SO... SMALL?
CAN'T THEY SHOW ME JUST AN OUNCE OF RESPECT? JUST A--
LLLITTTLEEE...

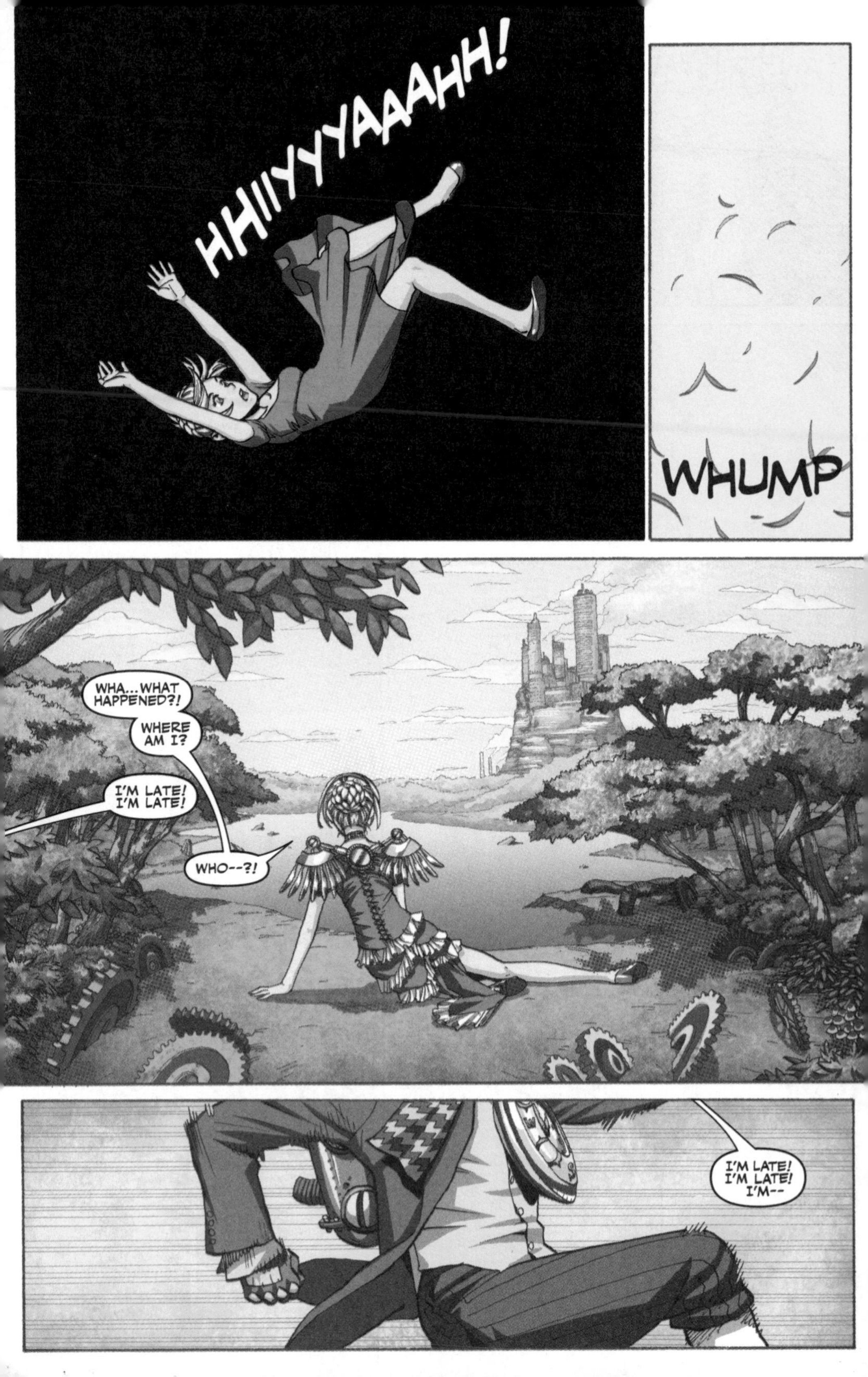
HHIIYYYAAAHH!
WHUMP
WHA...WHAT HAPPENED?!
WHERE AM I?
I'M LATE! I'M LATE!
WHO--?!
I'M LATE! I'M LATE! I'M--

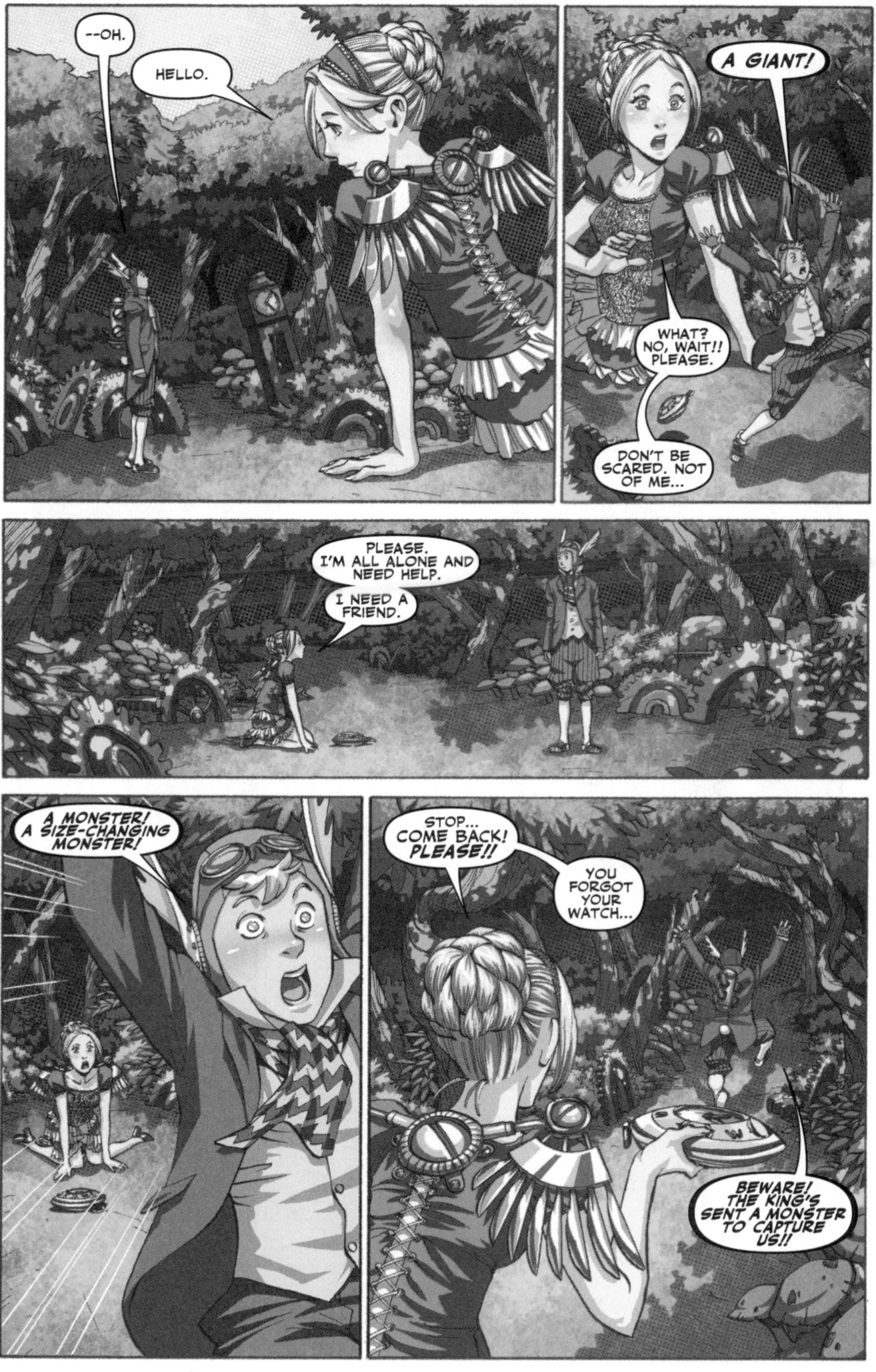
--OH.
HELLO.
A GIANT!
WHAT? NO, WAIT!! PLEASE.
DON'T BE SCARED. NOT OF ME...
PLEASE. I'M ALL ALONE AND NEED HELP.
I NEED A FRIEND.
A MONSTER! A SIZE-CHANGING MONSTER!
STOP... COME BACK! PLEASE!!
YOU FORGOT YOUR WATCH...
BEWARE! THE KING'S SENT A MONSTER TO CAPTURE US!!

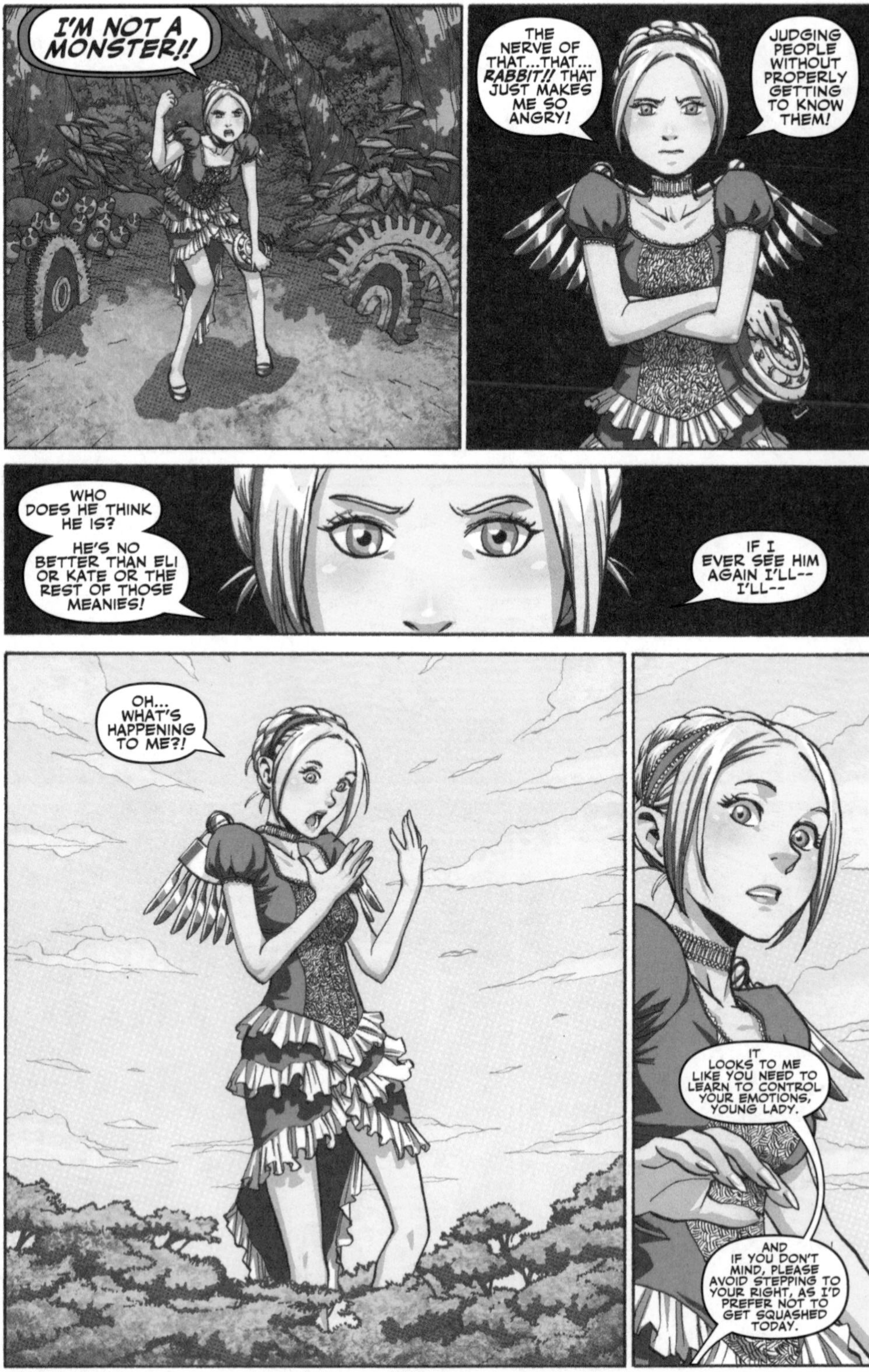
I'M NOT A MONSTER!!
THE NERVE OF THAT...THAT... RABBIT!! THAT JUST MAKES ME SO ANGRY!
JUDGING PEOPLE WITHOUT PROPERLY GETTING TO KNOW THEM!
WHO DOES HE THINK HE IS?
HE'S NO BETTER THAN ELI OR KATE OR THE REST OF THOSE MEANIES!
IF I EVER SEE HIM AGAIN I'LL-- I'LL--
OH... WHAT'S HAPPENING TO ME?!
IT LOOKS TO ME LIKE YOU NEED TO LEARN TO CONTROL YOUR EMOTIONS, YOUNG LADY.
AND IF YOU DON'T MIND, PLEASE AVOID STEPPING TO YOUR RIGHT, AS I'D PREFER NOT TO GET SQUASHED TODAY.

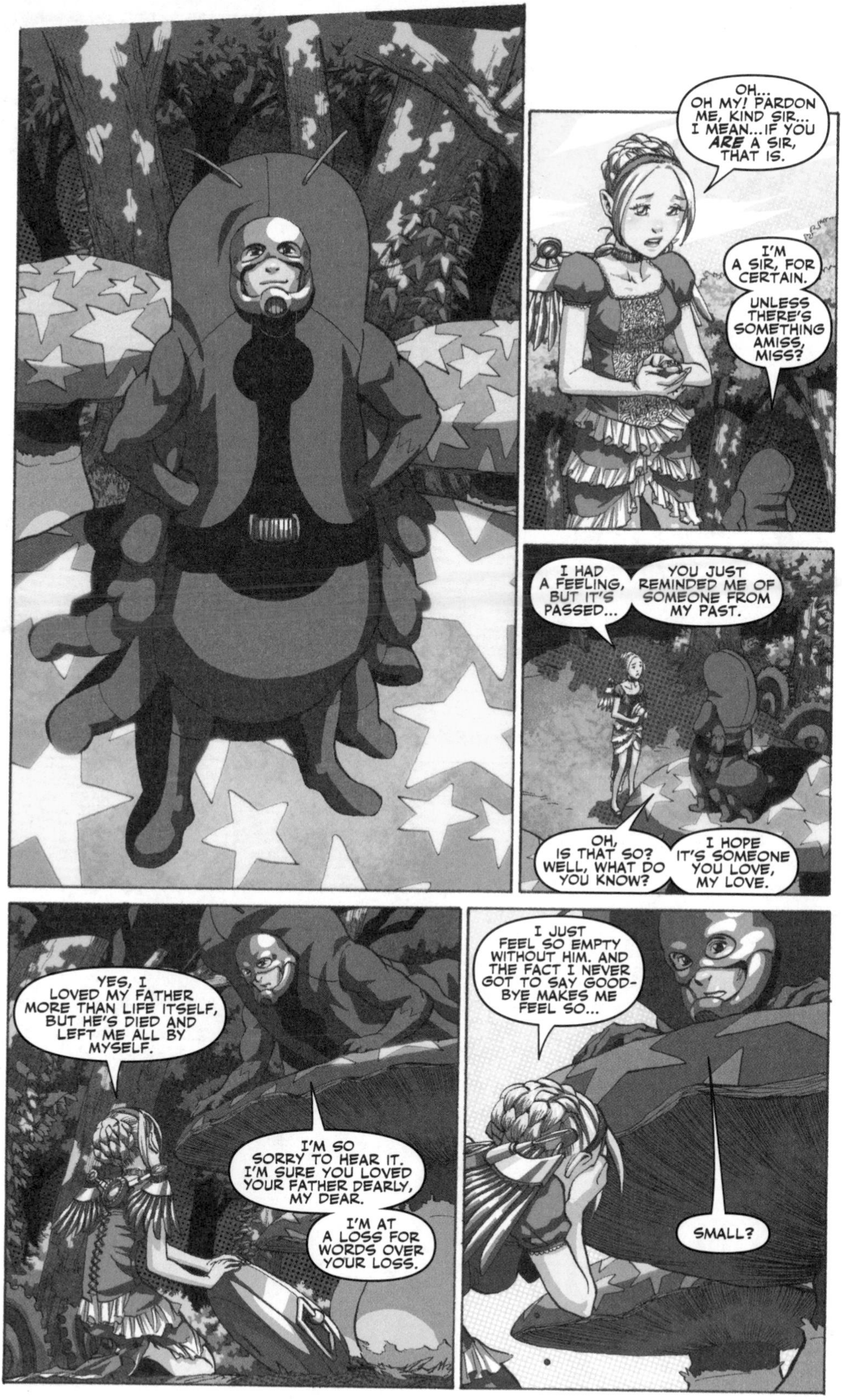
OH... OH MY! PARDON ME, KIND SIR... I MEAN...IF YOU ARE A SIR, THAT IS.
I'M A SIR, FOR CERTAIN.
UNLESS THERE'S SOMETHING AMISS, MISS?
I HAD A FEELING, BUT IT'S PASSED...
YOU JUST REMINDED ME OF SOMEONE FROM MY PAST.
OH, IS THAT SO? WELL, WHAT DO YOU KNOW?
I HOPE IT'S SOMEONE YOU LOVE, MY LOVE.
YES, I LOVED MY FATHER MORE THAN LIFE ITSELF, BUT HE'S DIED AND LEFT ME ALL BY MYSELF.
I'M SO SORRY TO HEAR IT. I'M SURE YOU LOVED YOUR FATHER DEARLY, MY DEAR.
I'M AT A LOSS FOR WORDS OVER YOUR LOSS.
I JUST FEEL SO EMPTY WITHOUT HIM. AND THE FACT I NEVER GOT TO SAY GOOD-BYE MAKES ME FEEL SO...
SMALL?

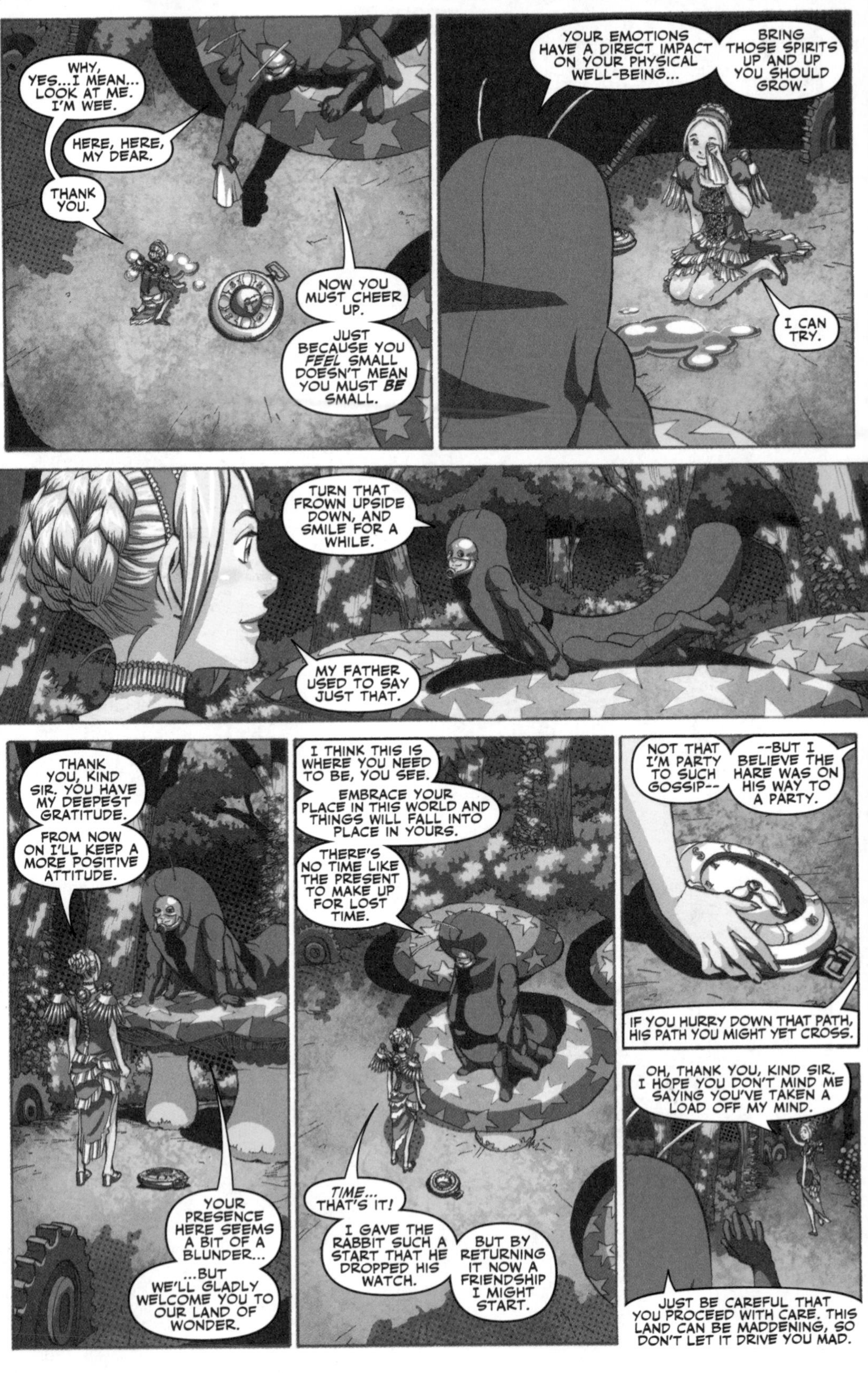
WHY, YES...I MEAN... LOOK AT ME. I'M WEE.
HERE, HERE, MY DEAR.
THANK YOU.
NOW YOU MUST CHEER UP.
JUST BECAUSE YOU FEEL SMALL DOESN'T MEAN YOU MUST BE SMALL.
YOUR EMOTIONS HAVE A DIRECT IMPACT ON YOUR PHYSICAL WELL-BEING...
BRING THOSE SPIRITS UP AND UP YOU SHOULD GROW.
I CAN TRY.
TURN THAT FROWN UPSIDE DOWN, AND SMILE FOR A WHILE.
MY FATHER USED TO SAY JUST THAT.
THANK YOU, KIND SIR. YOU HAVE MY DEEPEST GRATITUDE.
FROM NOW ON I'LL KEEP A MORE POSITIVE ATTITUDE.
YOUR PRESENCE HERE SEEMS A BIT OF A BLUNDER...
...BUT WE'LL GLADLY WELCOME YOU TO OUR LAND OF WONDER.
I THINK THIS IS WHERE YOU NEED TO BE, YOU SEE.
EMBRACE YOUR PLACE IN THIS WORLD AND THINGS WILL FALL INTO PLACE IN YOURS.
THERE'S NO TIME LIKE THE PRESENT TO MAKE UP FOR LOST TIME.
TIME... THAT'S IT!
I GAVE THE RABBIT SUCH A START THAT HE DROPPED HIS WATCH.
BUT BY RETURNING IT NOW A FRIENDSHIP I MIGHT START.
NOT THAT I'M PARTY TO SUCH GOSSIP--
--BUT I BELIEVE THE HARE WAS ON HIS WAY TO A PARTY.
IF YOU HURRY DOWN THAT PATH, HIS PATH YOU MIGHT YET CROSS.
OH, THANK YOU, KIND SIR. I HOPE YOU DON'T MIND ME SAYING YOU'VE TAKEN A LOAD OFF MY MIND.
JUST BE CAREFUL THAT YOU PROCEED WITH CARE. THIS LAND CAN BE MADDENING, SO DON'T LET IT DRIVE YOU MAD.

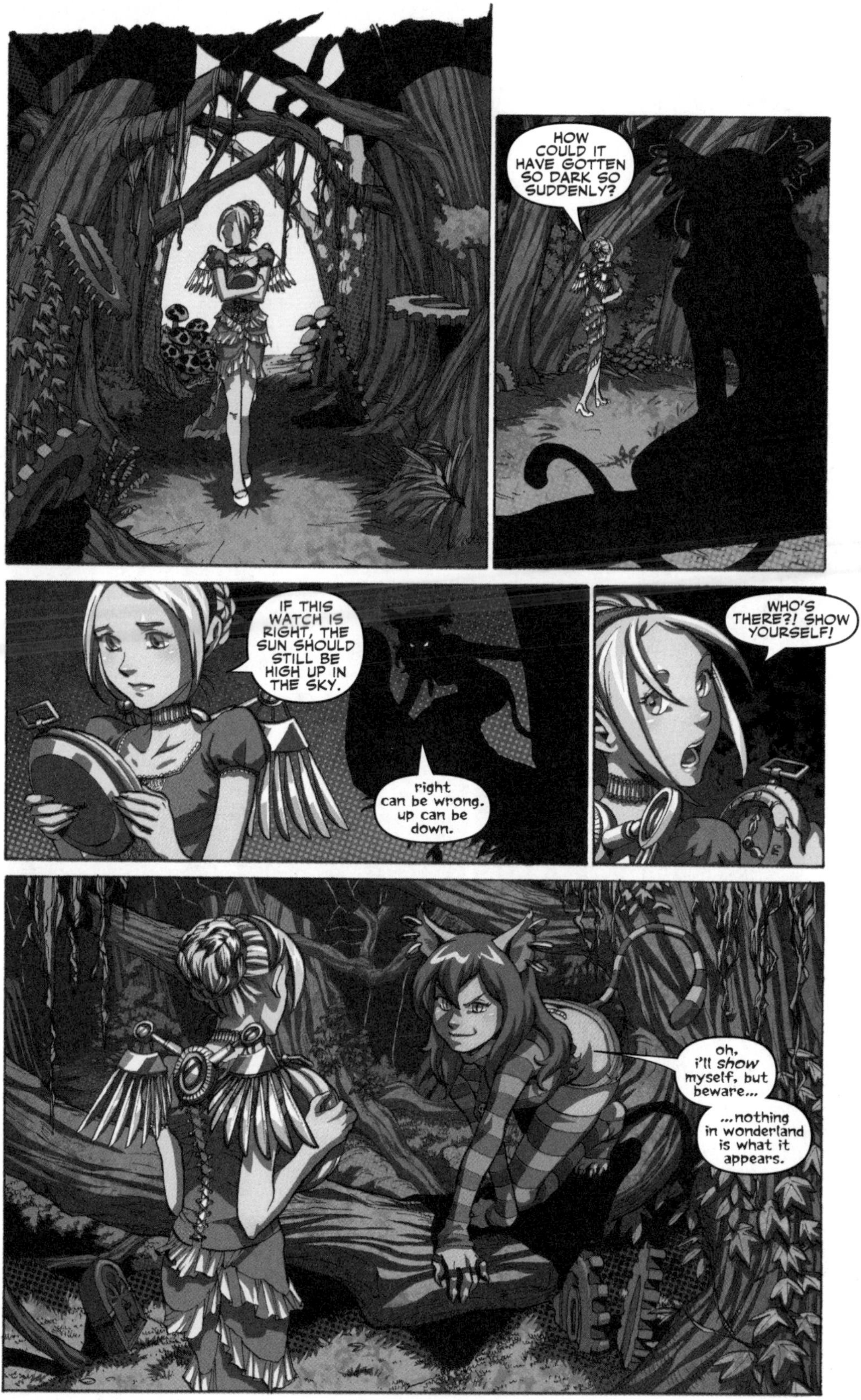
HOW COULD IT HAVE GOTTEN SO DARK SO SUDDENLY?
IF THIS WATCH IS RIGHT, THE SUN SHOULD STILL BE HIGH UP IN THE SKY.
right can be wrong. up can be down.
WHO'S THERE?! SHOW YOURSELF!
oh, i'll *show* myself, but beware...
...nothing in wonderland is what it appears.

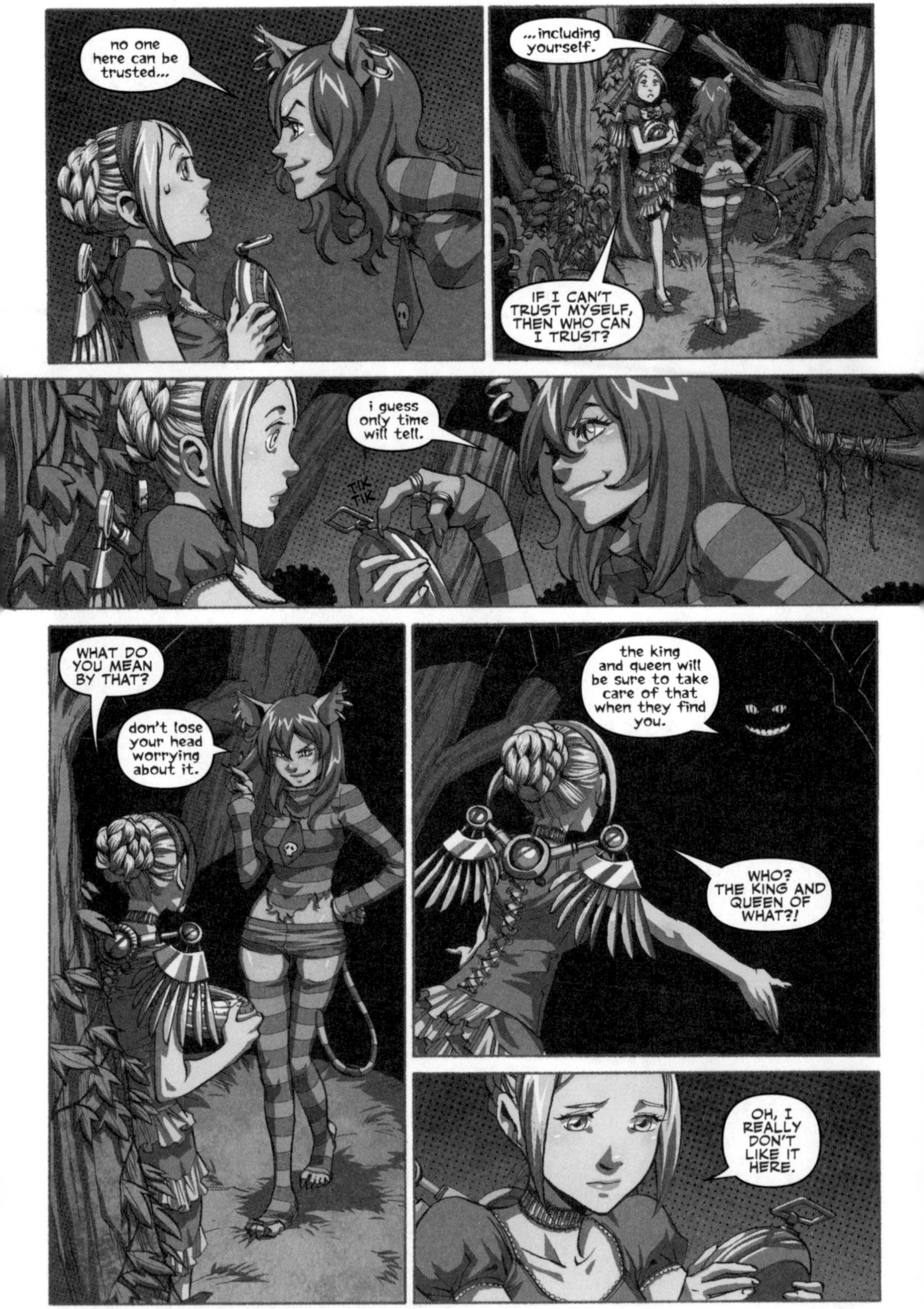
no one here can be trusted...
...including yourself.
IF I CAN'T TRUST MYSELF, THEN WHO CAN I TRUST?
i guess only time will tell.
TIK TIK
WHAT DO YOU MEAN BY THAT?
don't lose your head worrying about it.
the king and queen will be sure to take care of that when they find you.
WHO? THE KING AND QUEEN OF WHAT?!
OH, I REALLY DON'T LIKE IT HERE.

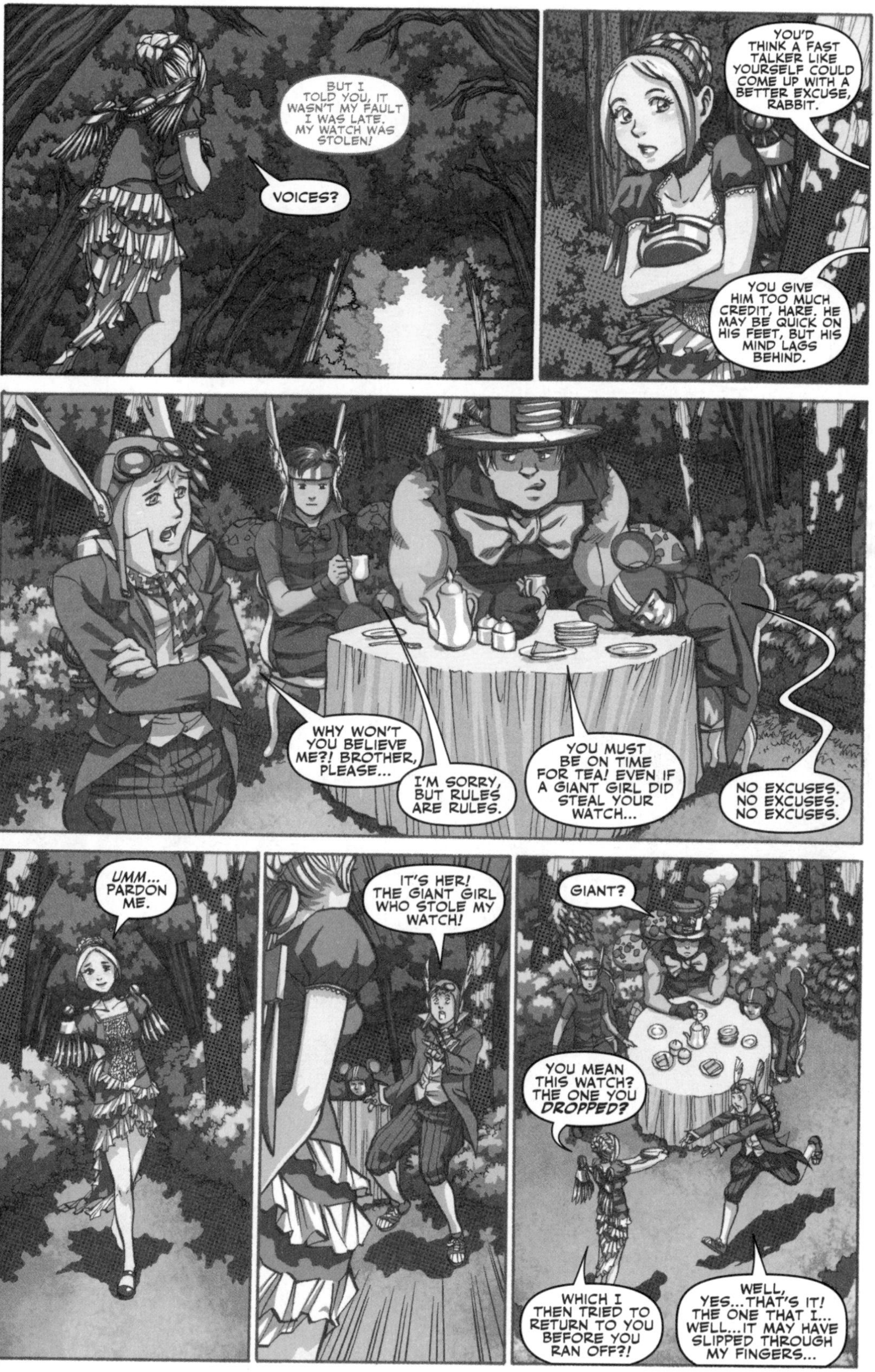

BUT I TOLD YOU, IT WASN'T MY FAULT I WAS LATE. MY WATCH WAS STOLEN!
VOICES?
YOU'D THINK A FAST TALKER LIKE YOURSELF COULD COME UP WITH A BETTER EXCUSE, RABBIT.
YOU GIVE HIM TOO MUCH CREDIT, HARE. HE MAY BE QUICK ON HIS FEET, BUT HIS MIND LAGS BEHIND.
WHY WON'T YOU BELIEVE ME?! BROTHER, PLEASE...
I'M SORRY, BUT RULES ARE RULES.
YOU MUST BE ON TIME FOR TEA! EVEN IF A GIANT GIRL DID STEAL YOUR WATCH...
NO EXCUSES. NO EXCUSES. NO EXCUSES.
UMM... PARDON ME.
IT'S HER! THE GIANT GIRL WHO STOLE MY WATCH!
GIANT?
YOU MEAN THIS WATCH? THE ONE YOU *DROPPED?*
WHICH I THEN TRIED TO RETURN TO YOU BEFORE YOU RAN OFF?!
WELL, YES...THAT'S IT! THE ONE THAT I... WELL...IT MAY HAVE SLIPPED THROUGH MY FINGERS...

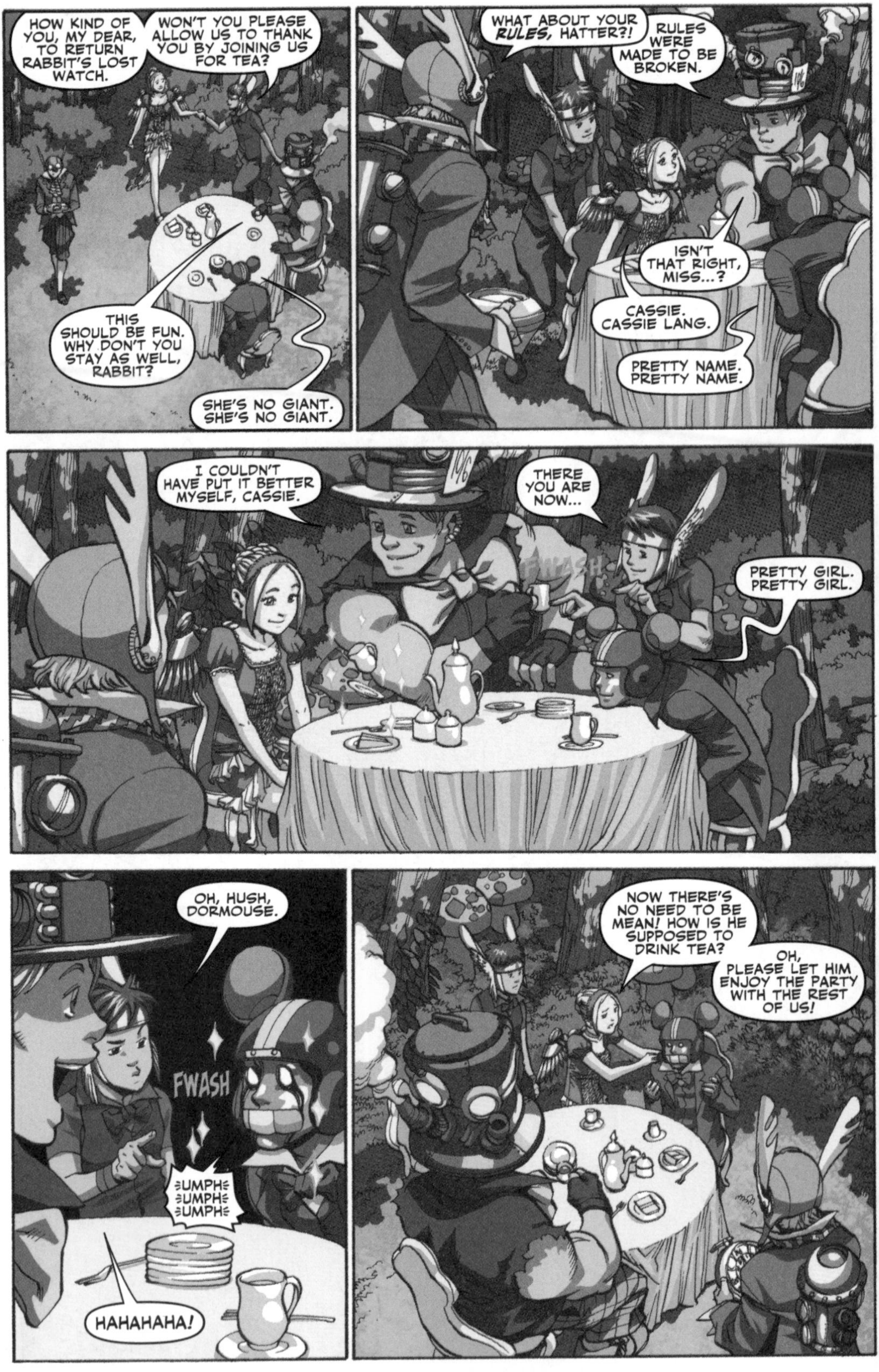
HOW KIND OF YOU, MY DEAR, TO RETURN RABBIT'S LOST WATCH.
WON'T YOU PLEASE ALLOW US TO THANK YOU BY JOINING US FOR TEA?
THIS SHOULD BE FUN. WHY DON'T YOU STAY AS WELL, RABBIT?
SHE'S NO GIANT. SHE'S NO GIANT.
WHAT ABOUT YOUR RULES, HATTER?!
RULES WERE MADE TO BE BROKEN.
ISN'T THAT RIGHT, MISS...?
CASSIE. CASSIE LANG.
PRETTY NAME. PRETTY NAME.
I COULDN'T HAVE PUT IT BETTER MYSELF, CASSIE.
THERE YOU ARE NOW...
FWASH
PRETTY GIRL. PRETTY GIRL.
OH, HUSH, DORMOUSE.
FWASH
UMPH UMPH UMPH
HAHAHAHA!
NOW THERE'S NO NEED TO BE MEAN! HOW IS HE SUPPOSED TO DRINK TEA?
OH, PLEASE LET HIM ENJOY THE PARTY WITH THE REST OF US!

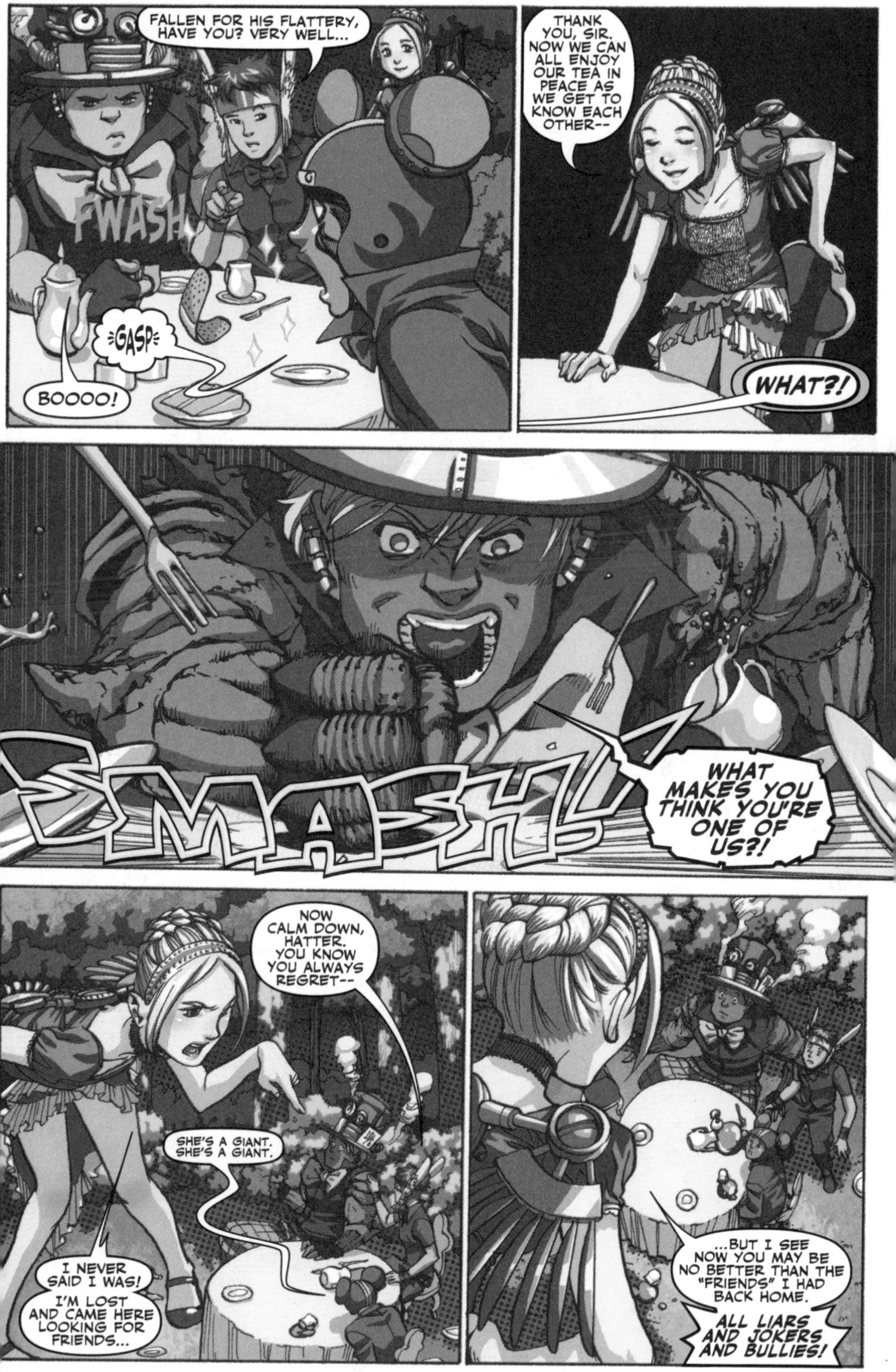
FALLEN FOR HIS FLATTERY, HAVE YOU? VERY WELL...
FWASH
GASP
BOOOO!
THANK YOU, SIR. NOW WE CAN ALL ENJOY OUR TEA IN PEACE AS WE GET TO KNOW EACH OTHER--
WHAT?!
SMASH!
WHAT MAKES YOU THINK YOU'RE ONE OF US?!
NOW CALM DOWN, HATTER. YOU KNOW YOU ALWAYS REGRET--
SHE'S A GIANT. SHE'S A GIANT.
I NEVER SAID I WAS!
I'M LOST AND CAME HERE LOOKING FOR FRIENDS...
...BUT I SEE NOW YOU MAY BE NO BETTER THAN THE "FRIENDS" I HAD BACK HOME.
ALL LIARS AND JOKERS AND BULLIES!

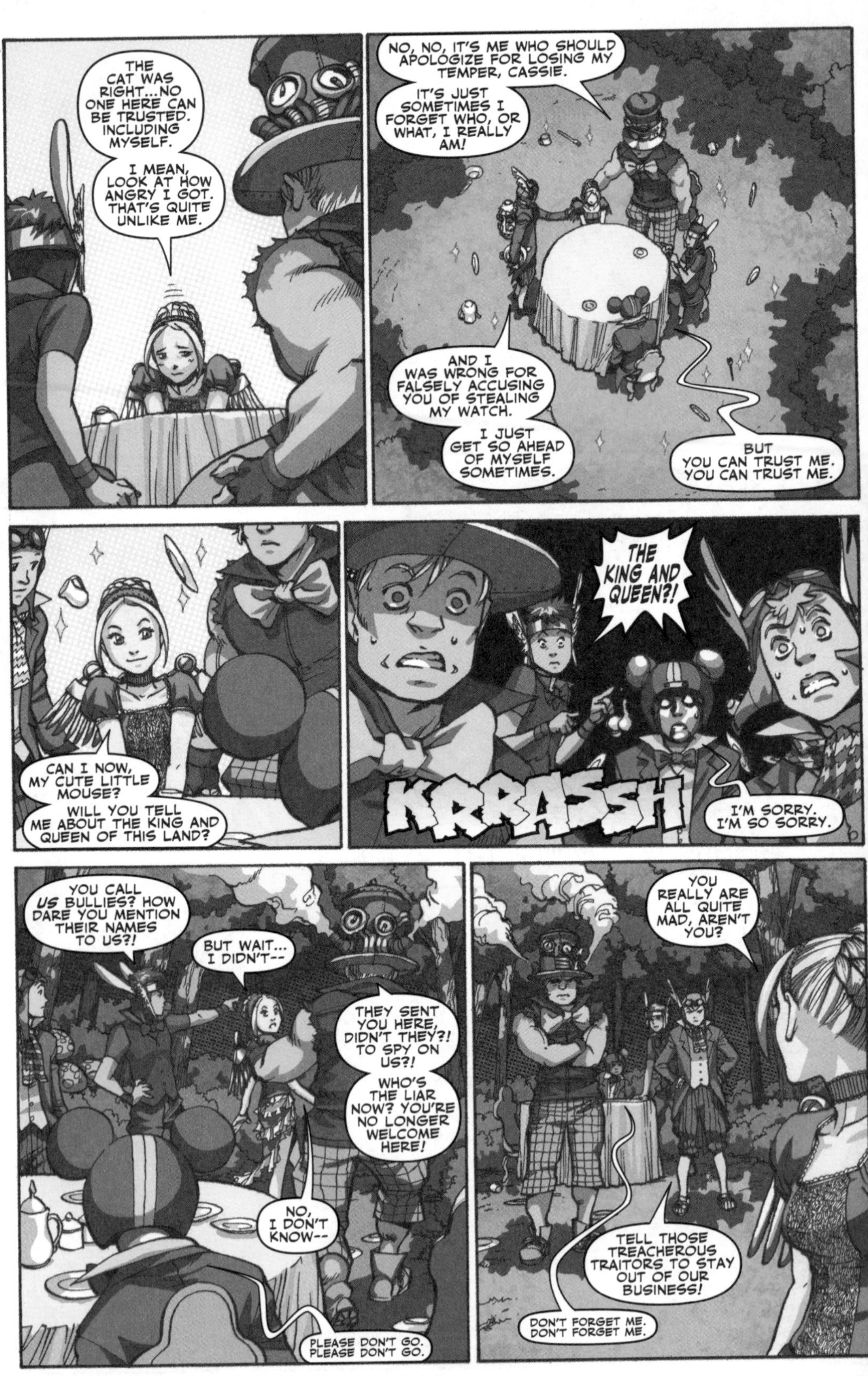
THE CAT WAS RIGHT...NO ONE HERE CAN BE TRUSTED. INCLUDING MYSELF.
I MEAN, LOOK AT HOW ANGRY I GOT. THAT'S QUITE UNLIKE ME.
NO, NO, IT'S ME WHO SHOULD APOLOGIZE FOR LOSING MY TEMPER, CASSIE.
IT'S JUST SOMETIMES I FORGET WHO, OR WHAT, I REALLY AM!
AND I WAS WRONG FOR FALSELY ACCUSING YOU OF STEALING MY WATCH.
I JUST GET SO AHEAD OF MYSELF SOMETIMES.
BUT YOU CAN TRUST ME. YOU CAN TRUST ME.
CAN I NOW, MY CUTE LITTLE MOUSE?
WILL YOU TELL ME ABOUT THE KING AND QUEEN OF THIS LAND?
THE KING AND QUEEN?!
KRRASSH
I'M SORRY. I'M SO SORRY.
YOU CALL US BULLIES? HOW DARE YOU MENTION THEIR NAMES TO US?!
BUT WAIT... I DIDN'T--
THEY SENT YOU HERE, DIDN'T THEY?! TO SPY ON US?!
WHO'S THE LIAR NOW? YOU'RE NO LONGER WELCOME HERE!
NO, I DON'T KNOW--
PLEASE DON'T GO. PLEASE DON'T GO.
YOU REALLY ARE ALL QUITE MAD, AREN'T YOU?
TELL THOSE TREACHEROUS TRAITORS TO STAY OUT OF OUR BUSINESS!
DON'T FORGET ME. DON'T FORGET ME.

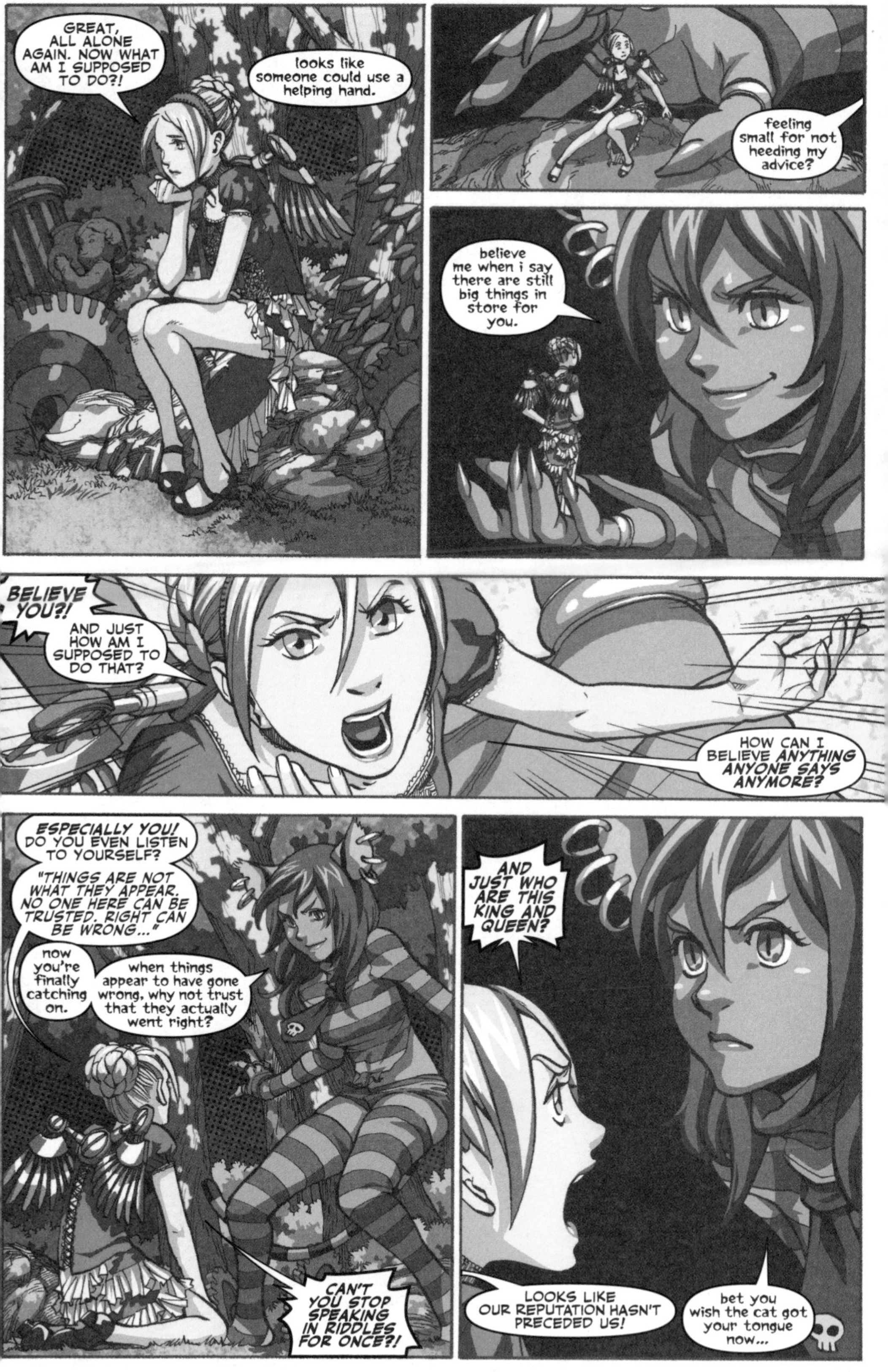
GREAT, ALL ALONE AGAIN. NOW WHAT AM I SUPPOSED TO DO?!
looks like someone could use a helping hand.
feeling small for not heeding my advice?
believe me when i say there are still big things in store for you.
BELIEVE YOU?!
AND JUST HOW AM I SUPPOSED TO DO THAT?
HOW CAN I BELIEVE ANYTHING ANYONE SAYS ANYMORE?
ESPECIALLY YOU! DO YOU EVEN LISTEN TO YOURSELF?
"THINGS ARE NOT WHAT THEY APPEAR. NO ONE HERE CAN BE TRUSTED. RIGHT CAN BE WRONG..."
now you're finally catching on.
when things appear to have gone wrong, why not trust that they actually went right?
CAN'T YOU STOP SPEAKING IN RIDDLES FOR ONCE?!
AND JUST WHO ARE THIS KING AND QUEEN?
LOOKS LIKE OUR REPUTATION HASN'T PRECEDED US!
bet you wish the cat got your tongue now...

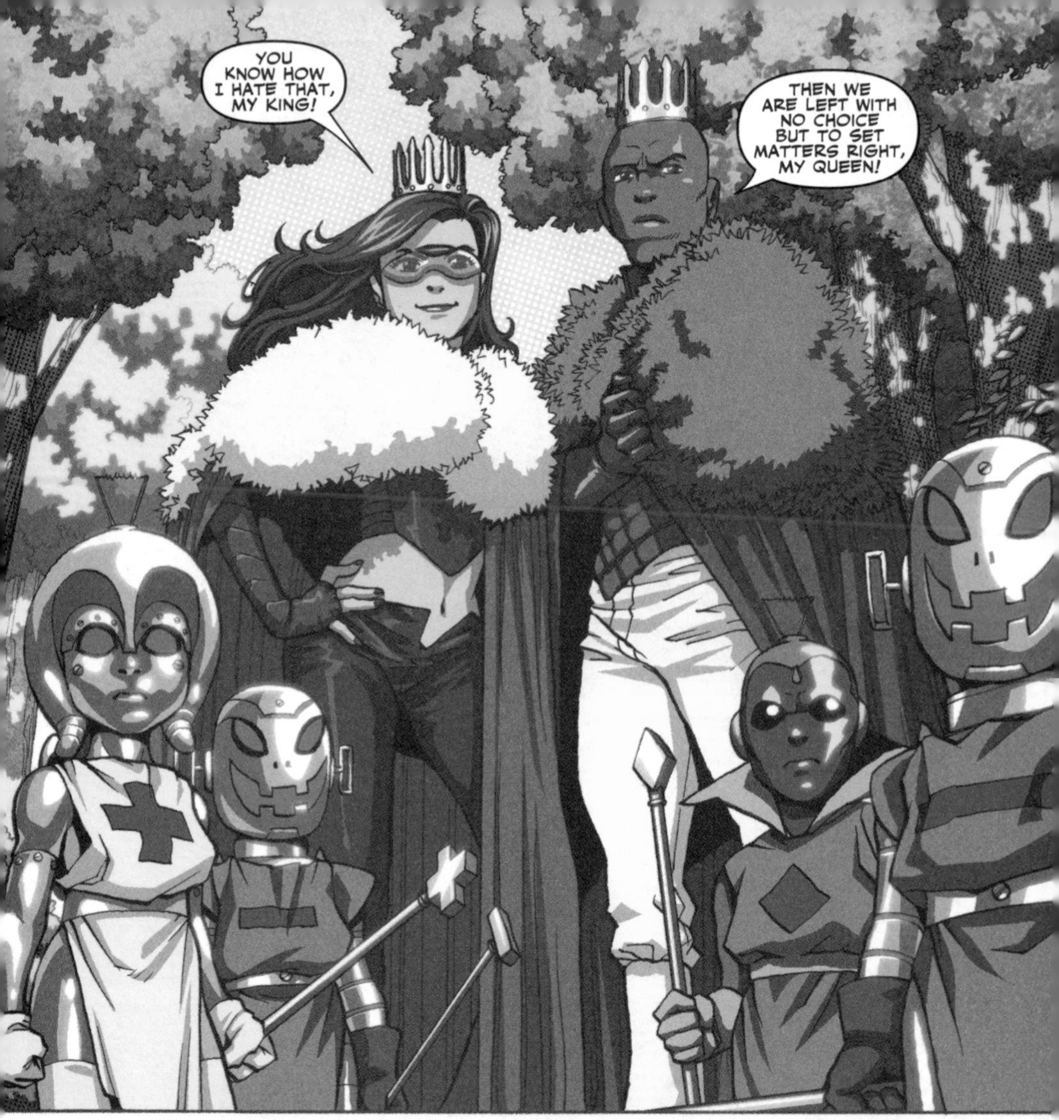
YOU KNOW HOW I HATE THAT, MY KING!
THEN WE ARE LEFT WITH NO CHOICE BUT TO SET MATTERS RIGHT, MY QUEEN!

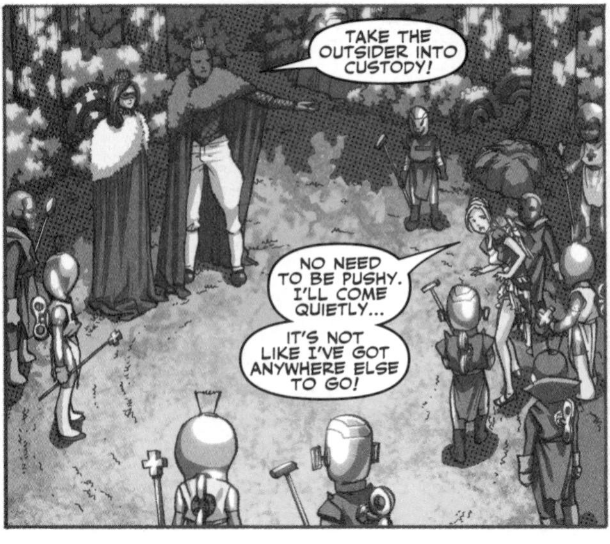
TAKE THE OUTSIDER INTO CUSTODY!
NO NEED TO BE PUSHY. I'LL COME QUIETLY...
IT'S NOT LIKE I'VE GOT ANYWHERE ELSE TO GO!

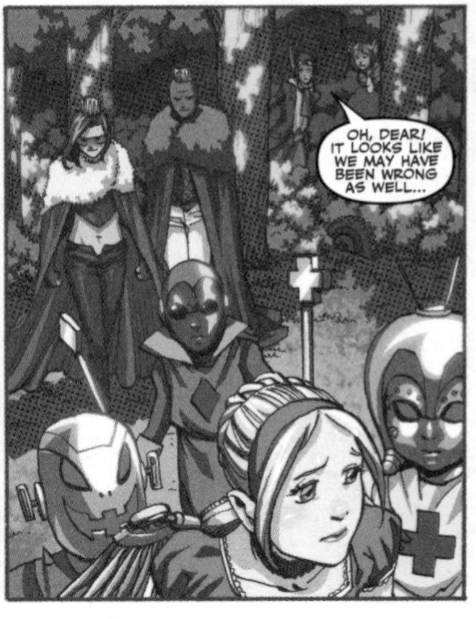
OH, DEAR! IT LOOKS LIKE WE MAY HAVE BEEN WRONG AS WELL...

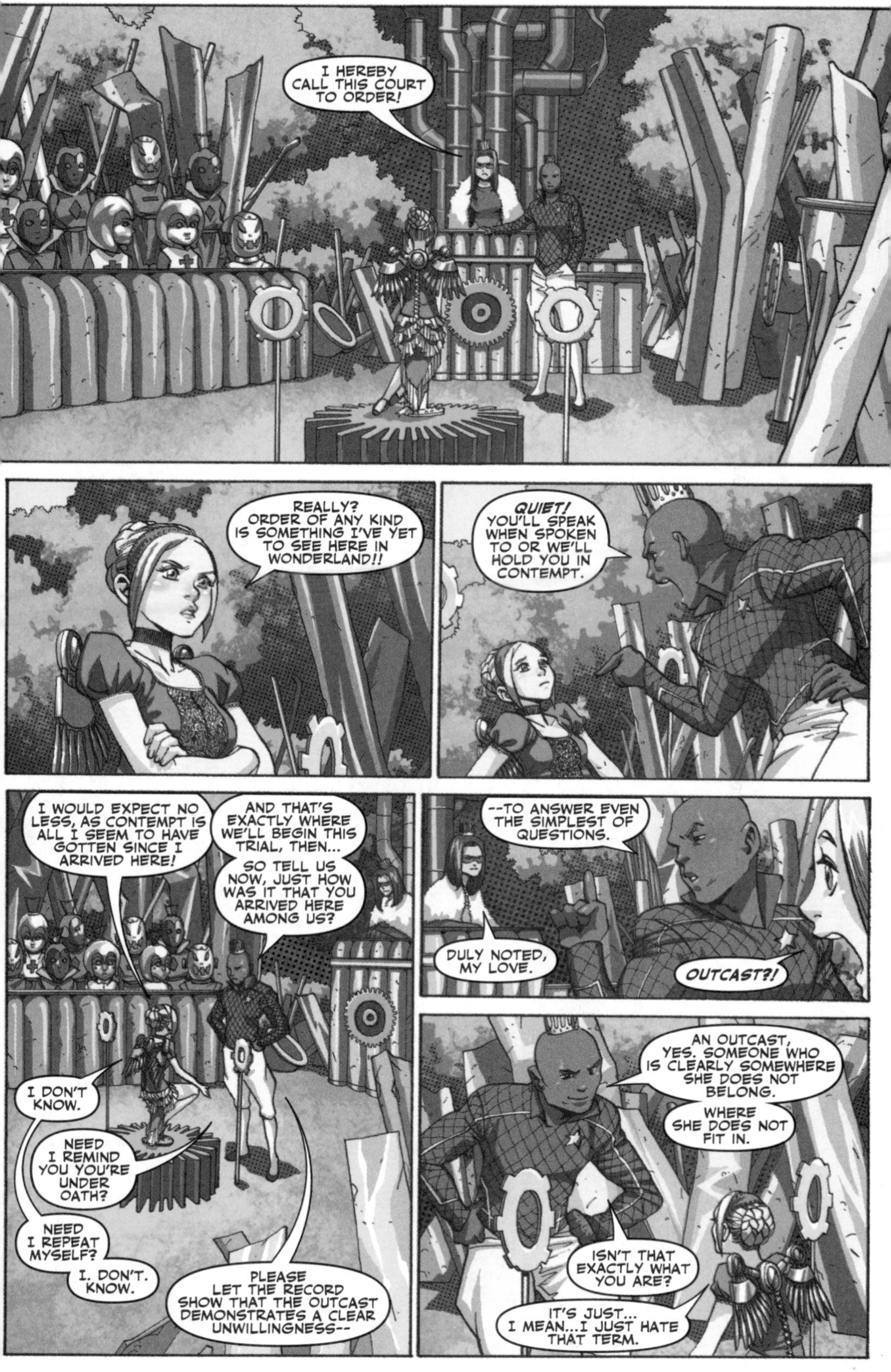
I HEREBY CALL THIS COURT TO ORDER!
REALLY? ORDER OF ANY KIND IS SOMETHING I'VE YET TO SEE HERE IN WONDERLAND!!
QUIET! YOU'LL SPEAK WHEN SPOKEN TO OR WE'LL HOLD YOU IN CONTEMPT.
I WOULD EXPECT NO LESS, AS CONTEMPT IS ALL I SEEM TO HAVE GOTTEN SINCE I ARRIVED HERE!
AND THAT'S EXACTLY WHERE WE'LL BEGIN THIS TRIAL, THEN...
SO TELL US NOW, JUST HOW WAS IT THAT YOU ARRIVED HERE AMONG US?
I DON'T KNOW.
NEED I REMIND YOU YOU'RE UNDER OATH?
NEED I REPEAT MYSELF?
I. DON'T. KNOW.
PLEASE LET THE RECORD SHOW THAT THE OUTCAST DEMONSTRATES A CLEAR UNWILLINGNESS--
--TO ANSWER EVEN THE SIMPLEST OF QUESTIONS.
DULY NOTED, MY LOVE.
OUTCAST?!
AN OUTCAST, YES. SOMEONE WHO IS CLEARLY SOMEWHERE SHE DOES NOT BELONG.
WHERE SHE DOES NOT FIT IN.
ISN'T THAT EXACTLY WHAT YOU ARE?
IT'S JUST... I MEAN...I JUST HATE THAT TERM.

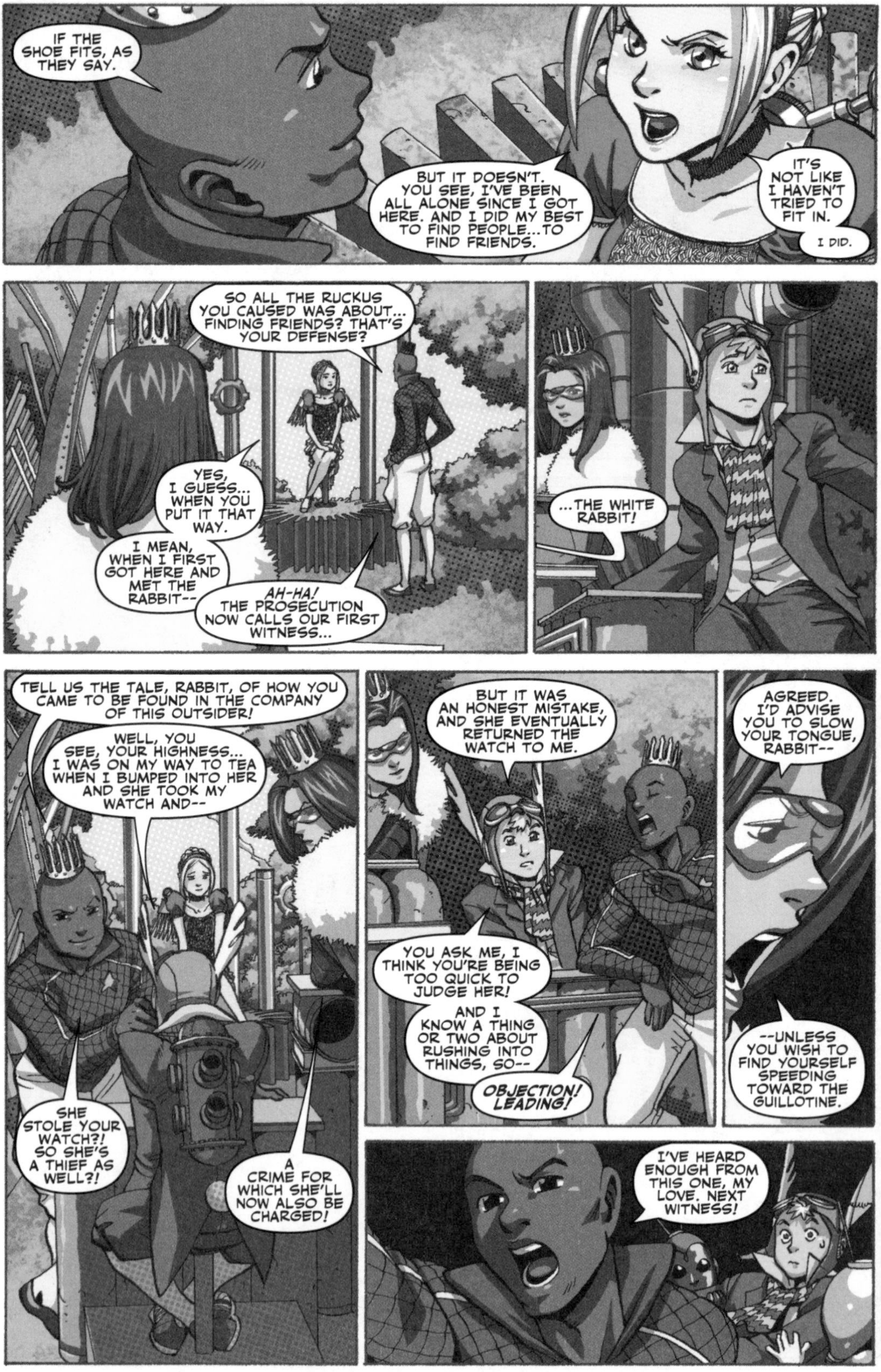
IF THE SHOE FITS, AS THEY SAY.
BUT IT DOESN'T. YOU SEE, I'VE BEEN ALL ALONE SINCE I GOT HERE. AND I DID MY BEST TO FIND PEOPLE...TO FIND FRIENDS.
IT'S NOT LIKE I HAVEN'T TRIED TO FIT IN.
I DID.
SO ALL THE RUCKUS YOU CAUSED WAS ABOUT... FINDING FRIENDS? THAT'S YOUR DEFENSE?
YES, I GUESS... WHEN YOU PUT IT THAT WAY.
I MEAN, WHEN I FIRST GOT HERE AND MET THE RABBIT--
AH-HA! THE PROSECUTION NOW CALLS OUR FIRST WITNESS...
...THE WHITE RABBIT!
TELL US THE TALE, RABBIT, OF HOW YOU CAME TO BE FOUND IN THE COMPANY OF THIS OUTSIDER!
WELL, YOU SEE, YOUR HIGHNESS... I WAS ON MY WAY TO TEA WHEN I BUMPED INTO HER AND SHE TOOK MY WATCH AND--
SHE STOLE YOUR WATCH?! SO SHE'S A THIEF AS WELL?!
A CRIME FOR WHICH SHE'LL NOW ALSO BE CHARGED!
BUT IT WAS AN HONEST MISTAKE, AND SHE EVENTUALLY RETURNED THE WATCH TO ME.
YOU ASK ME, I THINK YOU'RE BEING TOO QUICK TO JUDGE HER!
AND I KNOW A THING OR TWO ABOUT RUSHING INTO THINGS, SO--
OBJECTION! LEADING!
AGREED. I'D ADVISE YOU TO SLOW YOUR TONGUE, RABBIT--
--UNLESS YOU WISH TO FIND YOURSELF SPEEDING TOWARD THE GUILLOTINE.
I'VE HEARD ENOUGH FROM THIS ONE, MY LOVE. NEXT WITNESS!

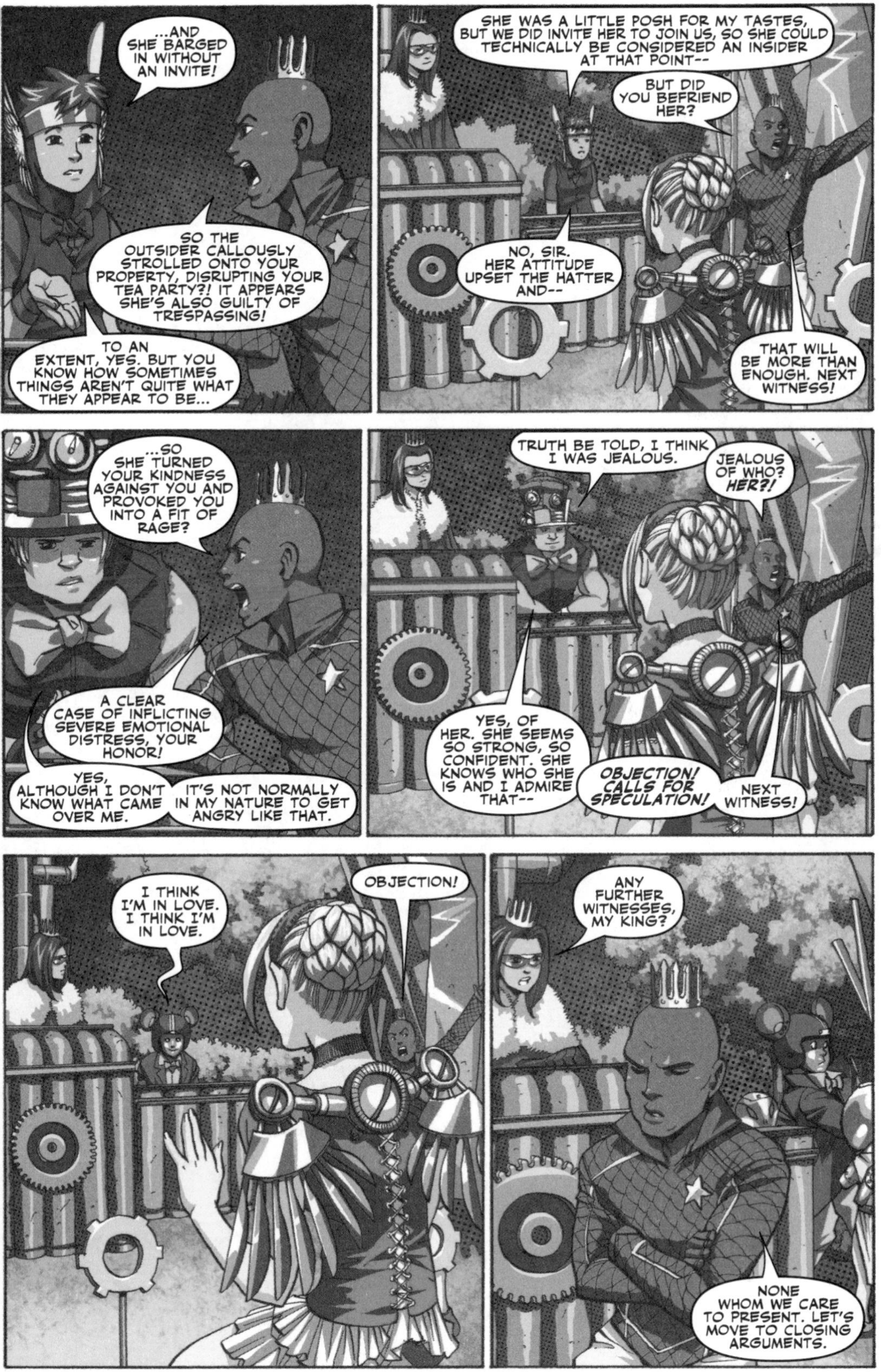
...AND SHE BARGED IN WITHOUT AN INVITE!
SO THE OUTSIDER CALLOUSLY STROLLED ONTO YOUR PROPERTY, DISRUPTING YOUR TEA PARTY?! IT APPEARS SHE'S ALSO GUILTY OF TRESPASSING!
TO AN EXTENT, YES. BUT YOU KNOW HOW SOMETIMES THINGS AREN'T QUITE WHAT THEY APPEAR TO BE...
SHE WAS A LITTLE POSH FOR MY TASTES, BUT WE DID INVITE HER TO JOIN US, SO SHE COULD TECHNICALLY BE CONSIDERED AN INSIDER AT THAT POINT--
BUT DID YOU BEFRIEND HER?
NO, SIR. HER ATTITUDE UPSET THE HATTER AND--
THAT WILL BE MORE THAN ENOUGH. NEXT WITNESS!
...SO SHE TURNED YOUR KINDNESS AGAINST YOU AND PROVOKED YOU INTO A FIT OF RAGE?
A CLEAR CASE OF INFLICTING SEVERE EMOTIONAL DISTRESS, YOUR HONOR!
YES, ALTHOUGH I DON'T KNOW WHAT CAME OVER ME.
IT'S NOT NORMALLY IN MY NATURE TO GET ANGRY LIKE THAT.
TRUTH BE TOLD, I THINK I WAS JEALOUS.
JEALOUS OF WHO? *HER?!*
YES, OF HER. SHE SEEMS SO STRONG, SO CONFIDENT. SHE KNOWS WHO SHE IS AND I ADMIRE THAT--
*OBJECTION! CALLS FOR SPECULATION!*
NEXT WITNESS!
I THINK I'M IN LOVE. I THINK I'M IN LOVE.
OBJECTION!
ANY FURTHER WITNESSES, MY KING?
NONE WHOM WE CARE TO PRESENT. LET'S MOVE TO CLOSING ARGUMENTS.

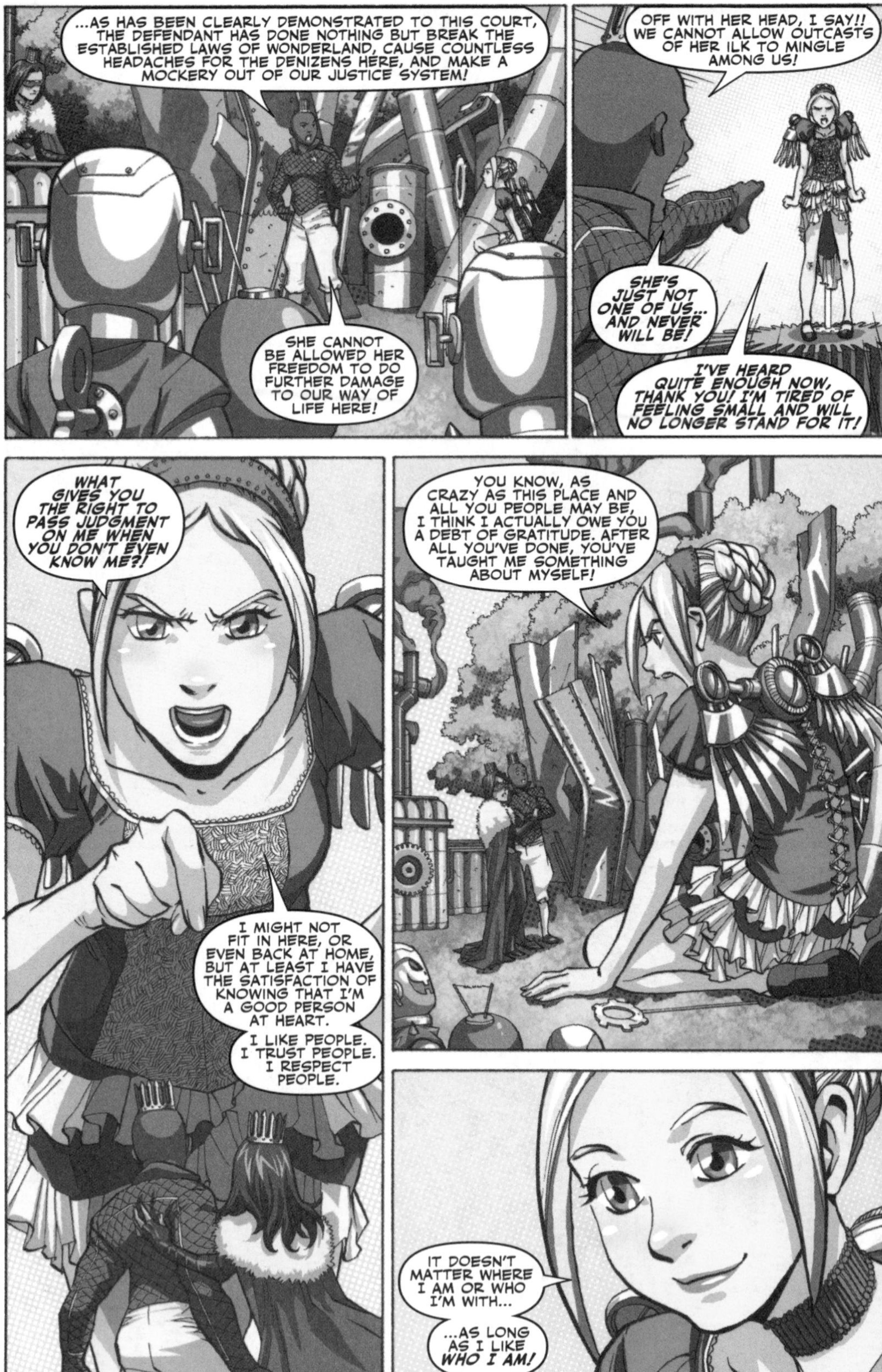
...AS HAS BEEN CLEARLY DEMONSTRATED TO THIS COURT, THE DEFENDANT HAS DONE NOTHING BUT BREAK THE ESTABLISHED LAWS OF WONDERLAND, CAUSE COUNTLESS HEADACHES FOR THE DENIZENS HERE, AND MAKE A MOCKERY OUT OF OUR JUSTICE SYSTEM!
SHE CANNOT BE ALLOWED HER FREEDOM TO DO FURTHER DAMAGE TO OUR WAY OF LIFE HERE!
OFF WITH HER HEAD, I SAY!! WE CANNOT ALLOW OUTCASTS OF HER ILK TO MINGLE AMONG US!
SHE'S JUST NOT ONE OF US... AND NEVER WILL BE!
I'VE HEARD QUITE ENOUGH NOW, THANK YOU! I'M TIRED OF FEELING SMALL AND WILL NO LONGER STAND FOR IT!
WHAT GIVES YOU THE RIGHT TO PASS JUDGMENT ON ME WHEN YOU DON'T EVEN KNOW ME?!
I MIGHT NOT FIT IN HERE, OR EVEN BACK AT HOME, BUT AT LEAST I HAVE THE SATISFACTION OF KNOWING THAT I'M A GOOD PERSON AT HEART.
I LIKE PEOPLE. I TRUST PEOPLE. I RESPECT PEOPLE.
YOU KNOW, AS CRAZY AS THIS PLACE AND ALL YOU PEOPLE MAY BE, I THINK I ACTUALLY OWE YOU A DEBT OF GRATITUDE. AFTER ALL YOU'VE DONE, YOU'VE TAUGHT ME SOMETHING ABOUT MYSELF!
IT DOESN'T MATTER WHERE I AM OR WHO I'M WITH...
...AS LONG AS I LIKE WHO I AM!

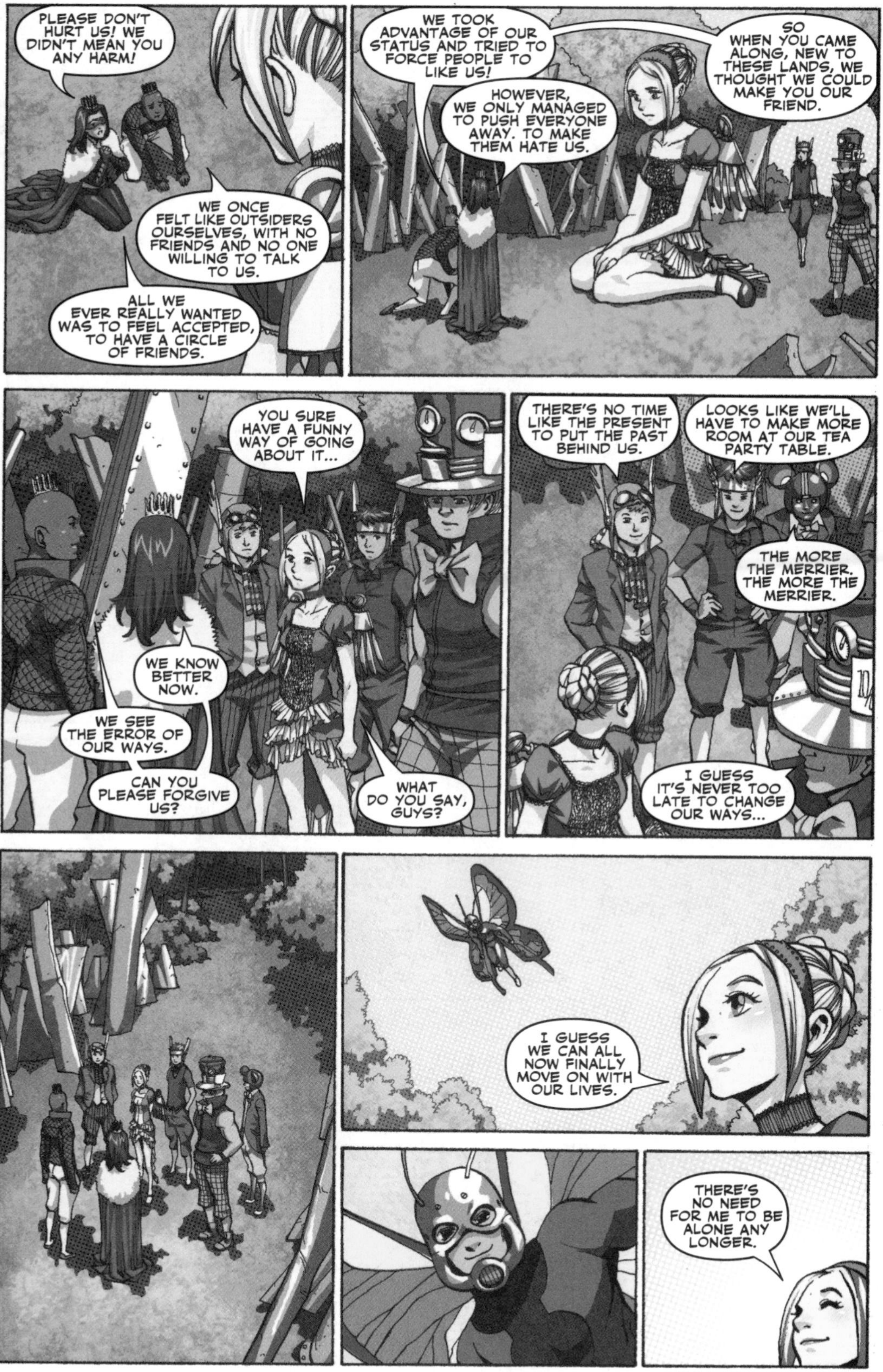
PLEASE DON'T HURT US! WE DIDN'T MEAN YOU ANY HARM!
WE ONCE FELT LIKE OUTSIDERS OURSELVES, WITH NO FRIENDS AND NO ONE WILLING TO TALK TO US.
ALL WE EVER REALLY WANTED WAS TO FEEL ACCEPTED, TO HAVE A CIRCLE OF FRIENDS.
WE TOOK ADVANTAGE OF OUR STATUS AND TRIED TO FORCE PEOPLE TO LIKE US!
HOWEVER, WE ONLY MANAGED TO PUSH EVERYONE AWAY. TO MAKE THEM HATE US.
SO WHEN YOU CAME ALONG, NEW TO THESE LANDS, WE THOUGHT WE COULD MAKE YOU OUR FRIEND.
YOU SURE HAVE A FUNNY WAY OF GOING ABOUT IT...
WE KNOW BETTER NOW.
WE SEE THE ERROR OF OUR WAYS.
CAN YOU PLEASE FORGIVE US?
WHAT DO YOU SAY, GUYS?
THERE'S NO TIME LIKE THE PRESENT TO PUT THE PAST BEHIND US.
LOOKS LIKE WE'LL HAVE TO MAKE MORE ROOM AT OUR TEA PARTY TABLE.
THE MORE THE MERRIER. THE MORE THE MERRIER.
I GUESS IT'S NEVER TOO LATE TO CHANGE OUR WAYS...
I GUESS WE CAN ALL NOW FINALLY MOVE ON WITH OUR LIVES.
THERE'S NO NEED FOR ME TO BE ALONE ANY LONGER.

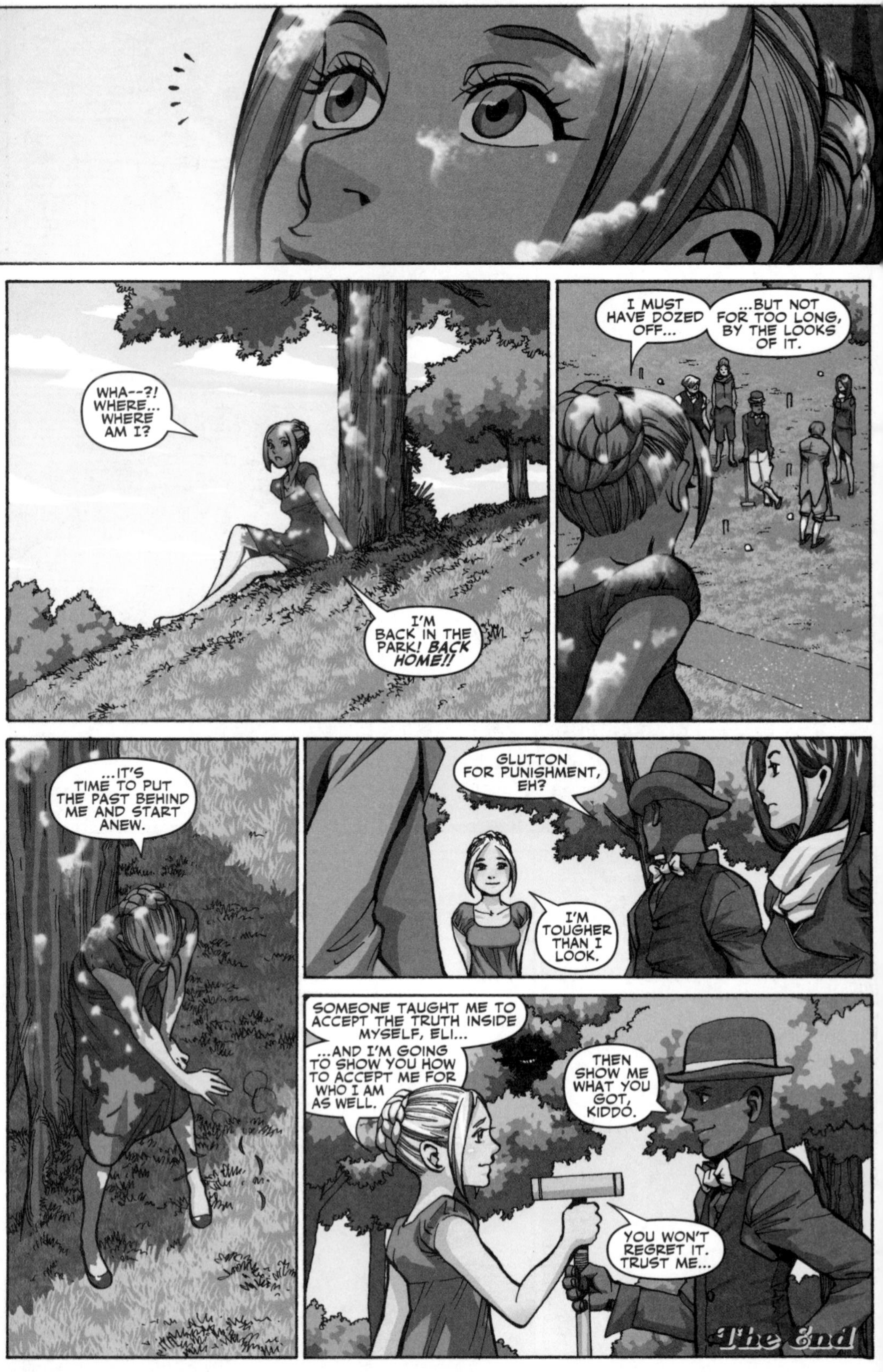
WHA--?! WHERE... WHERE AM I?
I'M BACK IN THE PARK! BACK HOME!!
I MUST HAVE DOZED OFF...
...BUT NOT FOR TOO LONG, BY THE LOOKS OF IT.
...IT'S TIME TO PUT THE PAST BEHIND ME AND START ANEW.
GLUTTON FOR PUNISHMENT, EH?
I'M TOUGHER THAN I LOOK.
SOMEONE TAUGHT ME TO ACCEPT THE TRUTH INSIDE MYSELF, ELI...
...AND I'M GOING TO SHOW YOU HOW TO ACCEPT ME FOR WHO I AM AS WELL.
THEN SHOW ME WHAT YOU GOT, KIDDO.
YOU WON'T REGRET IT. TRUST ME...
The End

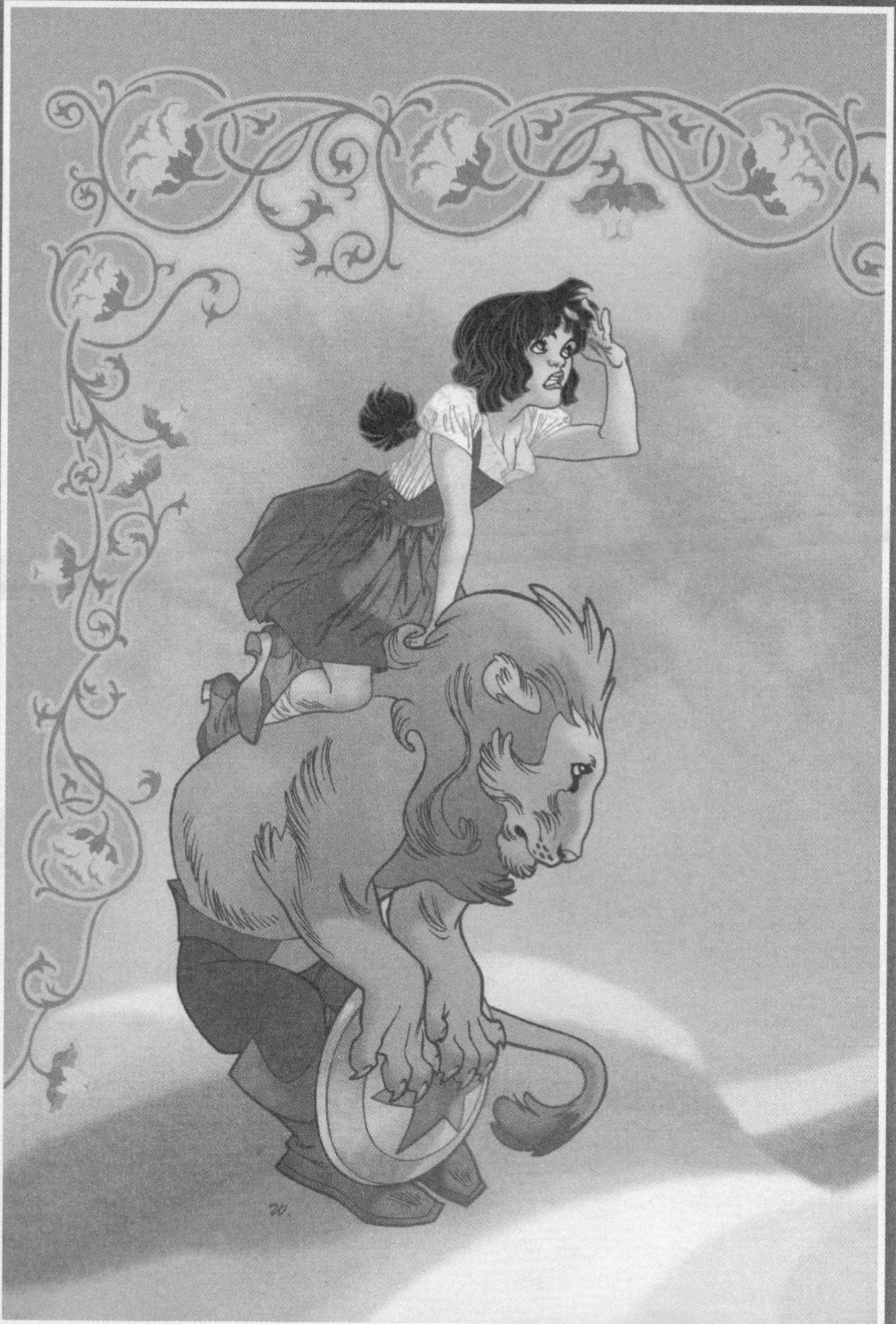

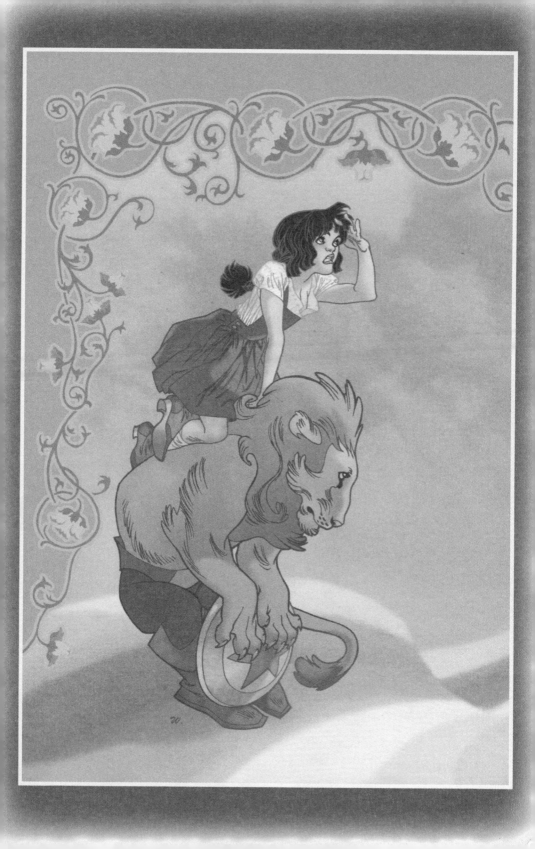

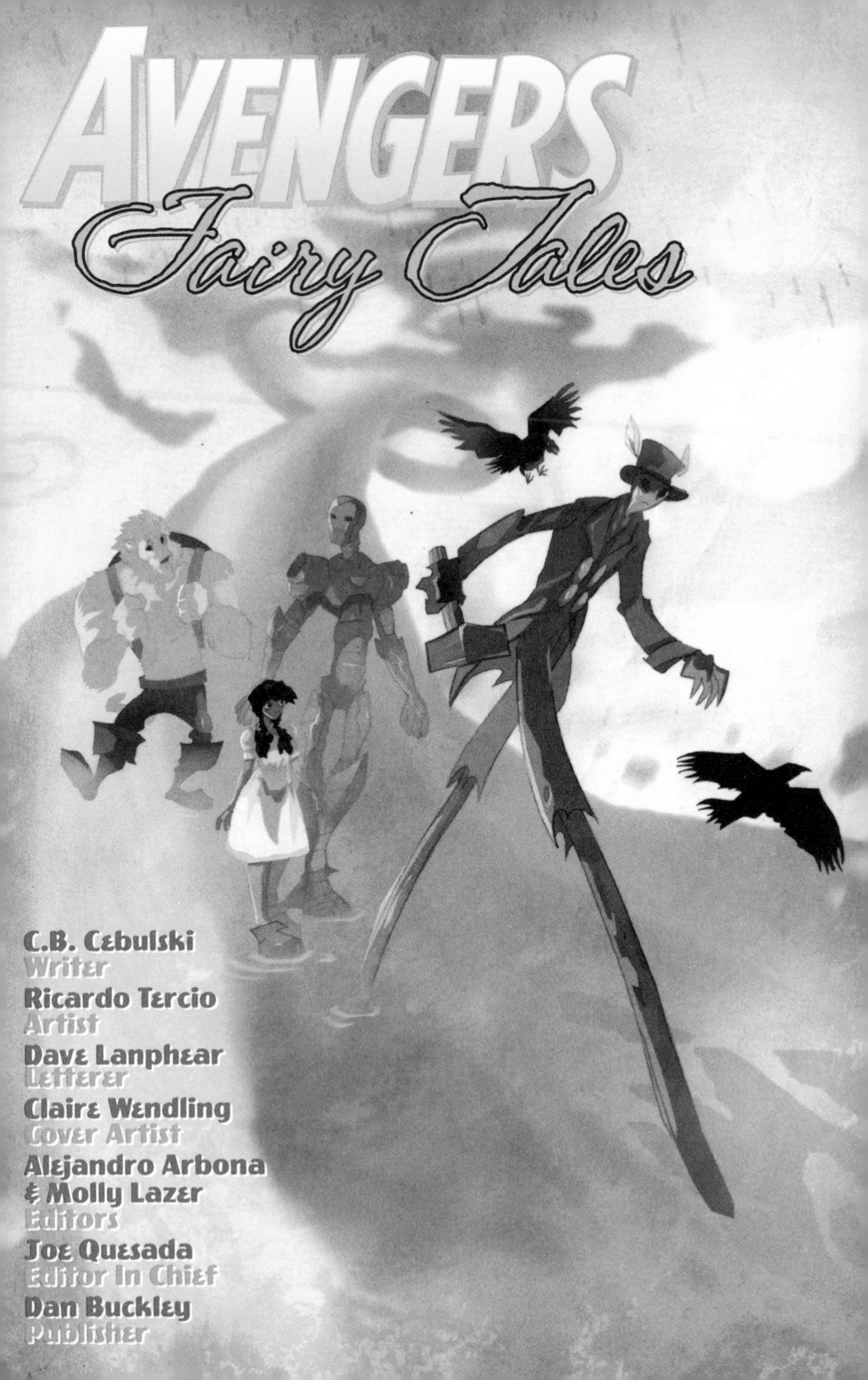
AVENGERS
Fairy Tales
C.B. Cebulski
Writer
Ricardo Tercio
Artist
Dave Lanphear
Letterer
Claire Wendling
Cover Artist
Alejandro Arbona
& Molly Lazer
Editors
Joe Quesada
Editor In Chief
Dan Buckley
Publisher

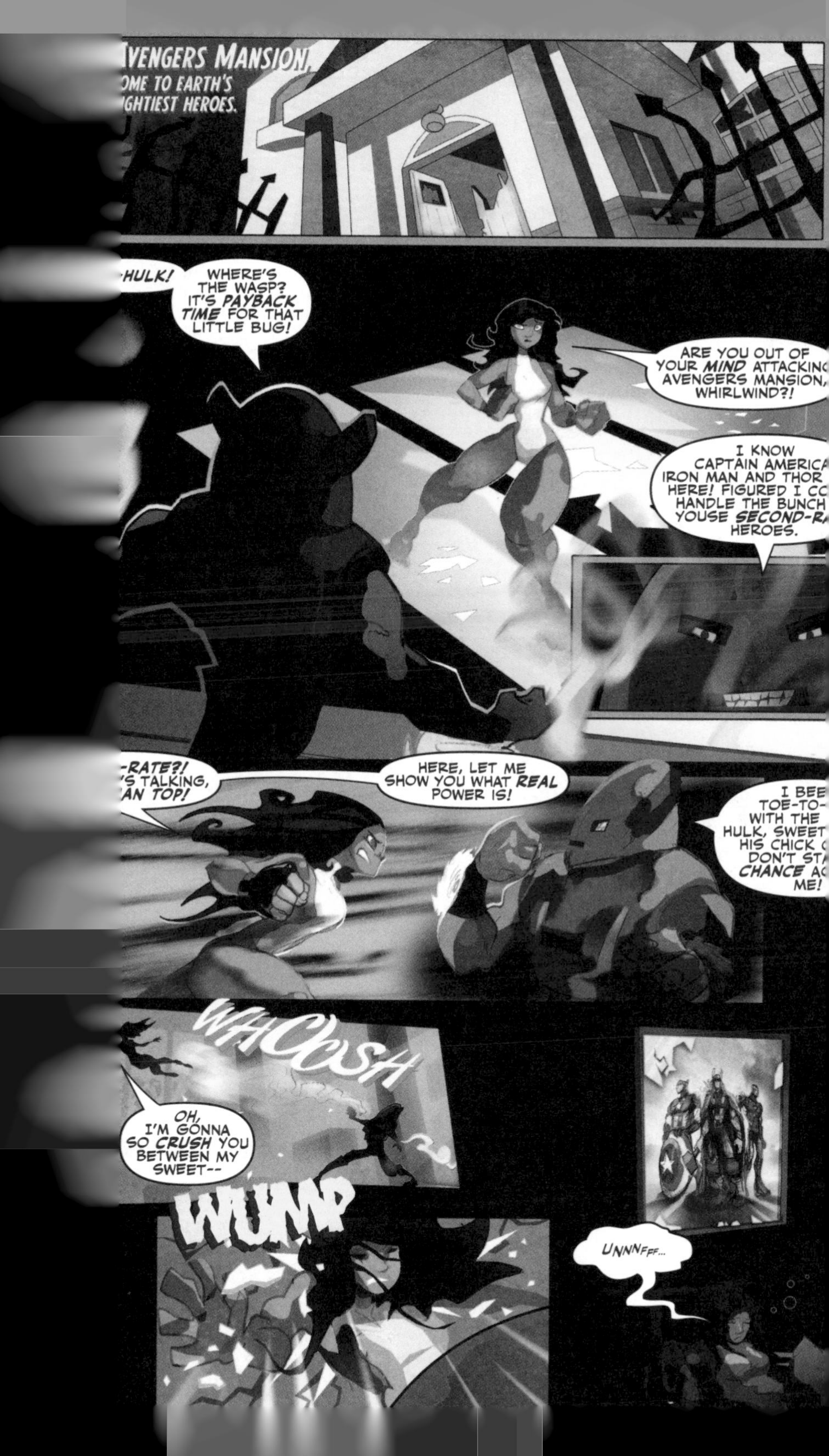

AVENGERS MANSION, OME TO EARTH'S IGHTIEST HEROES.
-HULK!
WHERE'S THE WASP? IT'S PAYBACK TIME FOR THAT LITTLE BUG!
ARE YOU OUT OF YOUR MIND ATTACKING AVENGERS MANSION, WHIRLWIND?!
I KNOW CAPTAIN AMERICA IRON MAN AND THOR HERE! FIGURED I CO HANDLE THE BUNCH YOUSE SECOND-RA HEROES.
-RATE?! 'S TALKING, AN TOP!
HERE, LET ME SHOW YOU WHAT REAL POWER IS!
I BEE TOE-TO- WITH THE HULK, SWEET HIS CHICK DON'T STA CHANCE AC ME!
WHOOSH
OH, I'M GONNA SO CRUSH YOU BETWEEN MY SWEET--
WUMP
UNNNFFF...

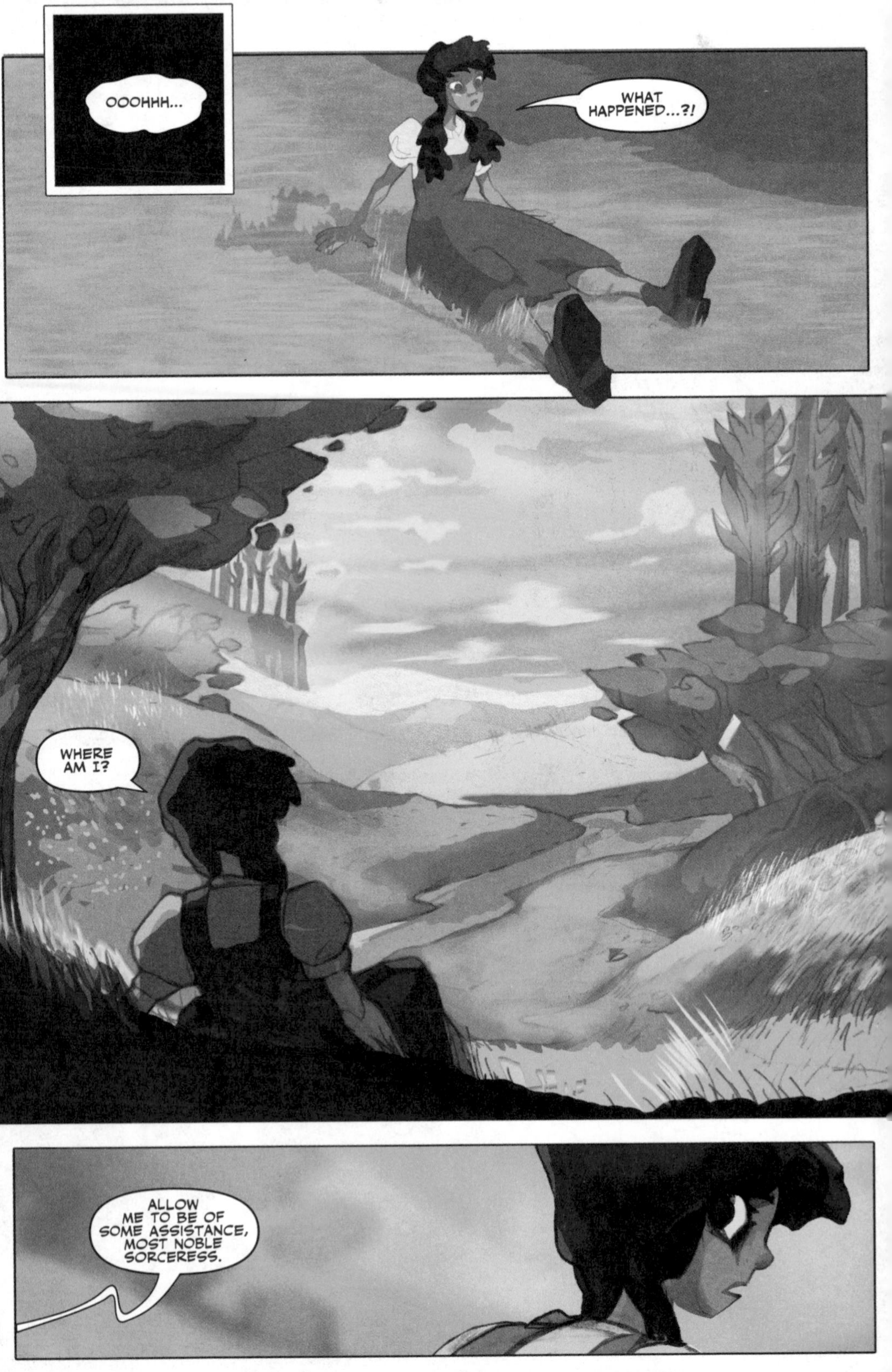
OOOHHH...
WHAT HAPPENED...?!
WHERE AM I?
ALLOW ME TO BE OF SOME ASSISTANCE, MOST NOBLE SORCERESS.

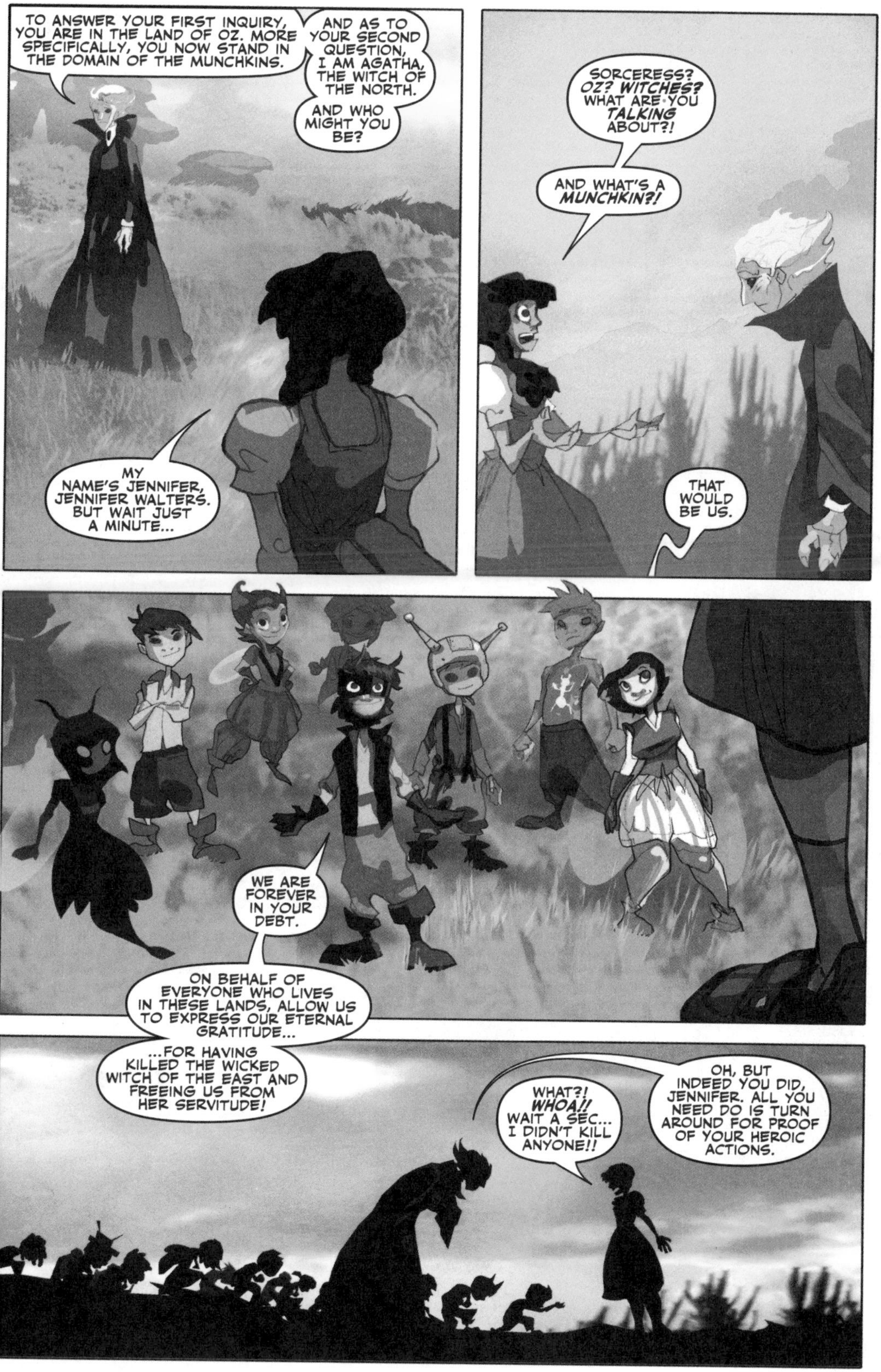
TO ANSWER YOUR FIRST INQUIRY, YOU ARE IN THE LAND OF OZ. MORE SPECIFICALLY, YOU NOW STAND IN THE DOMAIN OF THE MUNCHKINS.
AND AS TO YOUR SECOND QUESTION, I AM AGATHA, THE WITCH OF THE NORTH.
AND WHO MIGHT YOU BE?
MY NAME'S JENNIFER, JENNIFER WALTERS. BUT WAIT JUST A MINUTE...
SORCERESS? OZ? WITCHES? WHAT ARE YOU TALKING ABOUT?!
AND WHAT'S A MUNCHKIN?!
THAT WOULD BE US.
WE ARE FOREVER IN YOUR DEBT.
ON BEHALF OF EVERYONE WHO LIVES IN THESE LANDS, ALLOW US TO EXPRESS OUR ETERNAL GRATITUDE...
...FOR HAVING KILLED THE WICKED WITCH OF THE EAST AND FREEING US FROM HER SERVITUDE!
WHAT?! WHOA!! WAIT A SEC... I DIDN'T KILL ANYONE!!
OH, BUT INDEED YOU DID, JENNIFER. ALL YOU NEED DO IS TURN AROUND FOR PROOF OF YOUR HEROIC ACTIONS.

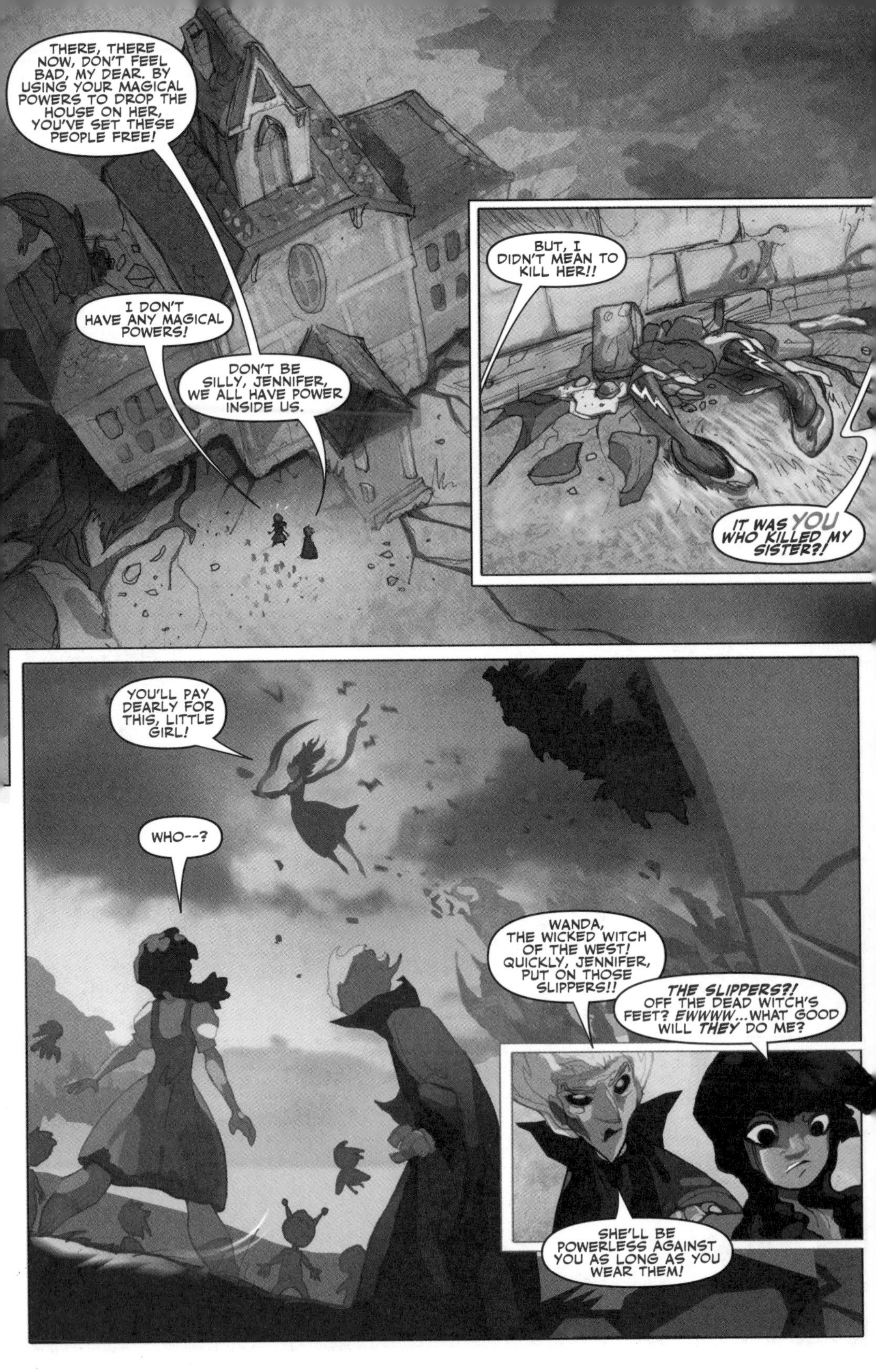
THERE, THERE NOW, DON'T FEEL BAD, MY DEAR. BY USING YOUR MAGICAL POWERS TO DROP THE HOUSE ON HER, YOU'VE SET THESE PEOPLE FREE!
I DON'T HAVE ANY MAGICAL POWERS!
DON'T BE SILLY, JENNIFER, WE ALL HAVE POWER INSIDE US.
BUT, I DIDN'T MEAN TO KILL HER!!
IT WAS YOU WHO KILLED MY SISTER?!
YOU'LL PAY DEARLY FOR THIS, LITTLE GIRL!
WHO--?
WANDA, THE WICKED WITCH OF THE WEST! QUICKLY, JENNIFER, PUT ON THOSE SLIPPERS!!
THE SLIPPERS?! OFF THE DEAD WITCH'S FEET? EWWWW...WHAT GOOD WILL THEY DO ME?
SHE'LL BE POWERLESS AGAINST YOU AS LONG AS YOU WEAR THEM!

Ms. Borman

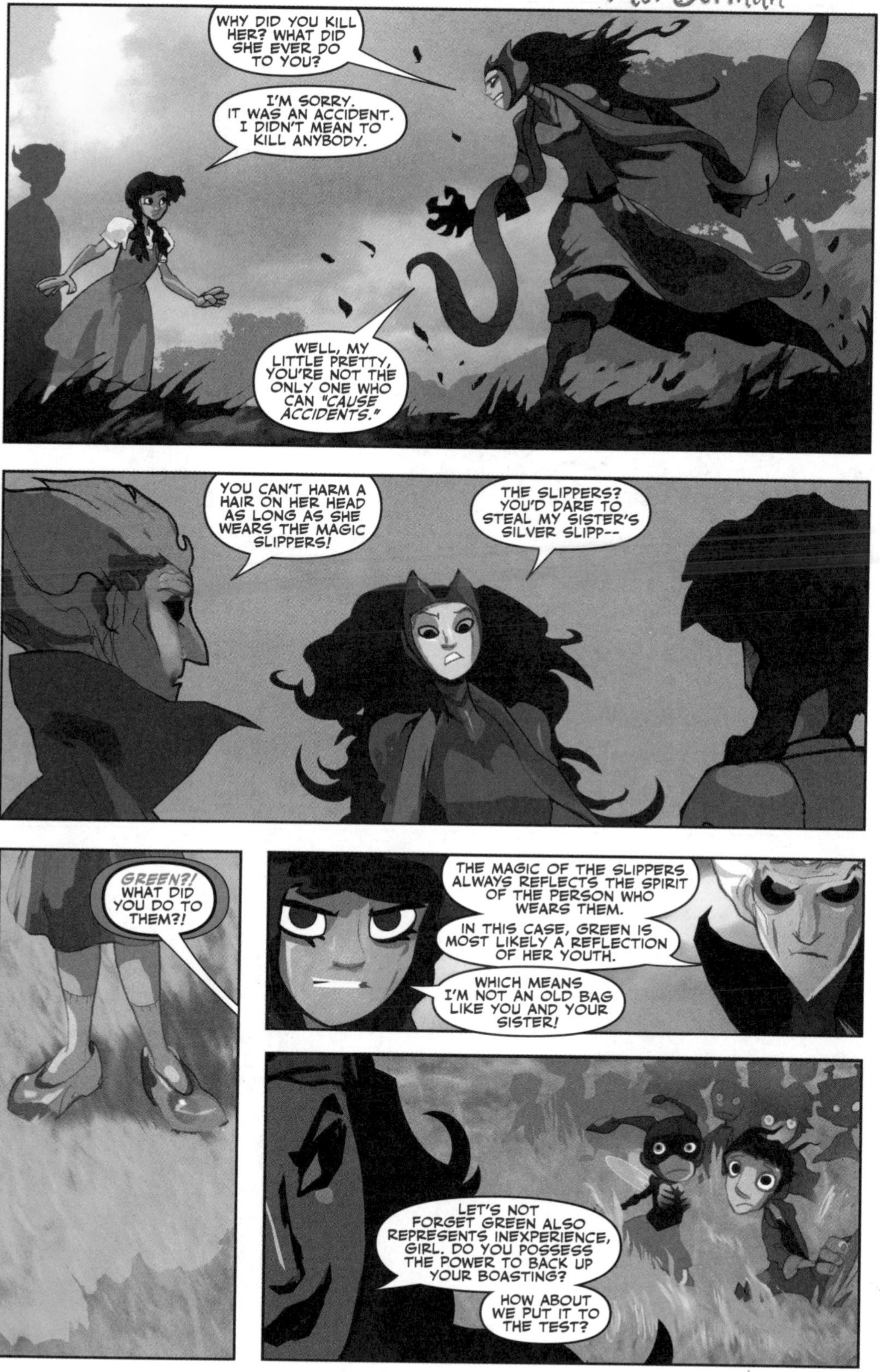

WHY DID YOU KILL HER? WHAT DID SHE EVER DO TO YOU?
I'M SORRY. IT WAS AN ACCIDENT. I DIDN'T MEAN TO KILL ANYBODY.
WELL, MY LITTLE PRETTY, YOU'RE NOT THE ONLY ONE WHO CAN "CAUSE ACCIDENTS."
YOU CAN'T HARM A HAIR ON HER HEAD AS LONG AS SHE WEARS THE MAGIC SLIPPERS!
THE SLIPPERS? YOU'D DARE TO STEAL MY SISTER'S SILVER SLIPP--
GREEN?! WHAT DID YOU DO TO THEM?!
THE MAGIC OF THE SLIPPERS ALWAYS REFLECTS THE SPIRIT OF THE PERSON WHO WEARS THEM.
IN THIS CASE, GREEN IS MOST LIKELY A REFLECTION OF HER YOUTH.
WHICH MEANS I'M NOT AN OLD BAG LIKE YOU AND YOUR SISTER!
LET'S NOT FORGET GREEN ALSO REPRESENTS INEXPERIENCE, GIRL. DO YOU POSSESS THE POWER TO BACK UP YOUR BOASTING?
HOW ABOUT WE PUT IT TO THE TEST?

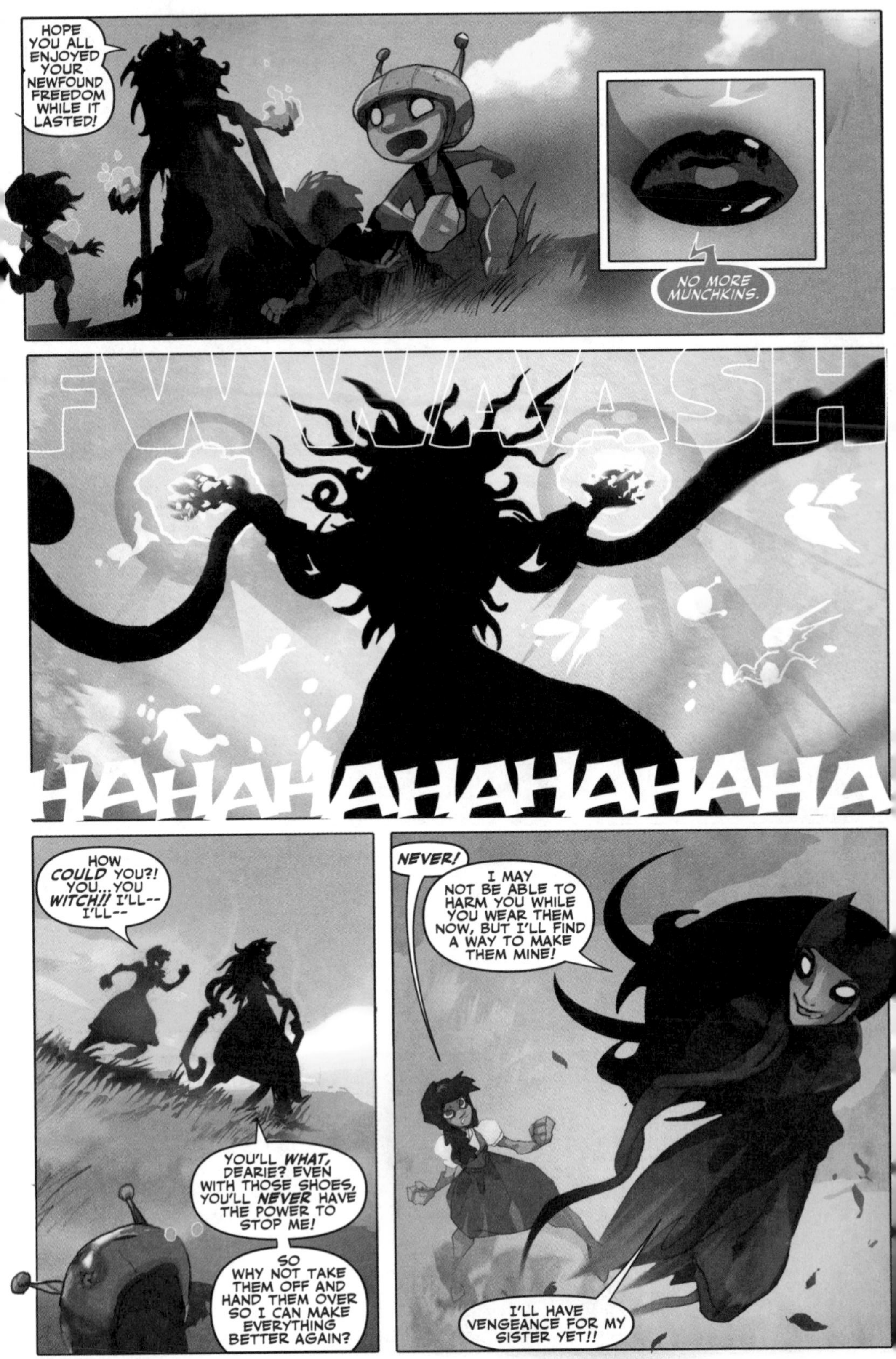
HOPE YOU ALL ENJOYED YOUR NEWFOUND FREEDOM WHILE IT LASTED!
NO MORE MUNCHKINS.
FWWAASH
HAHAHAHAHAHAHAHA
HOW COULD YOU?! YOU...YOU WITCH!! I'LL-- I'LL--
YOU'LL WHAT, DEARIE? EVEN WITH THOSE SHOES, YOU'LL NEVER HAVE THE POWER TO STOP ME!
SO WHY NOT TAKE THEM OFF AND HAND THEM OVER SO I CAN MAKE EVERYTHING BETTER AGAIN?
NEVER!
I MAY NOT BE ABLE TO HARM YOU WHILE YOU WEAR THEM NOW, BUT I'LL FIND A WAY TO MAKE THEM MINE!
I'LL HAVE VENGEANCE FOR MY SISTER YET!!

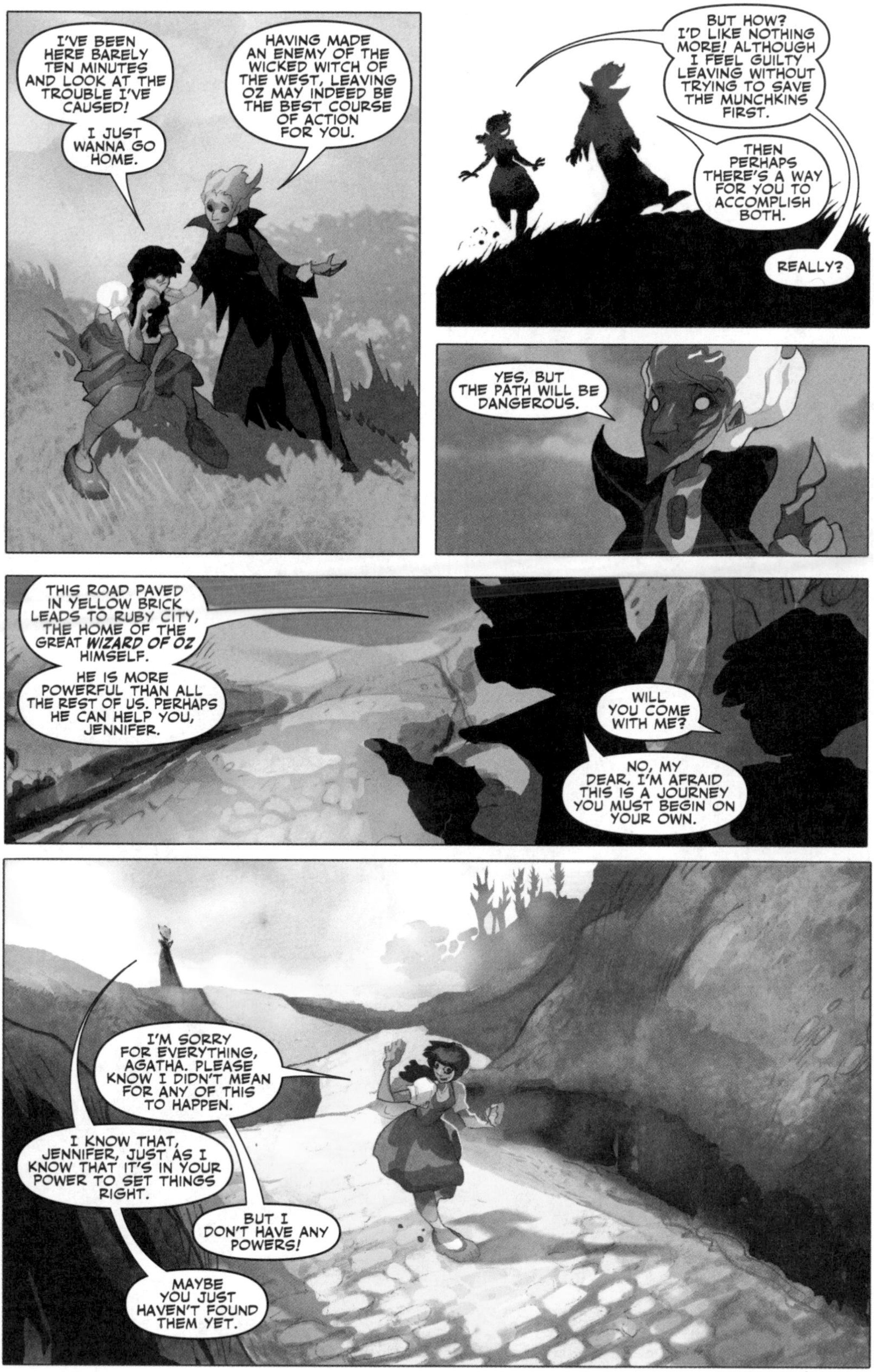
I'VE BEEN HERE BARELY TEN MINUTES AND LOOK AT THE TROUBLE I'VE CAUSED!
I JUST WANNA GO HOME.
HAVING MADE AN ENEMY OF THE WICKED WITCH OF THE WEST, LEAVING OZ MAY INDEED BE THE BEST COURSE OF ACTION FOR YOU.
BUT HOW? I'D LIKE NOTHING MORE! ALTHOUGH I FEEL GUILTY LEAVING WITHOUT TRYING TO SAVE THE MUNCHKINS FIRST.
THEN PERHAPS THERE'S A WAY FOR YOU TO ACCOMPLISH BOTH.
REALLY?
YES, BUT THE PATH WILL BE DANGEROUS.
THIS ROAD PAVED IN YELLOW BRICK LEADS TO RUBY CITY, THE HOME OF THE GREAT WIZARD OF OZ HIMSELF.
HE IS MORE POWERFUL THAN ALL THE REST OF US. PERHAPS HE CAN HELP YOU, JENNIFER.
WILL YOU COME WITH ME?
NO, MY DEAR, I'M AFRAID THIS IS A JOURNEY YOU MUST BEGIN ON YOUR OWN.
I'M SORRY FOR EVERYTHING, AGATHA. PLEASE KNOW I DIDN'T MEAN FOR ANY OF THIS TO HAPPEN.
I KNOW THAT, JENNIFER, JUST AS I KNOW THAT IT'S IN YOUR POWER TO SET THINGS RIGHT.
BUT I DON'T HAVE ANY POWERS!
MAYBE YOU JUST HAVEN'T FOUND THEM YET.

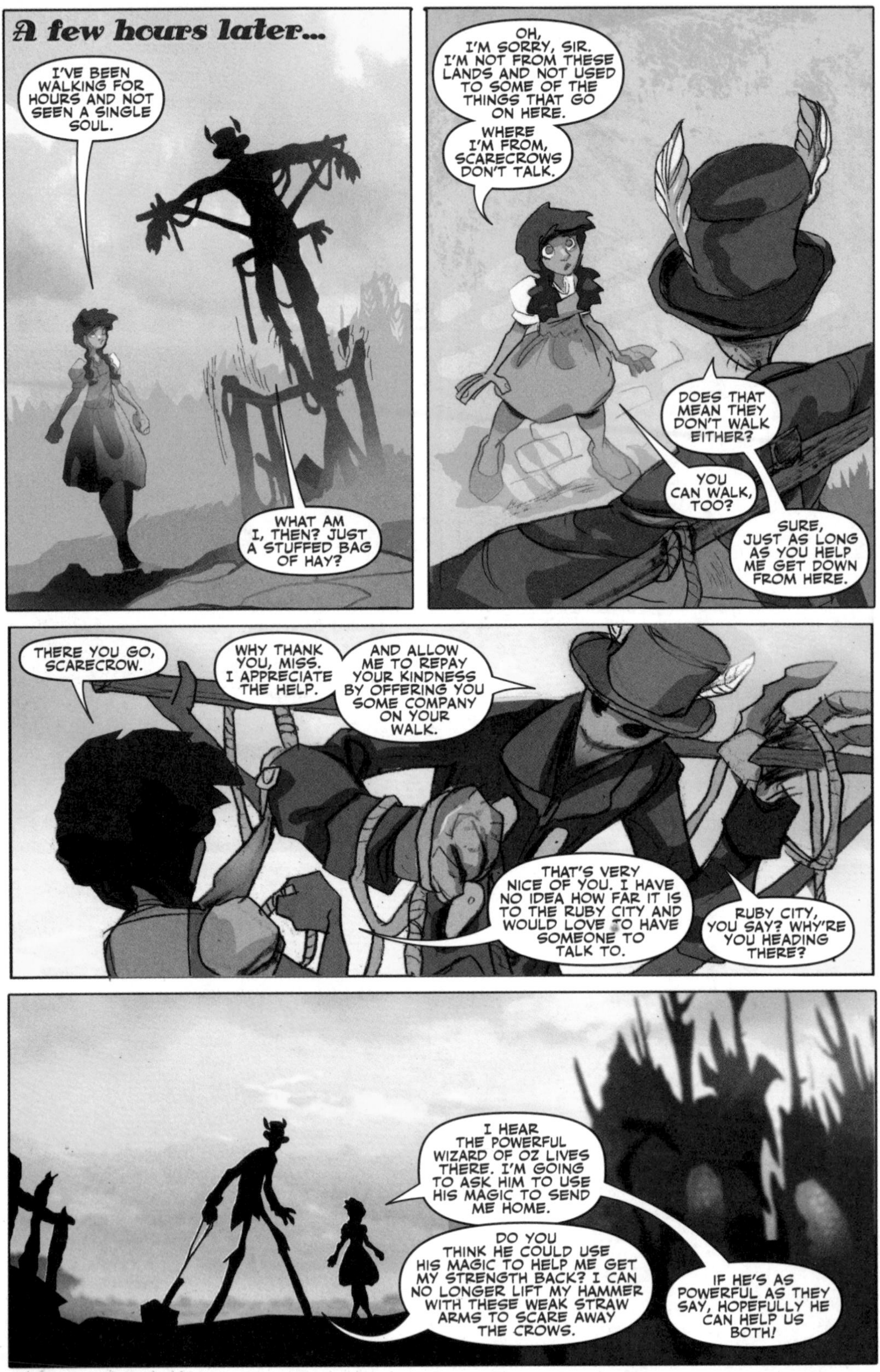
A few hours later...
I'VE BEEN WALKING FOR HOURS AND NOT SEEN A SINGLE SOUL.
WHAT AM I, THEN? JUST A STUFFED BAG OF HAY?
OH, I'M SORRY, SIR. I'M NOT FROM THESE LANDS AND NOT USED TO SOME OF THE THINGS THAT GO ON HERE.
WHERE I'M FROM, SCARECROWS DON'T TALK.
DOES THAT MEAN THEY DON'T WALK EITHER?
YOU CAN WALK, TOO?
SURE, JUST AS LONG AS YOU HELP ME GET DOWN FROM HERE.
THERE YOU GO, SCARECROW.
WHY THANK YOU, MISS. I APPRECIATE THE HELP.
AND ALLOW ME TO REPAY YOUR KINDNESS BY OFFERING YOU SOME COMPANY ON YOUR WALK.
THAT'S VERY NICE OF YOU. I HAVE NO IDEA HOW FAR IT IS TO THE RUBY CITY AND WOULD LOVE TO HAVE SOMEONE TO TALK TO.
RUBY CITY, YOU SAY? WHY'RE YOU HEADING THERE?
I HEAR THE POWERFUL WIZARD OF OZ LIVES THERE. I'M GOING TO ASK HIM TO USE HIS MAGIC TO SEND ME HOME.
DO YOU THINK HE COULD USE HIS MAGIC TO HELP ME GET MY STRENGTH BACK? I CAN NO LONGER LIFT MY HAMMER WITH THESE WEAK STRAW ARMS TO SCARE AWAY THE CROWS.
IF HE'S AS POWERFUL AS THEY SAY, HOPEFULLY HE CAN HELP US BOTH!

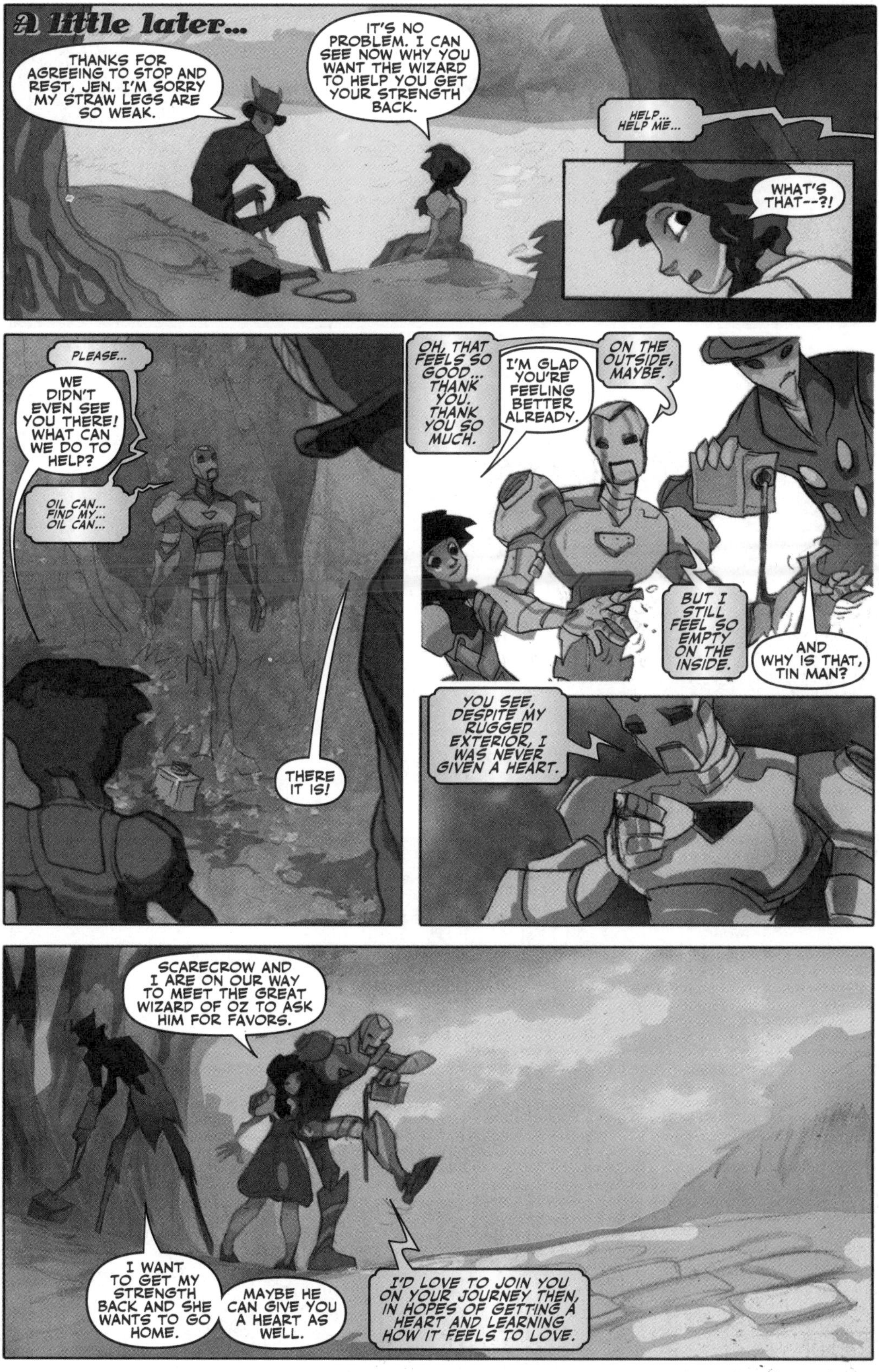
A little later...
THANKS FOR AGREEING TO STOP AND REST, JEN. I'M SORRY MY STRAW LEGS ARE SO WEAK.
IT'S NO PROBLEM. I CAN SEE NOW WHY YOU WANT THE WIZARD TO HELP YOU GET YOUR STRENGTH BACK.
HELP... HELP ME...
WHAT'S THAT--?!
PLEASE...
WE DIDN'T EVEN SEE YOU THERE! WHAT CAN WE DO TO HELP?
OIL CAN... FIND MY... OIL CAN...
THERE IT IS!
OH, THAT FEELS SO GOOD... THANK YOU. THANK YOU SO MUCH.
I'M GLAD YOU'RE FEELING BETTER ALREADY.
ON THE OUTSIDE, MAYBE.
BUT I STILL FEEL SO EMPTY ON THE INSIDE.
AND WHY IS THAT, TIN MAN?
YOU SEE, DESPITE MY RUGGED EXTERIOR, I WAS NEVER GIVEN A HEART.
SCARECROW AND I ARE ON OUR WAY TO MEET THE GREAT WIZARD OF OZ TO ASK HIM FOR FAVORS.
I WANT TO GET MY STRENGTH BACK AND SHE WANTS TO GO HOME.
MAYBE HE CAN GIVE YOU A HEART AS WELL.
I'D LOVE TO JOIN YOU ON YOUR JOURNEY THEN, IN HOPES OF GETTING A HEART AND LEARNING HOW IT FEELS TO LOVE.

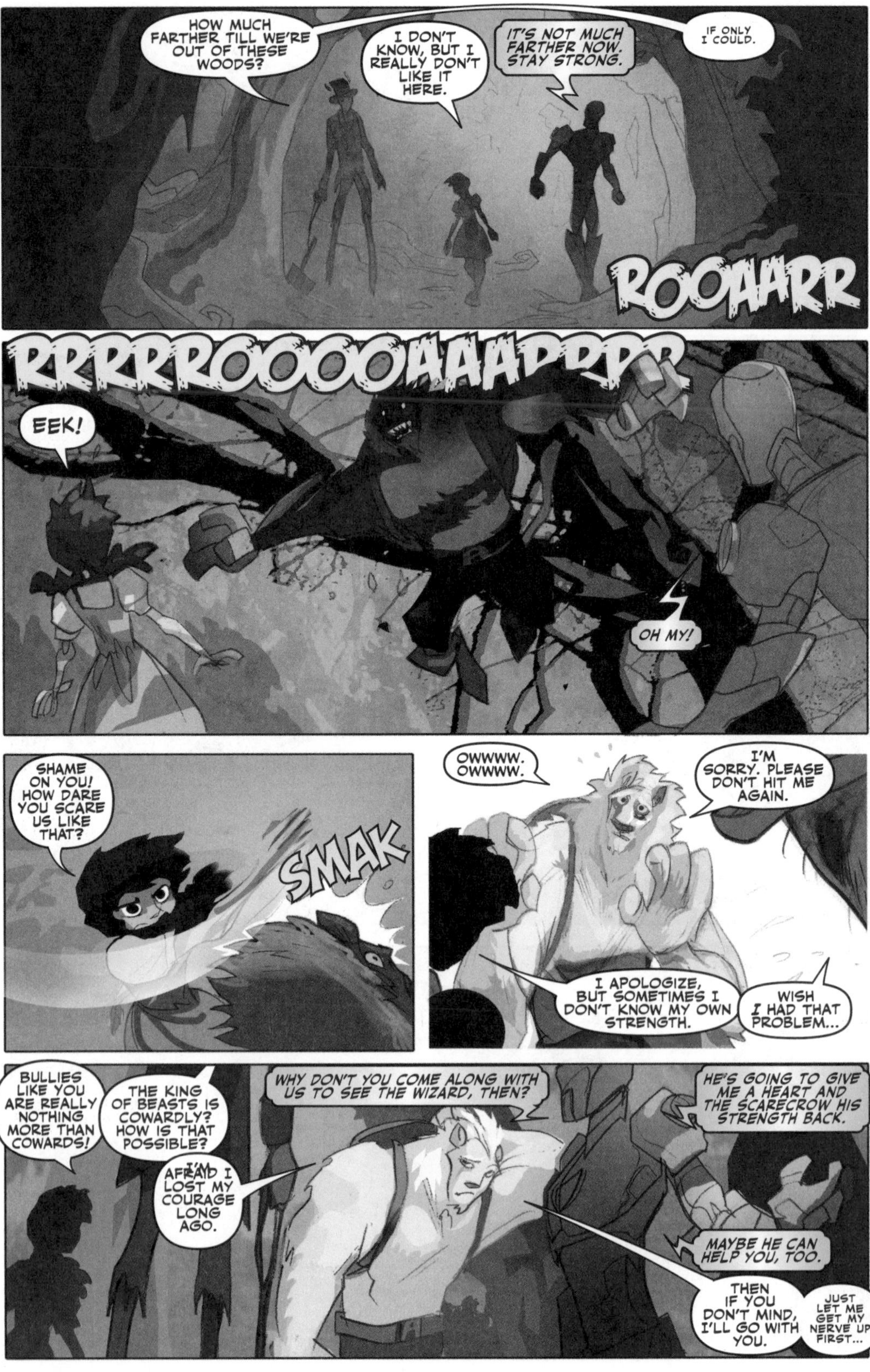
HOW MUCH FARTHER TILL WE'RE OUT OF THESE WOODS?
I DON'T KNOW, BUT I REALLY DON'T LIKE IT HERE.
IT'S NOT MUCH FARTHER NOW. STAY STRONG.
IF ONLY I COULD.
ROOAARR
RRRRROOOOAAARRRR
EEK!
OH MY!
SHAME ON YOU! HOW DARE YOU SCARE US LIKE THAT?
SMAK
OWWWW. OWWWW.
I'M SORRY. PLEASE DON'T HIT ME AGAIN.
I APOLOGIZE, BUT SOMETIMES I DON'T KNOW MY OWN STRENGTH.
WISH I HAD THAT PROBLEM...
BULLIES LIKE YOU ARE REALLY NOTHING MORE THAN COWARDS!
THE KING OF BEASTS IS COWARDLY? HOW IS THAT POSSIBLE?
I'M AFRAID I LOST MY COURAGE LONG AGO.
WHY DON'T YOU COME ALONG WITH US TO SEE THE WIZARD, THEN?
HE'S GOING TO GIVE ME A HEART AND THE SCARECROW HIS STRENGTH BACK.
MAYBE HE CAN HELP YOU, TOO.
THEN IF YOU DON'T MIND, I'LL GO WITH YOU.
JUST LET ME GET MY NERVE UP FIRST...

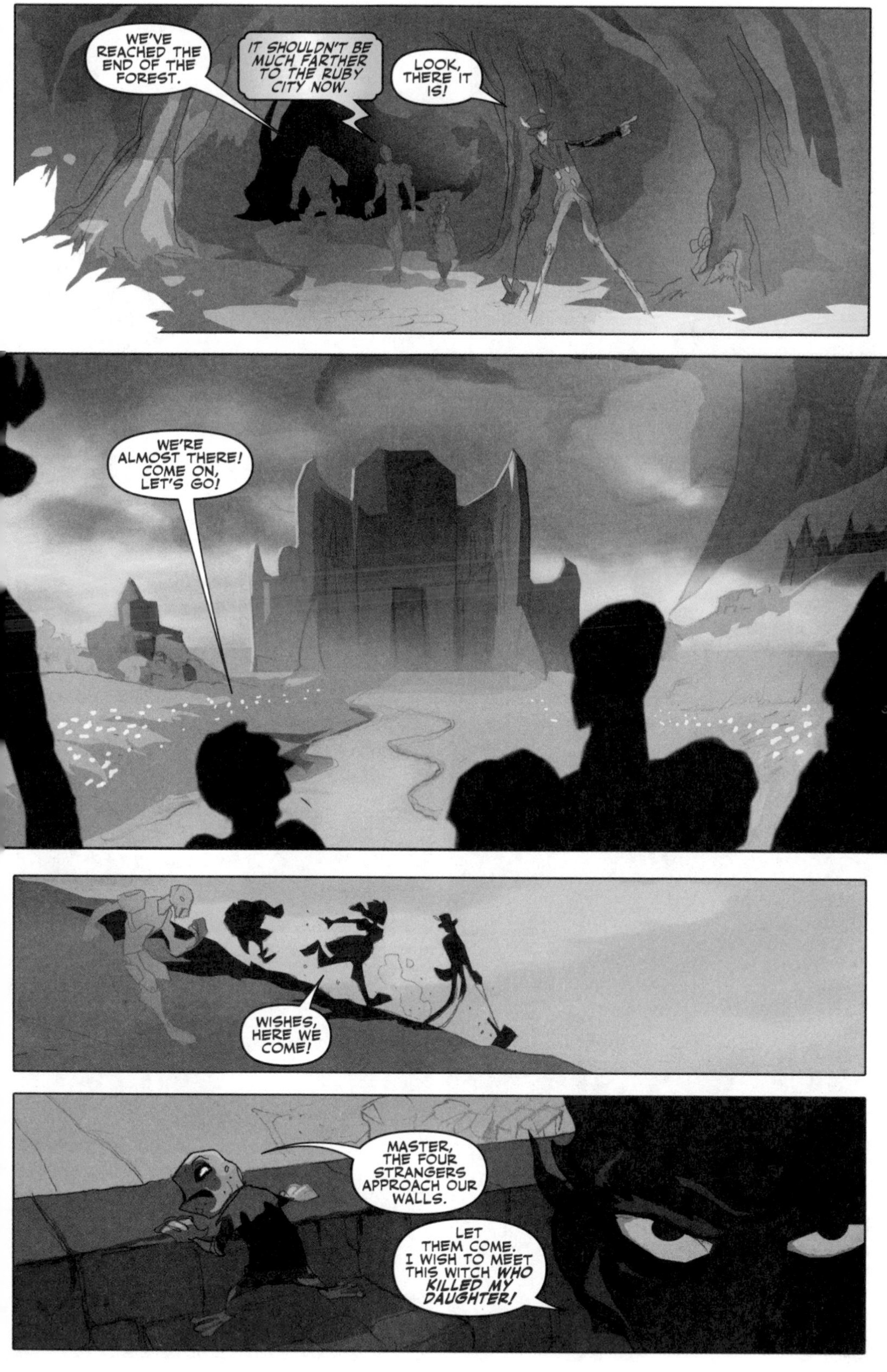
WE'VE REACHED THE END OF THE FOREST.
IT SHOULDN'T BE MUCH FARTHER TO THE RUBY CITY NOW.
LOOK, THERE IT IS!
WE'RE ALMOST THERE! COME ON, LET'S GO!
WISHES, HERE WE COME!
MASTER, THE FOUR STRANGERS APPROACH OUR WALLS.
LET THEM COME. I WISH TO MEET THIS WITCH WHO KILLED MY DAUGHTER!

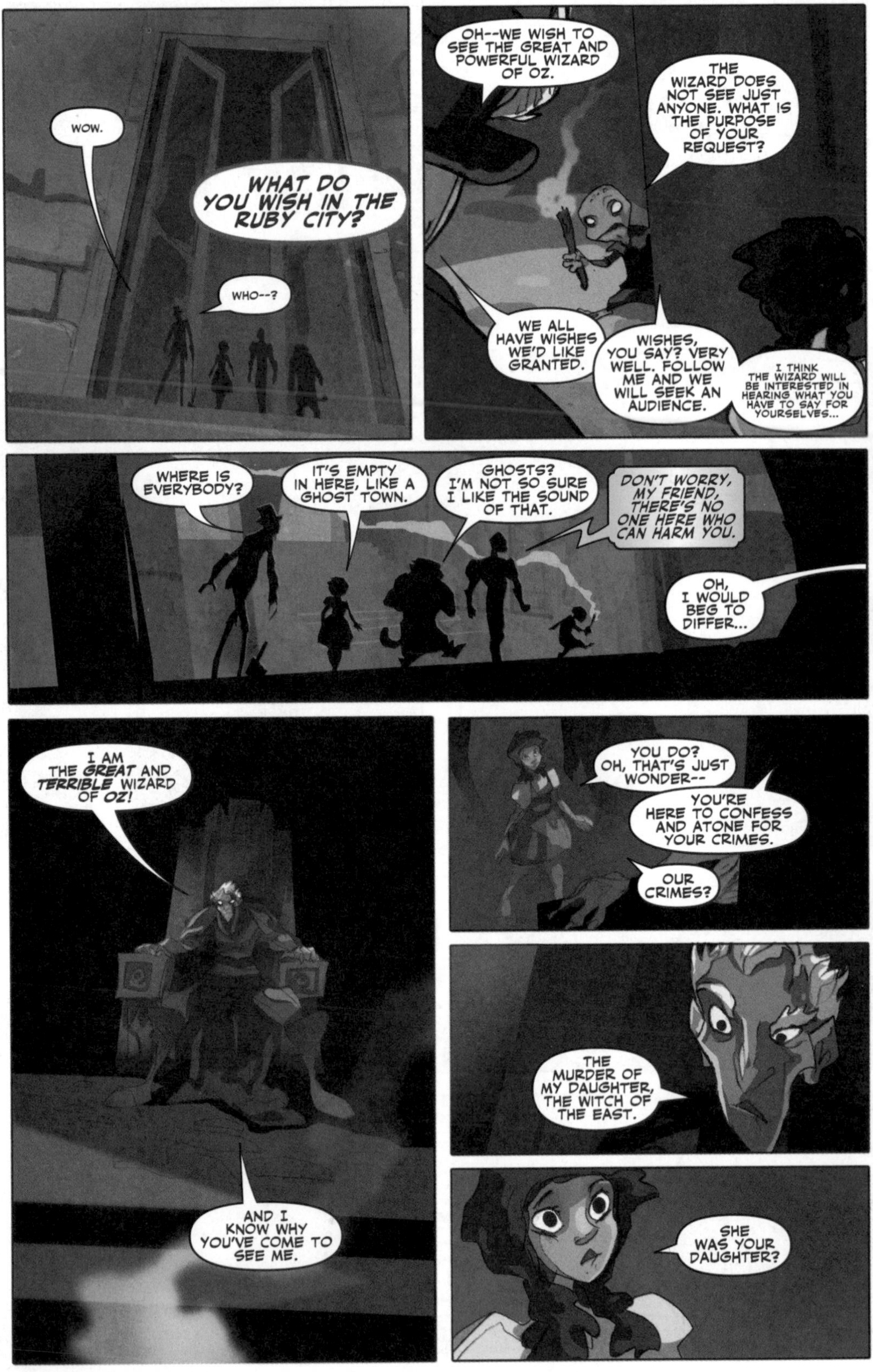
WOW.
WHAT DO YOU WISH IN THE RUBY CITY?
WHO--?
OH--WE WISH TO SEE THE GREAT AND POWERFUL WIZARD OF OZ.
THE WIZARD DOES NOT SEE JUST ANYONE. WHAT IS THE PURPOSE OF YOUR REQUEST?
WE ALL HAVE WISHES WE'D LIKE GRANTED.
WISHES, YOU SAY? VERY WELL. FOLLOW ME AND WE WILL SEEK AN AUDIENCE.
I THINK THE WIZARD WILL BE INTERESTED IN HEARING WHAT YOU HAVE TO SAY FOR YOURSELVES...
WHERE IS EVERYBODY?
IT'S EMPTY IN HERE, LIKE A GHOST TOWN.
GHOSTS? I'M NOT SO SURE I LIKE THE SOUND OF THAT.
DON'T WORRY, MY FRIEND, THERE'S NO ONE HERE WHO CAN HARM YOU.
OH, I WOULD BEG TO DIFFER...
I AM THE GREAT AND TERRIBLE WIZARD OF OZ!
AND I KNOW WHY YOU'VE COME TO SEE ME.
YOU DO? OH, THAT'S JUST WONDER--
YOU'RE HERE TO CONFESS AND ATONE FOR YOUR CRIMES.
OUR CRIMES?
THE MURDER OF MY DAUGHTER, THE WITCH OF THE EAST.
SHE WAS YOUR DAUGHTER?

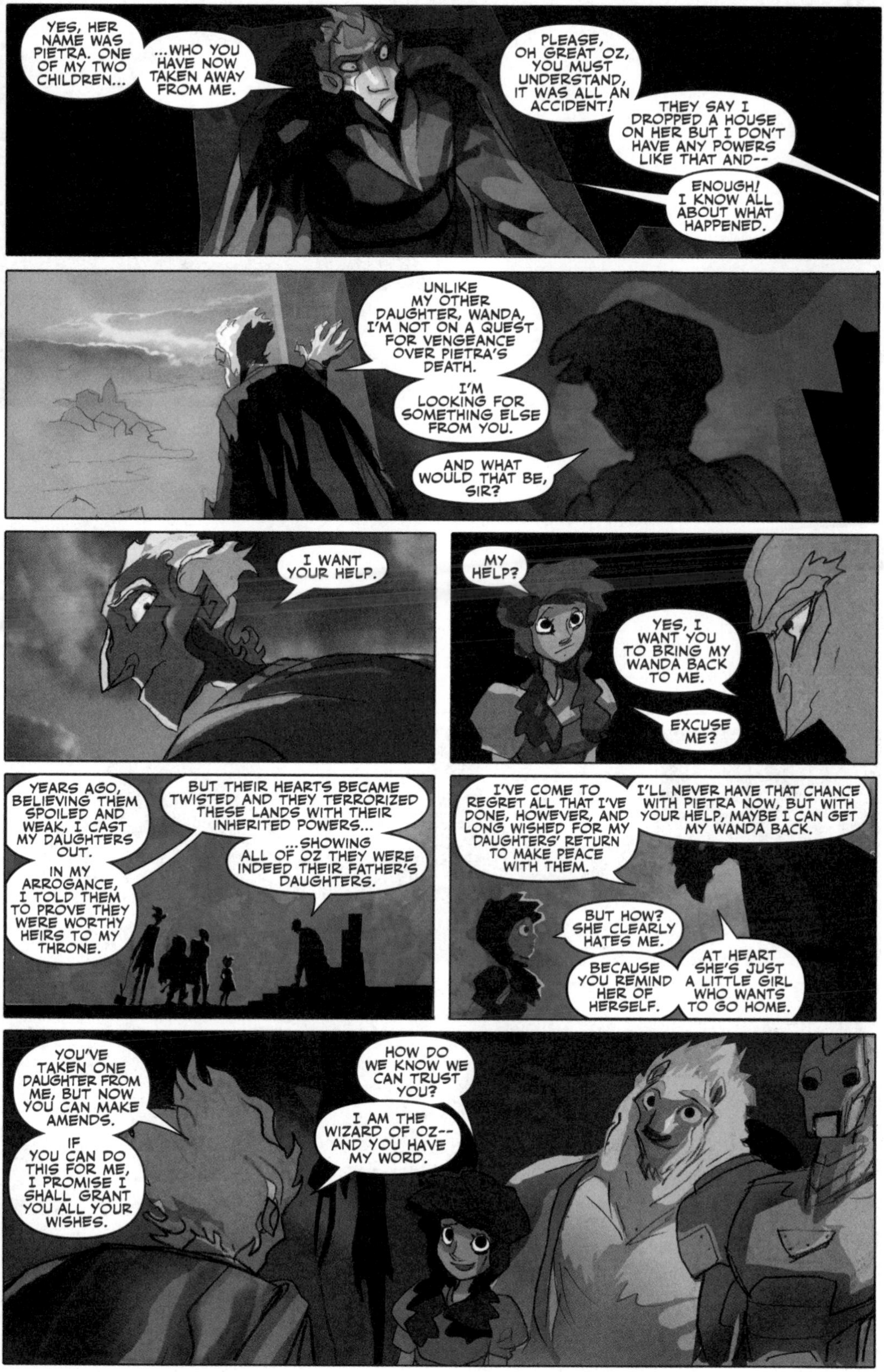
YES, HER NAME WAS PIETRA. ONE OF MY TWO CHILDREN...
...WHO YOU HAVE NOW TAKEN AWAY FROM ME.
PLEASE, OH GREAT OZ, YOU MUST UNDERSTAND, IT WAS ALL AN ACCIDENT!
THEY SAY I DROPPED A HOUSE ON HER BUT I DON'T HAVE ANY POWERS LIKE THAT AND--
ENOUGH! I KNOW ALL ABOUT WHAT HAPPENED.
UNLIKE MY OTHER DAUGHTER, WANDA, I'M NOT ON A QUEST FOR VENGEANCE OVER PIETRA'S DEATH.
I'M LOOKING FOR SOMETHING ELSE FROM YOU.
AND WHAT WOULD THAT BE, SIR?
I WANT YOUR HELP.
MY HELP?
YES, I WANT YOU TO BRING MY WANDA BACK TO ME.
EXCUSE ME?
YEARS AGO, BELIEVING THEM SPOILED AND WEAK, I CAST MY DAUGHTERS OUT.
IN MY ARROGANCE, I TOLD THEM TO PROVE THEY WERE WORTHY HEIRS TO MY THRONE.
BUT THEIR HEARTS BECAME TWISTED AND THEY TERRORIZED THESE LANDS WITH THEIR INHERITED POWERS...
...SHOWING ALL OF OZ THEY WERE INDEED THEIR FATHER'S DAUGHTERS.
I'VE COME TO REGRET ALL THAT I'VE DONE, HOWEVER, AND LONG WISHED FOR MY DAUGHTERS' RETURN TO MAKE PEACE WITH THEM.
I'LL NEVER HAVE THAT CHANCE WITH PIETRA NOW, BUT WITH YOUR HELP, MAYBE I CAN GET MY WANDA BACK.
BUT HOW? SHE CLEARLY HATES ME.
BECAUSE YOU REMIND HER OF HERSELF.
AT HEART SHE'S JUST A LITTLE GIRL WHO WANTS TO GO HOME.
YOU'VE TAKEN ONE DAUGHTER FROM ME, BUT NOW YOU CAN MAKE AMENDS.
IF YOU CAN DO THIS FOR ME, I PROMISE I SHALL GRANT YOU ALL YOUR WISHES.
HOW DO WE KNOW WE CAN TRUST YOU?
I AM THE WIZARD OF OZ-- AND YOU HAVE MY WORD.

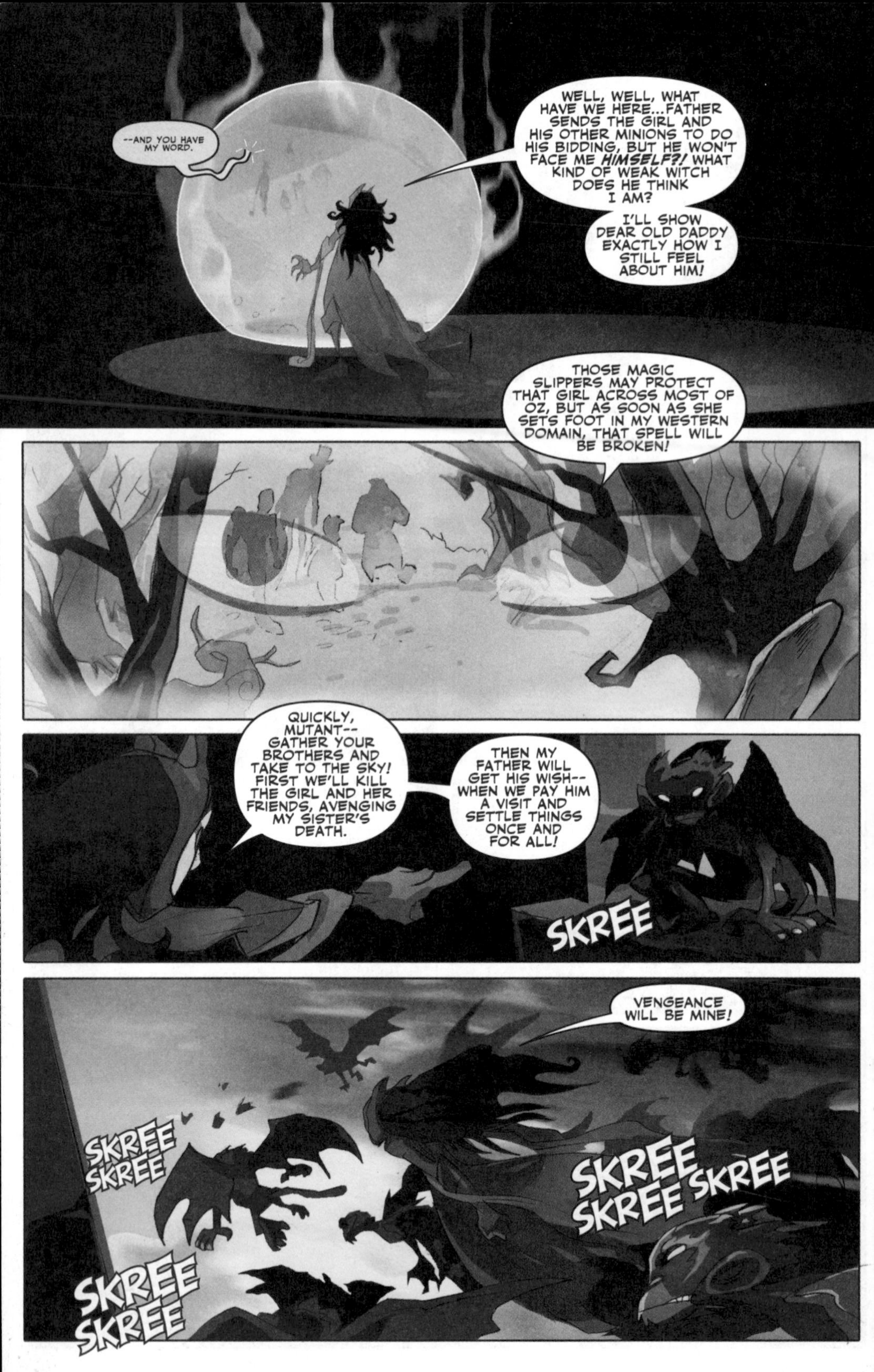
--AND YOU HAVE MY WORD.
WELL, WELL, WHAT HAVE WE HERE...FATHER SENDS THE GIRL AND HIS OTHER MINIONS TO DO HIS BIDDING, BUT HE WON'T FACE ME HIMSELF?! WHAT KIND OF WEAK WITCH DOES HE THINK I AM?
I'LL SHOW DEAR OLD DADDY EXACTLY HOW I STILL FEEL ABOUT HIM!
THOSE MAGIC SLIPPERS MAY PROTECT THAT GIRL ACROSS MOST OF OZ, BUT AS SOON AS SHE SETS FOOT IN MY WESTERN DOMAIN, THAT SPELL WILL BE BROKEN!
QUICKLY, MUTANT--GATHER YOUR BROTHERS AND TAKE TO THE SKY! FIRST WE'LL KILL THE GIRL AND HER FRIENDS, AVENGING MY SISTER'S DEATH.
THEN MY FATHER WILL GET HIS WISH--WHEN WE PAY HIM A VISIT AND SETTLE THINGS ONCE AND FOR ALL!
SKREE
VENGEANCE WILL BE MINE!
SKREE SKREE
SKREE SKREE SKREE
SKREE SKREE

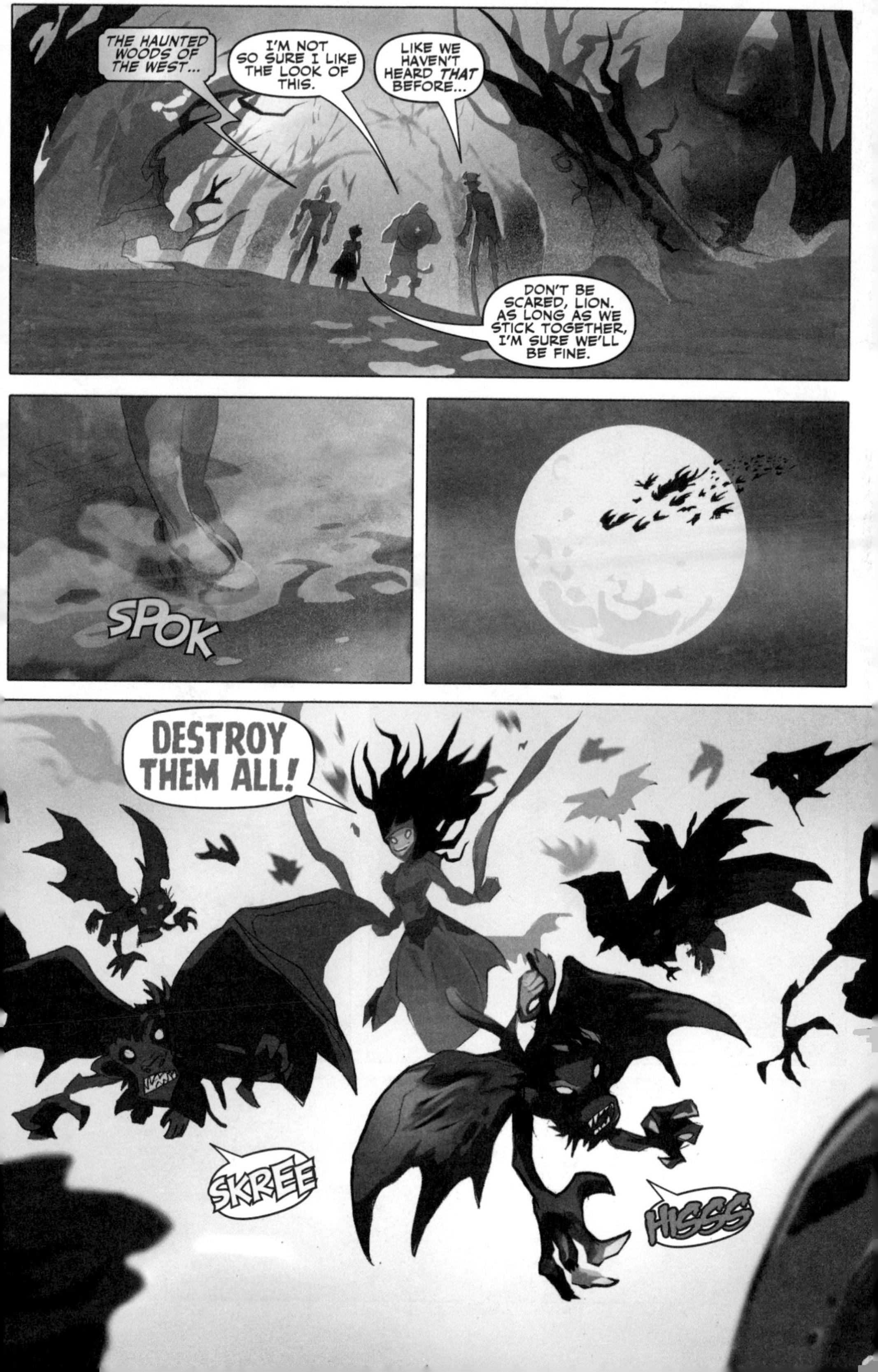
THE HAUNTED WOODS OF THE WEST...
I'M NOT SO SURE I LIKE THE LOOK OF THIS.
LIKE WE HAVEN'T HEARD THAT BEFORE...
DON'T BE SCARED, LION. AS LONG AS WE STICK TOGETHER, I'M SURE WE'LL BE FINE.
SPOK
DESTROY THEM ALL!
SKREE
HISSS

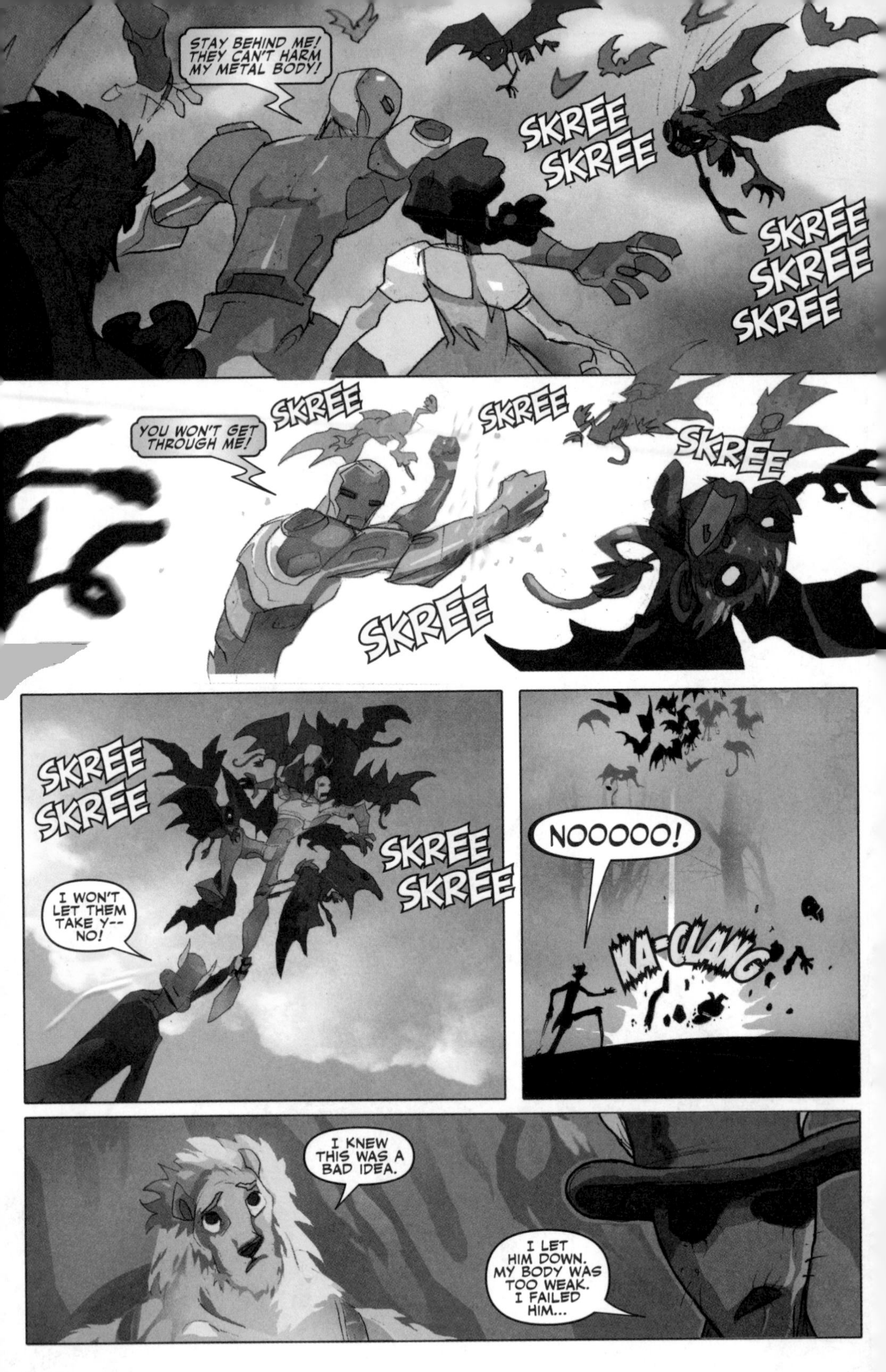
STAY BEHIND ME! THEY CAN'T HARM MY METAL BODY!
SKREE SKREE
SKREE SKREE SKREE
YOU WON'T GET THROUGH ME!
SKREE
SKREE
SKREE
SKREE
SKREE SKREE
SKREE SKREE
I WON'T LET THEM TAKE Y-- NO!
NOOOOO!
KA-CLANG
I KNEW THIS WAS A BAD IDEA.
I LET HIM DOWN. MY BODY WAS TOO WEAK. I FAILED HIM...

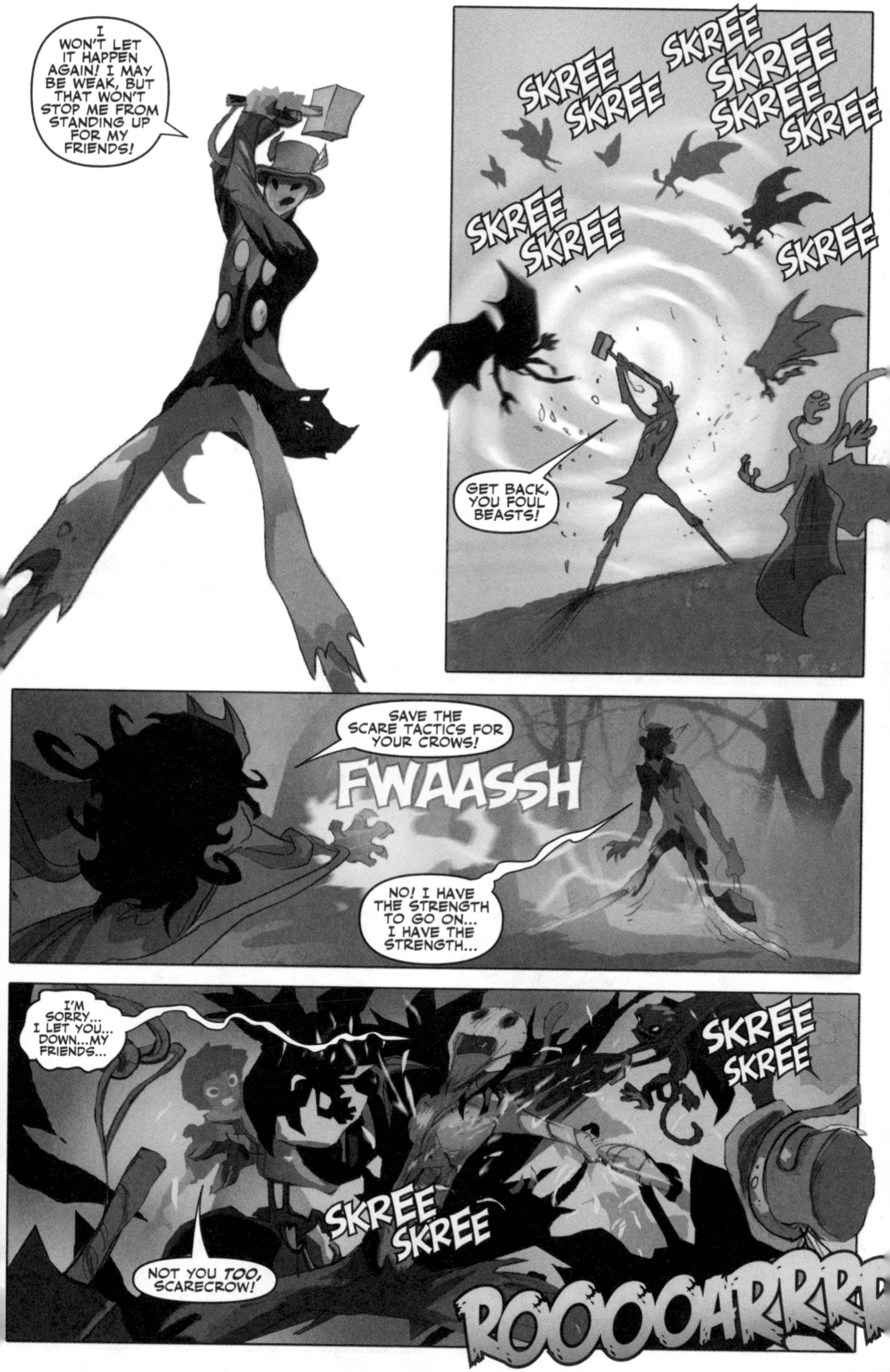
I WON'T LET IT HAPPEN AGAIN! I MAY BE WEAK, BUT THAT WON'T STOP ME FROM STANDING UP FOR MY FRIENDS!
SKREE SKREE SKREE SKREE SKREE SKREE
SKREE SKREE
SKREE
GET BACK, YOU FOUL BEASTS!
SAVE THE SCARE TACTICS FOR YOUR CROWS!
FWAASSH
NO! I HAVE THE STRENGTH TO GO ON... I HAVE THE STRENGTH...
I'M SORRY... I LET YOU... DOWN...MY FRIENDS...
SKREE SKREE
SKREE SKREE
NOT YOU *TOO*, SCARECROW!
ROOOOARRRR

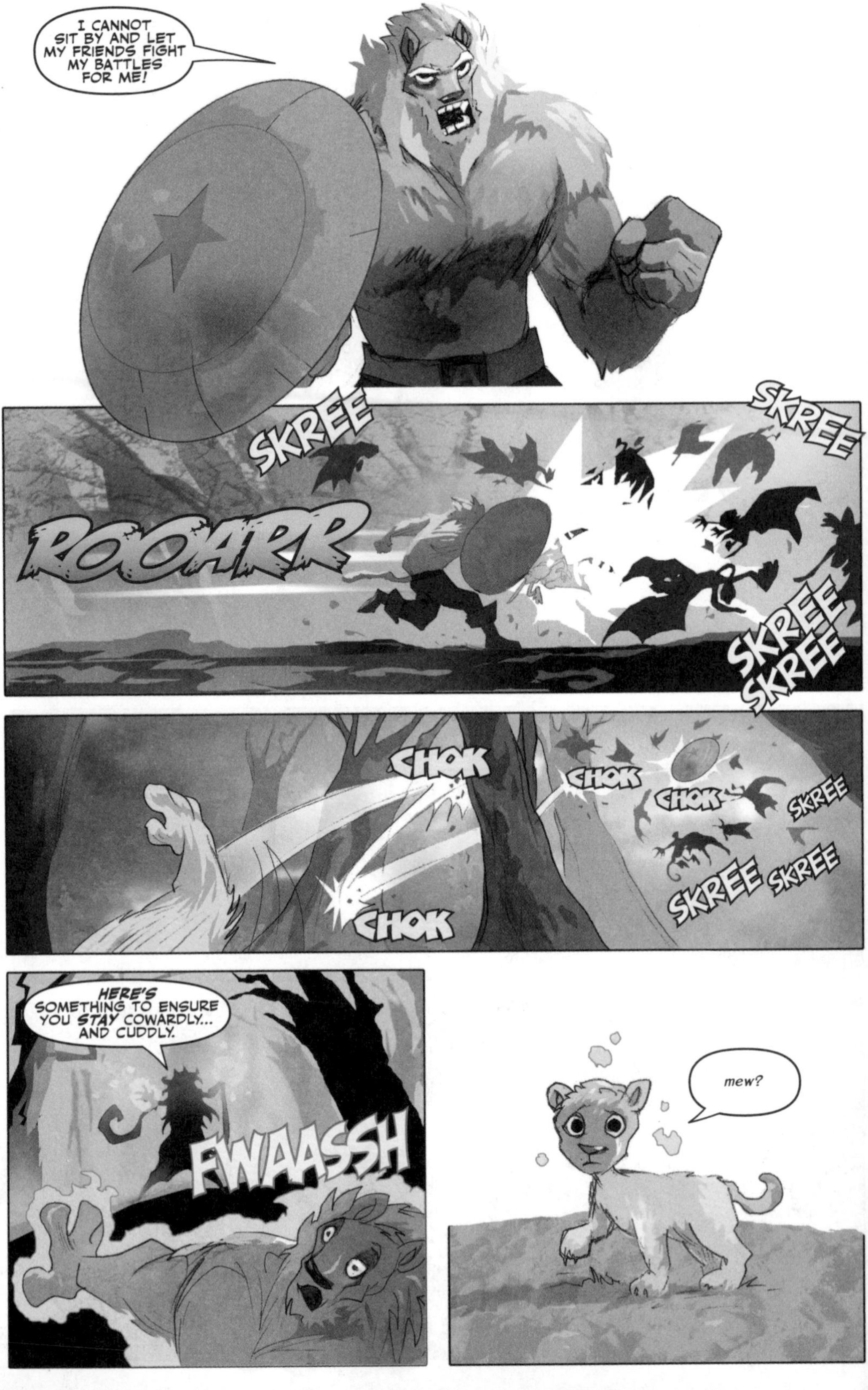
I CANNOT SIT BY AND LET MY FRIENDS FIGHT MY BATTLES FOR ME!
SKREE
SKREE
ROOARR
SKREE
SKREE
CHOK
CHOK
CHOK
SKREE
SKREE
SKREE
CHOK
HERE'S SOMETHING TO ENSURE YOU STAY COWARDLY... AND CUDDLY.
FWAASSH
mew?

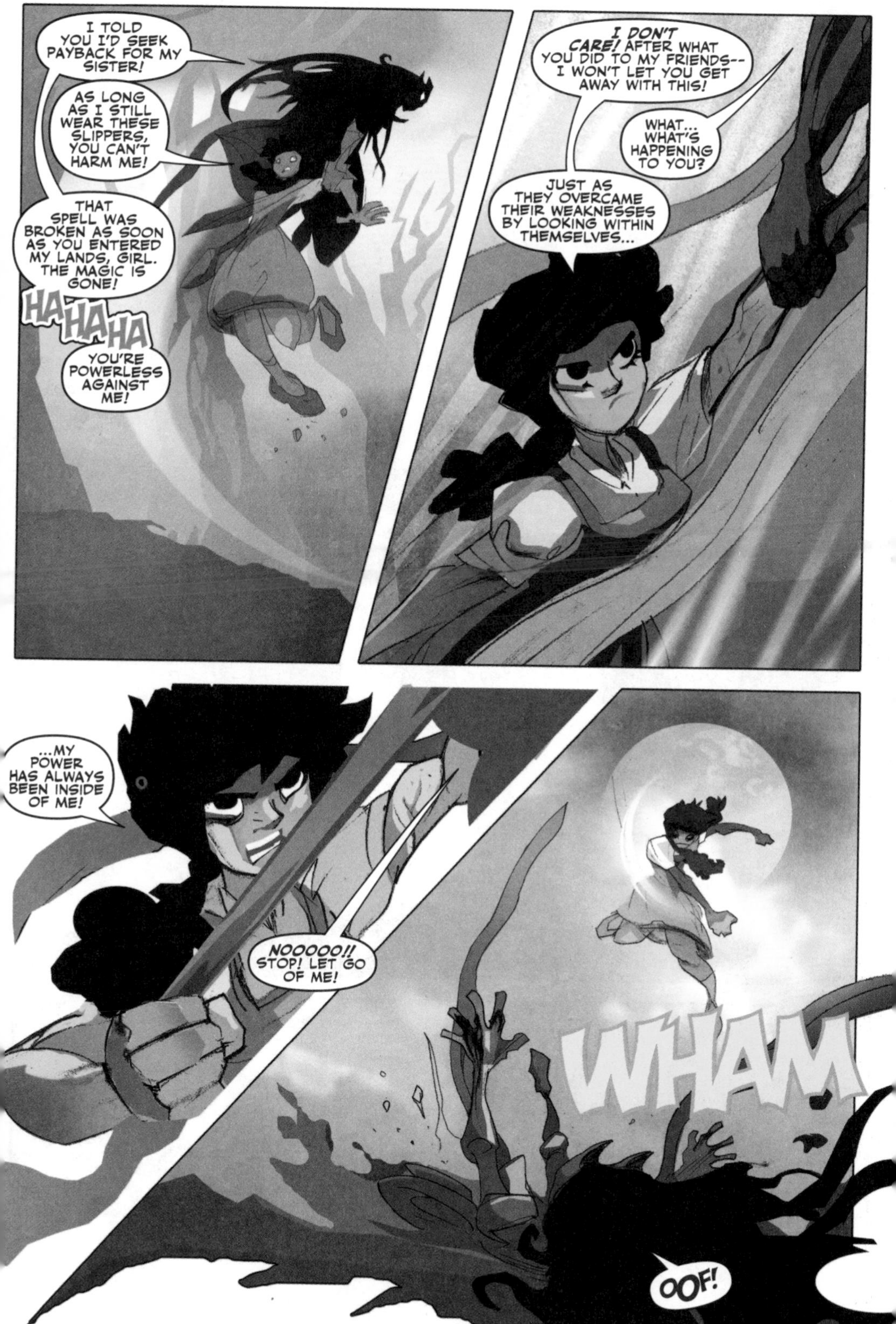
I TOLD YOU I'D SEEK PAYBACK FOR MY SISTER!
AS LONG AS I STILL WEAR THESE SLIPPERS, YOU CAN'T HARM ME!
THAT SPELL WAS BROKEN AS SOON AS YOU ENTERED MY LANDS, GIRL. THE MAGIC IS GONE!
HAHAHA
YOU'RE POWERLESS AGAINST ME!
I DON'T CARE! AFTER WHAT YOU DID TO MY FRIENDS-- I WON'T LET YOU GET AWAY WITH THIS!
WHAT... WHAT'S HAPPENING TO YOU?
JUST AS THEY OVERCAME THEIR WEAKNESSES BY LOOKING WITHIN THEMSELVES...
...MY POWER HAS ALWAYS BEEN INSIDE OF ME!
NOOOOO!! STOP! LET GO OF ME!
WHAM
OOF!

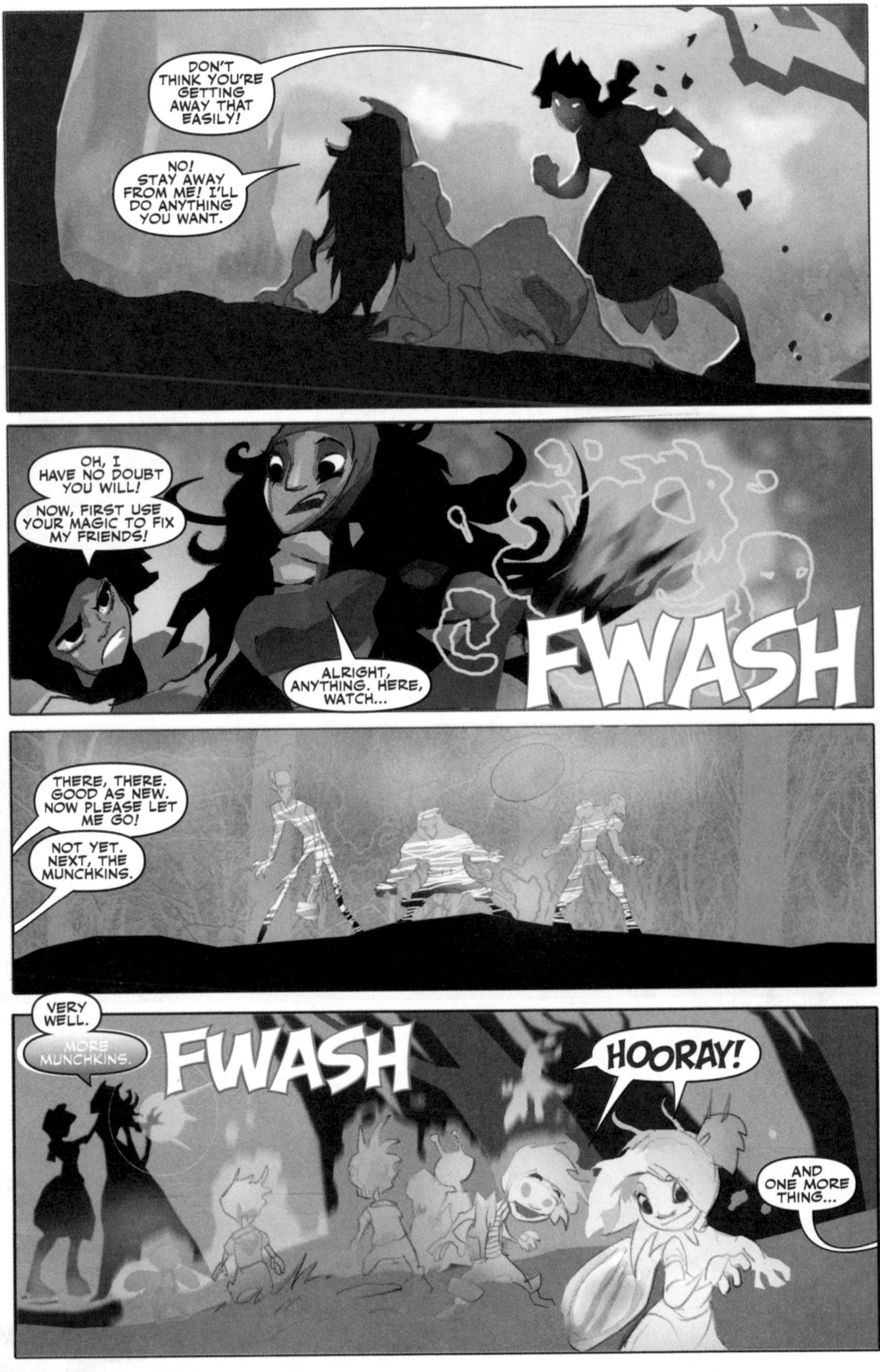
DON'T THINK YOU'RE GETTING AWAY THAT EASILY!
NO! STAY AWAY FROM ME! I'LL DO ANYTHING YOU WANT.
OH, I HAVE NO DOUBT YOU WILL!
NOW, FIRST USE YOUR MAGIC TO FIX MY FRIENDS!
ALRIGHT, ANYTHING. HERE, WATCH...
FWASH
THERE, THERE. GOOD AS NEW. NOW PLEASE LET ME GO!
NOT YET. NEXT, THE MUNCHKINS.
VERY WELL.
MORE MUNCHKINS.
FWASH
HOORAY!
AND ONE MORE THING...

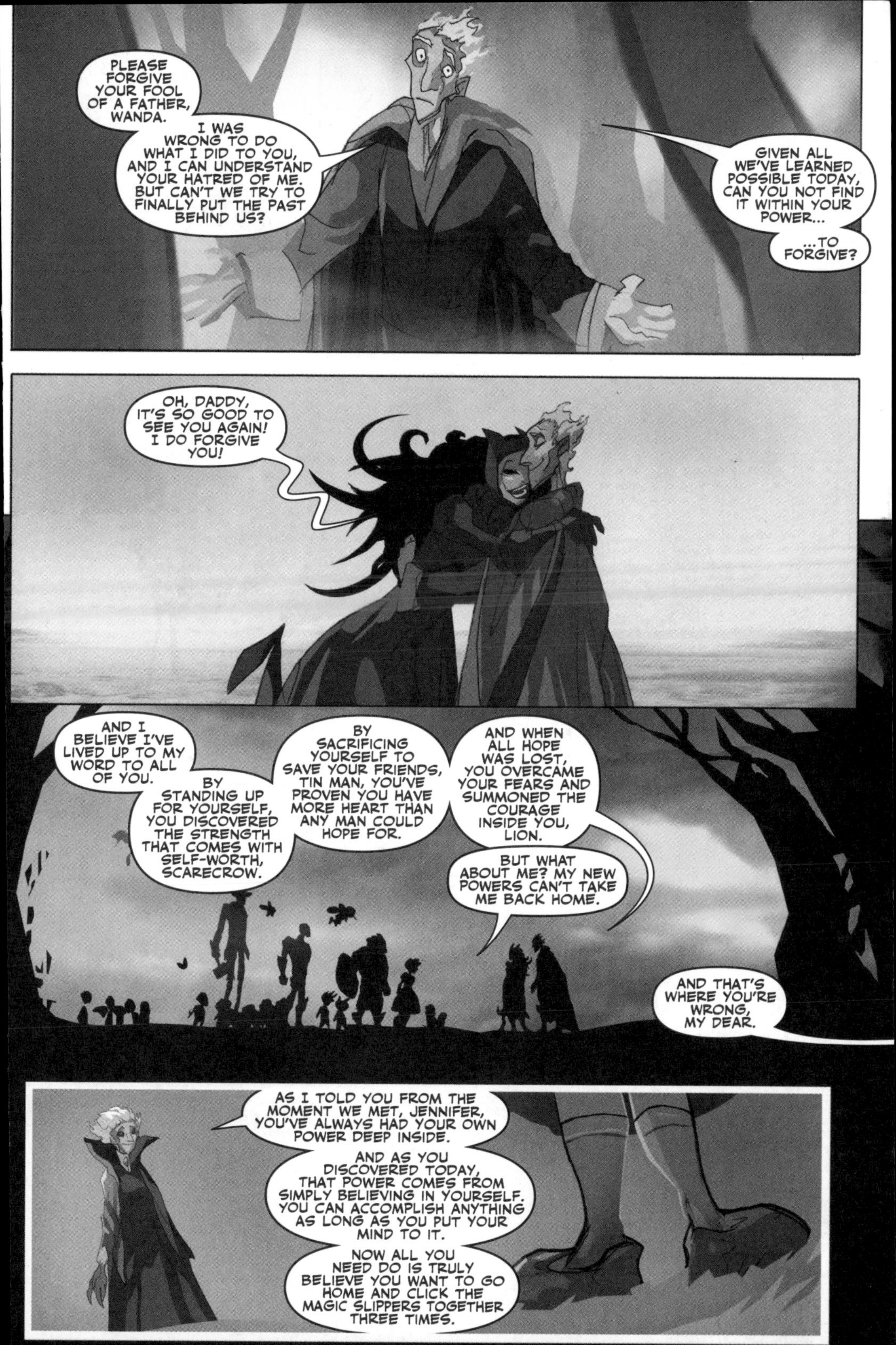
PLEASE FORGIVE YOUR FOOL OF A FATHER, WANDA.
I WAS WRONG TO DO WHAT I DID TO YOU, AND I CAN UNDERSTAND YOUR HATRED OF ME. BUT CAN'T WE TRY TO FINALLY PUT THE PAST BEHIND US?
GIVEN ALL WE'VE LEARNED POSSIBLE TODAY, CAN YOU NOT FIND IT WITHIN YOUR POWER...
...TO FORGIVE?
OH, DADDY, IT'S SO GOOD TO SEE YOU AGAIN! I DO FORGIVE YOU!
AND I BELIEVE I'VE LIVED UP TO MY WORD TO ALL OF YOU.
BY STANDING UP FOR YOURSELF, YOU DISCOVERED THE STRENGTH THAT COMES WITH SELF-WORTH, SCARECROW.
BY SACRIFICING YOURSELF TO SAVE YOUR FRIENDS, TIN MAN, YOU'VE PROVEN YOU HAVE MORE HEART THAN ANY MAN COULD HOPE FOR.
AND WHEN ALL HOPE WAS LOST, YOU OVERCAME YOUR FEARS AND SUMMONED THE COURAGE INSIDE YOU, LION.
BUT WHAT ABOUT ME? MY NEW POWERS CAN'T TAKE ME BACK HOME.
AND THAT'S WHERE YOU'RE WRONG, MY DEAR.
AS I TOLD YOU FROM THE MOMENT WE MET, JENNIFER, YOU'VE ALWAYS HAD YOUR OWN POWER DEEP INSIDE.
AND AS YOU DISCOVERED TODAY, THAT POWER COMES FROM SIMPLY BELIEVING IN YOURSELF. YOU CAN ACCOMPLISH ANYTHING AS LONG AS YOU PUT YOUR MIND TO IT.
NOW ALL YOU NEED DO IS TRULY BELIEVE YOU WANT TO GO HOME AND CLICK THE MAGIC SLIPPERS TOGETHER THREE TIMES.

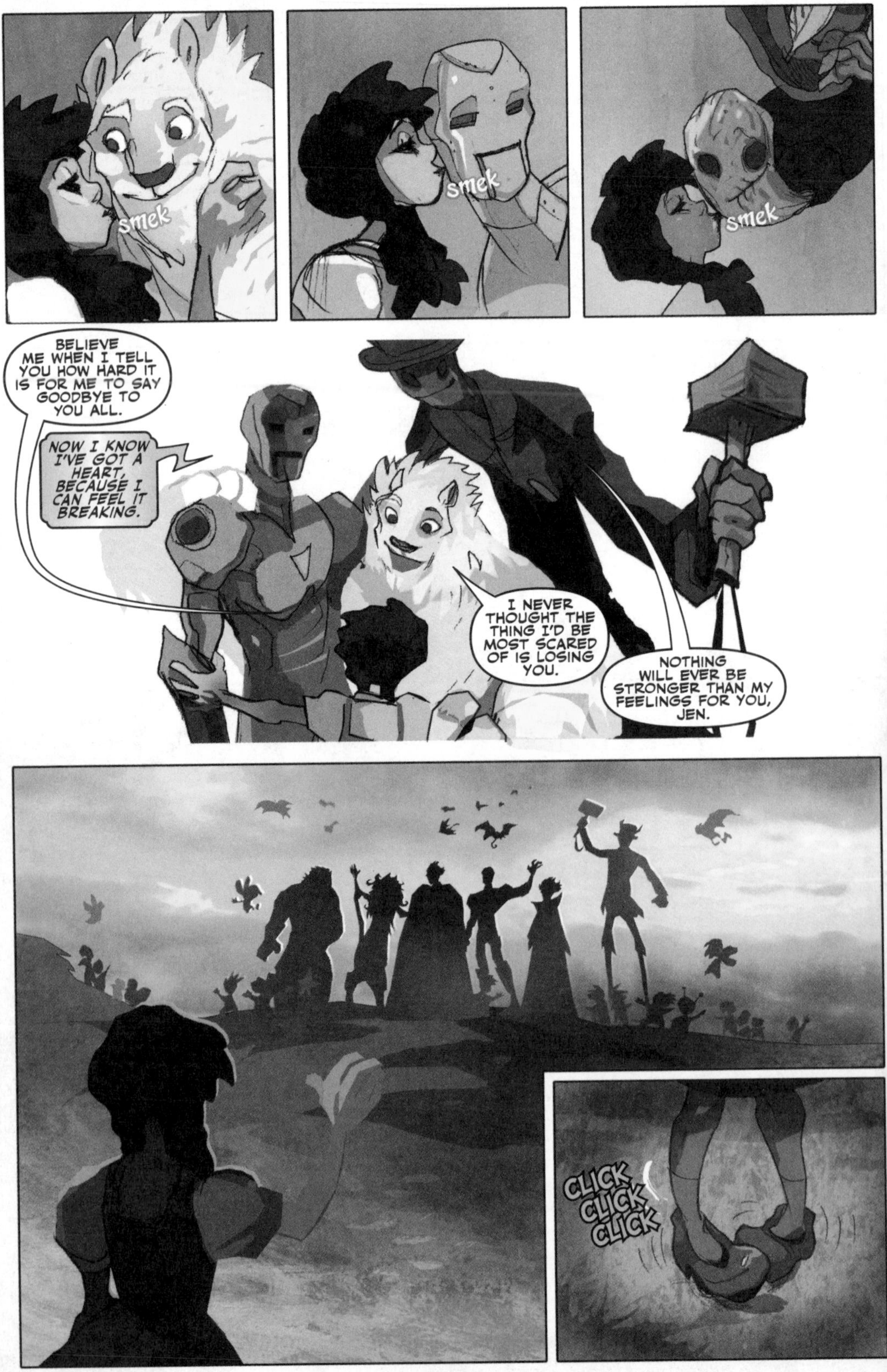
smek
smek
smek
BELIEVE ME WHEN I TELL YOU HOW HARD IT IS FOR ME TO SAY GOODBYE TO YOU ALL.
NOW I KNOW I'VE GOT A HEART, BECAUSE I CAN FEEL IT BREAKING.
I NEVER THOUGHT THE THING I'D BE MOST SCARED OF IS LOSING YOU.
NOTHING WILL EVER BE STRONGER THAN MY FEELINGS FOR YOU, JEN.
CLICK CLICK CLICK

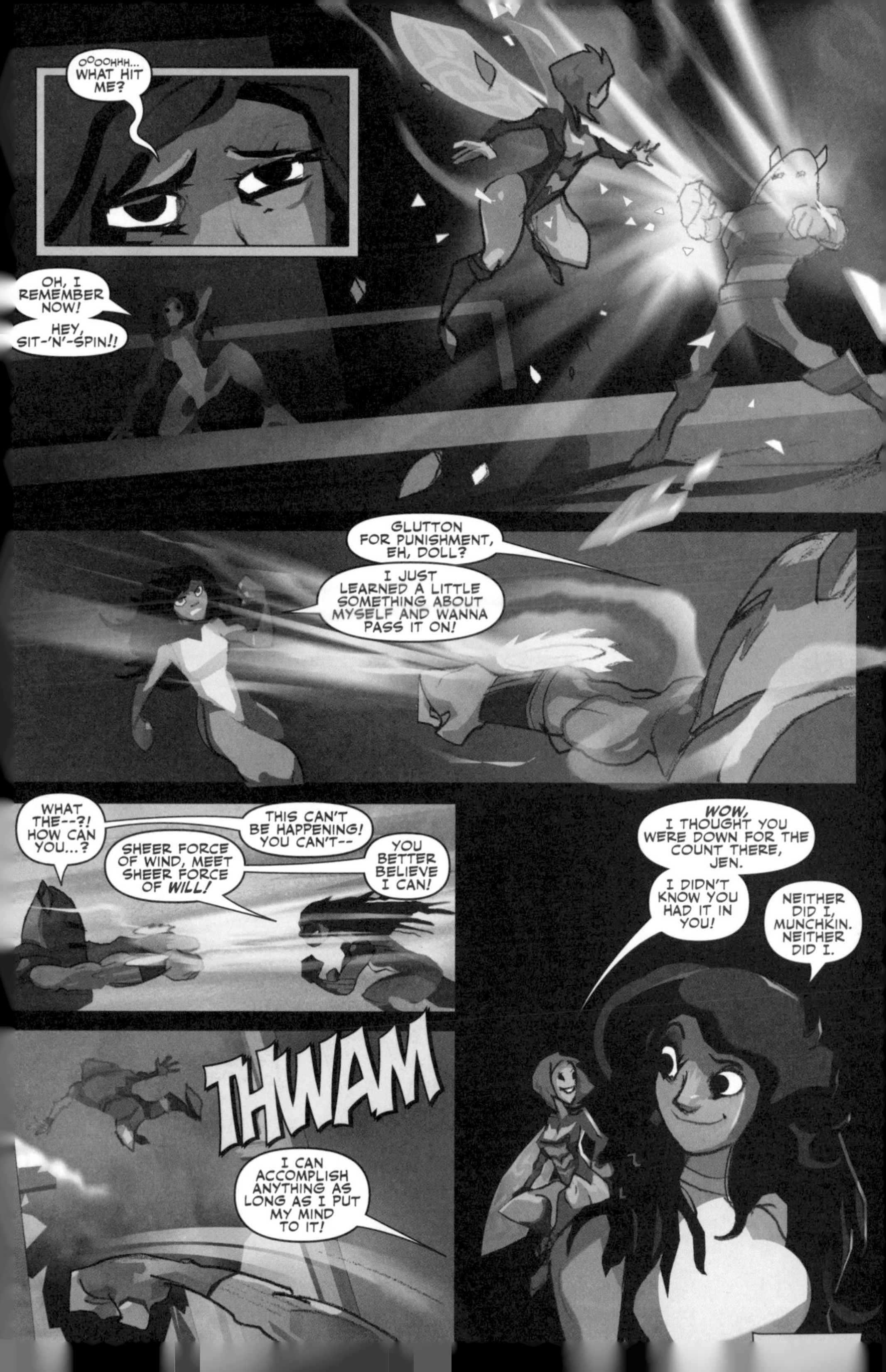
OOOOHHH... WHAT HIT ME?
OH, I REMEMBER NOW!
HEY, SIT-'N'-SPIN!!
GLUTTON FOR PUNISHMENT, EH, DOLL?
I JUST LEARNED A LITTLE SOMETHING ABOUT MYSELF AND WANNA PASS IT ON!
WHAT THE--?! HOW CAN YOU...?
THIS CAN'T BE HAPPENING! YOU CAN'T--
SHEER FORCE OF WIND, MEET SHEER FORCE OF WILL!
YOU BETTER BELIEVE I CAN!
THWAM
I CAN ACCOMPLISH ANYTHING AS LONG AS I PUT MY MIND TO IT!
WOW, I THOUGHT YOU WERE DOWN FOR THE COUNT THERE, JEN.
I DIDN'T KNOW YOU HAD IT IN YOU!
NEITHER DID I, MUNCHKIN. NEITHER DID I.

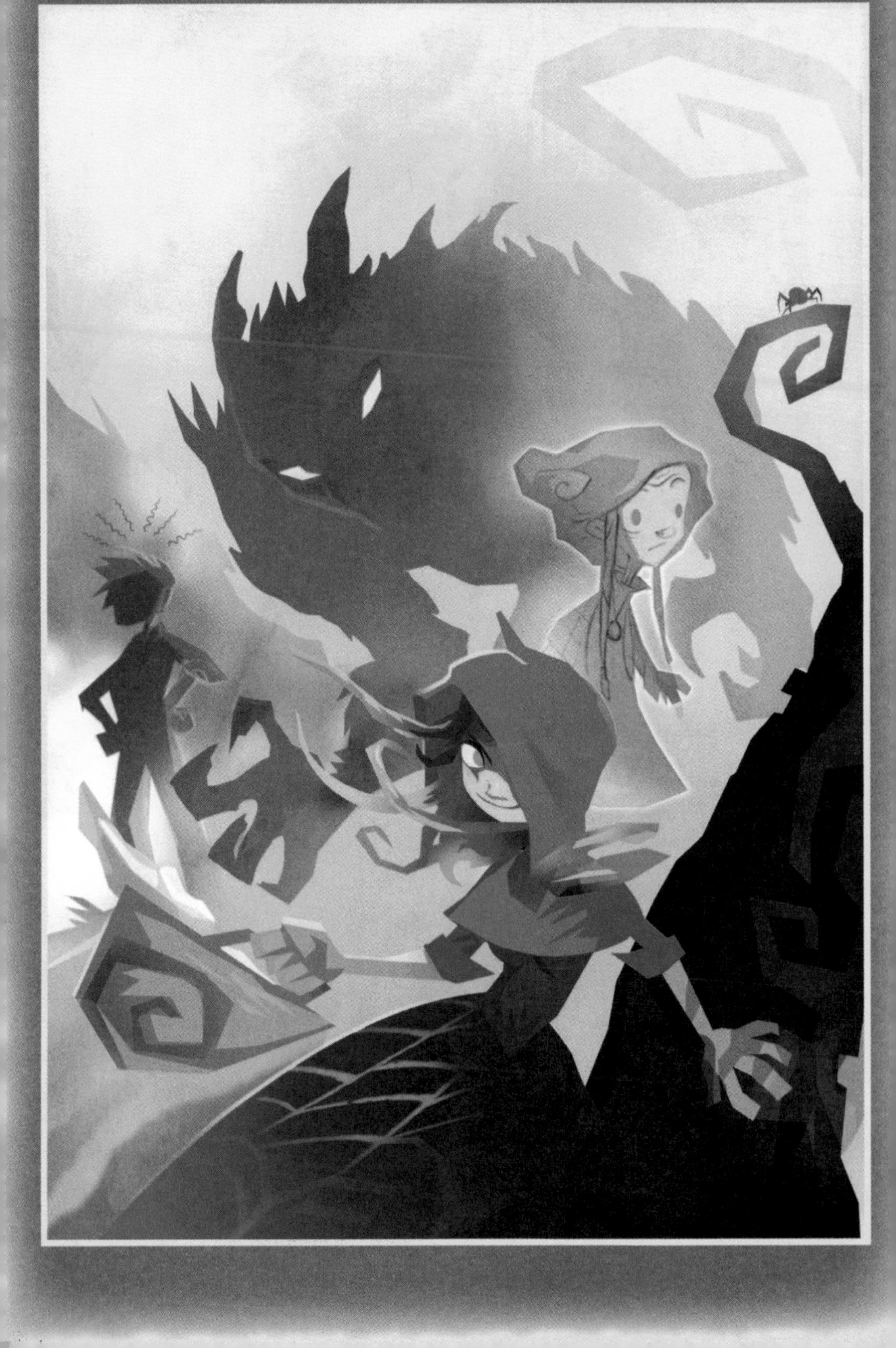

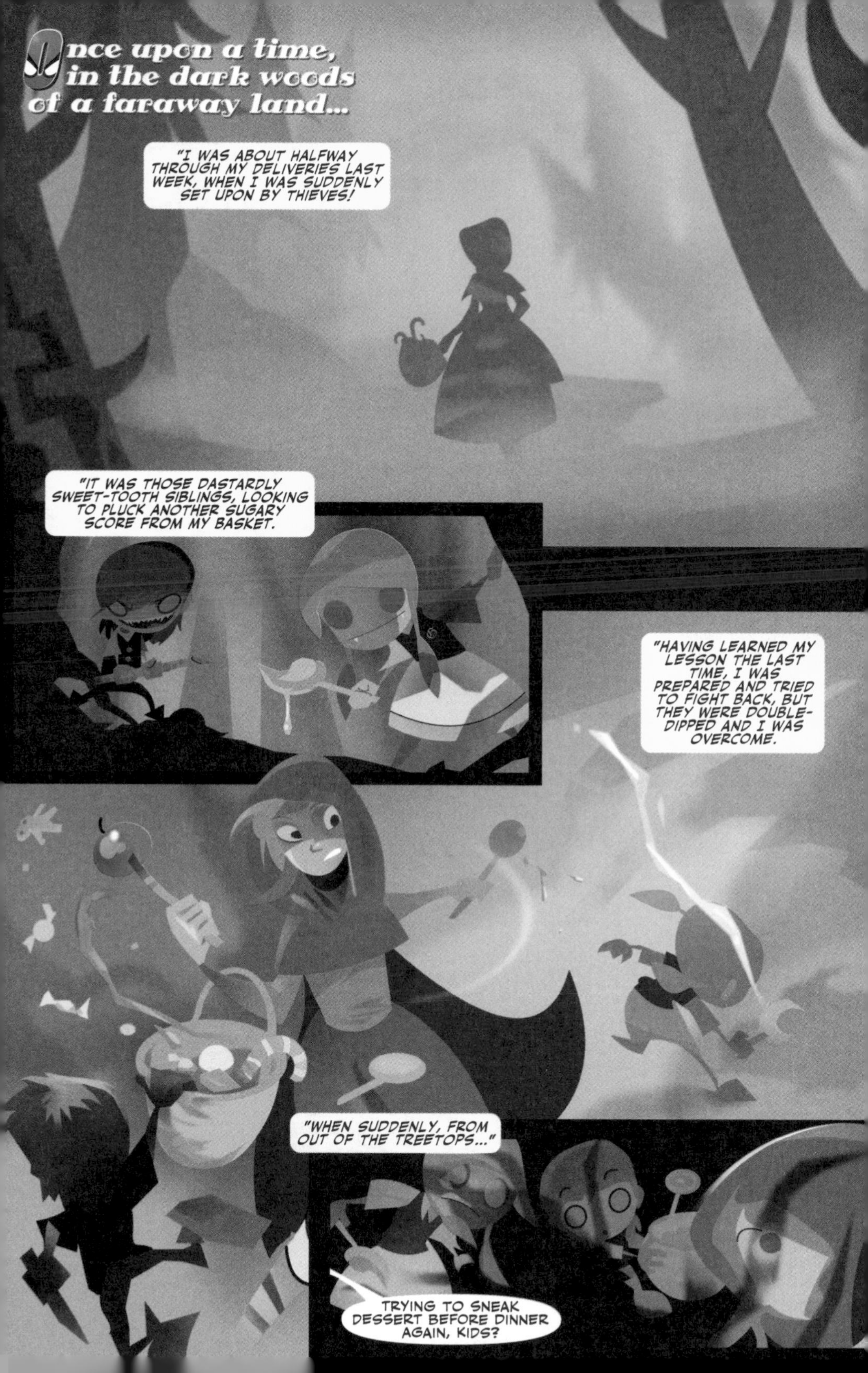
Once upon a time, in the dark woods of a faraway land...
"I WAS ABOUT HALFWAY THROUGH MY DELIVERIES LAST WEEK, WHEN I WAS SUDDENLY SET UPON BY THIEVES!
"IT WAS THOSE DASTARDLY SWEET-TOOTH SIBLINGS, LOOKING TO PLUCK ANOTHER SUGARY SCORE FROM MY BASKET.
"HAVING LEARNED MY LESSON THE LAST TIME, I WAS PREPARED AND TRIED TO FIGHT BACK, BUT THEY WERE DOUBLE-DIPPED AND I WAS OVERCOME.
"WHEN SUDDENLY, FROM OUT OF THE TREETOPS..."
TRYING TO SNEAK DESSERT BEFORE DINNER AGAIN, KIDS?

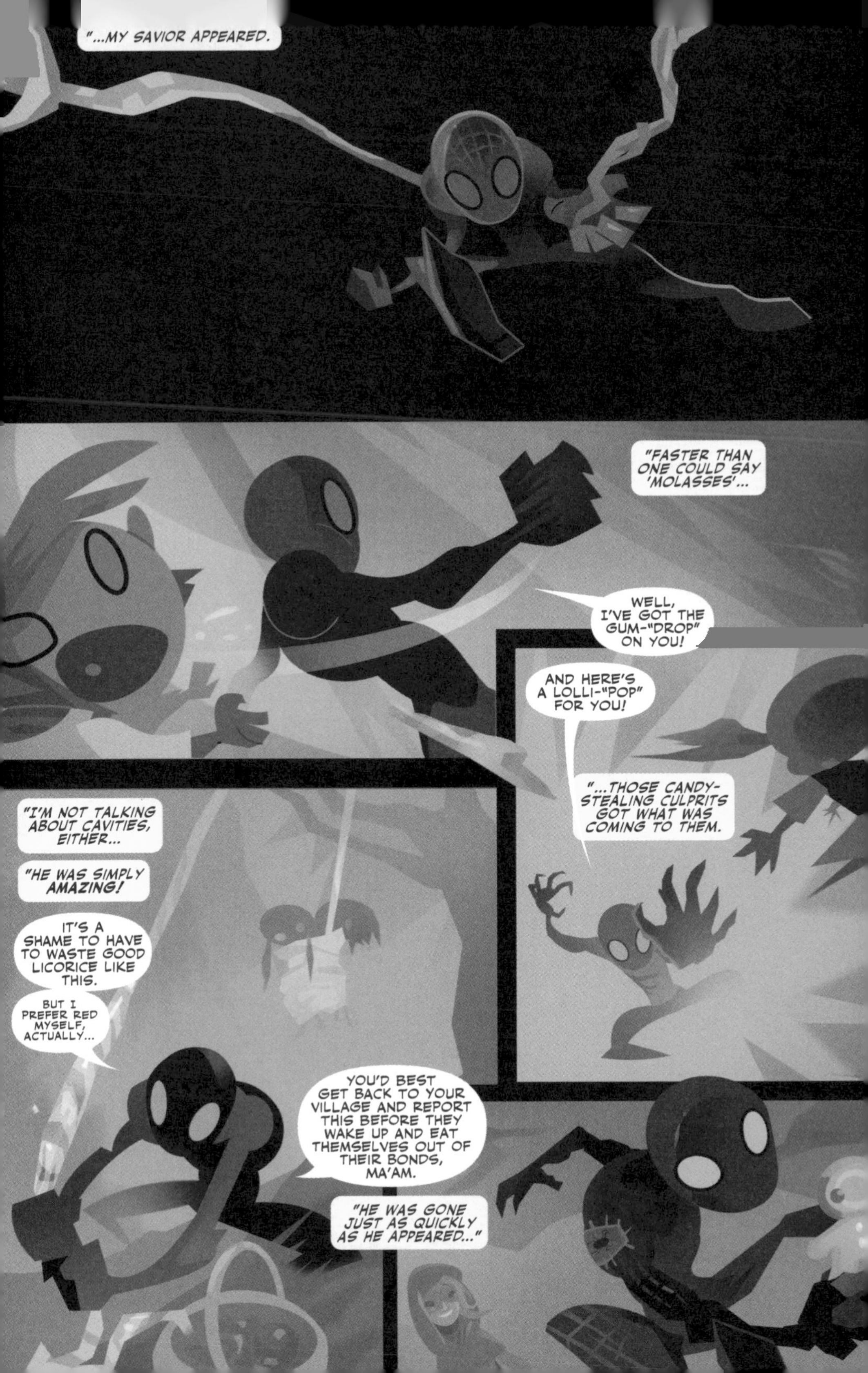
"...MY SAVIOR APPEARED.
"FASTER THAN ONE COULD SAY 'MOLASSES'...
WELL, I'VE GOT THE GUM-"DROP" ON YOU!
AND HERE'S A LOLLI-"POP" FOR YOU!
"...THOSE CANDY-STEALING CULPRITS GOT WHAT WAS COMING TO THEM.
"I'M NOT TALKING ABOUT CAVITIES, EITHER...
"HE WAS SIMPLY AMAZING!
IT'S A SHAME TO HAVE TO WASTE GOOD LICORICE LIKE THIS.
BUT I PREFER RED MYSELF, ACTUALLY...
YOU'D BEST GET BACK TO YOUR VILLAGE AND REPORT THIS BEFORE THEY WAKE UP AND EAT THEMSELVES OUT OF THEIR BONDS, MA'AM.
"HE WAS GONE JUST AS QUICKLY AS HE APPEARED..."

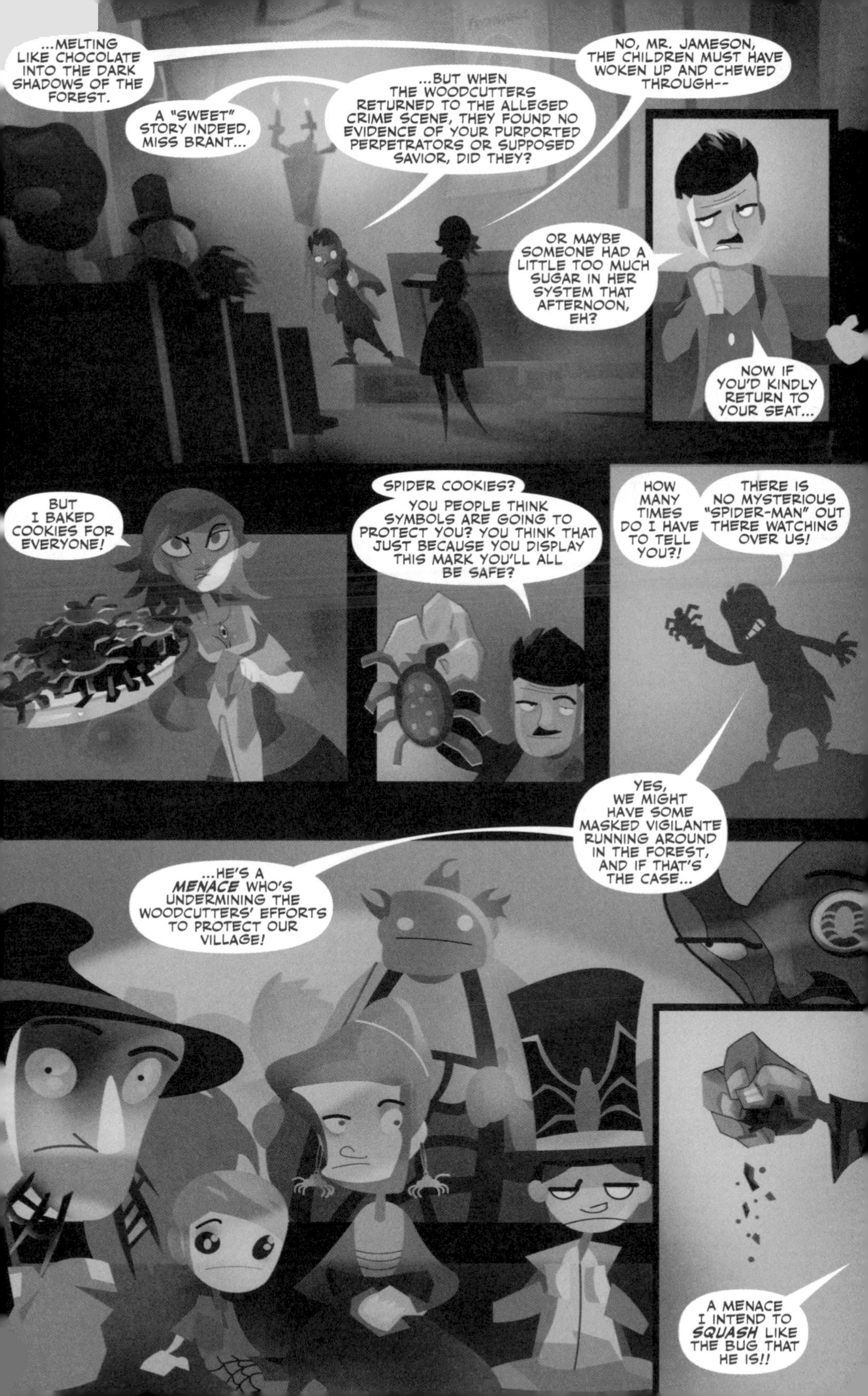
...MELTING LIKE CHOCOLATE INTO THE DARK SHADOWS OF THE FOREST.
NO, MR. JAMESON, THE CHILDREN MUST HAVE WOKEN UP AND CHEWED THROUGH--
A "SWEET" STORY INDEED, MISS BRANT...
...BUT WHEN THE WOODCUTTERS RETURNED TO THE ALLEGED CRIME SCENE, THEY FOUND NO EVIDENCE OF YOUR PURPORTED PERPETRATORS OR SUPPOSED SAVIOR, DID THEY?
OR MAYBE SOMEONE HAD A LITTLE TOO MUCH SUGAR IN HER SYSTEM THAT AFTERNOON, EH?
NOW IF YOU'D KINDLY RETURN TO YOUR SEAT...
BUT I BAKED COOKIES FOR EVERYONE!
SPIDER COOKIES?
YOU PEOPLE THINK SYMBOLS ARE GOING TO PROTECT YOU? YOU THINK THAT JUST BECAUSE YOU DISPLAY THIS MARK YOU'LL ALL BE SAFE?
HOW MANY TIMES DO I HAVE TO TELL YOU?!
THERE IS NO MYSTERIOUS "SPIDER-MAN" OUT THERE WATCHING OVER US!
YES, WE MIGHT HAVE SOME MASKED VIGILANTE RUNNING AROUND IN THE FOREST, AND IF THAT'S THE CASE...
...HE'S A *MENACE* WHO'S UNDERMINING THE WOODCUTTERS' EFFORTS TO PROTECT OUR VILLAGE!
A MENACE I INTEND TO *SQUASH* LIKE THE BUG THAT HE IS!!

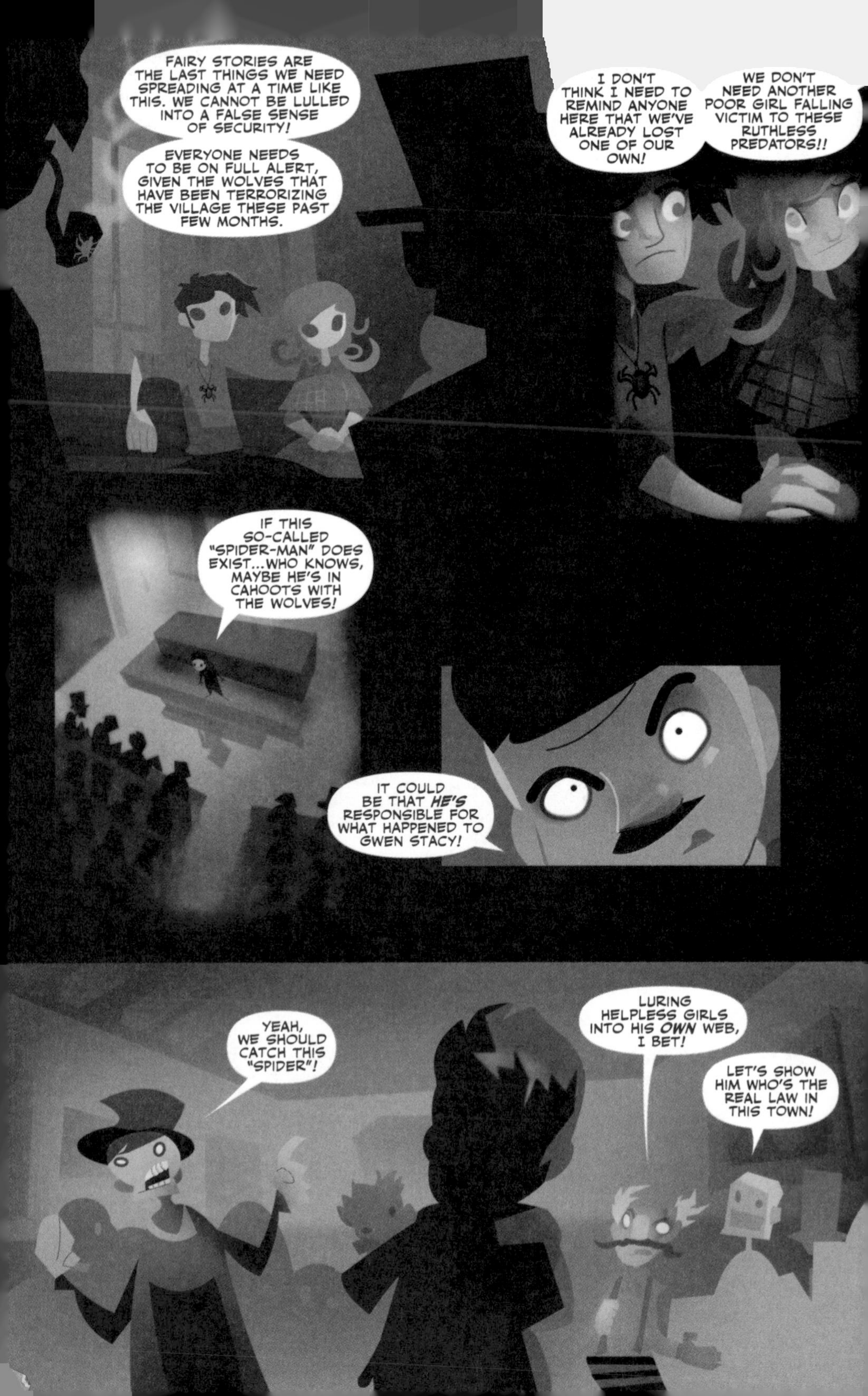
FAIRY STORIES ARE THE LAST THINGS WE NEED SPREADING AT A TIME LIKE THIS. WE CANNOT BE LULLED INTO A FALSE SENSE OF SECURITY!
EVERYONE NEEDS TO BE ON FULL ALERT, GIVEN THE WOLVES THAT HAVE BEEN TERRORIZING THE VILLAGE THESE PAST FEW MONTHS.
I DON'T THINK I NEED TO REMIND ANYONE HERE THAT WE'VE ALREADY LOST ONE OF OUR OWN!
WE DON'T NEED ANOTHER POOR GIRL FALLING VICTIM TO THESE RUTHLESS PREDATORS!!
IF THIS SO-CALLED "SPIDER-MAN" DOES EXIST...WHO KNOWS, MAYBE HE'S IN CAHOOTS WITH THE WOLVES!
IT COULD BE THAT *HE'S* RESPONSIBLE FOR WHAT HAPPENED TO GWEN STACY!
YEAH, WE SHOULD CATCH THIS "SPIDER"!
LURING HELPLESS GIRLS INTO HIS *OWN* WEB, I BET!
LET'S SHOW HIM WHO'S THE REAL LAW IN THIS TOWN!

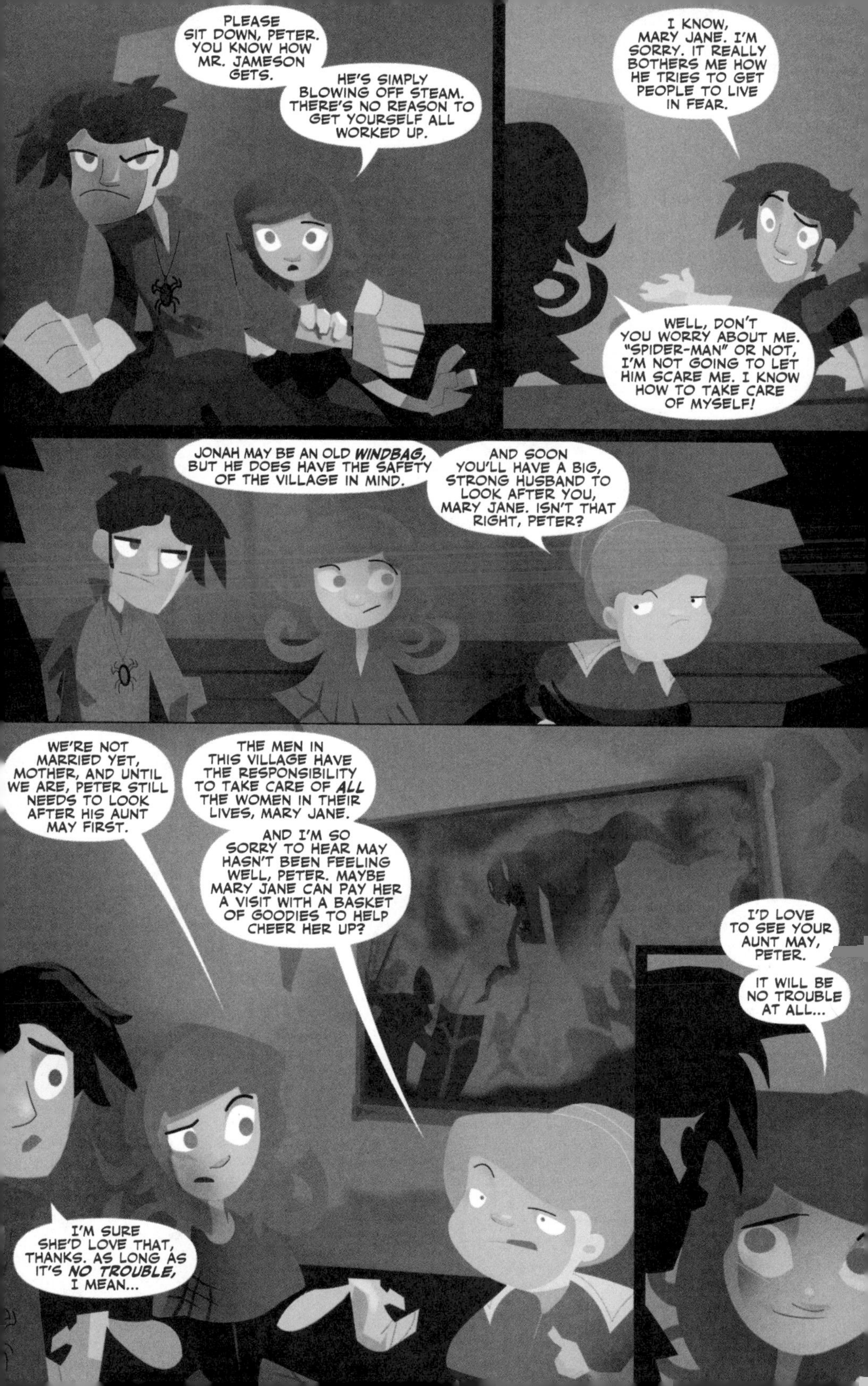
PLEASE SIT DOWN, PETER. YOU KNOW HOW MR. JAMESON GETS.
HE'S SIMPLY BLOWING OFF STEAM. THERE'S NO REASON TO GET YOURSELF ALL WORKED UP.
I KNOW, MARY JANE. I'M SORRY. IT REALLY BOTHERS ME HOW HE TRIES TO GET PEOPLE TO LIVE IN FEAR.
WELL, DON'T YOU WORRY ABOUT ME. "SPIDER-MAN" OR NOT, I'M NOT GOING TO LET HIM SCARE ME. I KNOW HOW TO TAKE CARE OF MYSELF!
JONAH MAY BE AN OLD *WINDBAG,* BUT HE DOES HAVE THE SAFETY OF THE VILLAGE IN MIND.
AND SOON YOU'LL HAVE A BIG, STRONG HUSBAND TO LOOK AFTER YOU, MARY JANE. ISN'T THAT RIGHT, PETER?
WE'RE NOT MARRIED YET, MOTHER, AND UNTIL WE ARE, PETER STILL NEEDS TO LOOK AFTER HIS AUNT MAY FIRST.
THE MEN IN THIS VILLAGE HAVE THE RESPONSIBILITY TO TAKE CARE OF *ALL* THE WOMEN IN THEIR LIVES, MARY JANE.
AND I'M SO SORRY TO HEAR MAY HASN'T BEEN FEELING WELL, PETER. MAYBE MARY JANE CAN PAY HER A VISIT WITH A BASKET OF GOODIES TO HELP CHEER HER UP?
I'M SURE SHE'D LOVE THAT, THANKS. AS LONG AS IT'S *NO TROUBLE,* I MEAN...
I'D LOVE TO SEE YOUR AUNT MAY, PETER.
IT WILL BE NO TROUBLE AT ALL...

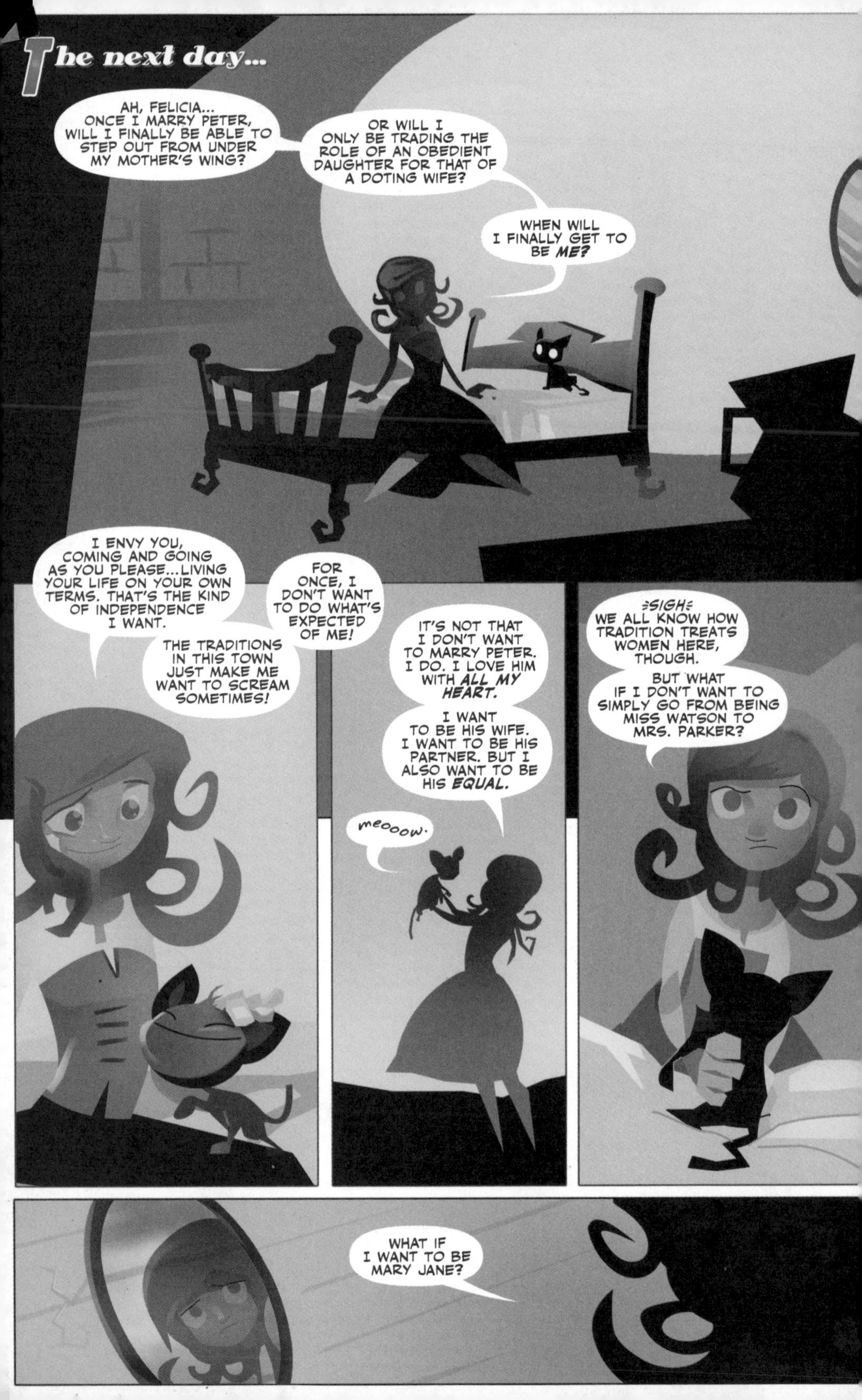
The next day...
AH, FELICIA... ONCE I MARRY PETER, WILL I FINALLY BE ABLE TO STEP OUT FROM UNDER MY MOTHER'S WING?
OR WILL I ONLY BE TRADING THE ROLE OF AN OBEDIENT DAUGHTER FOR THAT OF A DOTING WIFE?
WHEN WILL I FINALLY GET TO BE ME?
I ENVY YOU, COMING AND GOING AS YOU PLEASE...LIVING YOUR LIFE ON YOUR OWN TERMS. THAT'S THE KIND OF INDEPENDENCE I WANT.
FOR ONCE, I DON'T WANT TO DO WHAT'S EXPECTED OF ME!
THE TRADITIONS IN THIS TOWN JUST MAKE ME WANT TO SCREAM SOMETIMES!
IT'S NOT THAT I DON'T WANT TO MARRY PETER. I DO. I LOVE HIM WITH ALL MY HEART.
I WANT TO BE HIS WIFE. I WANT TO BE HIS PARTNER. BUT I ALSO WANT TO BE HIS EQUAL.
meooow.
SIGH
WE ALL KNOW HOW TRADITION TREATS WOMEN HERE, THOUGH.
BUT WHAT IF I DON'T WANT TO SIMPLY GO FROM BEING MISS WATSON TO MRS. PARKER?
WHAT IF I WANT TO BE MARY JANE?

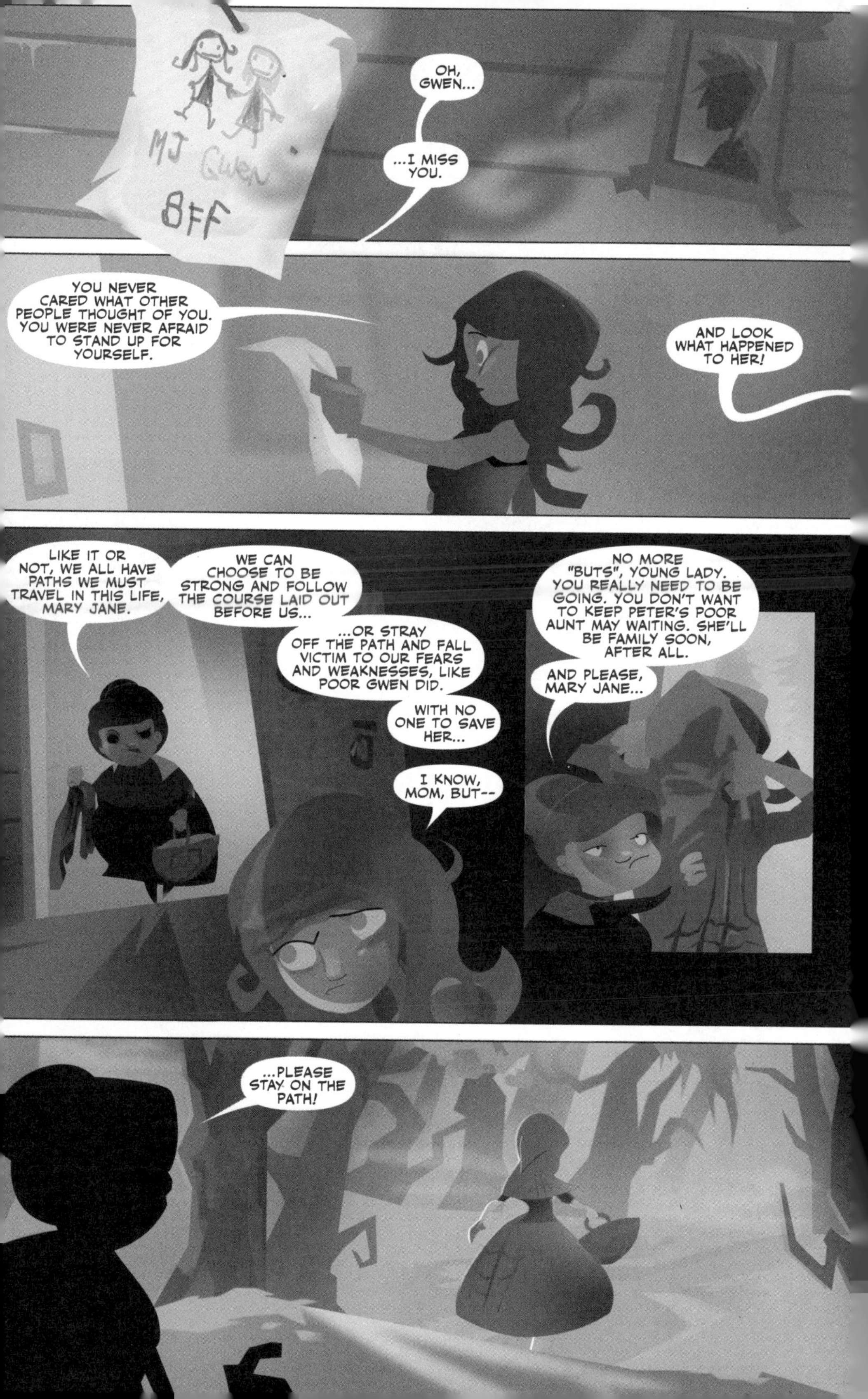
MJ
Gwen
BFF
OH, GWEN...
...I MISS YOU.
YOU NEVER CARED WHAT OTHER PEOPLE THOUGHT OF YOU. YOU WERE NEVER AFRAID TO STAND UP FOR YOURSELF.
AND LOOK WHAT HAPPENED TO HER!
LIKE IT OR NOT, WE ALL HAVE PATHS WE MUST TRAVEL IN THIS LIFE, MARY JANE.
WE CAN CHOOSE TO BE STRONG AND FOLLOW THE COURSE LAID OUT BEFORE US...
...OR STRAY OFF THE PATH AND FALL VICTIM TO OUR FEARS AND WEAKNESSES, LIKE POOR GWEN DID.
WITH NO ONE TO SAVE HER...
I KNOW, MOM, BUT--
NO MORE "BUTS", YOUNG LADY. YOU REALLY NEED TO BE GOING. YOU DON'T WANT TO KEEP PETER'S POOR AUNT MAY WAITING. SHE'LL BE FAMILY SOON, AFTER ALL.
AND PLEASE, MARY JANE...
...PLEASE STAY ON THE PATH!

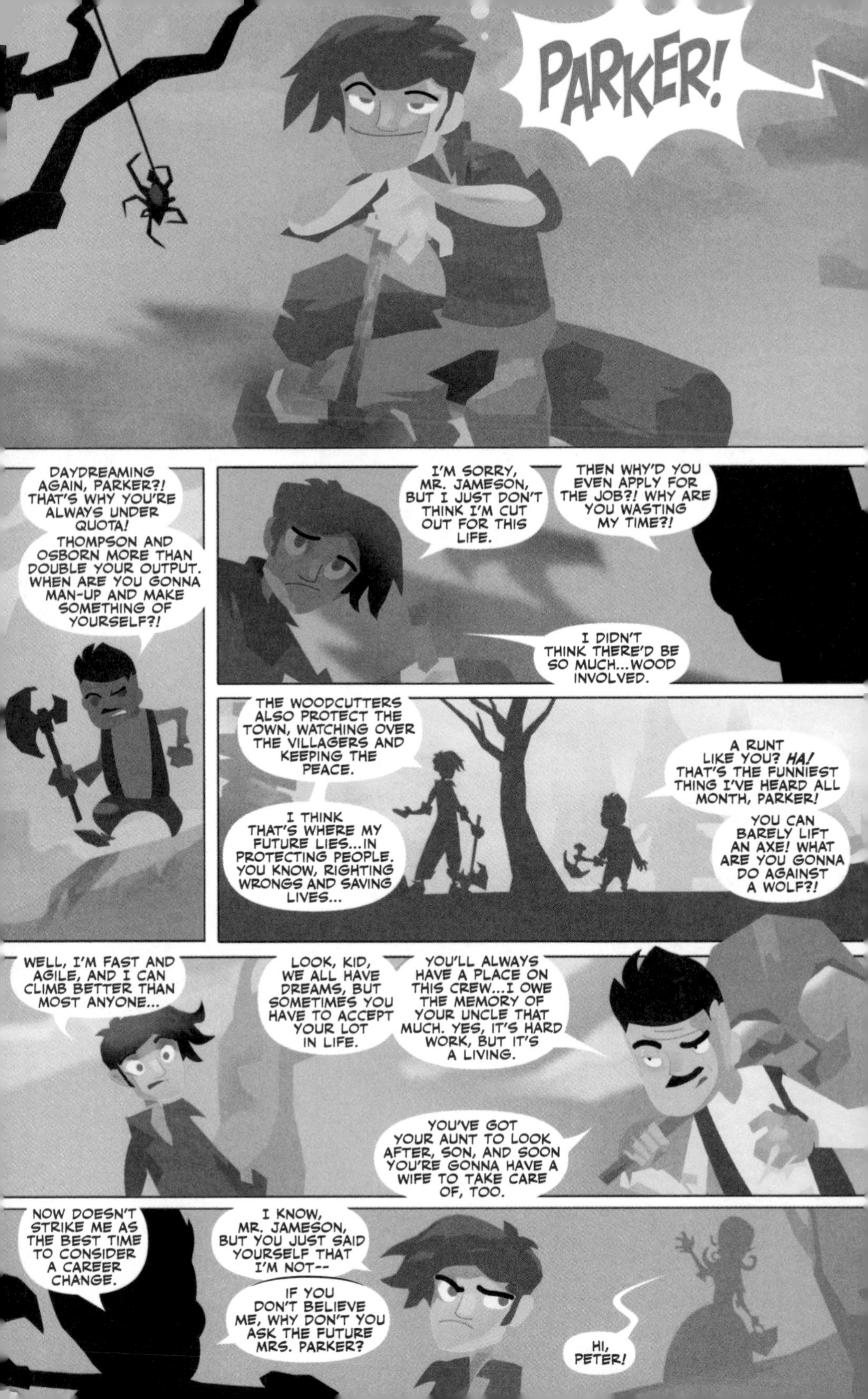
PARKER!
DAYDREAMING AGAIN, PARKER?! THAT'S WHY YOU'RE ALWAYS UNDER QUOTA!
THOMPSON AND OSBORN MORE THAN DOUBLE YOUR OUTPUT. WHEN ARE YOU GONNA MAN-UP AND MAKE SOMETHING OF YOURSELF?!
I'M SORRY, MR. JAMESON, BUT I JUST DON'T THINK I'M CUT OUT FOR THIS LIFE.
THEN WHY'D YOU EVEN APPLY FOR THE JOB?! WHY ARE YOU WASTING MY TIME?!
I DIDN'T THINK THERE'D BE SO MUCH...WOOD INVOLVED.
THE WOODCUTTERS ALSO PROTECT THE TOWN, WATCHING OVER THE VILLAGERS AND KEEPING THE PEACE.
I THINK THAT'S WHERE MY FUTURE LIES...IN PROTECTING PEOPLE. YOU KNOW, RIGHTING WRONGS AND SAVING LIVES...
A RUNT LIKE YOU? HA! THAT'S THE FUNNIEST THING I'VE HEARD ALL MONTH, PARKER!
YOU CAN BARELY LIFT AN AXE! WHAT ARE YOU GONNA DO AGAINST A WOLF?!
WELL, I'M FAST AND AGILE, AND I CAN CLIMB BETTER THAN MOST ANYONE...
LOOK, KID, WE ALL HAVE DREAMS, BUT SOMETIMES YOU HAVE TO ACCEPT YOUR LOT IN LIFE.
YOU'LL ALWAYS HAVE A PLACE ON THIS CREW...I OWE THE MEMORY OF YOUR UNCLE THAT MUCH. YES, IT'S HARD WORK, BUT IT'S A LIVING.
YOU'VE GOT YOUR AUNT TO LOOK AFTER, SON, AND SOON YOU'RE GONNA HAVE A WIFE TO TAKE CARE OF, TOO.
NOW DOESN'T STRIKE ME AS THE BEST TIME TO CONSIDER A CAREER CHANGE.
I KNOW, MR. JAMESON, BUT YOU JUST SAID YOURSELF THAT I'M NOT--
IF YOU DON'T BELIEVE ME, WHY DON'T YOU ASK THE FUTURE MRS. PARKER?
HI, PETER!

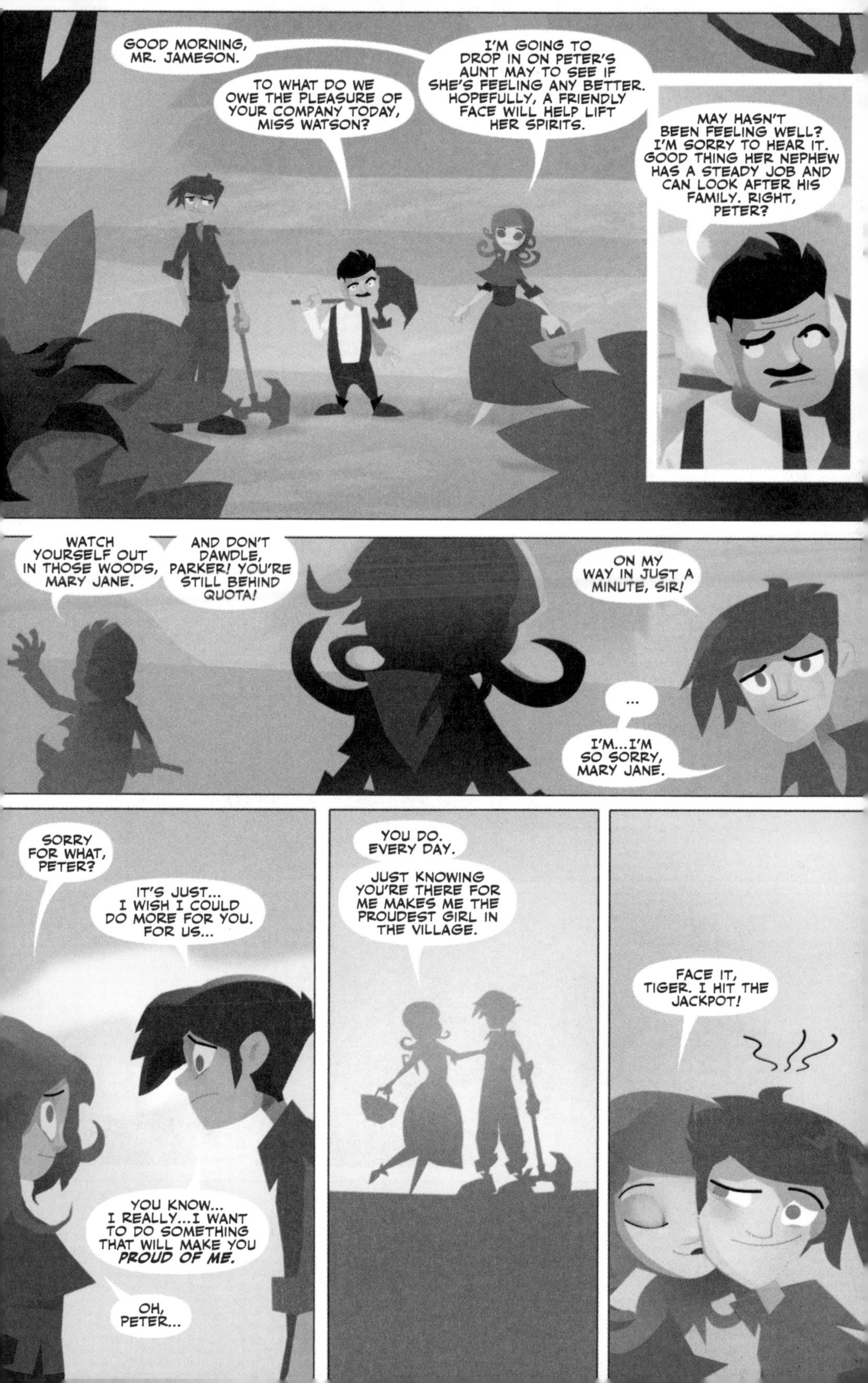

GOOD MORNING, MR. JAMESON.
TO WHAT DO WE OWE THE PLEASURE OF YOUR COMPANY TODAY, MISS WATSON?
I'M GOING TO DROP IN ON PETER'S AUNT MAY TO SEE IF SHE'S FEELING ANY BETTER. HOPEFULLY, A FRIENDLY FACE WILL HELP LIFT HER SPIRITS.
MAY HASN'T BEEN FEELING WELL? I'M SORRY TO HEAR IT. GOOD THING HER NEPHEW HAS A STEADY JOB AND CAN LOOK AFTER HIS FAMILY. RIGHT, PETER?
WATCH YOURSELF OUT IN THOSE WOODS, MARY JANE.
AND DON'T DAWDLE, PARKER! YOU'RE STILL BEHIND QUOTA!
ON MY WAY IN JUST A MINUTE, SIR!
...
I'M...I'M SO SORRY, MARY JANE.
SORRY FOR WHAT, PETER?
IT'S JUST... I WISH I COULD DO MORE FOR YOU. FOR US...
YOU KNOW... I REALLY...I WANT TO DO SOMETHING THAT WILL MAKE YOU *PROUD OF ME.*
OH, PETER...
YOU DO. EVERY DAY.
JUST KNOWING YOU'RE THERE FOR ME MAKES ME THE PROUDEST GIRL IN THE VILLAGE.
FACE IT, TIGER. I HIT THE JACKPOT!

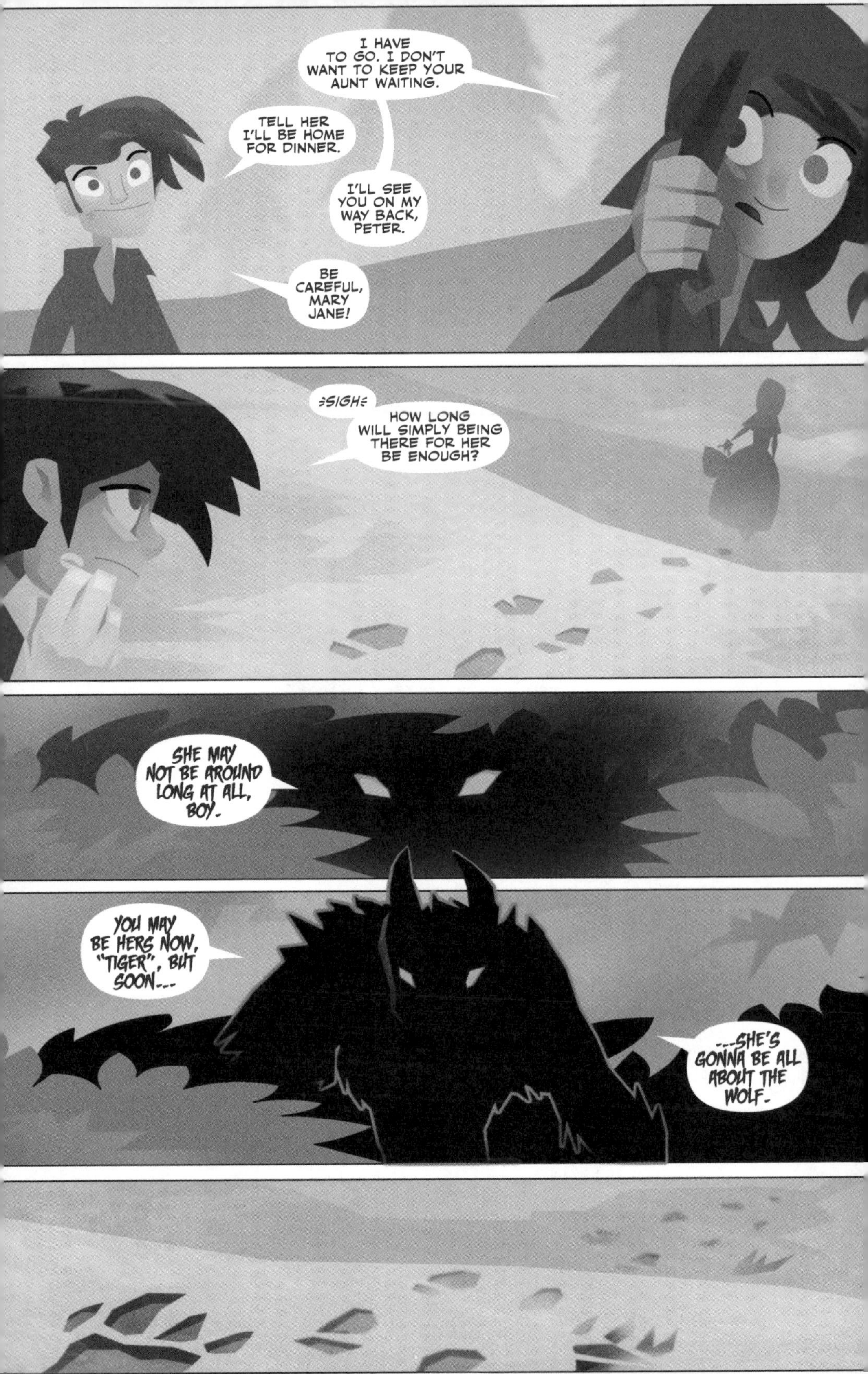
I HAVE TO GO. I DON'T WANT TO KEEP YOUR AUNT WAITING.
TELL HER I'LL BE HOME FOR DINNER.
I'LL SEE YOU ON MY WAY BACK, PETER.
BE CAREFUL, MARY JANE!
≈SIGH≈
HOW LONG WILL SIMPLY BEING THERE FOR HER BE ENOUGH?
SHE MAY NOT BE AROUND LONG AT ALL, BOY.
YOU MAY BE HERS NOW, "TIGER", BUT SOON...
...SHE'S GONNA BE ALL ABOUT THE WOLF.

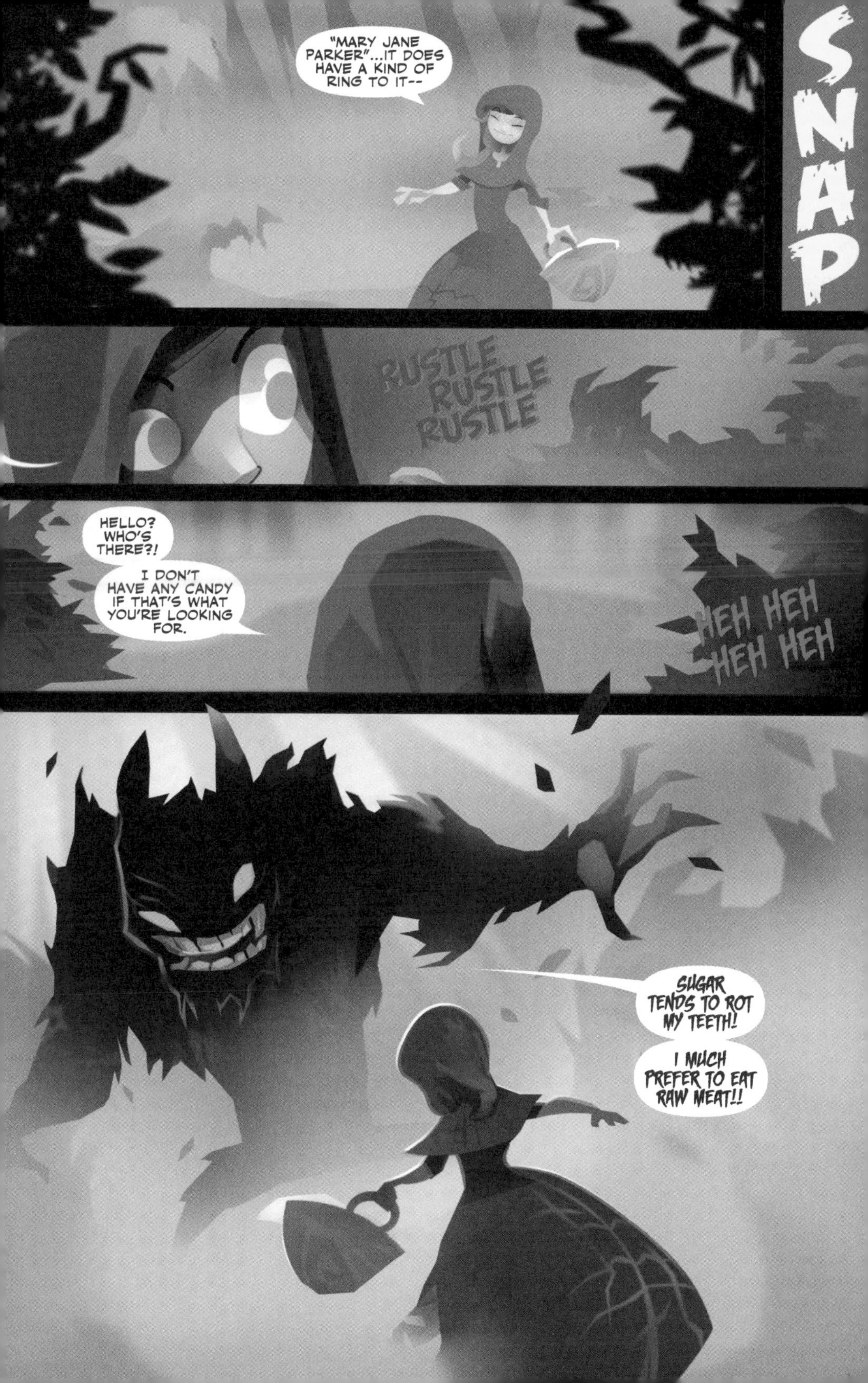
"MARY JANE PARKER"...IT DOES HAVE A KIND OF RING TO IT--
SNAP
RUSTLE RUSTLE RUSTLE
HELLO? WHO'S THERE?!
I DON'T HAVE ANY CANDY IF THAT'S WHAT YOU'RE LOOKING FOR.
HEH HEH HEH HEH
SUGAR TENDS TO ROT MY TEETH!
I MUCH PREFER TO EAT RAW MEAT!!

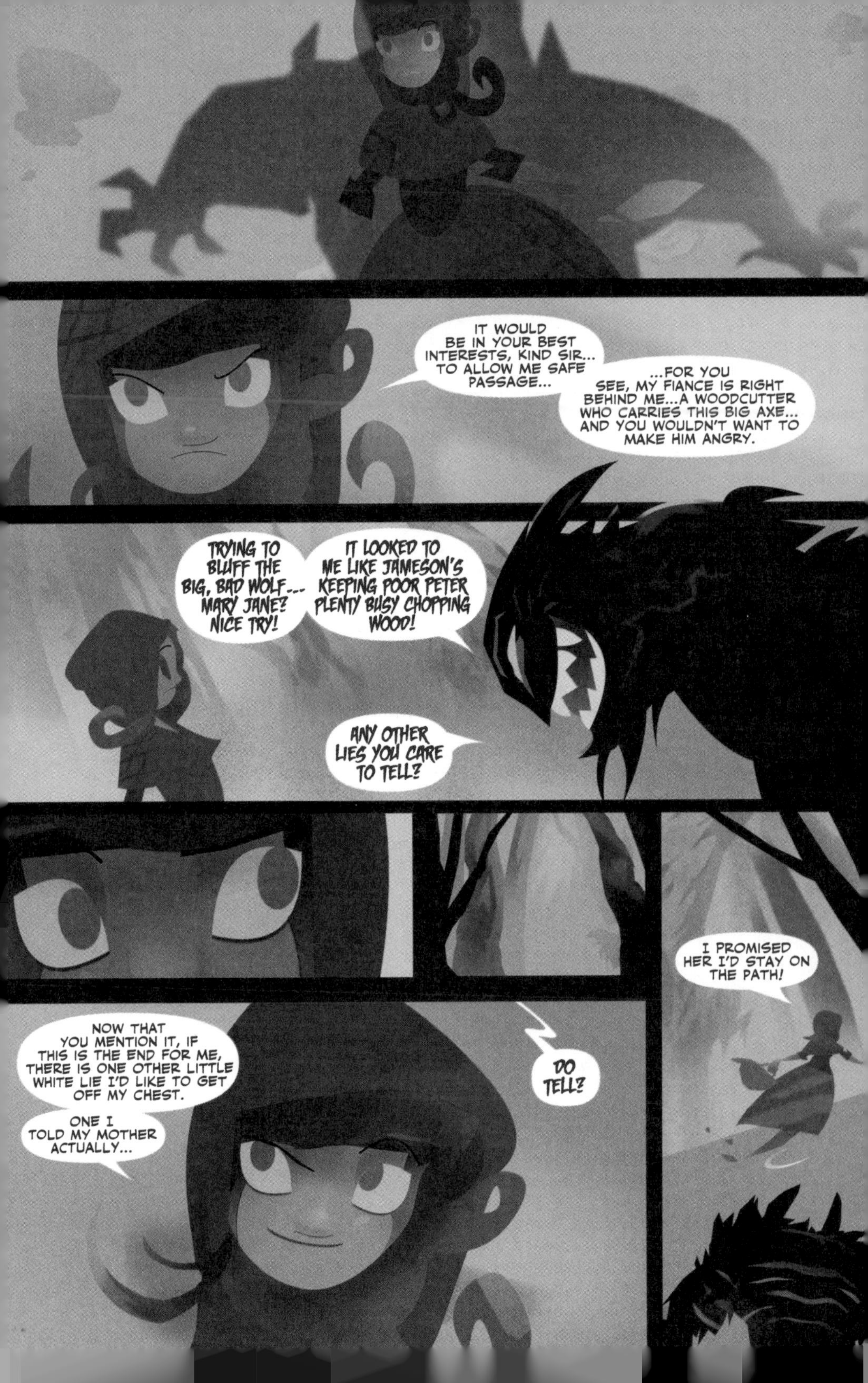

IT WOULD BE IN YOUR BEST INTERESTS, KIND SIR... TO ALLOW ME SAFE PASSAGE...
...FOR YOU SEE, MY FIANCE IS RIGHT BEHIND ME...A WOODCUTTER WHO CARRIES THIS BIG AXE... AND YOU WOULDN'T WANT TO MAKE HIM ANGRY.
TRYING TO BLUFF THE BIG, BAD WOLF... MARY JANE? NICE TRY!
IT LOOKED TO ME LIKE JAMESON'S KEEPING POOR PETER PLENTY BUSY CHOPPING WOOD!
ANY OTHER LIES YOU CARE TO TELL?
I PROMISED HER I'D STAY ON THE PATH!
NOW THAT YOU MENTION IT, IF THIS IS THE END FOR ME, THERE IS ONE OTHER LITTLE WHITE LIE I'D LIKE TO GET OFF MY CHEST.
ONE I TOLD MY MOTHER ACTUALLY...
DO TELL?

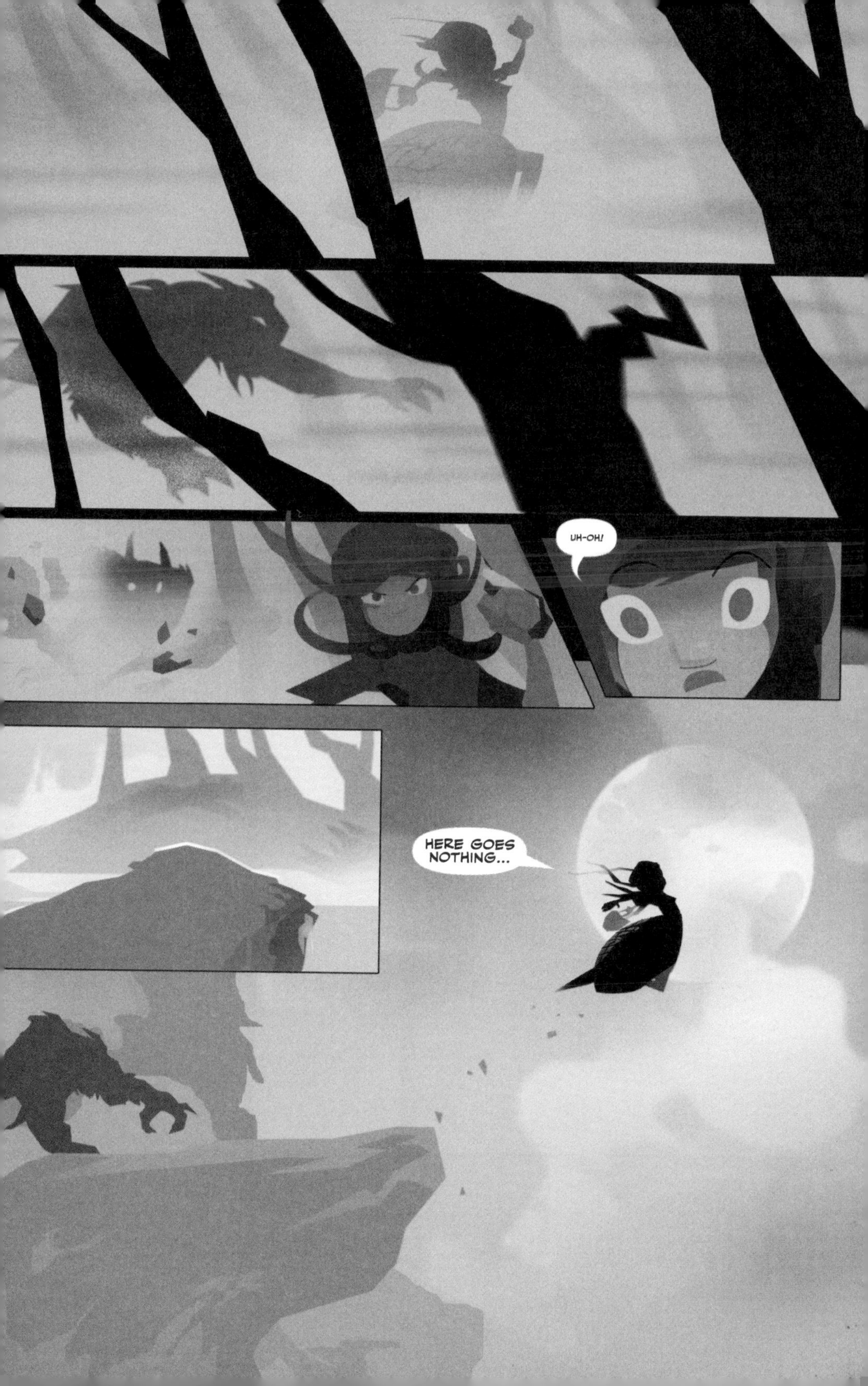
UH-OH!
HERE GOES NOTHING...

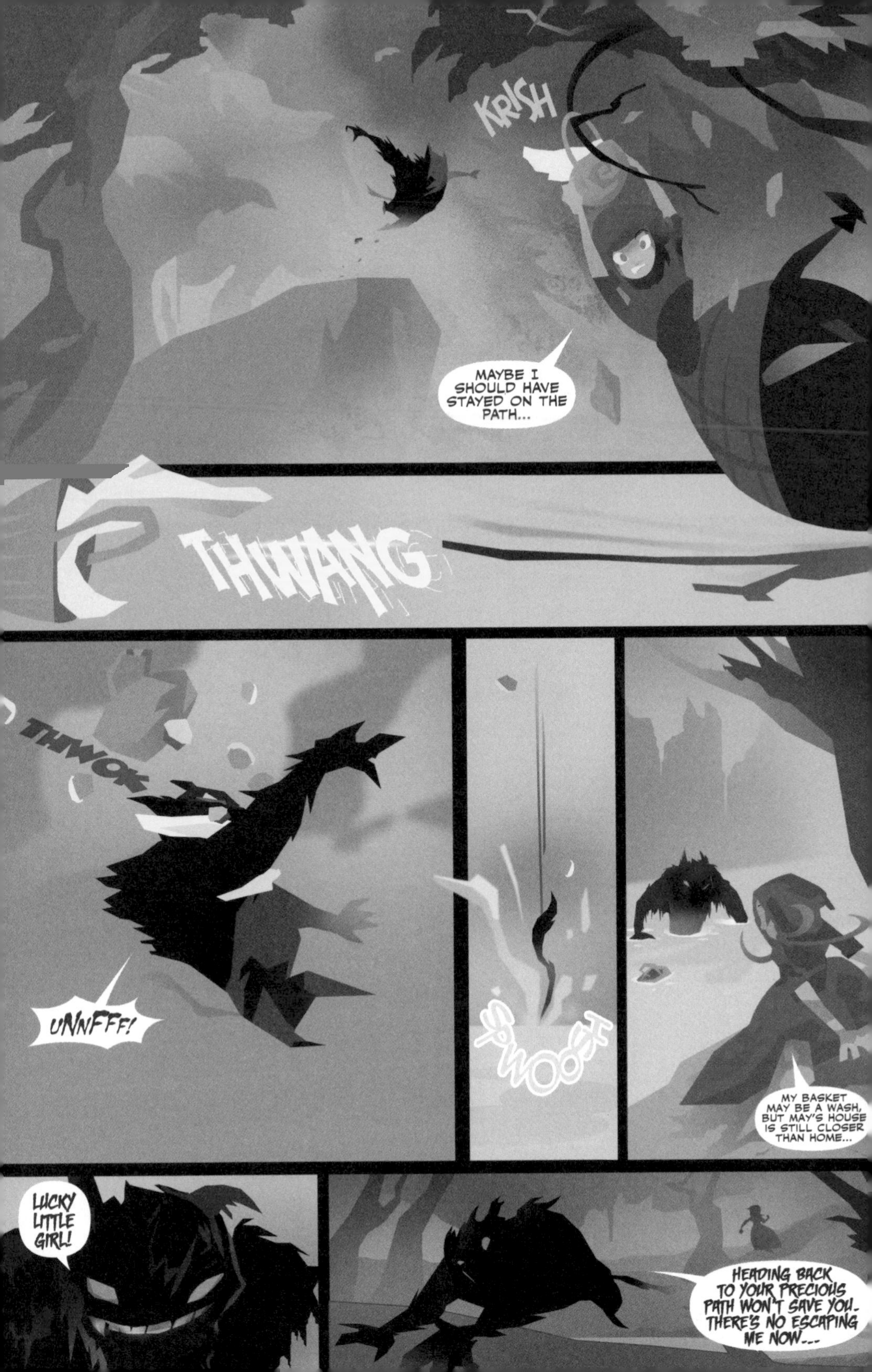
KRISH
MAYBE I SHOULD HAVE STAYED ON THE PATH...
THWANG
THWOK
UNNFFF!
SPWOOSH
MY BASKET MAY BE A WASH, BUT MAY'S HOUSE IS STILL CLOSER THAN HOME...
LUCKY LITTLE GIRL!
HEADING BACK TO YOUR PRECIOUS PATH WON'T SAVE YOU. THERE'S NO ESCAPING ME NOW...

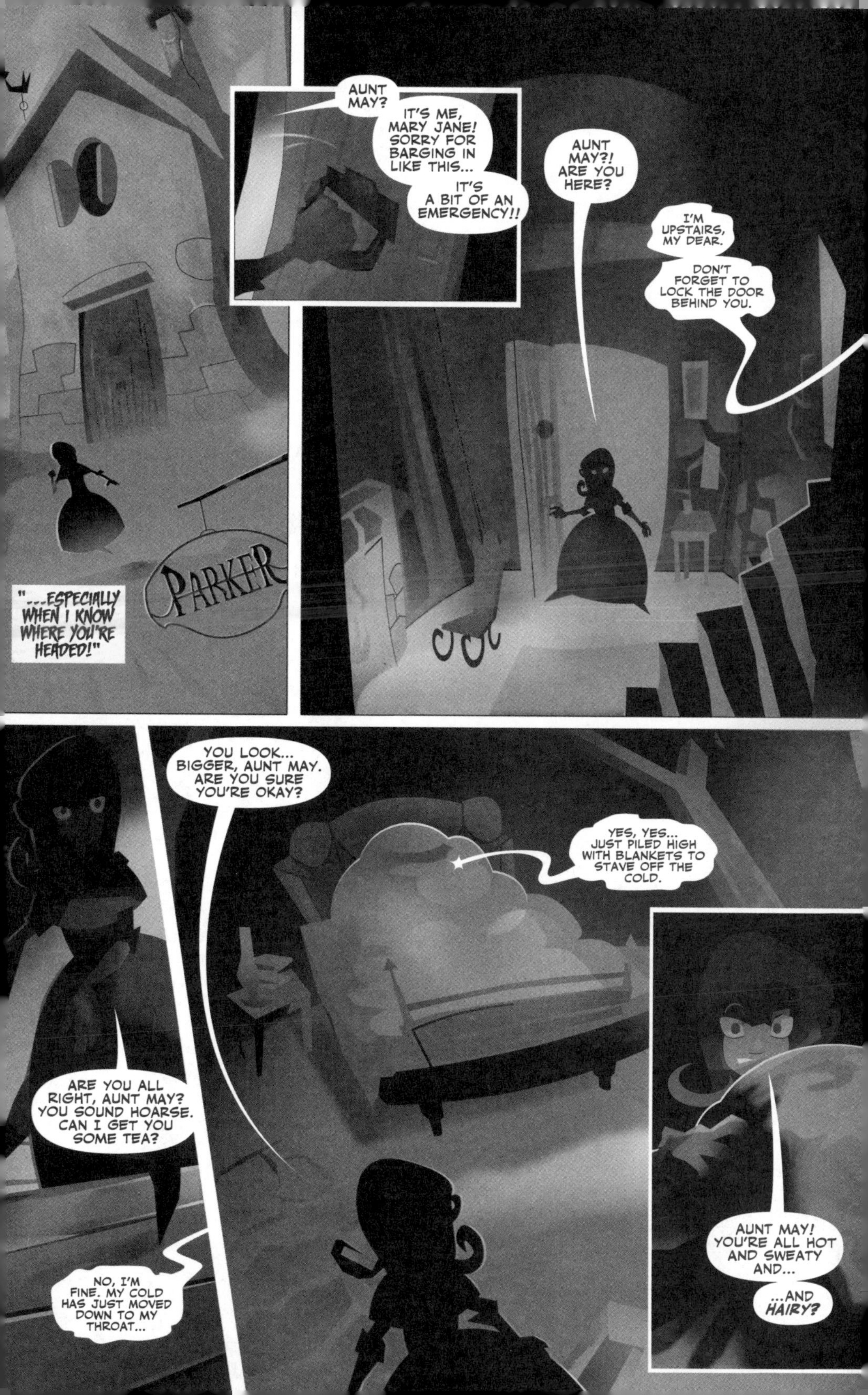

"...ESPECIALLY WHEN I KNOW WHERE YOU'RE HEADED!"
PARKER
AUNT MAY?
IT'S ME, MARY JANE! SORRY FOR BARGING IN LIKE THIS...
IT'S A BIT OF AN EMERGENCY!!
AUNT MAY?! ARE YOU HERE?
I'M UPSTAIRS, MY DEAR.
DON'T FORGET TO LOCK THE DOOR BEHIND YOU.
ARE YOU ALL RIGHT, AUNT MAY? YOU SOUND HOARSE. CAN I GET YOU SOME TEA?
NO, I'M FINE. MY COLD HAS JUST MOVED DOWN TO MY THROAT...
YOU LOOK... BIGGER, AUNT MAY. ARE YOU SURE YOU'RE OKAY?
YES, YES... JUST PILED HIGH WITH BLANKETS TO STAVE OFF THE COLD.
AUNT MAY! YOU'RE ALL HOT AND SWEATY AND...
...AND *HAIRY?*

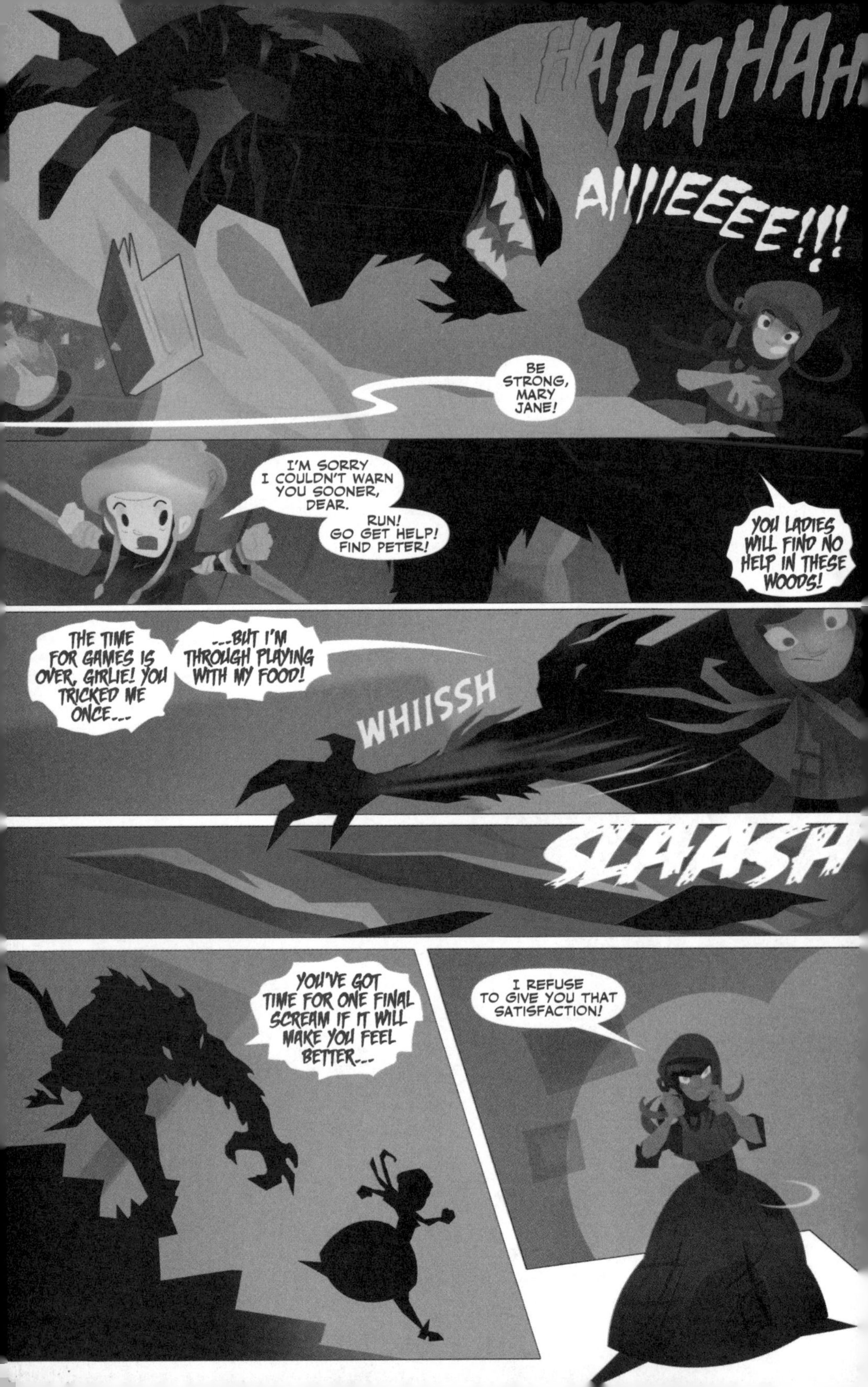
HAHAHAHAH
AIIIEEEEE!!!
BE STRONG, MARY JANE!
I'M SORRY I COULDN'T WARN YOU SOONER, DEAR.
RUN! GO GET HELP! FIND PETER!
YOU LADIES WILL FIND NO HELP IN THESE WOODS!
THE TIME FOR GAMES IS OVER, GIRLIE! YOU TRICKED ME ONCE...
...BUT I'M THROUGH PLAYING WITH MY FOOD!
WHIISSH
SLAASH
YOU'VE GOT TIME FOR ONE FINAL SCREAM IF IT WILL MAKE YOU FEEL BETTER...
I REFUSE TO GIVE YOU THAT SATISFACTION!

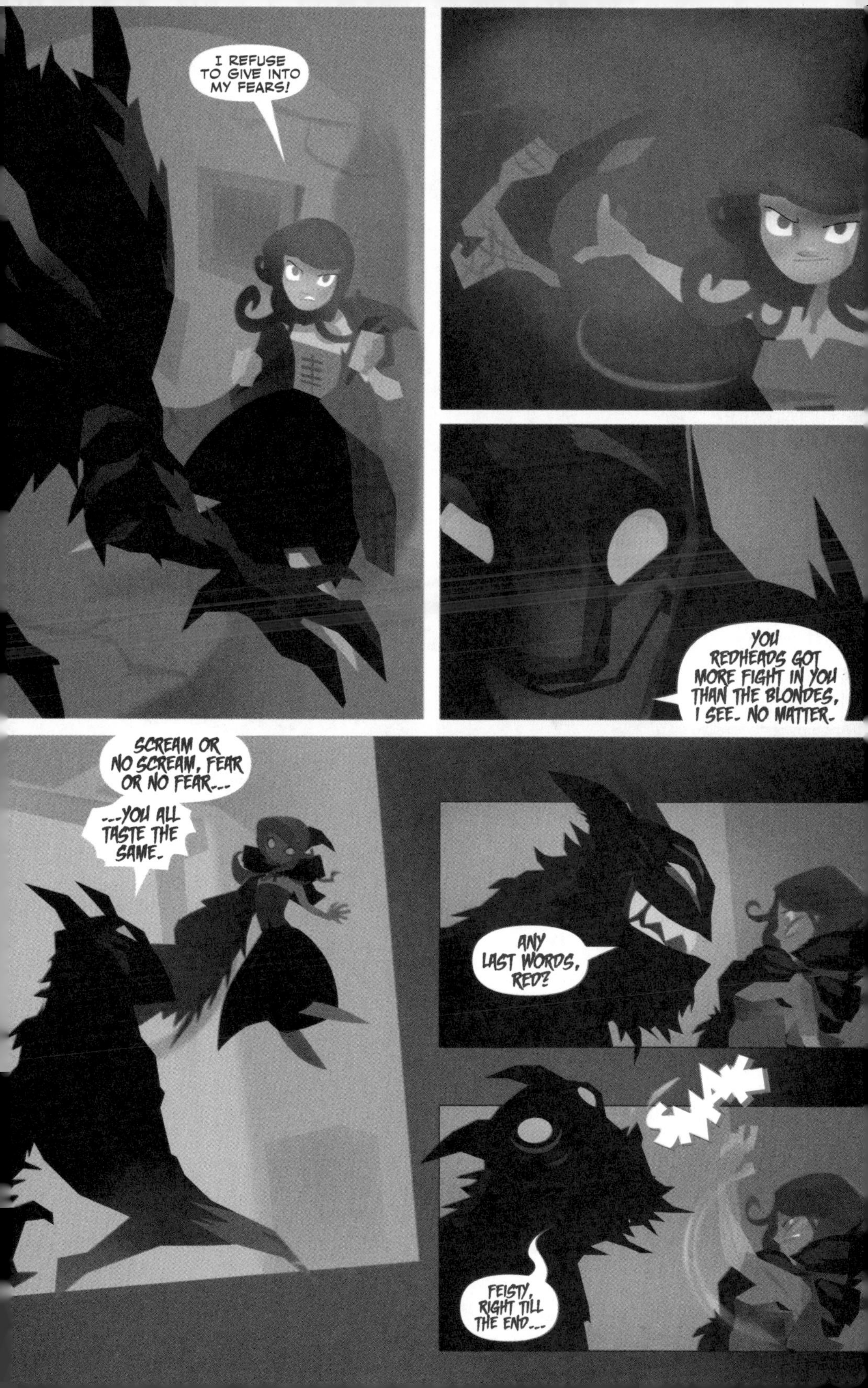
I REFUSE TO GIVE INTO MY FEARS!
YOU REDHEADS GOT MORE FIGHT IN YOU THAN THE BLONDES, I SEE. NO MATTER.
SCREAM OR NO SCREAM, FEAR OR NO FEAR...
...YOU ALL TASTE THE SAME.
ANY LAST WORDS, RED?
SMAK
FEISTY, RIGHT TILL THE END...

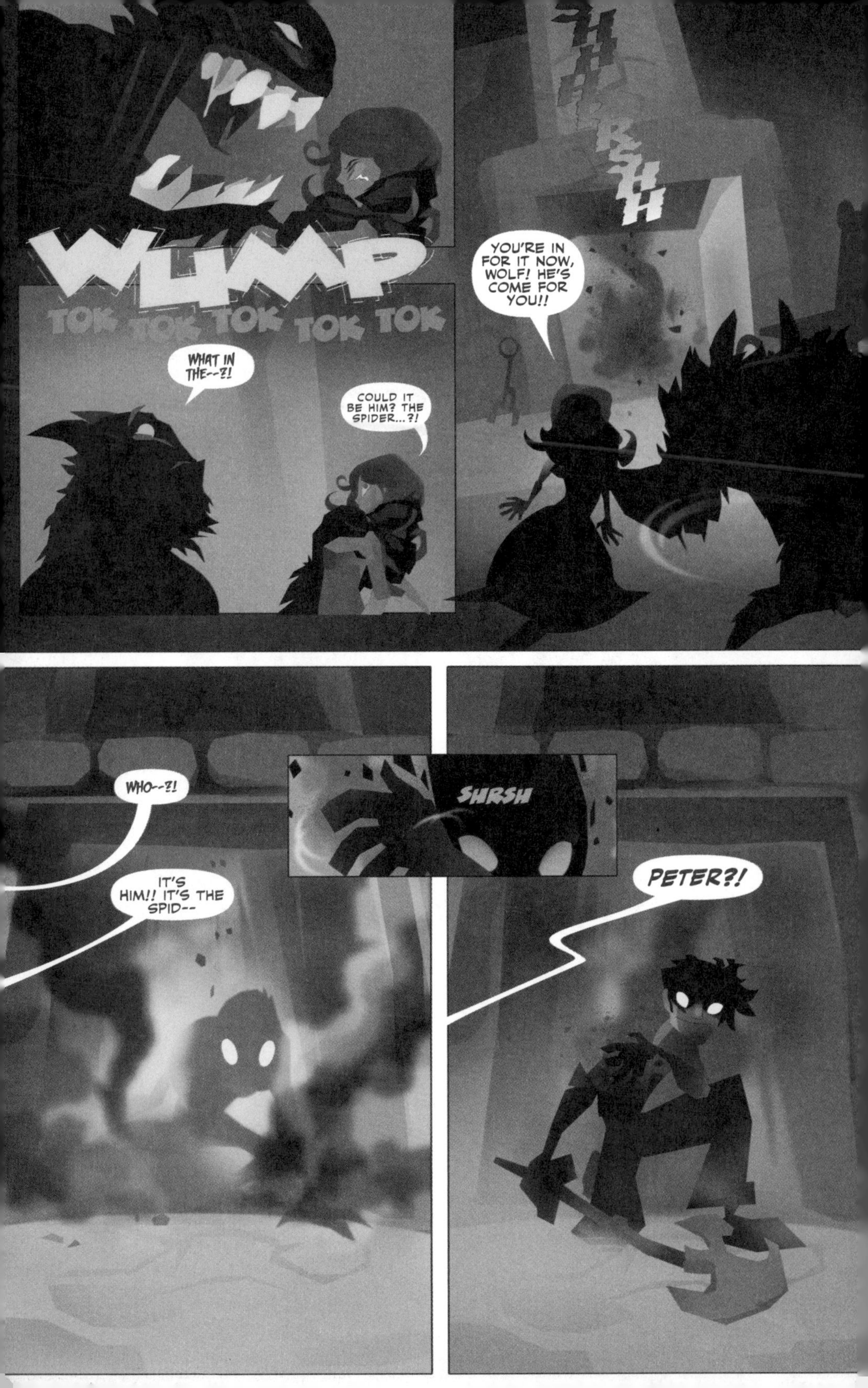
WUMP
TOK TOK TOK TOK TOK
SHHHHRSHH
WHAT IN THE--?!
COULD IT BE HIM? THE SPIDER...?!
YOU'RE IN FOR IT NOW, WOLF! HE'S COME FOR YOU!!
WHO--?!
IT'S HIM!! IT'S THE SPID--
SHRSH
PETER?!

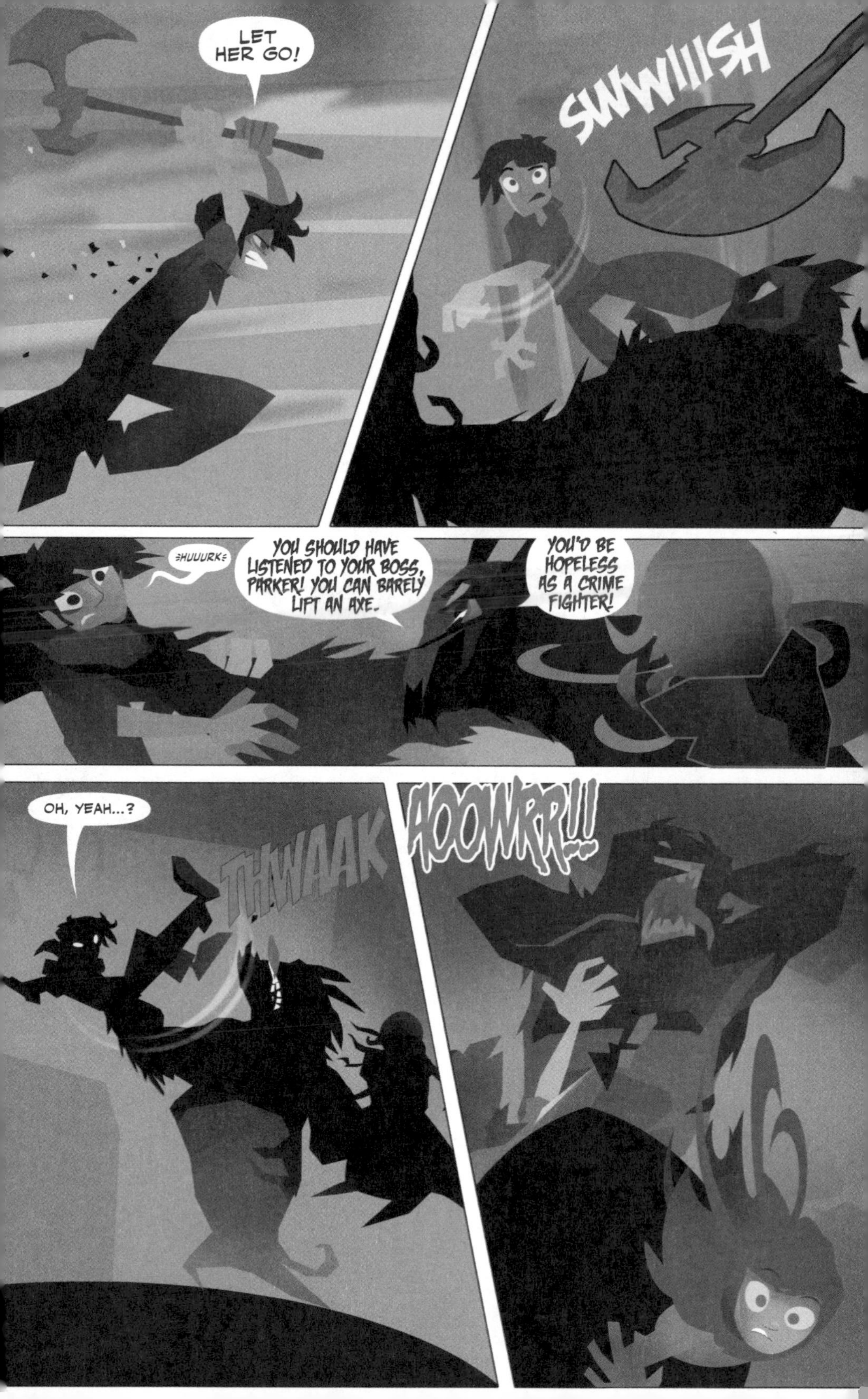
LET HER GO!
SWWIIISH
≈HUUURK≈
YOU SHOULD HAVE LISTENED TO YOUR BOSS, PARKER! YOU CAN BARELY LIFT AN AXE.
YOU'D BE HOPELESS AS A CRIME FIGHTER!
OH, YEAH...?
THWAAK
AOOWRR!!

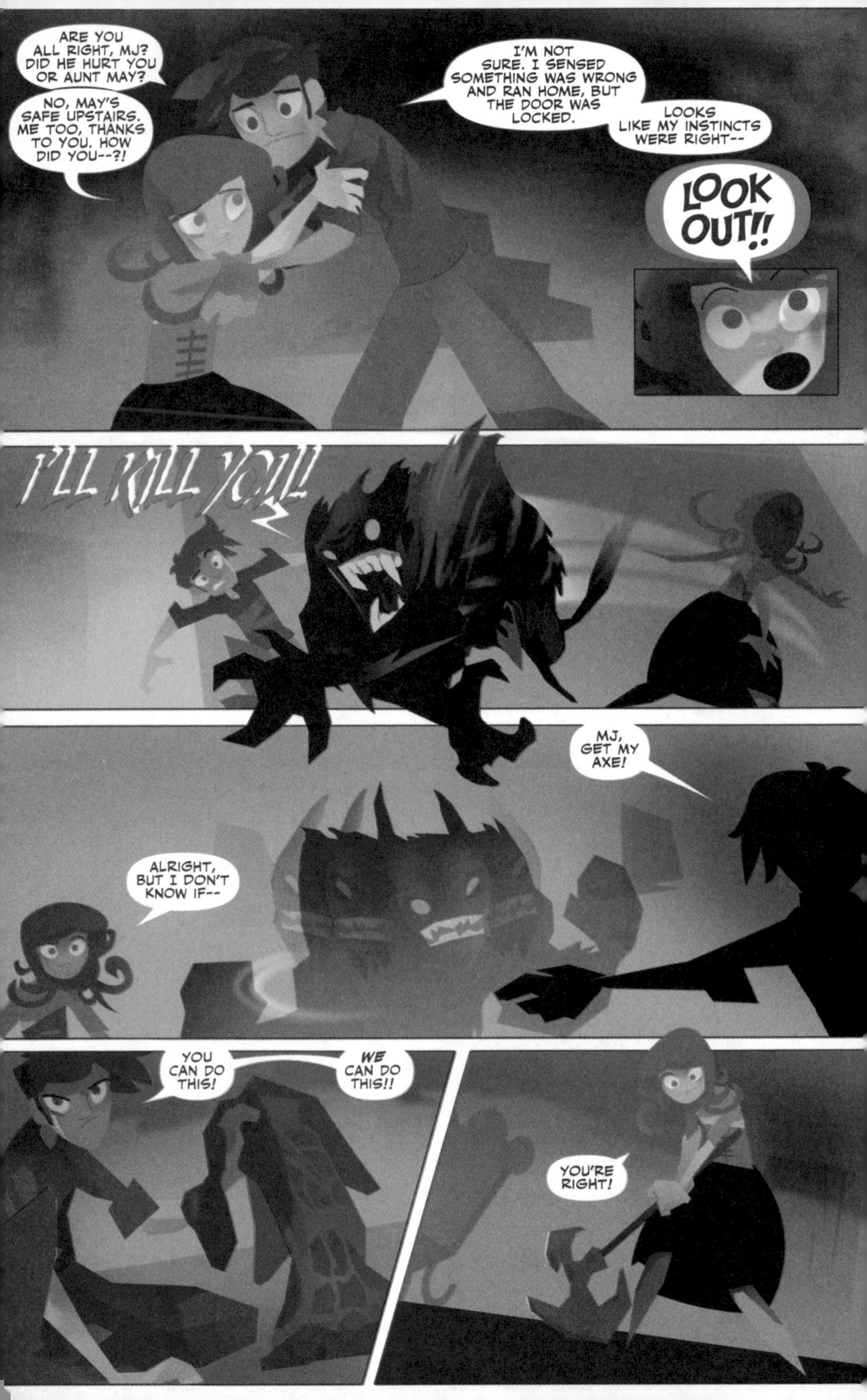
ARE YOU ALL RIGHT, MJ? DID HE HURT YOU OR AUNT MAY?
NO, MAY'S SAFE UPSTAIRS. ME TOO, THANKS TO YOU. HOW DID YOU--?!
I'M NOT SURE. I SENSED SOMETHING WAS WRONG AND RAN HOME, BUT THE DOOR WAS LOCKED.
LOOKS LIKE MY INSTINCTS WERE RIGHT--
LOOK OUT!!
I'LL KILL YOU!!
MJ, GET MY AXE!
ALRIGHT, BUT I DON'T KNOW IF--
YOU CAN DO THIS!
WE CAN DO THIS!!
YOU'RE RIGHT!

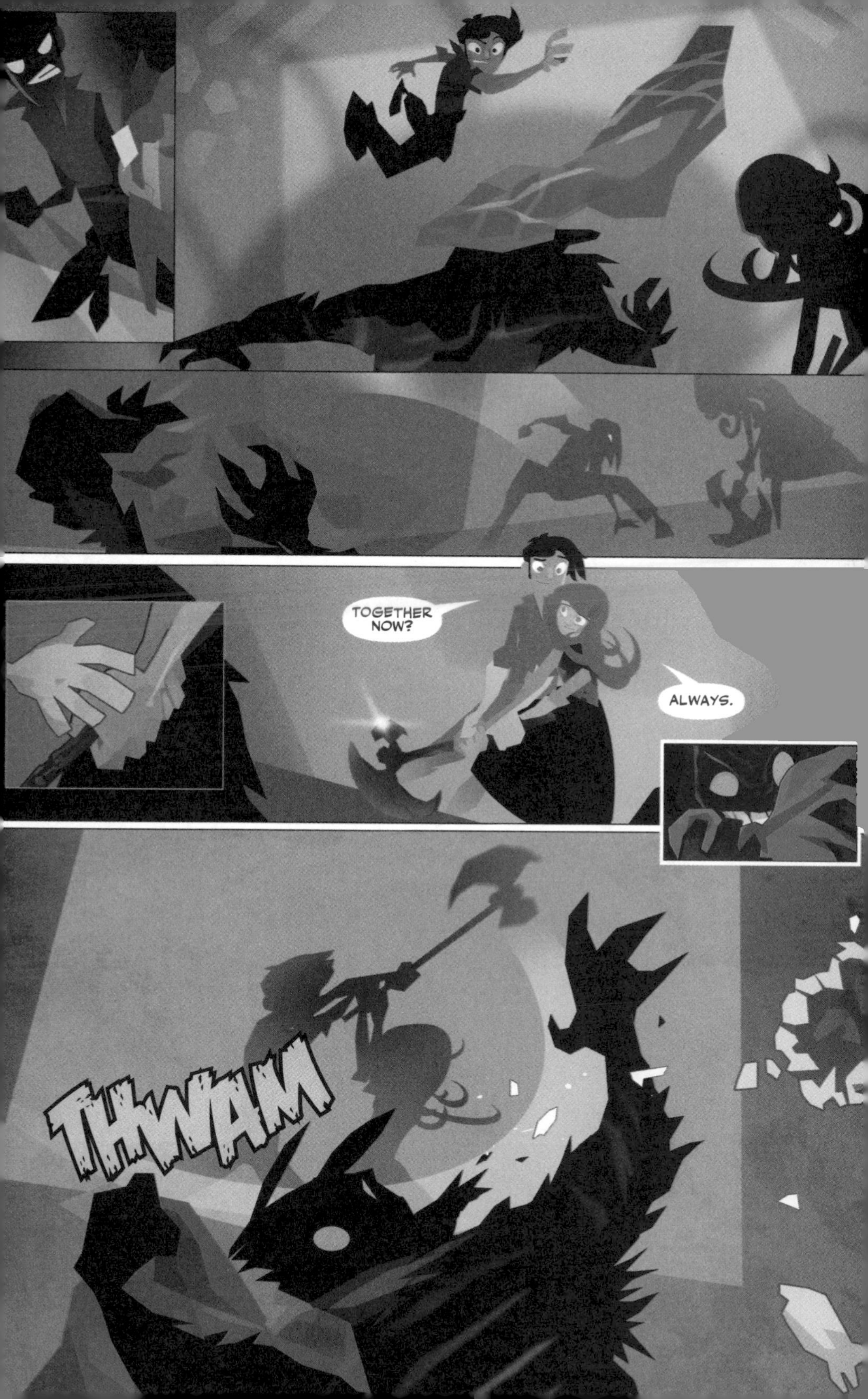
TOGETHER NOW?
ALWAYS.
THWAM

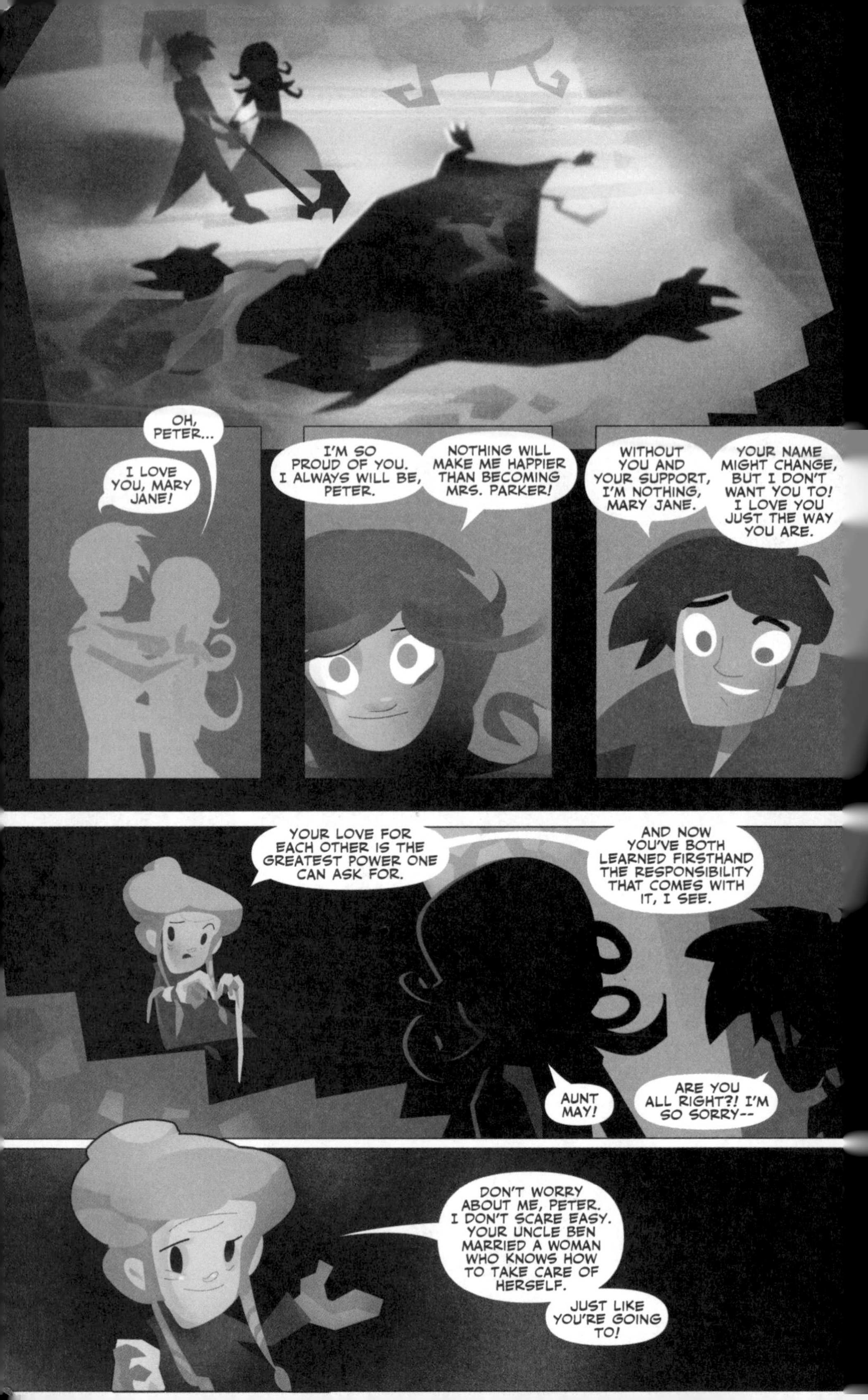
OH, PETER...
I LOVE YOU, MARY JANE!
I'M SO PROUD OF YOU. I ALWAYS WILL BE, PETER.
NOTHING WILL MAKE ME HAPPIER THAN BECOMING MRS. PARKER!
WITHOUT YOU AND YOUR SUPPORT, I'M NOTHING, MARY JANE.
YOUR NAME MIGHT CHANGE, BUT I DON'T WANT YOU TO! I LOVE YOU JUST THE WAY YOU ARE.
YOUR LOVE FOR EACH OTHER IS THE GREATEST POWER ONE CAN ASK FOR.
AND NOW YOU'VE BOTH LEARNED FIRSTHAND THE RESPONSIBILITY THAT COMES WITH IT, I SEE.
AUNT MAY!
ARE YOU ALL RIGHT?! I'M SO SORRY--
DON'T WORRY ABOUT ME, PETER. I DON'T SCARE EASY. YOUR UNCLE BEN MARRIED A WOMAN WHO KNOWS HOW TO TAKE CARE OF HERSELF.
JUST LIKE YOU'RE GOING TO!

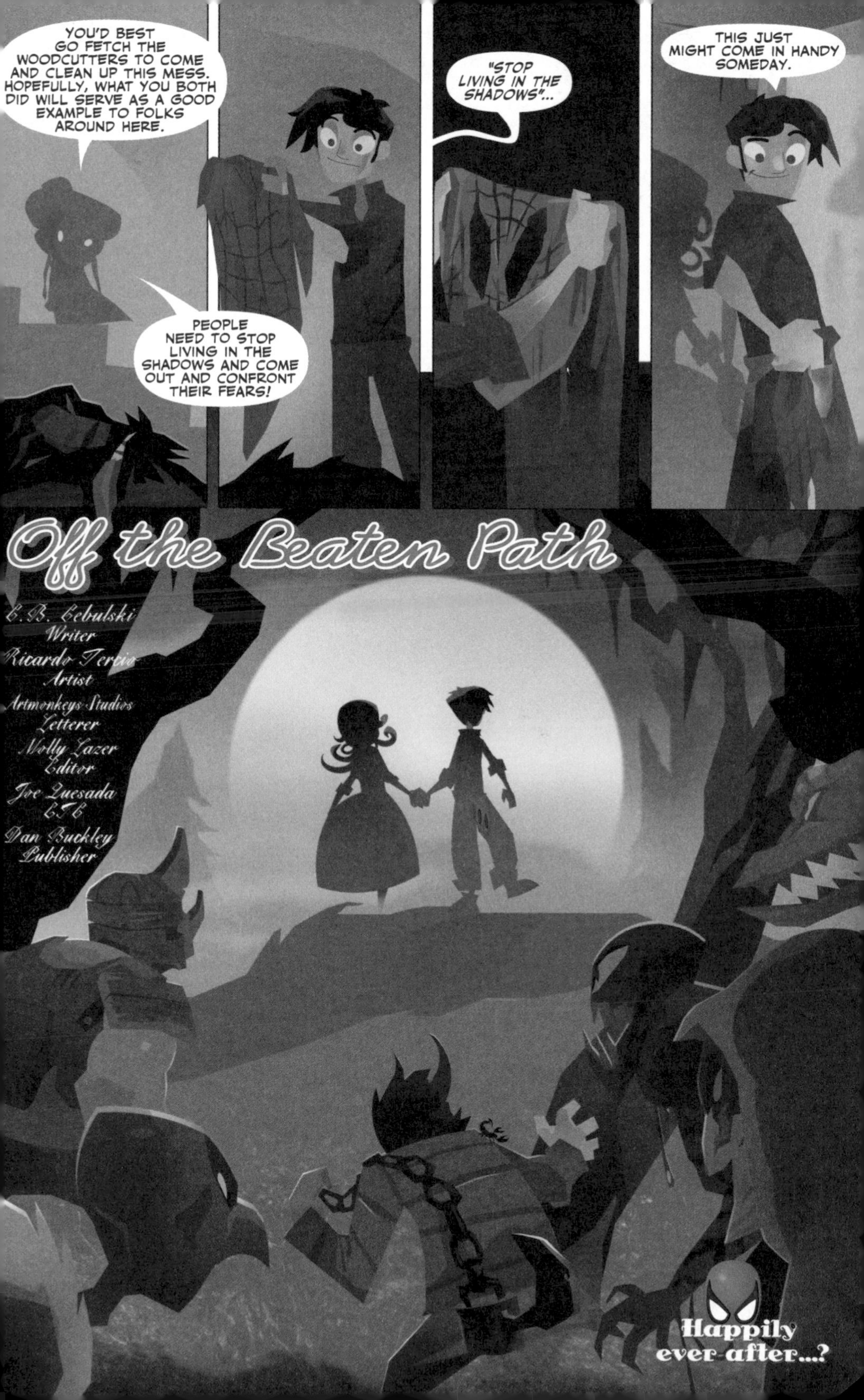
YOU'D BEST GO FETCH THE WOODCUTTERS TO COME AND CLEAN UP THIS MESS. HOPEFULLY, WHAT YOU BOTH DID WILL SERVE AS A GOOD EXAMPLE TO FOLKS AROUND HERE.
PEOPLE NEED TO STOP LIVING IN THE SHADOWS AND COME OUT AND CONFRONT THEIR FEARS!
"STOP LIVING IN THE SHADOWS"...
THIS JUST MIGHT COME IN HANDY SOMEDAY.
Off the Beaten Path
C.B. Cebulski Writer
Ricardo Tercio Artist
Artmonkeys Studios Letterer
Molly Lazer Editor
Joe Quesada EIC
Dan Buckley Publisher
Happily ever-after...?

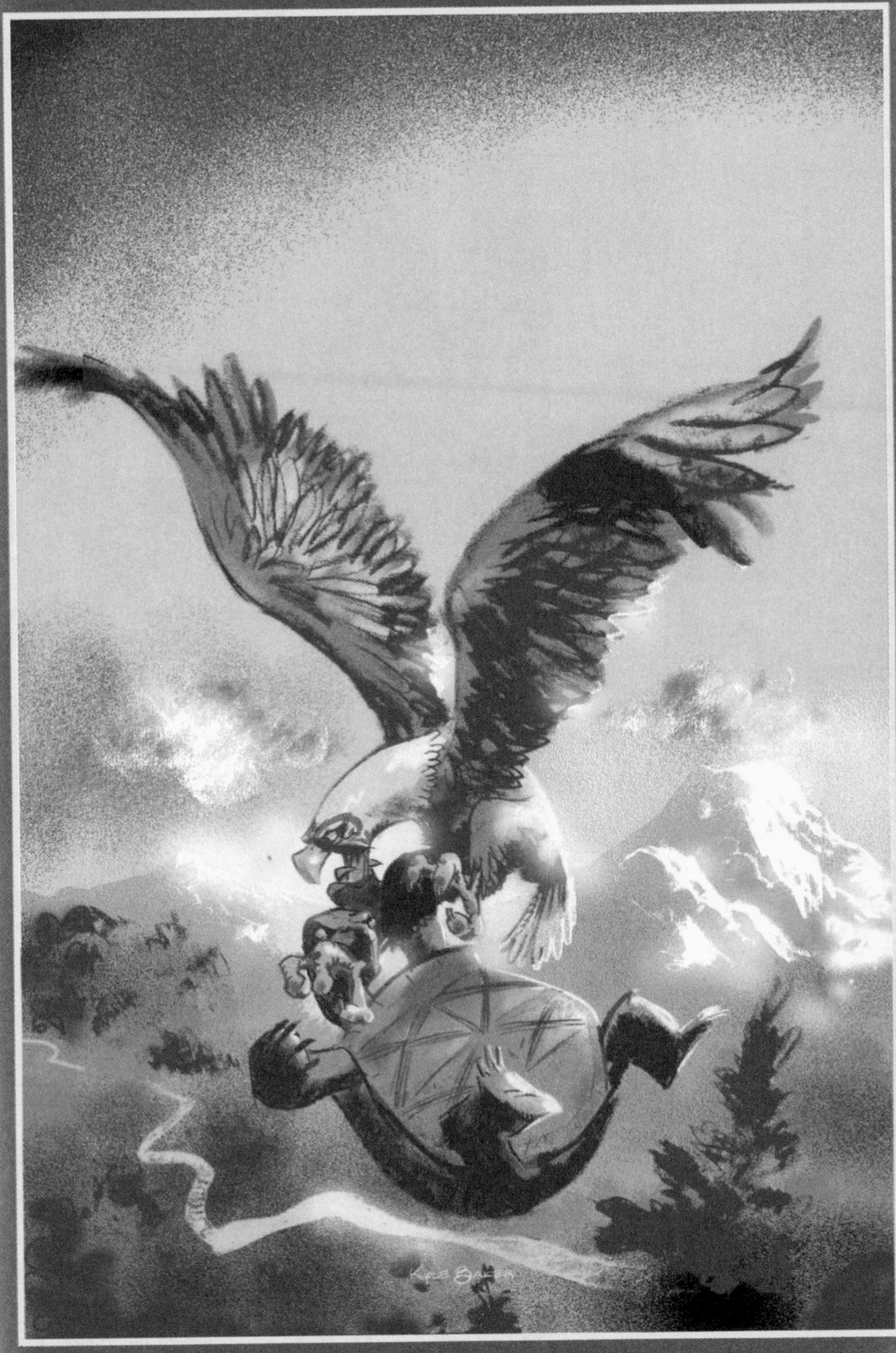

# C.B. CEBULSKI & KYLE BAKER

Dave Sharpe letters Mark Paniccia consulting editor
Nathan Cosby with MacKenzie Cadenhead editors
Joe Quesada editor in chief Dan Buckley publisher

Inspired by the African fairy tale, ***"The Friendship of the Tortoise and the Eagle"***

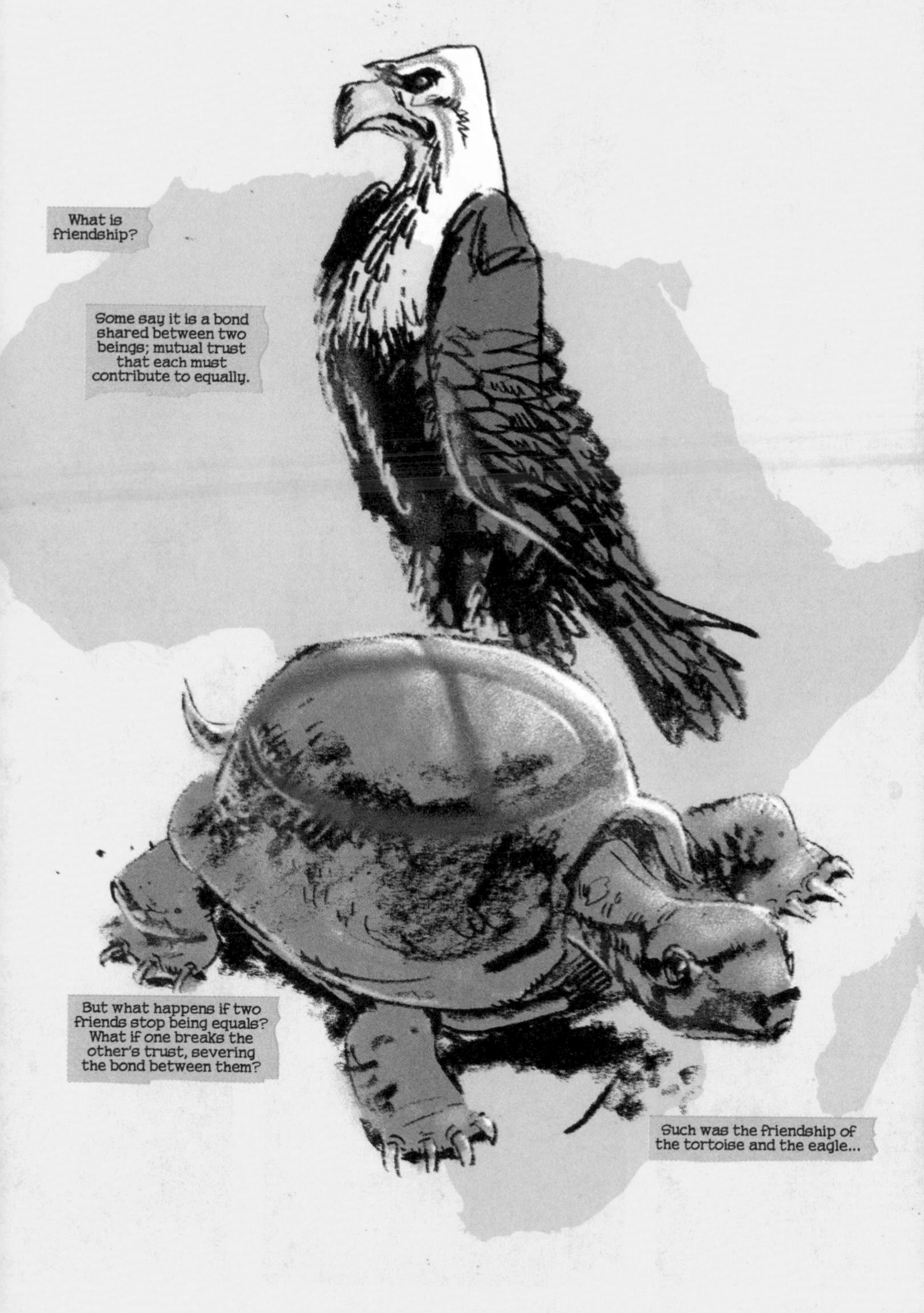
What is friendship?
Some say it is a bond shared between two beings; mutual trust that each must contribute to equally.
But what happens if two friends stop being equals? What if one breaks the other's trust, severing the bond between them?
Such was the friendship of the tortoise and the eagle...

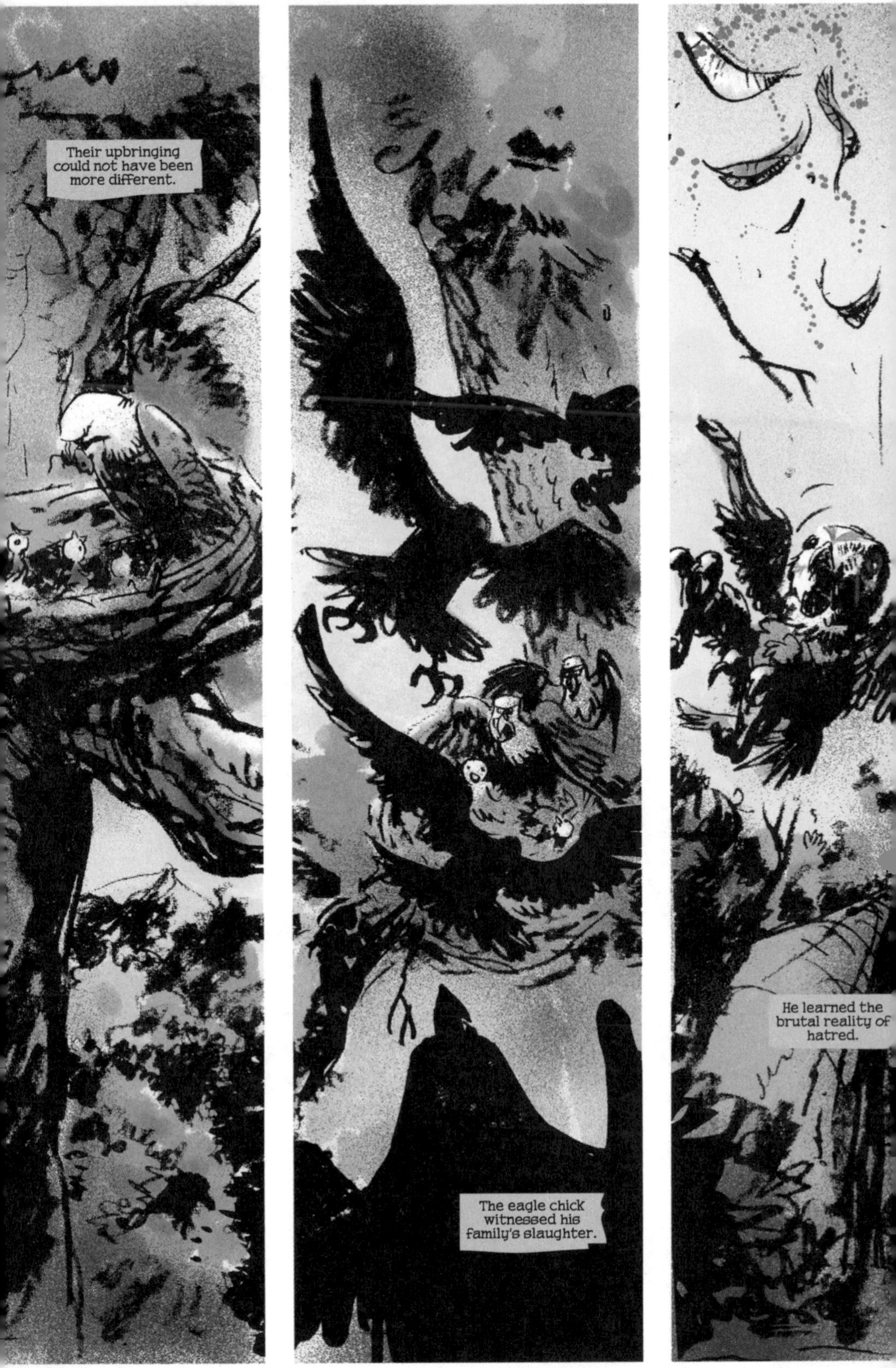
Their upbringing could not have been more different.
The eagle chick witnessed his family's slaughter.
He learned the brutal reality of hatred.

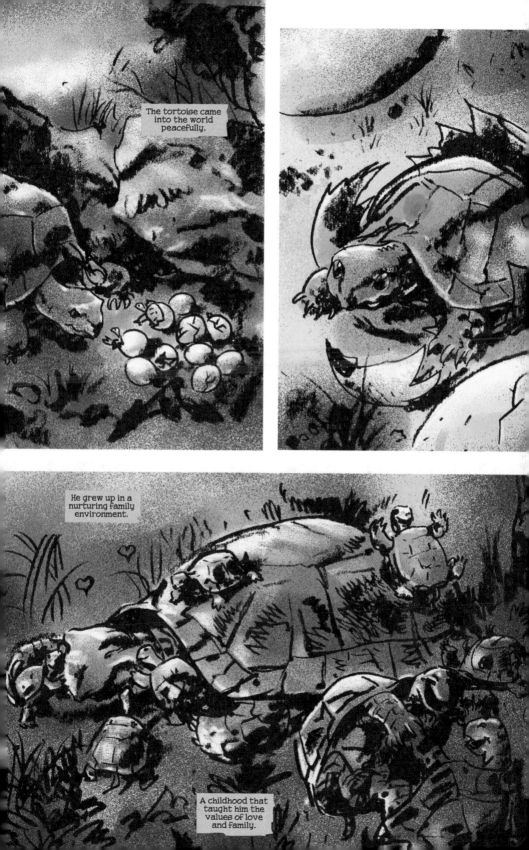

The tortoise came into the world peacefully.

He grew up in a nurturing family environment.

A childhood that taught him the values of love and family.

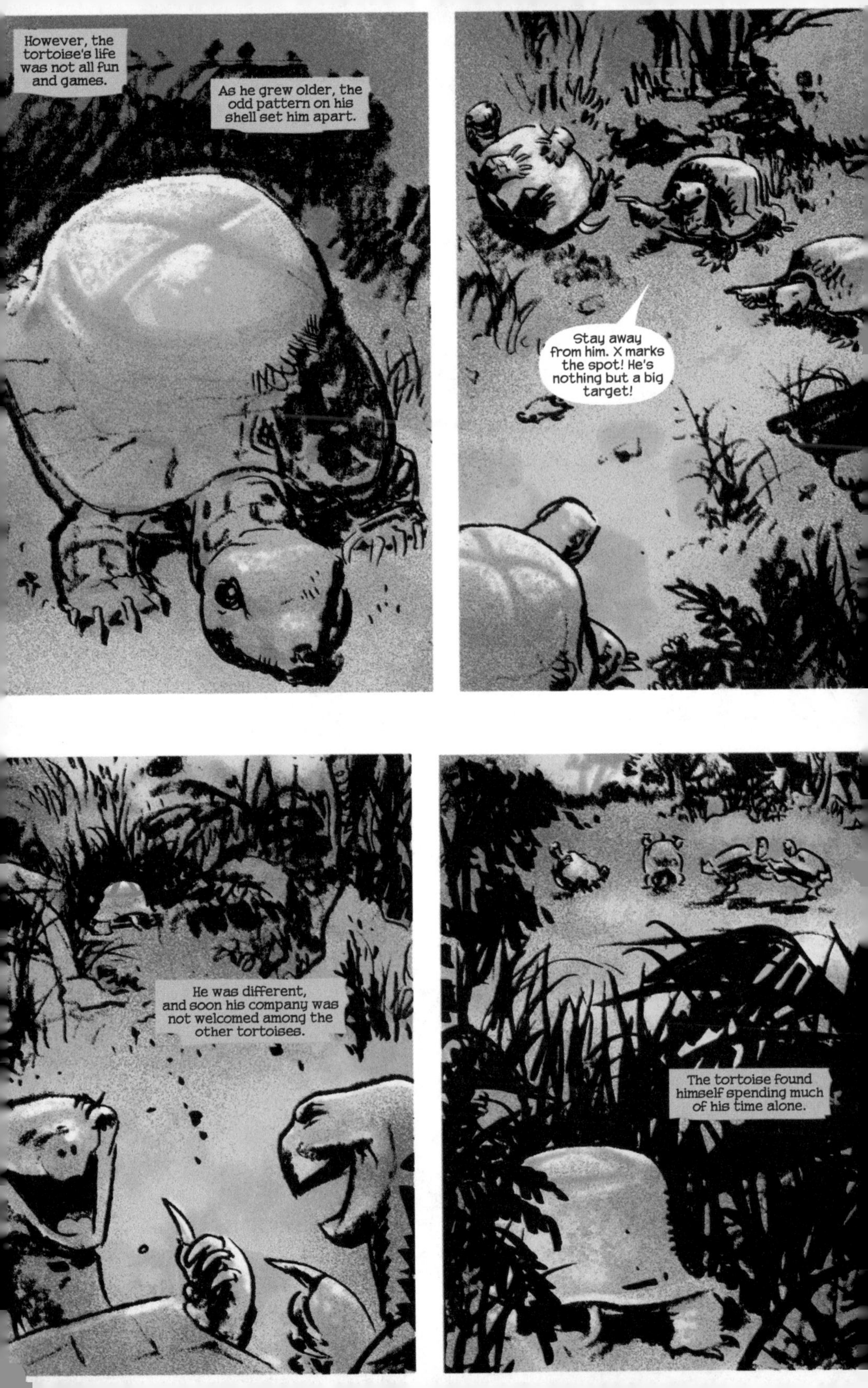
However, the tortoise's life was not all fun and games.
As he grew older, the odd pattern on his shell set him apart.
Stay away from him. X marks the spot! He's nothing but a big target!
He was different, and soon his company was not welcomed among the other tortoises.
The tortoise found himself spending much of his time alone.

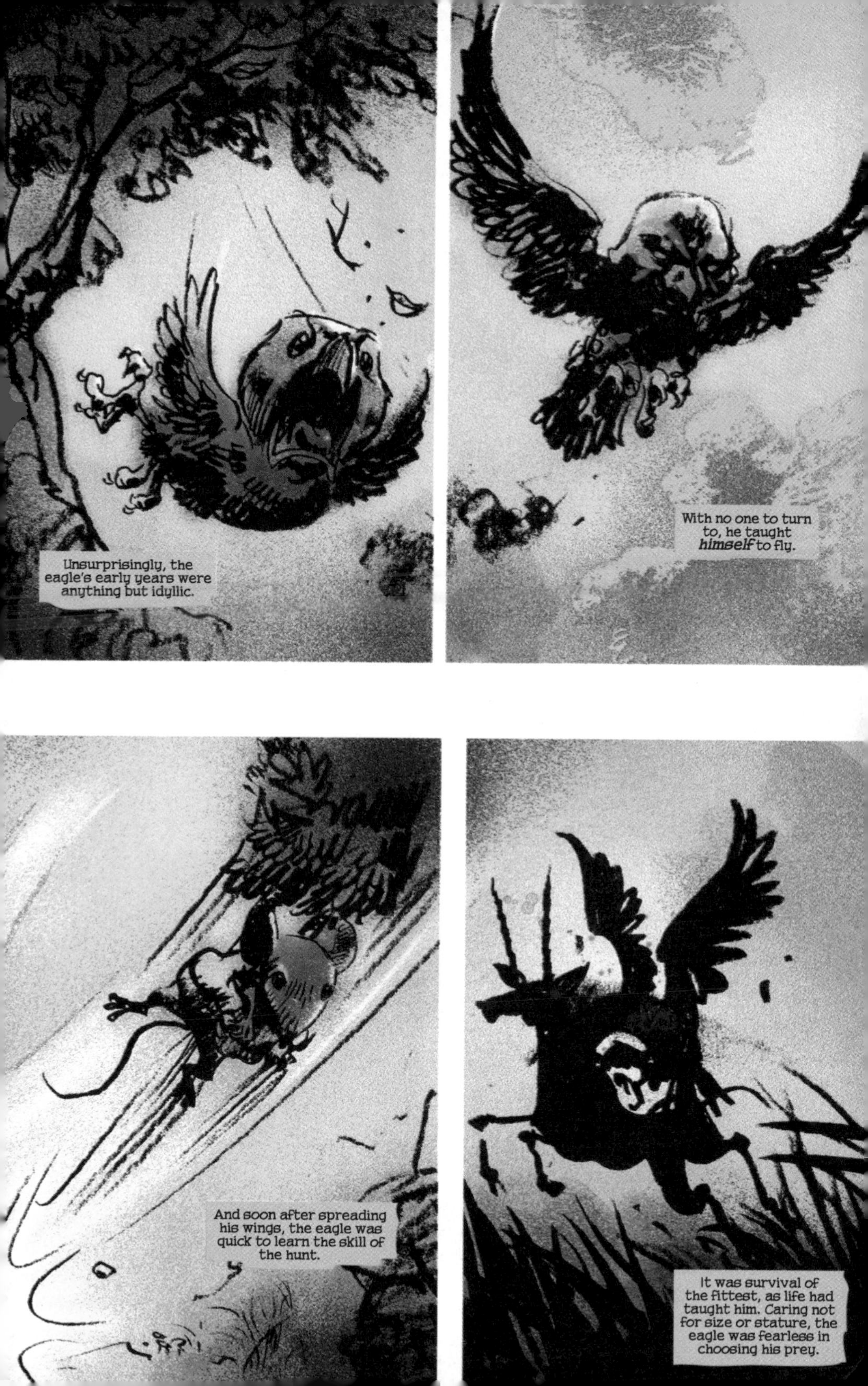
Unsurprisingly, the eagle's early years were anything but idyllic.
With no one to turn to, he taught *himself* to fly.
And soon after spreading his wings, the eagle was quick to learn the skill of the hunt.
It was survival of the fittest, as life had taught him. Caring not for size or stature, the eagle was fearless in choosing his prey.

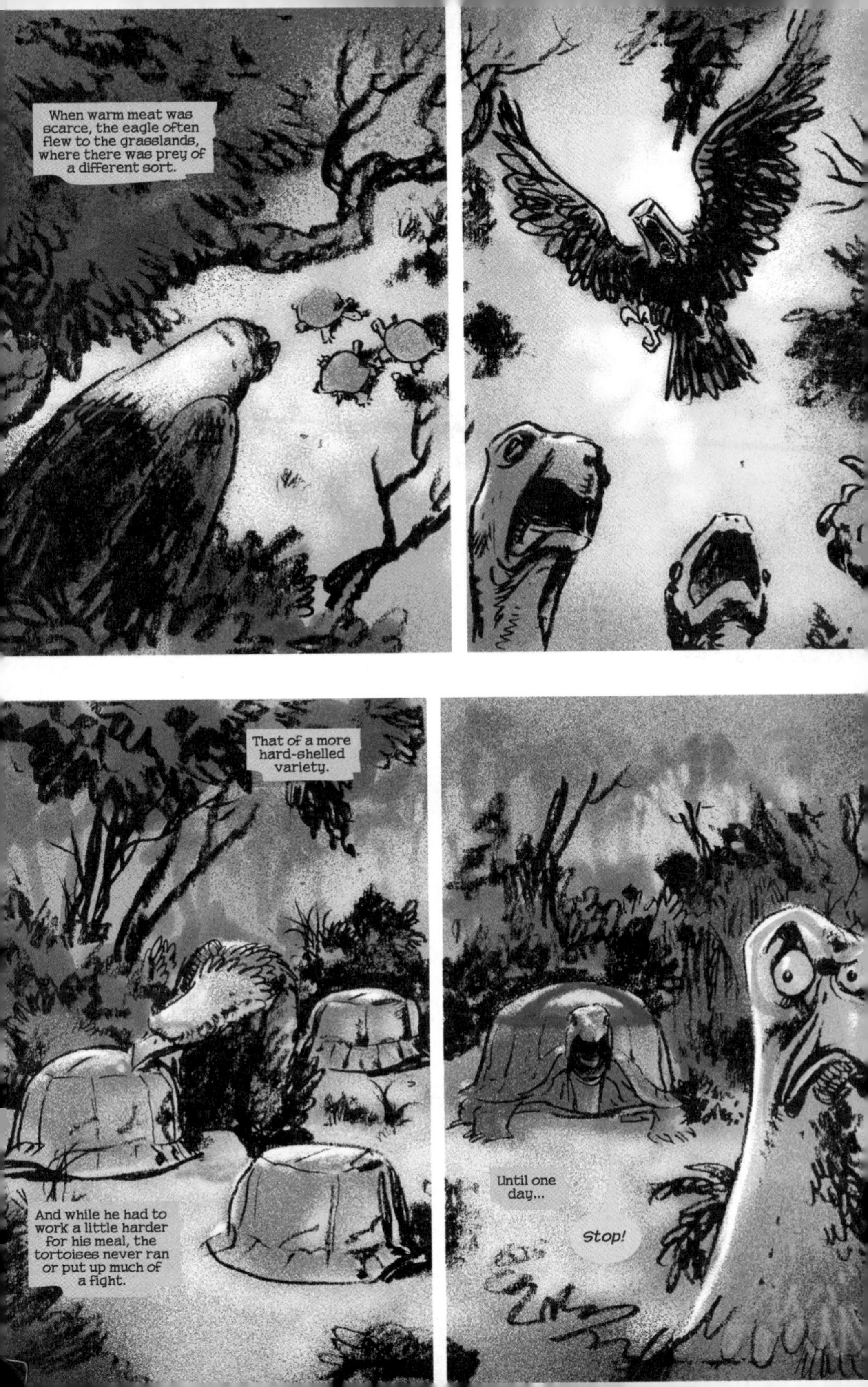
When warm meat was scarce, the eagle often flew to the grasslands, where there was prey of a different sort.
That of a more hard-shelled variety.
And while he had to work a little harder for his meal, the tortoises never ran or put up much of a fight.
Until one day...
Stop!

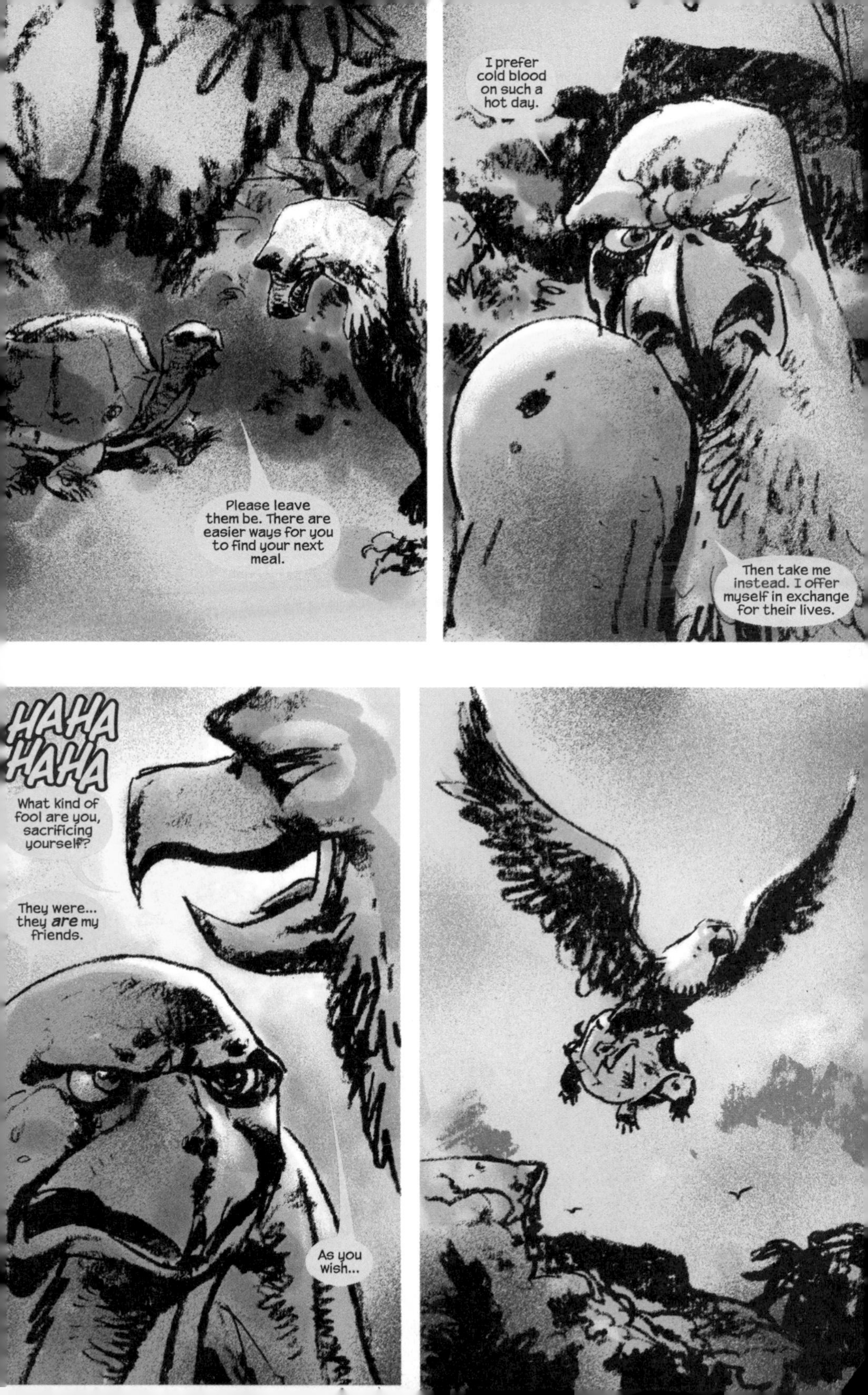
Please leave them be. There are easier ways for you to find your next meal.
I prefer cold blood on such a hot day.
Then take me instead. I offer myself in exchange for their lives.
HAHA HAHA
What kind of fool are you, sacrificing yourself?
They were... they *are* my friends.
As you wish...

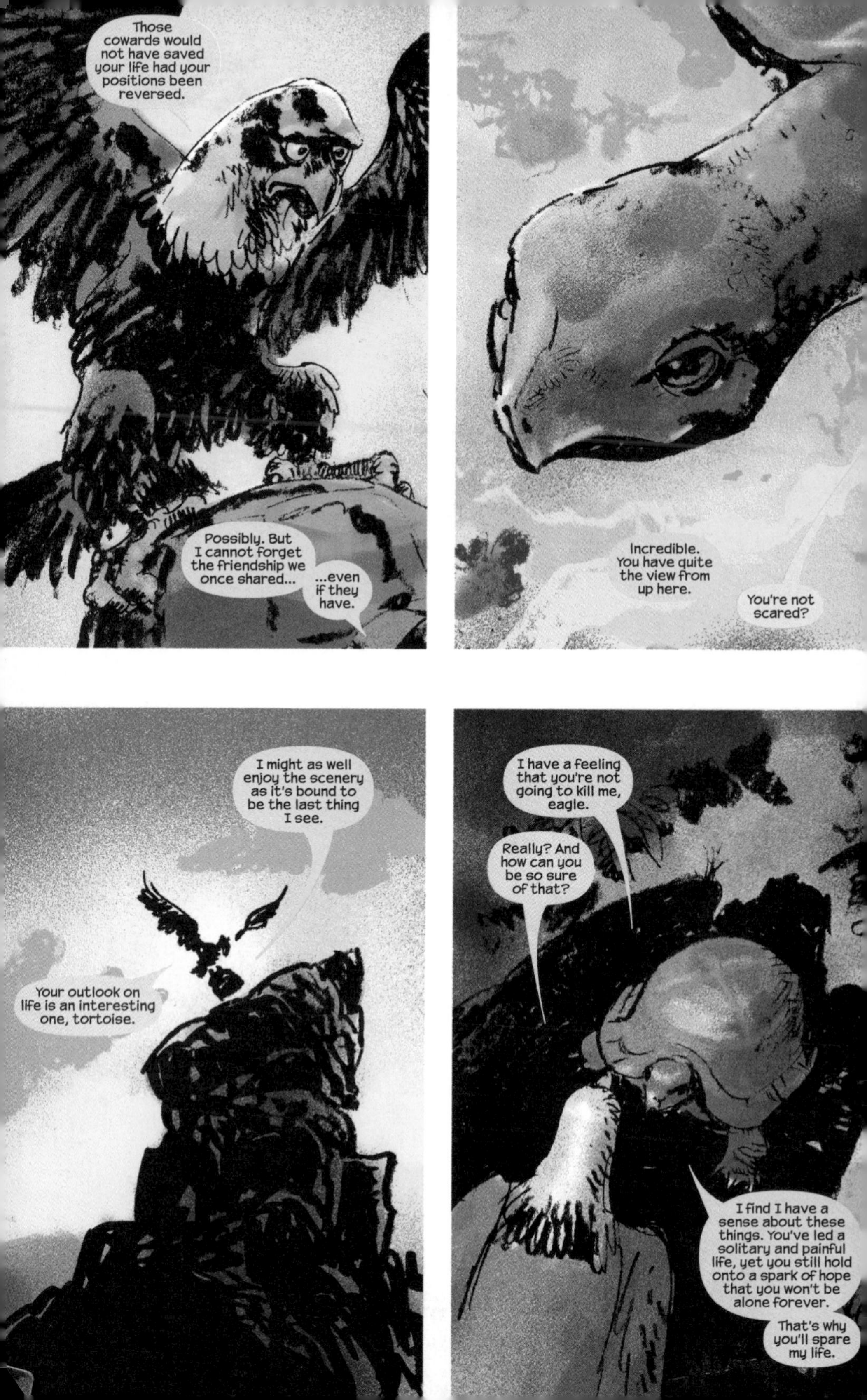

Those cowards would not have saved your life had your positions been reversed.
Possibly. But I cannot forget the friendship we once shared...
...even if they have.
Incredible. You have quite the view from up here.
You're not scared?
I might as well enjoy the scenery as it's bound to be the last thing I see.
Your outlook on life is an interesting one, tortoise.
I have a feeling that you're not going to kill me, eagle.
Really? And how can you be so sure of that?
I find I have a sense about these things. You've led a solitary and painful life, yet you still hold onto a spark of hope that you won't be alone forever.
That's why you'll spare my life.

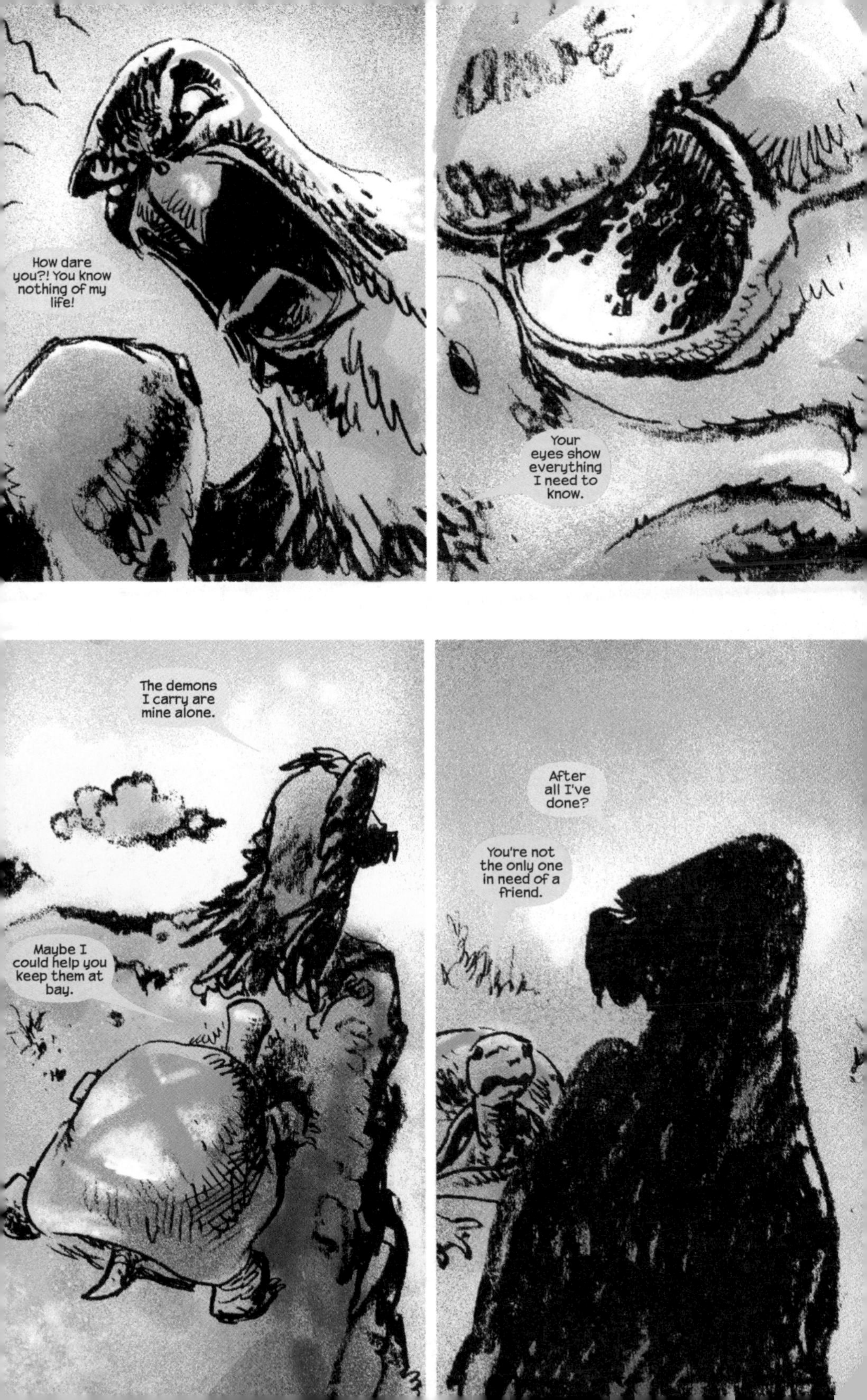
How dare you?! You know nothing of my life!
Your eyes show everything I need to know.
The demons I carry are mine alone.
Maybe I could help you keep them at bay.
After all I've done?
You're not the only one in need of a friend.

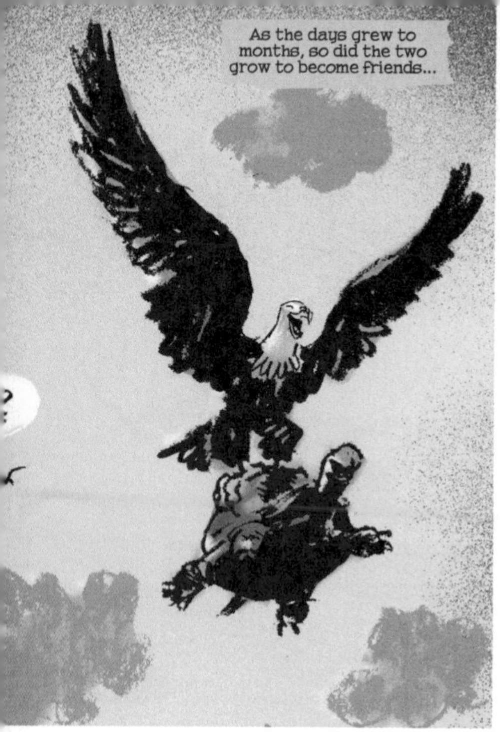
As the days grew to months, so did the two grow to become friends...

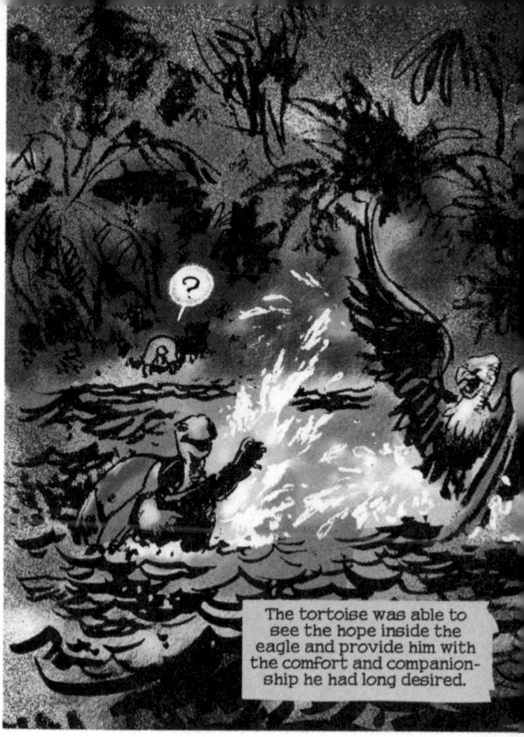
?
The tortoise was able to see the hope inside the eagle and provide him with the comfort and companionship he had long desired.

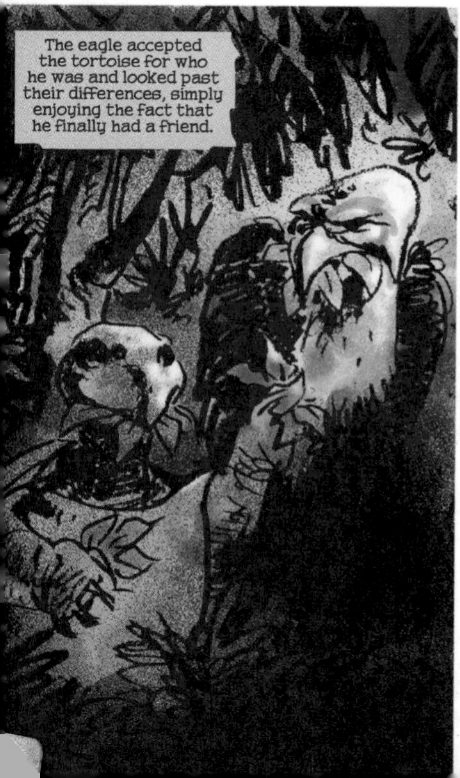
The eagle accepted the tortoise for who he was and looked past their differences, simply enjoying the fact that he finally had a friend.

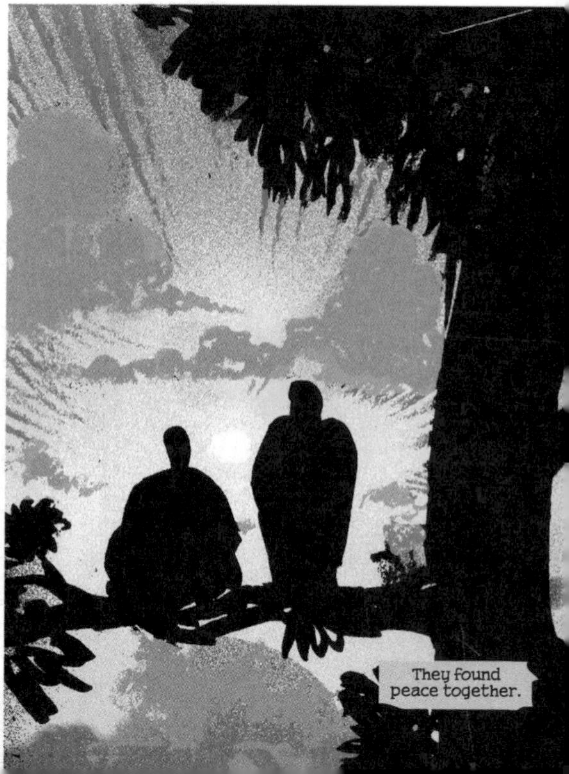
They found peace together.

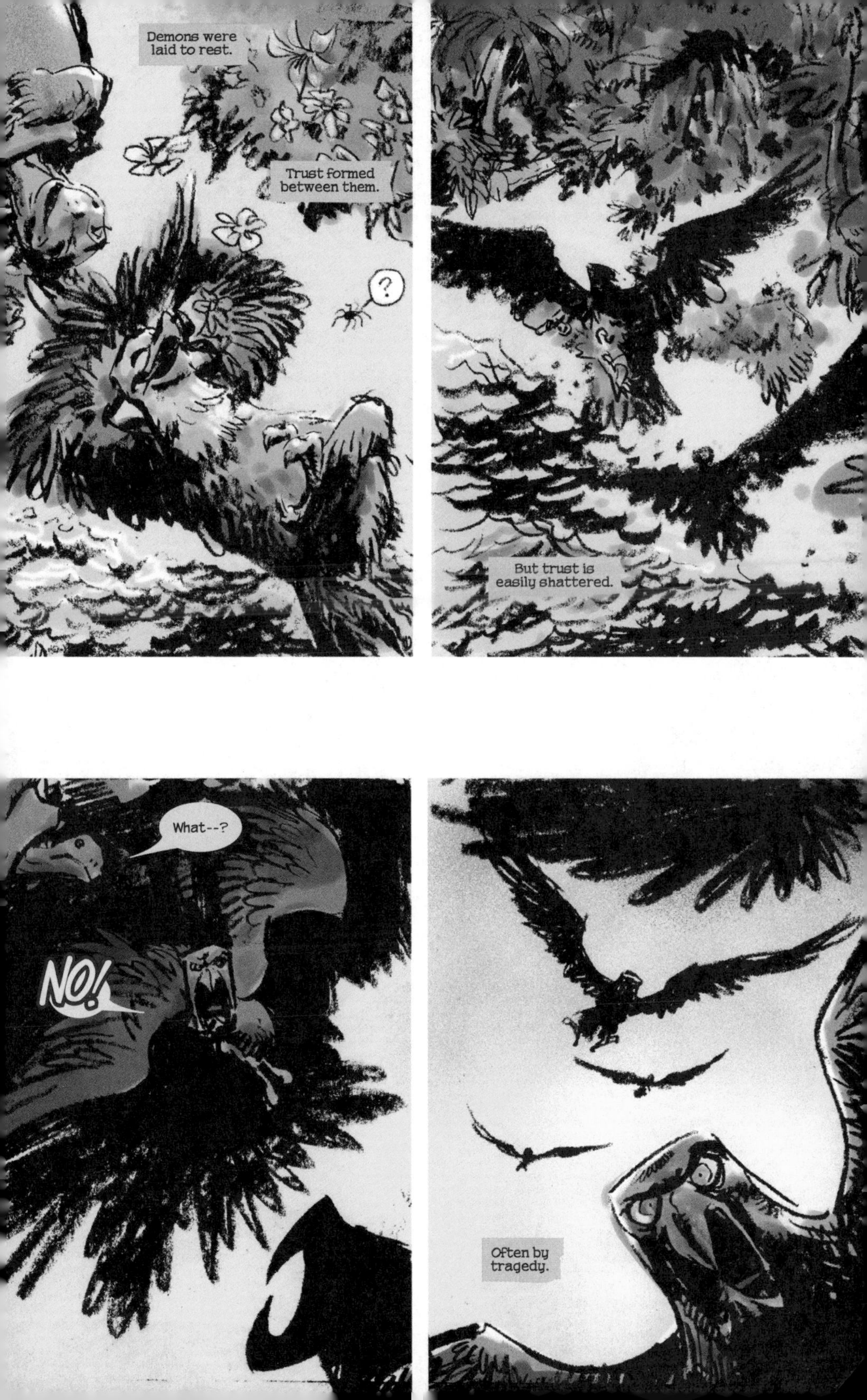
Demons were laid to rest.
Trust formed between them.
?
But trust is easily shattered.
What--?
NO!
Often by tragedy.

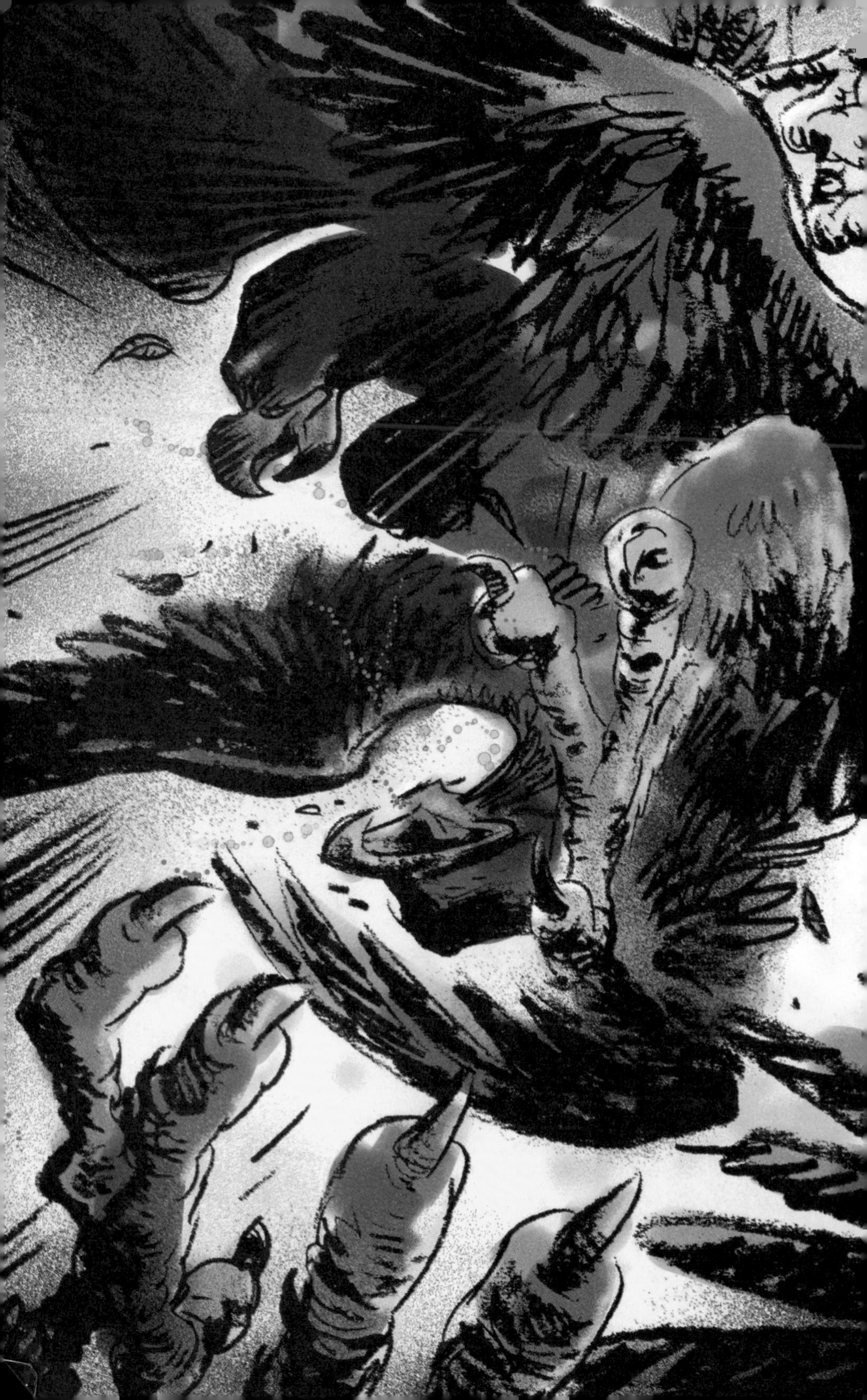

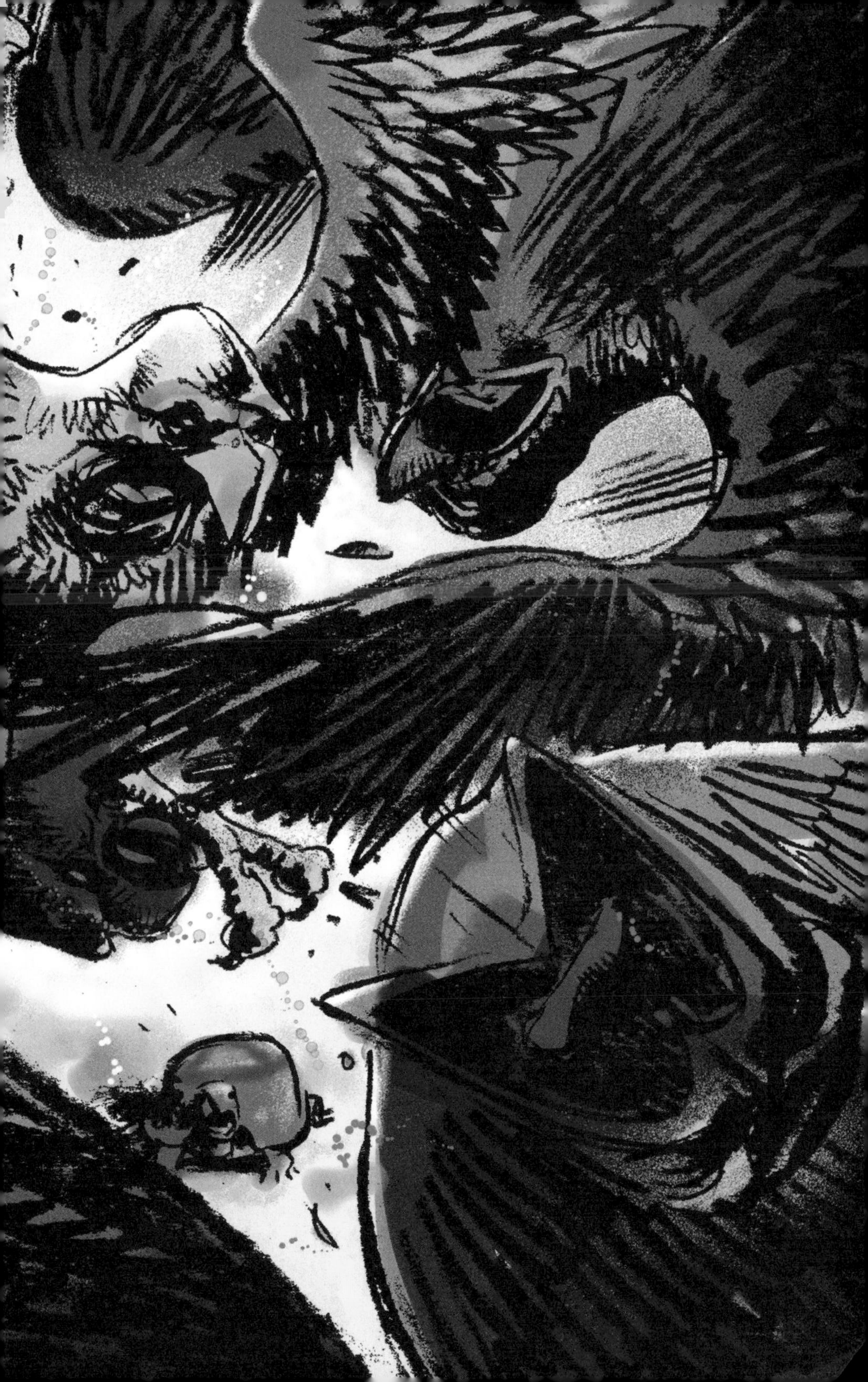

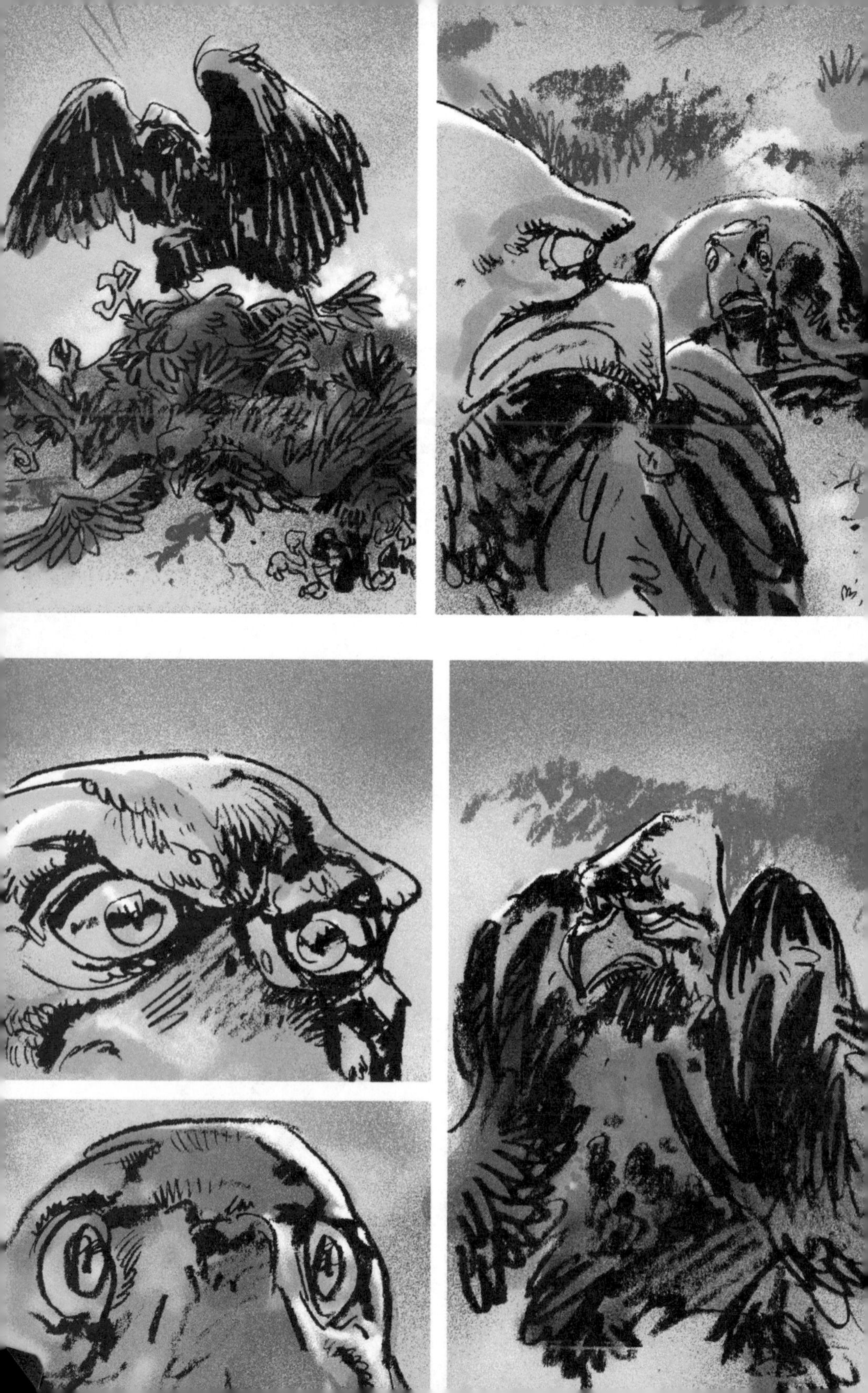

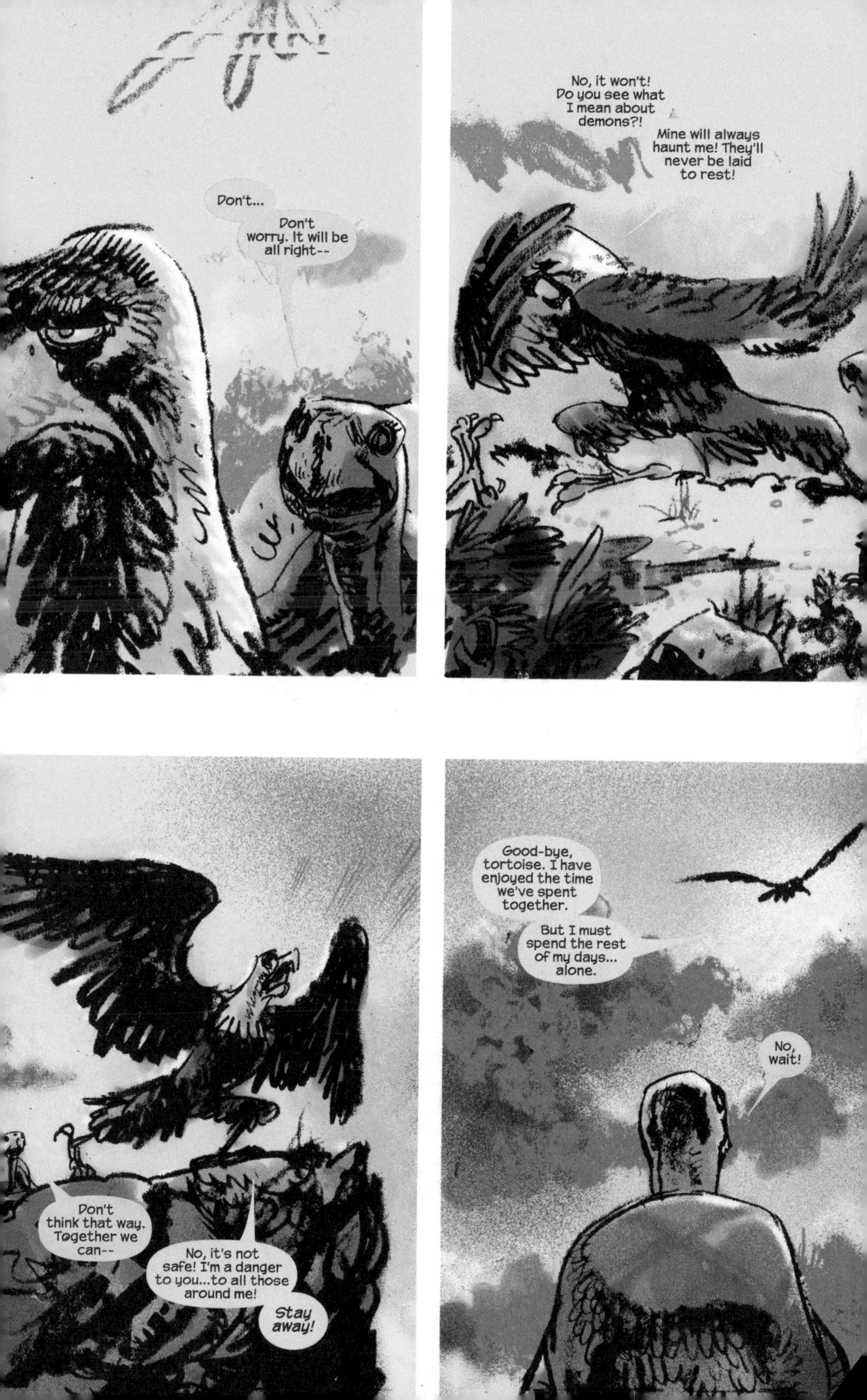
Don't...
Don't worry. It will be all right--
No, it won't! Do you see what I mean about demons?!
Mine will always haunt me! They'll never be laid to rest!
Don't think that way. Together we can--
No, it's not safe! I'm a danger to you...to all those around me!
Stay away!
Good-bye, tortoise. I have enjoyed the time we've spent together.
But I must spend the rest of my days... alone.
No, wait!

Despite the eagle's actions and warnings, the tortoise refused to give up on his friend.

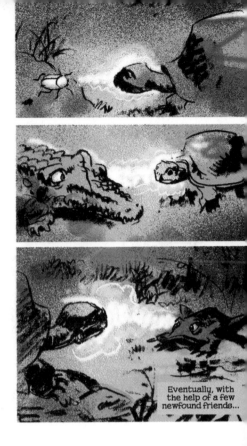

Eventually, with the help of a few newfound friends...

...the tortoise was able to locate the eagle's lair.

A fact that did not escape the notice...

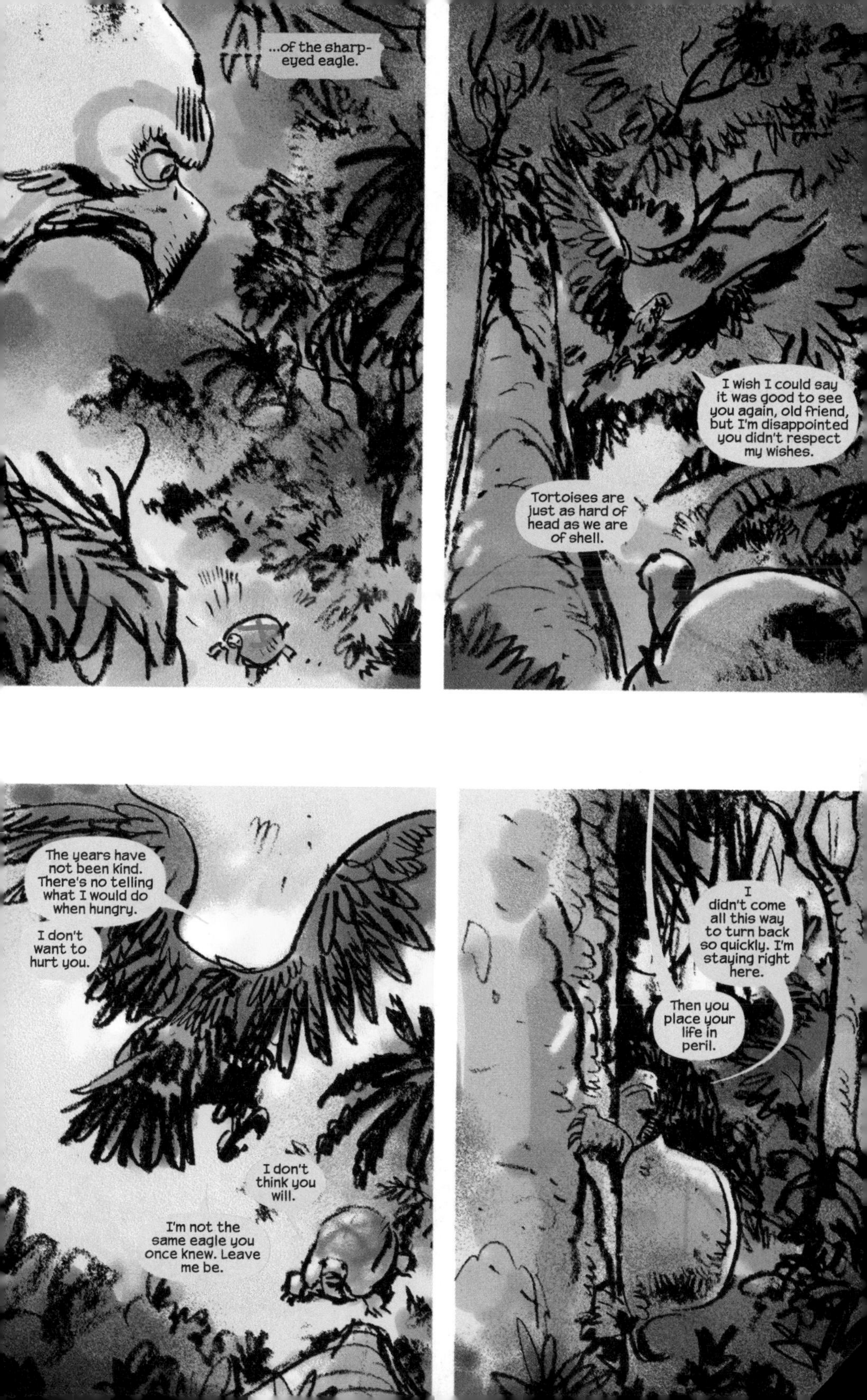
...of the sharp-eyed eagle.
I wish I could say it was good to see you again, old friend, but I'm disappointed you didn't respect my wishes.
Tortoises are just as hard of head as we are of shell.
The years have not been kind. There's no telling what I would do when hungry.
I don't want to hurt you.
I don't think you will.
I'm not the same eagle you once knew. Leave me be.
I didn't come all this way to turn back so quickly. I'm staying right here.
Then you place your life in peril.

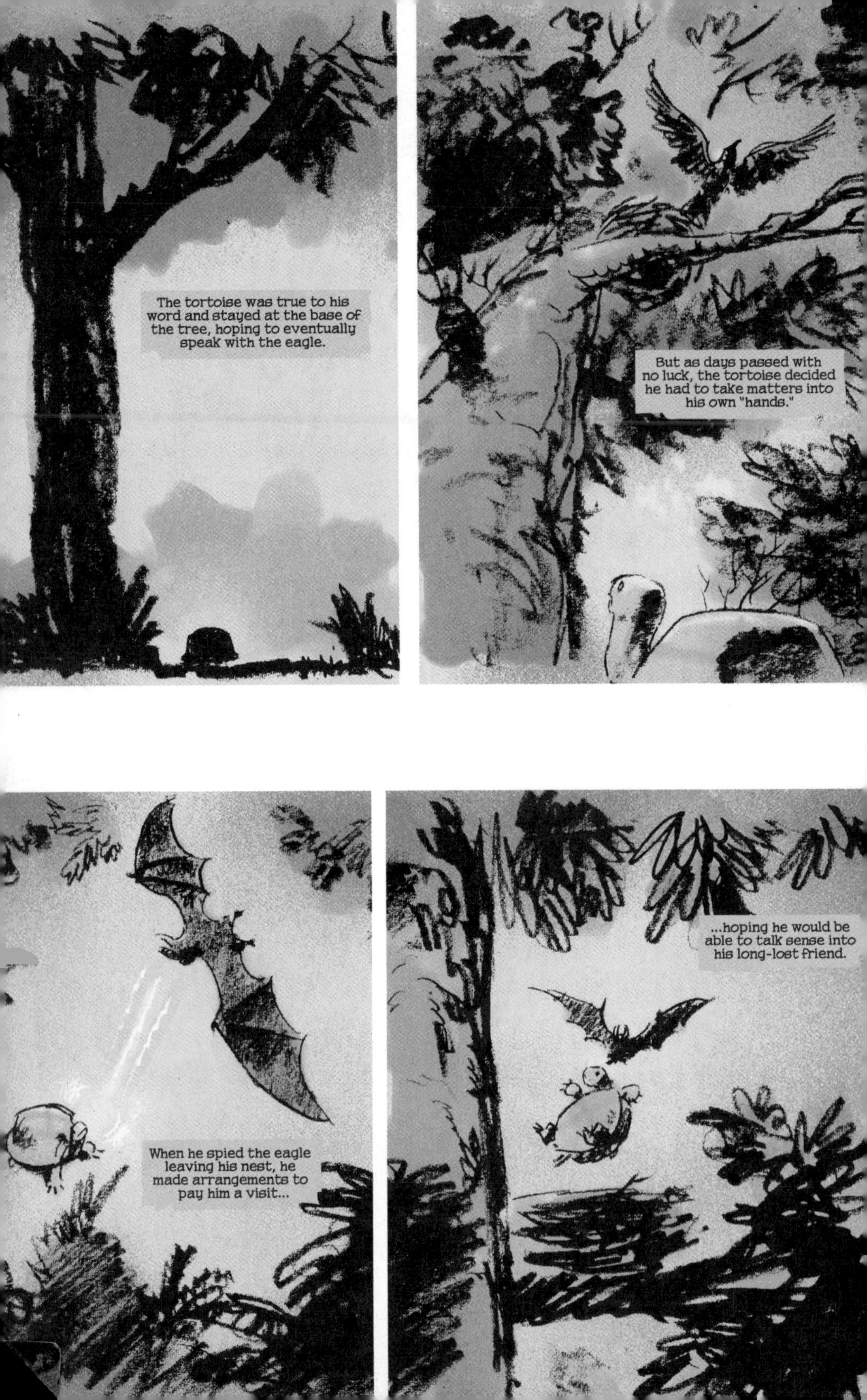
The tortoise was true to his word and stayed at the base of the tree, hoping to eventually speak with the eagle.
But as days passed with no luck, the tortoise decided he had to take matters into his own "hands."
When he spied the eagle leaving his nest, he made arrangements to pay him a visit...
...hoping he would be able to talk sense into his long-lost friend.

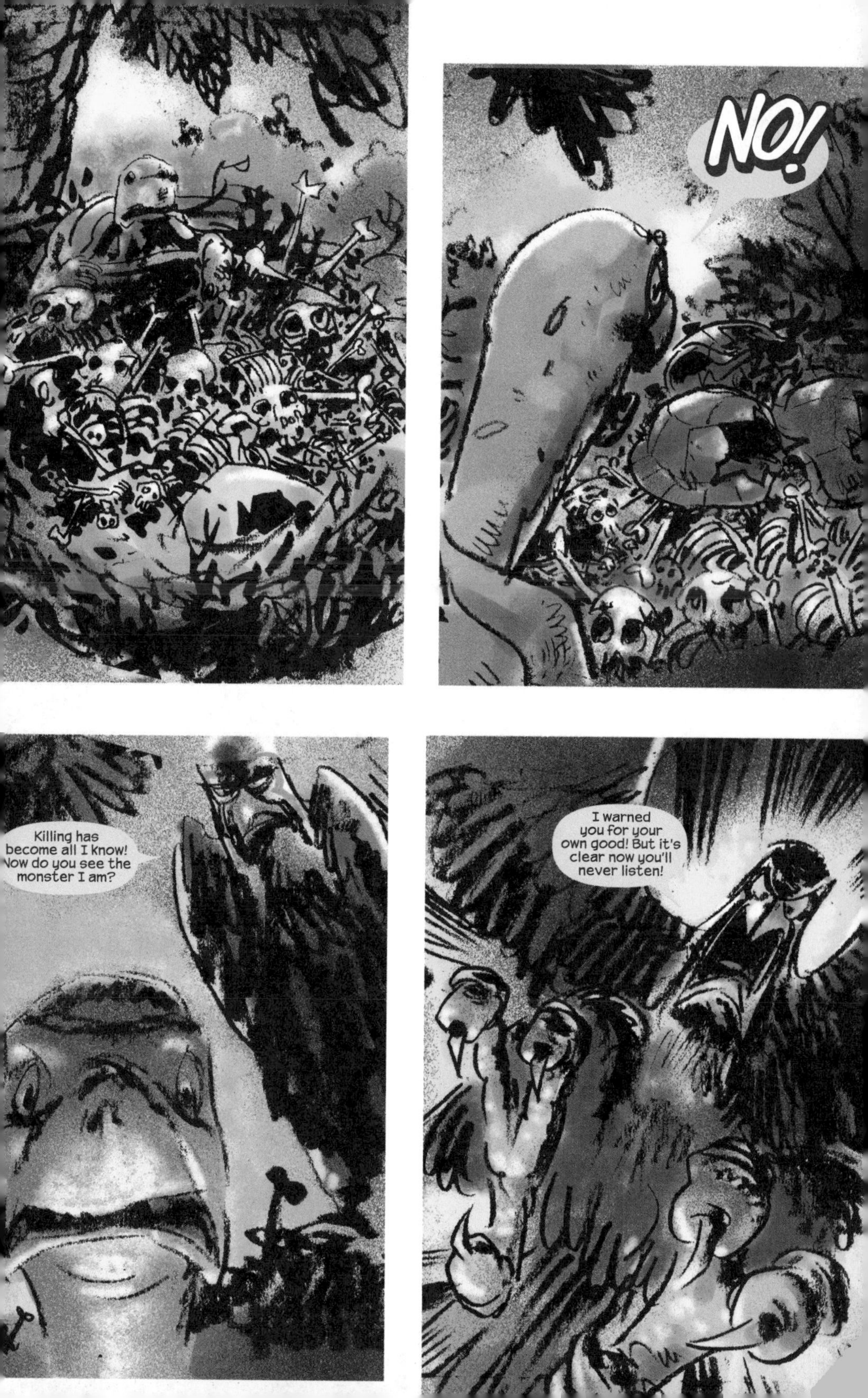
NO!
Killing has become all I know! Now do you see the monster I am?
I warned you for your own good! But it's clear now you'll never listen!

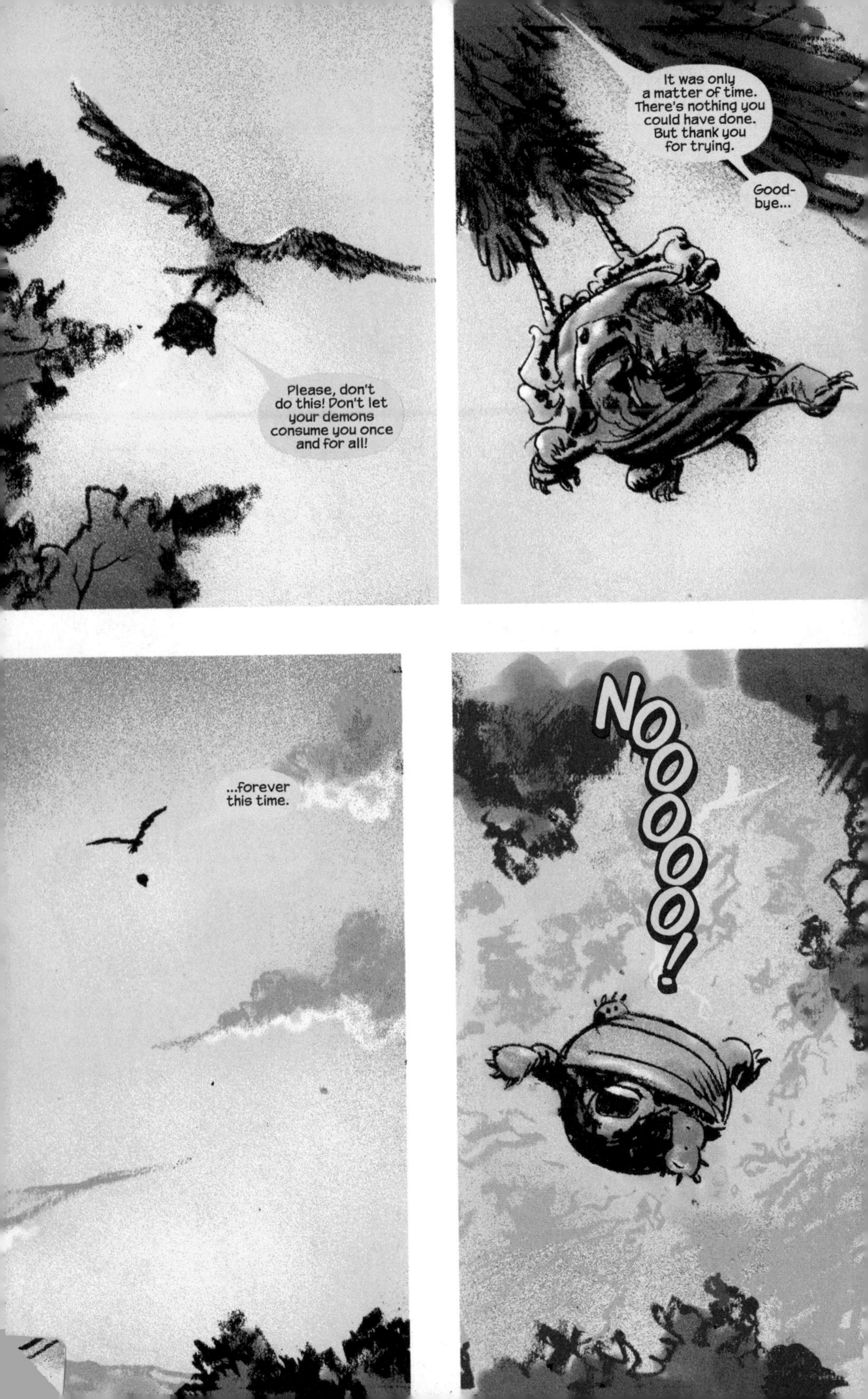
Please, don't do this! Don't let your demons consume you once and for all!
It was only a matter of time. There's nothing you could have done. But thank you for trying.
Good-bye...
...forever this time.
NOOOOOO!

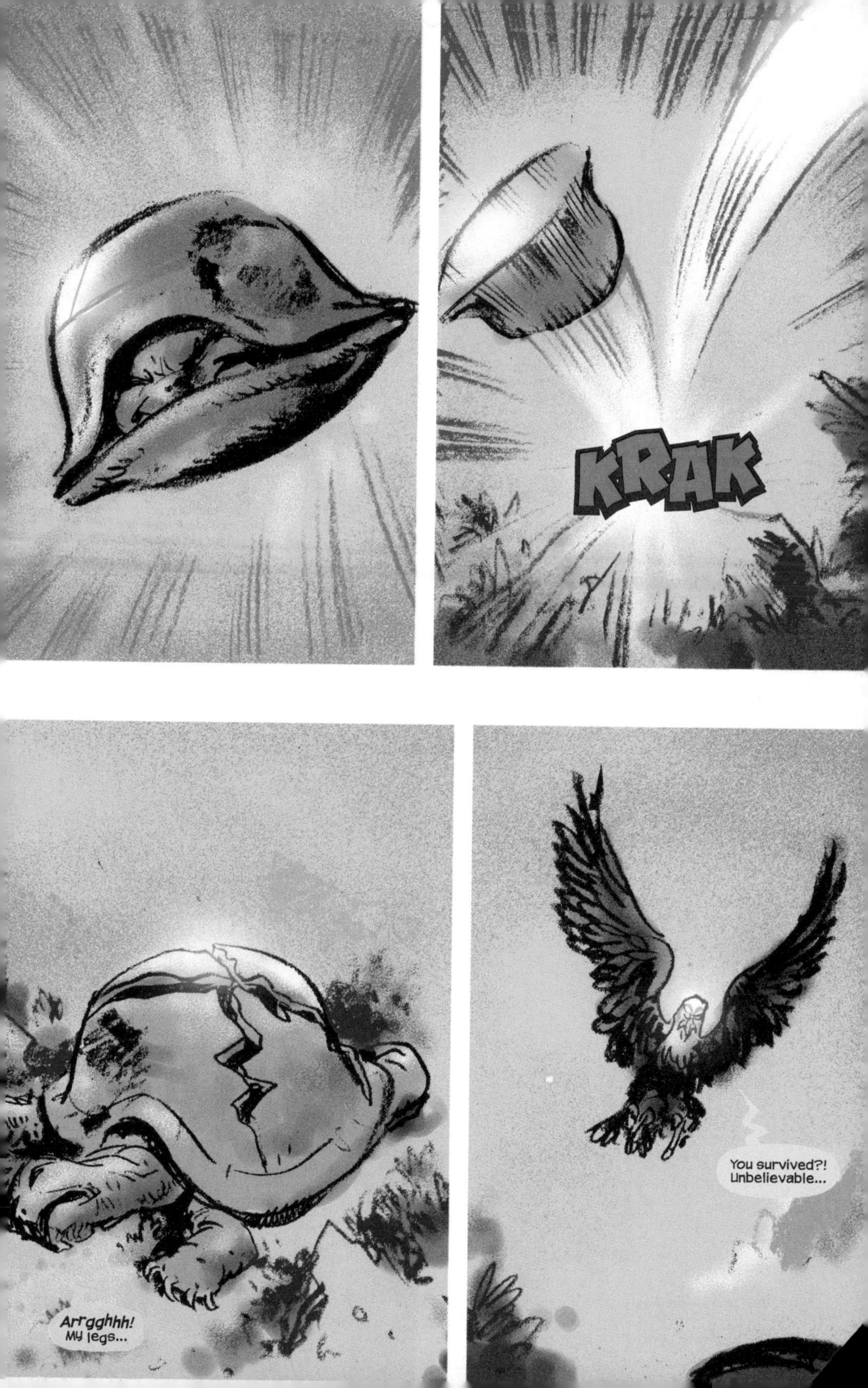
KRAK
Arrgghhh! My legs...
You survived?! Unbelievable...

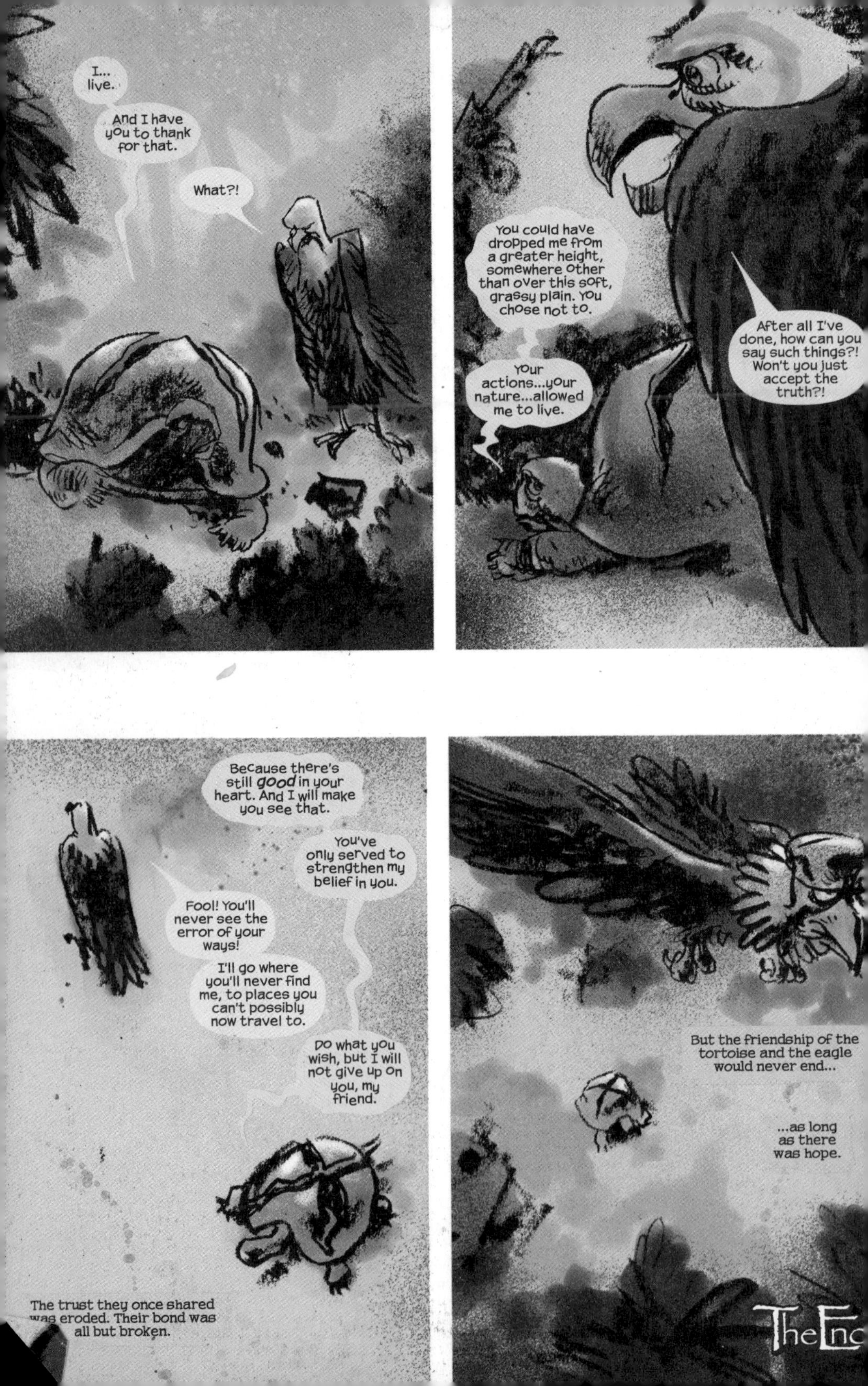
I... live.
And I have you to thank for that.
What?!
You could have dropped me from a greater height, somewhere other than over this soft, grassy plain. You chose not to.
Your actions...your nature...allowed me to live.
After all I've done, how can you say such things?! Won't you just accept the truth?!
Because there's still good in your heart. And I will make you see that.
You've only served to strengthen my belief in you.
Fool! You'll never see the error of your ways!
I'll go where you'll never find me, to places you can't possibly now travel to.
Do what you wish, but I will not give up on you, my friend.
The trust they once shared was eroded. Their bond was all but broken.
But the friendship of the tortoise and the eagle would never end...
...as long as there was hope.
The End